The Ethical Legitimization of Criminal Law

The Ethical Legitimization of Criminal Law

Krzysztof Szczucki

LEXINGTON BOOKS
Lanham • Boulder • New York • London

Published by Lexington Books
An imprint of The Rowman & Littlefield Publishing Group, Inc.
4501 Forbes Boulevard, Suite 200, Lanham, Maryland 20706
www.rowman.com

86-90 Paul Street, London EC2A 4NE, United Kingdom

The book was supported by the Polish National Science Center, project number: 2015/19/D/HS5/00526.

British Library Cataloguing in Publication Information Available

Library of Congress Cataloging-in-Publication Data

Names: Szczucki, Krzysztof, author.
Title: The ethical legitimization of criminal law / Krzysztof Szczucki.
Description: Lanham : Lexington Books, 2022. | Includes bibliographical references and index. | Summary: "The book focuses on one fundamental thesis: when creating the norms of criminal law, the legislator should strive for their compatibility with the principle of human dignity while taking into account the ethical legitimacy of criminal law"—Provided by publisher.
Identifiers: LCCN 2022005149 (print) | LCCN 2022005150 (ebook) | ISBN 9781666908053 (cloth) | ISBN 9781666908060 (epub)
Subjects: LCSH: Criminal law—Moral and ethical aspects. | Punishment—Moral and ethical aspects. | Criminal law—Philosophy. | Criminal justice, Administration of—Moral and ethical aspects. | Dignity. | Free will and determinism.
Classification: LCC K5018 .S93 2022 (print) | LCC K5018 (ebook) | DDC 345/.001—dc23/eng/20220208
LC record available at https://lccn.loc.gov/2022005149
LC ebook record available at https://lccn.loc.gov/2022005150

Contents

Introduction

The legislator, when creating norms of criminal law, should strive for their compatibility with the principle of human dignity and take into account the conclusions of the ethical legitimization of criminal law. The thesis formulated in this way is the axis around which this monograph has been built.

The ethical legitimization of criminal law requires the use of ethical considerations and analyses in the field of philosophical anthropology. Just note one of the legal maxims decorating the building of the Supreme Court in Warsaw: *Hominum causa omne ius constitutum sit*—Every law has been created for the sake of men. If it is to be the case that the fundamental point of reference for the establishment of the law is man, then it is necessary to establish an understanding of man, the essential characteristics of his nature, and also some understanding of his aspirations. Without this effort, which should be made by the legislator, it is impossible to pass a law that corresponds to what a person is. In the case of criminal law, this is a very visible problem. This branch of law, like no other, falls within the sphere of human decision-making, their internal experiences, and relations with other subjects. When determining the duty of a given person to take criminal responsibility, we often enter the realm of very intimate decisions and experiences. The making of criminal law for the benefit of man must therefore take into account who he is and what nature he has. Without this, the law will be made on the basis of the legislator's notion that is disconnected from reality, in a way that understands man ideologically. Such episodes are known from the history of law—the National Socialist man or the representative of the working class. The regime in these cases, instead of taking into account the abilities of the person and their rights in law, creates a new man, corresponding to the ideological image of the rulers.

Reconstructing a vision of a human being that corresponds to reality is certainly not an easy task. Even the best knowledge of biology, medicine, or even psychology is not enough. Each of these sciences describes a human being only in an aspect, in a fragment of their being. Therefore, it is justified to reach for the science that tries to describe man in his entirety, that is, philosophy, including above all philosophical anthropology and ethics. However, we find there—otherwise than in the case of the empirical sciences—numerous different descriptions of man, depending on the philosophical stand that we represent. Which vision of man is therefore to be chosen by the legislator?

First of all, as already noted above, it should validate the ideas with reality and thus make them real. A helpful tool here is also the reference to the principle of human dignity, which—as stated in Article 30 of the Constitution of the Republic of Poland as a "source of freedom and rights"—should become the main anthropological point of reference in the system of law, including criminal law. Human dignity in the constitutional sense is not only a principle that introduces a specific content into the legal system but also determines a specific direction of searching for and reconstructing a vision of man. After all, dignity resounds here in a certain philosophical context. This context was chosen by the founder, that is, the entire political community, as the preferred one. Reading this context, and its principles, then taking it into account in the process of making and applying criminal law—this is the fulfillment of the conditions for the establishment of criminal law on human grounds.

Human dignity is therefore interpreted as the central category of the ethical legitimization of criminal law. It is not only a direct source of specific content, which is extremely important in the process of establishing criminal law but also opens criminal law to a specific ethical and anthropological context.

It is impossible not to notice that before our very eyes, in many countries of our legal culture, serious changes in criminal law are taking place. One of the manifestations of this process is the transformation toward a much more preventive criminal law than so far, which has been observed in the doctrine of criminal law. The controversies related to this, concerning not only doubts about detailed solutions but the axiological premises themselves, require confrontation with the ethical paradigm of criminal law.

As early as 1984, Andrzej Wąsek, a renowned Polish expert on criminal law, noted the need to address the issue of morality in his studies of criminal law: "Criminal law, apart from family law, is one of the areas of the legal system which are most closely related to moral issues."[1] In another place, he diagnosed the necessity of taking notice of "whether and what aspects of a moral nature are connected with the issue of legality and punishment discussed, and what influence they may have on determining the basis and scope of criminal responsibility of the offender."[2] Individual institutions of criminal law and the solutions contained within them are not morally neutral.

In the case of criminal law, certain analogies to morality are self-imposed. Similarities—of various types and degrees—can be observed in the regulation of prohibited conduct, that is, detailed ethics, to the specific part of criminal law. Significant similarities, albeit limited in scope, can also be seen at first glance between general ethics and the general part of criminal law. It is therefore not only about these most obvious issues, such as whether the immorality of a certain behavior coincides with the criminalization of an offense. These are often noticed and commented on on various occasions, especially on successive modifications of a particular part of the criminal law. Much less attention is paid to the philosophical conditions of general criminal law institutions in the academic debate, particularly by lawyers. And yet they did not come from nowhere.

In his reflections on the ethical aspects of jurisprudence, Zygmunt Ziembiński noted that the court is expected to observe not only formal legal justice. Decisions taken by judges should also be morally correct and relevant from the point of view of social policy.[3] This rightness is achieved not only by means of general clauses enabling judges to move within the limits of a wider interpretative freedom but also by including evaluations and moral norms in the "determination of the normative content of legal norms and their consequences, i.e. by the influence of morality on the rules of interpretation and the rules of interference."[4]

The inspiration for the discussion on the ethical legitimization of criminal law was therefore the links and similarities between the law and morality that have been noticed in the Polish literature. They have been noticed, but so far no attempt, it seems, has been made to analyze and indicate the importance of morality in criminal law, especially in relation to the issue of principles and range of responsibilities. However, it is not only legal literature that has become the basis for the conviction that it is right to address this subject. I also see the sources of this belief in the conversations I have had with my friends, ethicists, and moralists. We have discussed various factual situations many times, whether in the form of case studies or commenting on media information about crimes discovered. It has very often turned out that we have come to similar solutions by recognizing the legitimization—or otherwise—of holding a person accountable. We used different tools, different nomenclatures, different methodologies for our deliberations, but in the end we had a common conclusion, usually on responsibility, but then, of course, different on the proposed sanctions. The observed regularity, which allowed me to reject the thesis of the randomness of such common conclusions, led me to seek the source of these coincidences.

What was intriguing was not so much the origin of similarities concerning moral evaluation of various types of human behaviors, namely the discussion about morality and lawlessness of more or less controversial acts. The issue of similarities in thinking about responsibility—its essence and scope—seemed to be more important and somehow universal. As a consequence, the considerations conducted here have been focused primarily on analyses concerning the general part of criminal law. References to the specific part are primarily for illustrative purposes. Such an assumption may raise questions and doubts as to the appropriateness of focusing primarily on the constructions regulated in the general part of criminal law. The first associations appearing in the reaction to the juxtaposition of the concepts of "criminal law" and "morality" relate primarily to the scope of criminalization. The debate on morality and criminal law often boils down to a discussion on the legitimization of criminalizing abortion, euthanasia, incest, or other equally controversial social behaviors. These issues are undoubtedly very important and need to be further developed and justified by their criminalization or, as the case may be, decriminalization. But they are not going to be the subject of this book. They may only appear on the margins. When considering criminal law in relation to ethics, we must not forget the importance of the general part of criminal law and, above all, the principles shaping the science of crime, which can also be presented as a theory of responsibility.

Michael S. Moore divides criminal law into a general and a specific part by dividing it into a theory of responsibility and a theory of unlawful conduct.[5] The theory of responsibility tries to answer the question of when a person is legally and morally responsible for behavior that has the characteristics of a criminal act. The theory of illegal behavior seeks to answer questions about which behaviors should be considered illegal and which behaviors are immoral.

The exhaustion of the legitimization potential of the categories still popular in the Polish theory of criminal law is also not without significance. Dagmara Gruszecka rightly pointed out that "the contemporary continental—if it can be defined as such—reflection on the model of legitimization of criminal law, concentrating on exploring still the same notions, willingly, struggles into a certain epigonism and reproducibility." It is therefore necessary to show hitherto not very popular prospects of legitimization.

Discussions on the relationship between criminal law and morality are carried out here in the perspective of the so-called modest version of moralism. This means that I assume that criminal law is not a matter of sanctioning morality but that it should not criminalize behavior that is considered morally good.[6]

This book consists of five chapters. The first deals with the issue of punishment, using the method proper to the Anglo-Saxon approach to the analysis of criminal law, where punishment becomes the starting point and theoretical issues of criminal law, including the science of crime—the destination. The fact that the very concept of punishment, fundamental to this branch of law, indicates the moral significance of not only the punishment itself but also of criminal responsibility and criminal law in general is so important in this first chapter. Disputes between representatives of retributive concepts and supporters of liberalism, as reflected in the debate between Patrick Devlin and Herbert L. Hart, among others, show that, regardless of which concept we choose, it is impossible to consider criminal law without reference to morality, and thus without reference to the vision of the person to whom the punishment is addressed. Analyzing criminal law from the inside, we acquire the conviction that it is necessary to go beyond its strictly formal framework.

Chapter 2 deals with the meaning and role of the principle of human dignity in criminal law, especially in the context of what I call the ethical legitimization of criminal law. The considerations carried out within it constitute the axis around which the thesis of this monograph is constructed and verified. Human dignity is an anthropological category in the philosophical sense, incorporated into the legal order for a specific purpose. This purpose is to orient the legal system to the good of the individual as they are. It is the legislator's duty to design solutions in a way that is subordinated to this approach.

The third chapter considers the issue of the capacity for responsibility in the context of free will. One of the fundamental issues to be resolved in the context of responsibility is whether a person can bear it at all. There are allegations of a real lack of free will. These doubts also arise from some scientific research or actually from the interpretation of its results. It is not possible today to consider the issue of criminal liability in a competent way without tackling, at least to some extent, the issue of neurobiological discoveries and their impact on legal constructions. At the same time, the already known problem of free will, that is, indeterminism and determinism, returns with the analysis of conclusions from these findings. The chapter discusses the doubts arising from the findings of empirical sciences, especially neuroscience, which can then be confronted with the conclusions of the vision of man reconstructed as described in chapter 4.

The fourth chapter attempts to reconstruct the vision of the human being in the area where it was necessary to establish the principles and scope of possible responsibility for a human being's actions. To this end, several philosophical traditions have been used, which in my opinion constitute the philosophical context of the principle of human dignity expressed in Article 30 of the Constitution of the Republic of Poland. The considerations carried out within the framework of classical and Christian philosophy, especially in the works of Aristotle and Thomas Aquinas, have been taken into account. The source of the search for a meaningful context was also the concept of the human being proposed by Karol Wojtyła. It also seemed appropriate to refer to the work of Roman Ingarden, in particular his considerations on responsibility. The discussion was supplemented by a reference to contemporary philosophy, including Anglo-Saxon work. My aim was not to present the concept of man according to one philosophical school, but rather to draw on various trends compatible with the principle of human dignity, and thus to indicate the sources of searching for a context appropriate to the ethical legitimization of criminal law.

The last chapter aims to make a form of application of previous considerations directly into criminal law. This has been done in relation to three selected theoretical constructions, two of which are the constructions that make up the shape of criminal responsibility, that is, omission and necessary defense, and the third—enemy criminal law—is a specific theoretical phenomenon that is gaining an increasing field of application. The application not only shows the scheme of conducting ethical legitimacy in criminal law but also provides a source of conclusions concerning the theoretical constructions discussed.

NOTES

1. A. Wąsek, *Prawo karne—minimum moralności?*, "Annales Universitatis Mariae Curie-Skłodowska. Sectio G. Ius" 1984, vol. 31, no. 3, p. 37. Similar thoughts were also expressed by Władysław Mącior: "Therefore, dealing with these problems by a criminal law theoretician is a difficult and responsible task, as it forces one to enter the territory of other disciplines, not in order to practise as a scientific partisan there, but only in order to use the appropriate achievements of these disciplines for the needs and purposes of criminal law science. Otherwise, the science of criminal law would be in danger not only of lagging behind, but also—and this would be even worse—of using formulas that more or less do not correspond to reality. In turn science has this attribute, that—being from the very beginning an aspiration to learn truth—must constantly develop. Of course, one must be aware of the fact that entering the area of other fields of knowledge, i.e. going beyond the borders of one's own specialty, hides an increased risk—because a certain risk always exists—of making a mistake in one's theoretical deliberations, but because of the necessity of such a procedure this risk is justified. Without this risk, it would not even be possible to get close to the desired goal," idem, *Czyn ludzki i jego znaczenie w prawie karnym. Zagadnienia podstawowe*, Warsaw 1990, pp. 9–10.
2. A. Wąsek, *Prawo karne. . .* , p. 37.
3. Z. Ziembiński, *Etyczne problemy prawoznawstwa*, Warsaw 1972, p. 126.
4. Ibid, p. 127.
5. M.S. Moore, *Placing Blame. A Theory of the Criminal Law*, Oxford 2012, p. 32.
6. For more on the topic of this conception, see R.A. Duff, *Towards a Modest Legal Moralism*, "Criminal Law and Philosophy" 2014, vol. 8, no. 1, p. 217 and note.

Chapter 1

The Validity and Legitimization of Criminal Law

Considerations carried out around the law, its legitimization, and interpretation usually concentrate in the legal debate on the issues within the system, possibly supplemented by a utility dimension, and thus transferring the axis of analysis to the issues of operability and functionality of the solutions adopted. The utility aspect, although significant for the assessment of the law adopted, is not a significant factor in the process of searching for grounds for the validity and legitimization of this adopted law. Moreover, the division into a justification of validity and legitimization of the law, also referred to as coming into effect, does not seem to be without significance. It seems that it may correspond or become the basis for distinguishing between two distinct, albeit closely related, trends in criminal law analysis.

The theory of law points to four basic categories: the binding nature of the law, the content of the law, the normativity of the law, and its legitimacy.[1] This book is mainly devoted to the issue of the legitimization of criminal law, in particular its ethical aspect. However, it seems necessary to at least outline the issue of its binding nature, because it is in this context that the most noticeable features of the phenomenon of legitimization of law are characteristic. The problem of the binding nature of law is very extensive, with many volumes of considerations conducted mainly on the basis of the philosophy of law being devoted to it. It is pointed out that there are at least a dozen or so theoretical and legal concepts of the binding nature of the law.[2] These include, but are not limited to, the theory of the validity of standards as belonging to the legal system, the theory of the validity as the application of standards, and the theory of the validity of standards in terms of compliance or effectiveness (efficiency) of standards.[3] In view of the assumptions made here, even if only the most important positions in this area were to be mentioned, this would go significantly beyond the framework. Therefore, it was decided to recall only the basic understanding of the binding nature, proposed by Zygmunt Ziembiński. This seems sufficient to distinguish legitimization from validity.

It is worth noting at this point that the binding nature of criminal law does not seem to differ from the applicability of other branches of law in terms of the basis. At the very beginning, one can use, as Ziembiński does, a far-reaching simplification, nevertheless showing a certain essence of a strictly positivist approach to the concept of validity of the law. The norms that have been set by a given community's sovereignty are understood as binding norms.[4] The sovereign, however, is that subject who has no habit of obedience to others, while obedience from others requires them to be able to force them to do so. At the same time, however, Ziembiński explicitly emphasizes that this does not release anyone from the obligation to reflect on sovereignty—its motivation and the sources of its position.[5] As Dan Priel suggests, enforceability can be established by stating that a norm is part of a set of standards that can be identified as belonging to a particular legal system. Enforceability means that the norm has a legal character, and not a moral, social, or any other.[6]

Undoubtedly, the image of sovereignty outlined above, which has been characterized as a subject exempt from obedience to others, is based on a certain simplification. Globalization—with an extensive international system, or in some cases even supranational order—no longer allows us to define sovereignty in this way, without at the same time depriving it of the attribute of being sovereign. Therefore, there is still a content in the name that would allow us to claim that, despite the fact that states operate in numerous dependencies, we can construct claims about their sovereignty. The determination of the minimum range of sovereignty, which determines the boundary between sovereignty and subjection, needs to be examined separately. The problem of searching for justifications and criteria for international and supranational processes influencing directly or indirectly the shape of national criminal law should also be the subject of another study. However, although the growing importance of international law *sensu largo*, also understood here as *soft law*, affects the content of national criminal law, it is not decisive for its enforceability.

The sovereign demands listening obedience from others through the establishment of legal norms that are the norm of conduct. Legal standards are standards of conduct qualified as standards established for other entities. Zygmunt Ziembiński points out that the establishment of a standard of conduct by man only for himself is not interesting for jurisprudence.[7] The author points out that jurisprudence is not interested in such a norm, because it is established privately and by man for himself. If, however, we assume that the norm of conduct occupying legal professions is only an act which is a norm for other entities, then the question whether a legal norm is a norm of conduct which is bound by sovereignty also or only by itself seems justified. Such a standard would, admittedly, be introduced in public, but not for external actors. It should be noted that, in a sense, the law is always made not only for external entities. If we assume that the legislator's mandate comes from the nation, and yet there is no one else, but members of that nation are the addressees of the vast majority of established legal norms, it is hard not to notice that the nation is—indirectly—a nation for itself. Even if we reduce this meta-level of lawmaking by one degree and assume that the law is made by a state body, the persons sitting on it or performing its functions may also, simply as citizens, be addressees of these legal norms. For a long time now, or rather since the twilight of the absolute monarchy, we cannot speak of a case in which the law would always be made only for entities external to the legislator himself. There is therefore no basis for claiming that it is not legally interesting that the legislator cannot bind itself to rules that would still be of a legal nature. However, such a link will also entail the possibility for the legislator concerned to modify or lift the restrictions imposed.

Ziembiński's considerations on legislative competences seem interesting. He points to a vicious circle in the concepts of normativism, describing it as "apparent": "A legal standard is what has been established by an entity defined by a legal standard in the manner specified by a legal standard."[8] At the same time, the author suggests that the problem lies primarily in the failure to distinguish between substantive norms and norms that grant normative competence, while this distinction alone does not yet completely eliminate the vicious circle. Moreover, he points out that the chain of competence norms must have its beginning not in legal competence but in axiological competence.[9] Another end to this chain of competence norms may be the situation in which the highest legislature and the entities acting under its authority have the means of effectively applying sanctions in the event of noncompliance with the legal norms laid down. However, this seems to be an ineffective means of dealing with the problem of the vicious circle, since the basis for applying sanctions are also legal norms, which must have their genesis in competence, probably also in the form of a legal norm. Thus, this axiological competence seems to be of key importance.

The sources of legitimization are sought primarily in norms that grant normative competences. Due to the specific nature of criminal law, it seems justified to talk about norms granting normative competences in the field of criminal law. They can be defined as norms "which require their addressees (entities subject to a given competence) to comply with such norms, which will be established by the entity obtaining a mandate to establish a given type of norm."[10]

The granting of normative competence to an authority does not yet mean that this authority is completely at liberty with regard to the manner of conduct and content of the legal norms created. This freedom, depending on the political position of the body, may be greater or lesser, sometimes even very large, which does not mean that it is absolute. This is because it is always associated, at least in a democratic state, with the need to carry out certain procedures and with the obligation to maintain the internal cohesion of the entire legal system, and thus also in compliance with higher order legal acts, assuming that a given legal system is built hierarchically.[11]

In the light of the above, it seems appropriate to describe the issue of the legitimization of law, which indicates that a judge, in order to settle a case, should first identify a legal norm that is appropriate in terms of its scope. To this end, knowledge of the principles for identifying legal standards is necessary.[12] Legal norms are adopted by the relevant entities, in an established procedure, and then promulgated accordingly. In the positivist understanding of the law, legitimation is not dependent on the content of the norm. The mere fact that a norm is binding does not necessarily mean that it must be complied with, which is not the case, however, with positivism in terms of its legitimative character.

Legitimization is a concept that we often use in our reflections on authority—its various aspects, including genesis. Some people pay attention to the abundance of definitions of this concept, pointing out that there are as many of them as there are authors dealing with the issue of legitimization.[13] In addition, it is recognized that the terms "legitimization," "legitimacy," "validity," and "lawfulness" are treated as synonyms in the literature.[14] Some interpretations show that legitimacy is rather a state of affairs, while legitimization is a process that leads to some state of affairs. Legitimacy is then seen as the end result of the legitimization process.[15]

The issue of legitimization of the law requires consideration of the issue of justifying the validity of the law and justifying the law.[16] The validation of the law is examined from an analytical and empirical perspective, while the justification of the law takes place in the area of argumentation and axiology. The procedure of determining the validity of a law must be accompanied by a procedure of axiological verification, that is, its justification.[17] It is understood as a procedure to confirm whether the law can be justified from an axiological point of view.

Legitimization of the law is far more than just a justification for its validity, especially if the justification is to be sought within the legal system itself. The statement that the validity of a given law can be justified by the procedure for its adoption, in accordance with the legislative procedure provided for in a given system and the validation rules related to it, is not legitimization, and therefore justification. Even more so, it is not a legitimization of the law to apply for its validity because of the accompanying state coercive apparatus. From these, but also from a number of other aspects, there may be a justification for the thesis that the law is in force. However, the validity itself does not yet imply legitimization of the law, unless it is supposed to legitimize itself, only for the sake of meeting formal criteria. However, then it would be unreasonable to distinguish between categories of legitimization as such.

The legitimization of law is related to its normative character. On the basis of considerations on the normativity of law, we ask about the sources of legal obligations, while on the basis of considerations on legitimization, the issue of conditions causing the law to be genuinely binding on the entities to which it is addressed.[18]

The legitimization of the law can be analyzed from the perspective of its development throughout the history of humanity. The search for legitimacy of individual solutions may vary depending on the political, historical, or social context prevailing at a given time. It is worth noting the historical specificity of the Western legal tradition, which translates into the nature of legitimization of particular legal orders. The specificity of criminal law and its legitimacy in the mentioned tradition seems particularly important here.[19]

According to Harold J. Berman, six major revolutions—Russian, French, American, English, Protestant, and Papal—transformed the Western legal tradition in the course of its development.[20] The author notes that periods of violent upheaval are typical of Western history, leading to the overthrow of existing social, legal, economic, and cultural relations. It was then that the existing system of institutions, values, and objectives were questioned. It is worth noting the recurring regularities of these revolutions. Each of them, according to Berman, was characterized by a fundamental, rapid, violent, and lasting change of the social system as such. Everyone searched for validation and justification in basic law, in the distant past or in the apocalyptic vision of the future. It took more than one generation for the revolution to take root. The result of each of them was a new legal system embodying the main objectives of the revolution, modifying the Western legal tradition, but—importantly—none of the revolutions except the canons of that tradition ultimately broke through.[21]

Interesting in this context are Berman's considerations regarding the possibility of the West avoiding the experience of these revolutions. In his opinion, this was impossible due to the inability of the Western political and legal system to introduce changes at the right time—in advance of any postulates raised on the revolutionary banners. Moreover, he notes that this inability to anticipate the desired changes is immanently inscribed in the essence of the Western legal tradition. The assumption that the purpose of this tradition is to maintain order highlights the tension between this order and the stability it entails and the need for change. Also the objective of ensuring justice can lead to tension between the protection of individual rights and the protection of the public good.[22] Revolutions are a kind of explosion, which take place when the system to date is unable to assimilate new conditions. Such an explosion destroys the old, but it also creates a new order. Ultimately, the passage of time usually shows that a revolution leads more to transformation than to a complete reversal of order.

LEGITIMIZATION OF THE LAW

Perhaps the most famous author who addressed the problem of legitimization was Max Weber.[23] He claimed, among other things, that "It is a principle (. . .) that those in power and those subject to such power internalise the rule, upholding it by referring to the legal basis, to the basis of its legitimacy, and the undermining of these beliefs of legitimization usually has far-reaching consequences."[24] The most popular is Weber's division of legitimization into three types: legal, traditional, and charismatic.

Legal legitimization is based on the established principle of determining to whom obedience is due:

> Obedience is not to a person by virtue of his own law, but to an established principle which determines to whom and to what extent it is due. Also, the commander is obedient to the principle when he gives an order, listens to the law, regulations, formal and abstract norms (. . .). The duty of obedience shall be framed within a certain hierarchy of posts subordinate to senior posts and governing the complaints procedure.[25]

Power based on traditional legitimization continues

> by virtue of faith in the sanctity of systems and powers that have existed for a long time (. . .). The content of the orders is determined by tradition, whose reckless violation by the ruler would threaten the legitimization of his authority, based solely on the sanctity of tradition. The creation of a new law, contrary to traditional norms, is seen as something fundamentally impossible.[26]

The charismatic legitimization of the authorities is based on different principles. It refers to the "emotional devotion to the person of the master and recognition of his extraordinary talents (charisma), in particular his magical abilities, heroism, power of spirit and speech. (. . .) One is obedient to a leader only because of his purely personal, unusual qualities, and not because of the position assigned to him or his traditionally accepted dignity."[27]

Perhaps the most appropriate legitimization of power in our part of the world is still the one based on the legal model, which refers to principles and procedures adopted. This does not in any way close off any other dimension of the legitimization issue. If power derives legitimization from the principles of law, then one can still ask about the sources of legitimization of this law. After all, one cannot claim that they are to be found in authority, because it is that which needs legitimization in law. The problem of legitimization is not limited to the search for justifications for exercising power but can also be understood as the search for contexts and criteria justifying the legal system as such.

At this point, even before going into the detailed considerations on legitimization, it is worth noting that the validity of using this concept or the phenomenon described with its help is sometimes questioned. Thomas Dewar Weldon clearly did so, stating that the question of the need to justify the law and its observance is as unjustified as the question of justification and observance of the rules of the game of cricket.[28] The mere determination of the applicability of a given norm shall entail the obligation to comply with it, without any other justification being necessary or needed.

In another approach, which does not go so far in the criticism of the legitimization analysis of law, it is pointed out that this phenomenon belongs more to political theory than to the legal sciences. Similarly to the area of political theory, the category of content of law is sometimes included. The science of law, on the other hand, should deal with what is covered by the categories of the lawfulness and normativity of the law. The binding nature of a norm would determine its normativity, while its content would determine its legitimization.[29] It seems that the qualification of legitimization to the scope of political theory is justified when we mean the legitimization of power. Legitimization of the law could then be a part of political theory, provided that it is acknowledged that all normative acts undertaken by the legitimized authority are also legitimized. It seems, however, that this statement would be too far-reaching, at least given the ethical aspect of the legitimization of the law discussed here. The mere fact that a criminal law has been passed by the appropriate authority, even in accordance with procedures, does not yet indicate that its content corresponds to certain ethical standards. Once again, it should be noted that this does not affect the formal validity of the law but rather its fairness and, to some extent at least, its effectiveness.

The problem of legitimization of law and power gains strength, especially in situations of various crises undermining trust in the legal system. This does not mean, however, that we have to agree with those authors who claim that the question of legitimization becomes relevant only when there is a legitimization crisis understood as a break in the relationship between society and the political organization of the social and legal system.[30] The question of legitimization is always relevant when considering the content of the law, especially in such a sensitive axiological scope as in the case of criminal law.

Zbigniew Pulka proposed the definition of legitimization taking into account not only the issues of the state and state authority but also the legal system in the Polish literature. By legitimization, he means "proving a legitimacy, which involves arguments of an evaluative nature. In other words, legitimization is an excusatory argument that aims to show the legal and state order as fulfilling certain values."[31] According to this author, legitimization has an axiological character, regardless of whether the justification is logical or empirical.

Mateusz Stępień proposed a different division of legitimization. He listed four types:

1) legitimization associated with legality, i.e. when the legal system can legitimize the legal order itself;
2) relational legitimacy, consisting in comparing the legal order with specific reference points; the degree of consistency between them translates into a degree of legitimization of the legal system;
3) social legitimization, seeking legitimization of the law in social reactions expressing trust, acceptance or consent;
4) political legitimization, understood not only as the identification of the legal system with the political doctrine in force at a given moment, but rather with the legitimization of political power.[32]

Richard H. Fallon proposes three types of legitimization: legal, sociological, and moral.[33] Legitimization refers to legal norms.[34] Legal legitimization is connected with the issue of the obligation to comply with the decisions on such legitimization of the deprived. This author makes a distinction between material legal legitimization, which allows for a critical assessment of decisions and not a refusal to enforce them, and a proprietary legal legitimization, which, on the one hand, allows for a wider margin for error on the part of the judge but, on the other, means that infringement of that legitimization exempts the subject from the obligation to comply with the judicature issued.[35]

However, sociological legitimization means that public opinion considers the object of legitimization, that is, power, its institutions and established law, to be justified, proper, deserving of support despite the sanctions that the legal system links with disobedience to decisions taken by institutions of power.[36]

Moral legitimization is understood by R. H. Fallon as a function of moral justification and deserving of respect. The existence of legal and sociological legitimization does not necessarily mean that the law is morally justified.[37] According to that author, moral legitimization can be understood in two ways. First of all, it can be interpreted as a form of consent to respect certain principles expressed by those governed by the act of entrusting power to the rulers. Second, moral legitimization can also be mentioned when the law implements the final standard of justice. This means that the fairer the law is, the more it deserves moral legitimization, even without the consent of those in power.[38] The key issues in the context of this type of legitimization are its scope and criteria. There are also questions about the general moral obligation to observe all norms and to comply with all decisions taken by a given authority.[39]

It is also worth noting the view of Massimo Renzo on this phenomenon. He bases it on the assumption that legitimization is directly connected with the right of public authority to govern. Legitimized authority allows for the imposition of burdens on individuals and other actors and, at the same time, for the use of different tools, including, most importantly, coercive tools.[40] Legitimization is therefore understood as an exclusive power of the state to impose and enforce civic obligations and the right to demand obedience.[41] It is considered to be a peculiar manifestation of an error in the attitude of anarchists refusing to join the state community, which to some extent deprives the state of the possibility to perform legislative, executive, and judicial functions. In this way, anarchists expose other people to the danger of living in a state of nature. If we accept that each of us has a duty to refrain from causing unjustified threats to others, we can recognize that each of us has a duty to become part of the state community at the same time.[42] This may also be achieved through the use of necessary defense by those living in the community. The legitimization of the state and its law is rooted in the duty of every human being to refrain from exposing others to dangers that would exist outside the state.[43]

Grażyna Skąpska and Jerzy Stelmach indicated two aspects of the legitimization of the law. In accordance with the first category, we can examine within this category the relationship between the political system and the law, paying particular attention to the subordination relationship. In the second aspect, the relationship between the law and society is visible, especially the law and nonlegal norms creating the social order.[44] Linking the law to the social order, which has been transforming itself over the centuries, allows us to claim that the law is also subject to processes of transformation that can be described as historical. This is a kind of historical legitimization of the law, which also opens the law to legitimization of another kind, which may result from social transformations, also in terms of axiology, taking place in time. These changes and a certain tangible continuity in the development of social, including legal, institutions are referred to as a tradition in which the law—despite the changes—tries to fit. It is impossible to disagree with Skąpska and Stelmach when they note that

> it is precisely the thinking in historical categories on the law, the analysis of the law against the backdrop of the traditions associated with it, that allows us to

> look at the law from a different point of view than only as an attribute of power or a technical means of regulation. Historical thinking leads to the formulation of the problem of the congruency of law with accepted customs, socially and culturally rooted systems of values, and inherited ideals.[45]

It is noted that the law is considered to be a historical phenomenon, since not only should it evolve, but it must also be seen as being constantly in the process of development.[46] This does not mean, however, that this process of evolution of the law has not been subjected to factors that could cause a disturbance within it. Such factors were different revolutions that attempted to reject the existing schemes of reasoning, although generally they did not lead to a break with legal tradition but rather to transform it or give it a new direction.[47] In some cases, it would be legitimate to say that revolutions have even become the cause of specific developmental leaps.[48]

The definition of Jürgen Habermas is worth noting, who by legitimization means the existence of good arguments for political order for it to be recognized as just and equitable. Legal validity for a political system means it is worthy of recognition. This definition may of course be called into question. In such situations when one criticizes the validity of the system, while another maintains the validity of the order in question, the need for consideration in this regard is usually revealed.[49]

David Beetham, on the other hand, focuses on the issue of legitimization of the power of the state authority.[50] He wonders what legitimizes the possibility for the state to enforce its provisions even by means of measures that significantly interfere with the interests of individuals. Although the subject of the considerations conducted here is the legitimization of law, in particular of a certain scope of criminal law, it is worth mentioning selected proposals from Beetham, as the legitimization of the law is not detached from the problem of legitimization of power. Nothing is more obvious than the fact that one of the basic means of exercising authority is precisely the law, which may be the basis for interference in the interests of an individual, for example, in the form of deprivation of liberty or other punishment.

The author rejects the view identifying the legitimization of the actions of the authorities with the legality of those actions.[51] Legality is rather within the scope of the enforceability of the law. Some concepts, however, point to the legal legitimization of the law, but even then it cannot be credibly stated that it exhausts the scope of legitimization criteria. Otherwise, the wording of the law itself, which would be the last resort for legitimization, could not be called into question. David Beetham rightly points out that the main subject of analysis in the area of legitimization is not what is required by the law in force but what should be ordered. It was undoubtedly not the intention of the author to separate legitimization analyses from the law in force but to state that the law is not the final point of reference. The law itself is subject to evaluation from the perspective of legitimization criteria. Legitimization, however, is what can be morally justified.[52] In a sociological context, the dimension of justification will not be universal as in a philosophical approach but will be interpreted in relation to the beliefs of the members of a given community in which the law is in force and assessed in the light of legitimization criteria.

A few other arguments also contend against identifying the legitimization of the law with legality, that is, compliance with the law, for example, with the legislative procedure or higher order legal acts. Although these are important aspects, they do not exhaust the issues of legitimization of the law. Legitimization is not limited to legal considerations only but also concerns philosophical and political issues. In addition, as Sergey Vasiliev notes, legality is binary in nature, which means that something is either legal or illegal. Legitimization is a dynamic, relative, and differentiated category,[53] as it can be graded and its assessment can be modified depending on the criteria adopted. Legality refers primarily to the sources of a given legal standard, its formal validity, and compliance with the relevant procedures. Legitimization, on the other hand, is assessed more frequently after taking into account the effects of a given decision.[54]

The adoption of a sociological approach should not mean—which can be achieved by accepting the view presented by M. Weber—understanding legitimization as the dominant conviction in society that the system is legitimized. The sociological criterion is rather based on the search for the compatibility of the introduced solutions with the convictions of citizens, which in consequence allows a conclusion on the legitimization of the system to be constructed. Legitimization of criminal law in this respect should not be understood in terms of verifying citizens' beliefs that the criminal law is legitimized. Rather, it is necessary to align the content of this law with the convictions and beliefs of the members of a given political community.[55]

The legitimization of legal norms derived from moral beliefs raises a number of questions about the subject assessing the level of legitimacy, the criteria for justifying norms or, finally, the method of selecting beliefs that become the basis for legitimizing the law. The entity legitimizing the norms is the community of citizens who are the addressees of the standards. It is ultimately the person whose behavior is regulated by a given norm who is entitled to judge whether that norm is justified or right. The criteria for the justification of norms and the methods of selecting justifiable beliefs may be sought in sources external to the social community and within the framework of that community.[56] External sources include religious motivations, natural law, and scientific doctrines. Among the internal sources, the most important are the traditions and beliefs of the members of the community.

LEGITIMIZATION OF THE LAW BY REFERENCE TO ETHICS

In light of the above, one might wonder to which collection the legitimization of the law referring to ethics should be qualified. If one assumes that criminal law is to correspond to the constructions adopted in a particular ethical system, understood as a complete and abstract set of norms, one should rather place it among external sources. On the other hand, if ethical legitimization is understood as justifying the accepted legal decisions by demonstrating their conformity with ethical decisions internalized by citizens, that is, with moral convictions accepted by them, it becomes a justification of the law with the use of internal sources for a given community. In fact, it is part of the legitimization referring to tradition and social attitudes.

Axiological justification of the law is connected with the concept of axiological competence, which would be the basis for the creation of a norm that would grant normative competence, and thus which would constitute a source of power for the state authority, at least in relation to criminal law, to establish appropriate norms, sanctioned with the help of criminal prohibitions and related criminal sanctions.[57] The problem of axiological competence of the legislator seems to be not only a problem of enforceability but also—perhaps even to a greater extent—the subject of analysis in the field of legitimization of criminal law.

The adoption of a positivist understanding of the law does not exclude the possibility of reaching for an axiological context which, accepted even in the narrowest possible function, may create conditions for the acceptance of the legislator's authority.[58] Furthermore, the ethical context, as well as the historical and cultural context, must be used in order to maintain the intrinsic value of law. Law devoid of these values, limited to the creation of a series of lawmaking facts, becomes impossible to internalize element of oppression, requiring sanctions by means of increasingly far-reaching coercive measures.

The existing arrangements allow us to assume that the legitimization of power may be interpreted as the conviction of members of a political community that entities of power deserve to exercise power, that is, to take decisions which are significant for all members of the community.[59] Legitimization of the law therefore means convincing the members of the political community that the legal norms enacted by a given authority should be observed. It is a conviction that they are right. The ethical legitimization of the law should be interpreted as a reading of the relation between the chosen legal norms and the reconstructed ethical system in the context of the principles and values that bind the community.

The literature discusses not only the validity and criteria for legitimization of power or law but also the legitimization of law enforcement bodies, including, first of all, police services. It is noted that it is not only procedural justice that legitimizes police action, although this is undoubtedly a very important premise. It is equally important for officers to act in a manner consistent with moral principles and, as it seems, to enforce ethically justified law.[60]

The correlation between the compatibility of the law with moral beliefs and its effectiveness was confirmed during research carried out on criminals within the framework of the "Chicago Gun Project."[61] One of the findings of this project is the observation that those who commit crimes using weapons—those who have been included in the study—are much more likely to act in accordance with the law when they believe in the legitimization of law enforcement agencies and believe that the content of the law is consistent with their moral systems.[62] It is worth noting, as has been pointed out by those responsible for carrying out these surveys, that even the most serious crimes in their daily lives generally comply with the law in force.

Legitimization is sometimes indicated as the cause of obedience to the law, often even as the basic cause. It can be defined as a value that induces a person to obey the law and to obey decisions taken by public authorities.[63] As David Smith notes, the preservation of social order is possible when it is not only the power but also its political and legal framework that are legitimate. Rightly, this author notes that as long as this belief is widespread, people will basically shape their behavior by reference to internalized values that correspond to the law and its principle. Coercion will be used only exceptionally when a legal limit is exceeded.[64] Linking this aspect to the above shows that the correlation of decisions taken by public authorities, including acts of lawmaking, with the moral systems of social community members is clearly noticeable from the perspective of law effectiveness. At the same time, it seems that the criterion relating to the conduct of state authorities should not be limited to procedural justice alone.[65] It was clearly indicated above that beliefs are consistent with the content of the law, which should not be limited only to procedural norms.

It therefore seems that the position that perceives legitimization as a feature of the legal system that makes its addressees obey it is correct. Legitimization also means that the members of a given political community, that is, citizens, internalize the aims of power that are consistent with their moral convictions. Moreover, citizens can also internalize the specific moral principles promoted by public authority if, in the general picture, the action of that authority is consistent with the cardinal moral principles. Such a process may also lead to the law not only being respected by citizens but also being justified and promoted.[66]

Research conducted in the United States confirms that a sense of moral community with law enforcement officers makes their actions more morally binding. The literature indicates that an important motive for observing the law is the conviction shared by the addressees of legal norms that behaviors typified as illegal are also immoral.[67] People are much more willing to voluntarily obey the law when they are convinced of its fairness.[68]

Research has also been carried out on the bases and criteria that guide us in assessing whether another person should be held criminally responsible. This applies, of course, to assessments made by nonprofessionals, that is, people who are not lawyers, who work out their positions mainly on the basis of personal beliefs, life experiences, and intuition. It turns out that people have a tendency to attribute the responsibility for causing a specific negative event to the one who caused the event—emerging from a series of events—the most morally charged. Behavior judged to be immoral does not even have to contribute to the cause of the event, which involves the need to identify a responsible person. It is enough that it made up the complex of behaviors of the person to whom responsibility is attributed. An example is responsibility for causing a car accident. It turns out that respondents much more often attribute responsibility to the driver if his or her journey had an immoral context than if he or she was carrying out an order in accordance with moral principles.[69] These proportions are not influenced by other factors that a professional should take into account, such as the state of the road, weather conditions, or even the behavior of others. The results of the research indicate that when trying to determine a fair punishment, the respondents usually seek a punishment proportional to the degree of moral guilt of the perpetrator.[70] This means that the size of the penalty is not directly affected by its preventive function.

The conclusions of these studies confirm that an individual who has undergone the process of socialization in a given culture has an image of a hierarchy of criminal acts, arranged according to their degree of deserving condemnation, and at the same time has a scale that allows for the imposition of specific punishments for such acts.[71]

Tom R. Tyler and Jonathan Jackson also point out that building such a moral community can be difficult in modern pluralized and multicultural societies.[72] This is undoubtedly a problem which is confirmed by reality, but it should not be understood as a statement that it is impossible to establish any values shared by citizens. If this were the case, it would be impossible at all to use the concept of community, which by definition is based on shared values. This problem also seems to be less relevant to the considerations conducted here, as it concerns more rights that would be the basis for a criminalization decision rather than the principles governing criminal liability. In other words, the divisions within society concern what should be included in the catalog of types of offenses rather than the rules governing responsibility as such.

John M. Darley, Kevin M. Carlsmith, and Paul H. Robinson presented an important analysis of this issue, based on empirical research, and based on the assumption that criminal law plays a preventive role, which they call an *ex ante* function. The authors of the study took into account that in the United States, criminal law is mostly passed by state legislatures. Closer analysis has shown that there are significant differences between state criminal law systems. Nevertheless, residents of individual states are convinced that they are able, even without knowing the law, to distinguish between legal and prohibited behavior. It may therefore be questioned what underlies a person's conviction that he or she knows the law, at least to the extent that he or she can avoid committing an act sanctioned by criminal law.[73] The reasons for this should be sought in the conviction of citizens that the law, and criminal law in particular, corresponds to their moral convictions.

At this point, it is worth briefly describing the course of these studies, as they are of great importance for the issue of the ethical legitimization of criminal law. The experiment involved 203 participants, selected in a manner appropriate to the methodology of scientific activity of this kind. Four short stories were presented to them which described potentially illegal behaviors.[74]

1. The obligation to provide assistance. In most states in the United States there is no criminal law sanctioned obligation to provide assistance to a person in a situation of imminent danger to life or health.[75] The issue of granting assistance was regulated differently in the state of Wisconsin, where the law imposes an obligation to grant assistance, provided that such assistance does not directly threaten the assisting person. In the case study presented to the participants of the study, the facts were described when a person indifferently passed by another person—unconscious, lying on the street, a victim of an assault.
2. The obligation to retreat. Most state legislatures allow violence to be used to repel unlawful assault even if the perpetrator of the attack were to die as a result. In North Dakota and Wisconsin, the use of necessary defense to kill an attacker should be preceded by an attempt at retreat, that is, escape from the danger area. In the case study presented to the participants of the study, the facts were described when a person whose life was undoubtedly endangered by an attacker decided to defend themselves by killing the attacker instead of trying to escape, when it was possible to safely move away from the place of danger.
3. Notification of the commission of a crime. South Dakota has introduced an obligation to report a crime committed, while the rest of the United States has not. The case study concerned a case in which a citizen did not notify the law enforcement authorities of a crime committed by a friend.
4. Defending property at the cost of life. In some states of the United States, it is permissible to kill an attacker if their behavior threatens another human being or, if the attack threatens not human life but property, to use

violence to repel them. An exception is Texas, where property can also be defended at the expense of the life of the perpetrator. However, it is then necessary to demonstrate a reasonable belief in the threat to life or the use of unlawful violence before the attacker is killed. The case study presented the actual state of affairs in which a burglar was shot during his escape in order to recover the property stolen by him.

In the first round, after reading each of the stories, the participants' task was to indicate whether the described person committed a crime and then, if the answer is affirmative, to indicate a penalty adequate to the crime committed. In the second round, it was not so much for the participants to express their views as to what they thought would be the decision to be taken by the law enforcement bodies.

In the conclusions of the survey, it was indicated that the participants were not aware of the content of the applicable law. At the same time, it was stressed that the case studies presented to the respondents concerned important issues that may be of public interest.[76] The respondents, despite not knowing the content of the applicable law, did not have any difficulties with formulating opinions on the legality or illegality of the particular behaviors described in the case studies. The results of the research allow us to claim that the moral beliefs of the respondents turned out to be the decisive criterion. The authors of the experiment formulated the thesis that the moral beliefs of citizens are quite an important factor influencing the content of the law passed by state legislatures, which may explain the convergence of assessments with the actual wording of norms.[77]

The research presented above was conducted in the United States. It seems that cultural and legal differences, in some aspects very important, do not, however, make it impossible to relate the above conclusions also to Polish conditions. However, it is reasonable to confront this thesis with domestic work. Adam Podgórecki conducted interesting research in this area,[78] It took place several decades ago, but the theses resulting from it not only deserve attention, but still seem to be valid.

In this research, one can find the basis for reversing the relationship presented above. The relationship between beliefs in relation to morality and in relation to the law may result not only from the influence of moral norms on the establishment of legal norms but also from the influence of legal norms on moral beliefs. The research indicated that not all behaviors that they condemn morally should be reflected in legal sanction. At the same time, however, they considered all the behaviors forbidden by the law, which were included in the research, were considered to be immoral. The conclusion from the research indicated that legal condemnation induces moral condemnation.[79] At the same time, it was pointed out that the increasing moral condemnation of certain behaviors is connected with the feeling that these behaviors should be condemned legally.[80]

Another important issue raised in A. Podgórecki's research was social knowledge of the law. It follows from this that one cannot speak of a universal knowledge of the law, nor even of a degree approaching universality. However, it also follows from the same research that there is widespread knowledge of the principles of law, which the author understands as certain basic norms concerning what is allowed and what is not allowed.[81] These norms indicate to what extent and under what conditions certain typical behavior is allowed. These rules, as noted further on by A. Podgórecki, are based on social knowledge and social values.[82] Thus, they have a moral foundation. This leads to the conclusion that the strengthening of legal sense, and thus of legal awareness, is possible by aligning legal norms with other norms of social life, including moral ones.[83]

As far as the ethical legitimization of criminal law is concerned, it is worth noting that it seems particularly important to determine the typical tendency of people to influence criminal legislation with their moral beliefs, especially when the state of public debate does not cause a person to reasonably believe that their opinion is in a minority. This means that the desire to ensure the effectiveness of the criminal law should be linked to taking into account the ethical context. It can therefore be concluded with conviction that the incompatibility between citizens' convictions and the content of criminal law is always a sufficient basis for considering the need for legislative changes, and that this incompatibility does not always have to lead to real changes. Arguments against adapting the law to social expectations may in some cases be so important that it would be justified to seek to change social assessments.[84]

The empirical studies described in the literature indicate that the level of compliance with the law in the past and the intention of people to comply with it in the future correlate with the degree to which, in their opinion, criminal law corresponds to a moral justification. The convergence between the moral convictions of a community and the content of criminal law gives it a moral credibility.[85] However, it is necessary to make one fundamental reservation, which has already been mentioned. The moral convictions of individual members of society may differ, and may also be subjected to critical judgments, or may even be mutually contradictory. Ethical legitimization should not be understood as an attempt to reconcile the established law with the moral convictions of all or even the majority of citizens. Rather, it is based on the assumption that upbringing, or socialization processes, takes place in a certain ethical culture, which is an important element of culture in the broad sense. Undoubtedly, we may very much differ in our beliefs about particular behaviors and their moral evaluation. However, this does not imply the necessary differentiation in terms of the understanding of responsibility and its principles, that is, what is usually included as part of the general criminal codification. Therefore, it can be assumed that the rejection by the authorities of the moral view of a part of society should be conscious and connected with an appropriate information campaign explaining the adopted law in such a way as to counteract the decrease in the level of trust in the state and in the law enacted by it. It is relatively less risky to fail to pass legislation that is desired by the majority. Authority risks disobedience when it enacts laws considered unjust.[86]

The findings so far allow us to agree with the claim that the moral force of a law acts independently of the coercion it legitimizes.[87] The more the content of the Criminal Act corresponds to the moral convictions of citizens, and thus is consistent with their intuitions concerning the basis and scope of criminal responsibility, the more likely it is to be observed. This is an important argument in favor of the need to seek the ethical legitimization of criminal law.

Legitimization can be understood as seeking justification for the use of force by the state. What's more, according to D. Priel, the motif of legitimization allows us to correctly determine and understand the place of law in the broader political and social structure of the state.[88] At the same time, he states that it is the category of legitimization that explains why the final decision of the court can be both morally justified and legally erroneous. Courts are to play an important role in the legitimization of this author, who to a large extent refers to the works of Ronald Dworkin. However, it seems more legitimate to argue that the obligation to seek the ethical legitimization of the law is first and foremost the responsibility of the legislator and then of the courts and other law enforcement authorities.[89]

Legitimization in the dimension of confronting the rightfulness of the law may take on a legal–natural character, that is, it consists in aiming at the realization of absolute values that are always in force, regardless of the current conditions.[90] Legal and natural legitimization, that is, the legitimization of the binding legal system by reference to absolute norms and values, is, however, sometimes understood incorrectly. It happens that these concepts, especially the classical approach of St. Thomas Aquinas, are attributed to the theses which do not at all result from the works they left behind. At this point, it seems justified to note only the basic assumptions of the classical legal and natural trend in order to indicate possible grounds for legitimization of the legal system, including—most importantly from the perspective of this issue—the legitimization of criminal law.

From the perspective of criminal law, the legal–natural concept presented by Javier Hervada, rooted in the issue of the virtue of justice, seems particularly interesting.[91] Ensuring justice is undoubtedly a general objective of the law as such. It comes to the fore especially in the case of criminal law. The provision of justice is one of its most important functions. Thus, legal and natural legitimization becomes in this concept at the same time a legitimization of justice. An act of justice is always understood here as secondary to an act that confers something on someone, something that is imputable to them. For the act by which the subject received what belongs to him is just. Justice alone, however, does not prejudge what belongs to a subject, as it is the domain of the original act.[92] This author notes:

> The law, whether we understand it as an act or as a fair thing, does not derive from the virtue of justice, which in turn is not prior to or superior to the law. The virtue of justice presupposes the presence of the law, in this sense it is always something later in relation to the law. Every act of justice provides for the existence of a pre-established right; it shall therefore constitute a secondary act.[93]

It follows from the above that, as the said author notes, the law can be verified and assessed from the perspective of the criterion of justice only if there is some initial positive system in relation to it, which would be a point of reference for determining what is due. If there is no such perspective, it is also impossible to say whether the positive law gives everyone what they deserve, i.e. whether it is fair.

This method of reasoning forms the basis not only for legal and natural legitimacy, but also, in a sense, for an ethical legitimization similar to it. The reason for this is the attempt to orient the system of law, including of course criminal law, toward an external context which allows us to assess whether a given set of normative decisions is justified, right or just. Ethical legitimization differs from the legal–natural approach, however, in that it entails much more modest postulates, although it does not eliminate the potential of legal–natural legitimization at the same time. The basic criterion is the justification of the law by its compliance with certain moral standards. In the case of the principle of criminal responsibility, which is the fundamental subject of the analyses conducted here, the rules governing it should correlate with how responsibility and its scope are understood by ethics. Once again it should be recalled that the correlation postulated here should not be understood as an overlap. Criminal liability, due to its specific nature, can and should be narrower in scope than moral liability. But simultaneously, it should not include in its scope such behaviors, which are morally judged to be good, and thus which are even recommended. However, this thread is not the most important in the analyses conducted here, as it concerns more criminalization than the general principles shaping criminal responsibility.

The legitimacy of seeking the ethical legitimization of the law is also confirmed by J. Hervada's reflections on the notion of a person.[94] It is impossible not to notice that these terms are sometimes understood differently in the language of philosophy and the language of law. In the language of philosophy, a person is an entity with special characteristics, characterized by rationality and freedom. A person has ontological and moral control over his or her being, that is, he or she is, by nature, incapable of belonging to another being and controls the course of his or her actions. The language of the law draws attention to selected aspects of the "person," unlike philosophy, which endeavors to make a holistic description. Differences in the understanding of the term "person" in philosophy and law should not be interpreted as an indication that they describe two completely different realities. Reality is one, it is human, and the differences in the abovementioned interpretations have their source in the priority treatment of various aspects of humanity, understandable due to the specificity of individual sciences.

The aforementioned boundary between philosophical and legal interpretations of the concept of "person" does not consist in a clear separation of the two, as well as in many other cases it is impossible to separate the legal interpretation of reality from its philosophical approach. This means that the law in the process of analyzing a subject of law—a person—by assigning to them particular features relevant to legal transactions, more or less consciously reaches to a philosophical description of a human being. Not only to the philosophical but also to the biological, psychological, economic, and probably also to various others. For if the scope of criminal law includes interest in the subject's ability to control themselves, including the management of his or her own conduct, and—as noted above—this aspect also belongs to the interest of philosophy, it is difficult not to reach conclusions on the basis of this science whenever one considers the legitimacy and correctness of legal solutions finally adopted.

J. Hervada's concept is neither the only one nor the most widespread. However, since it is built around a formula explaining the virtue of justice, it focuses on the search for criteria that would allow the law to be recognized as just and therefore legitimized. At least in this respect, it deserves attention to the extent to which it essentially rejects the positivist thesis that the law is legitimate by its very establishment, since we do not have any criteria for verifying its legitimization at other levels in any way.[95] It seems, however, that contemporary legal systems themselves are demanding the search for criteria for their legitimization beyond themselves. Such a direction of reasoning is indicated by the openness of the positivist system of law by referring, for example, to the category of natural and inalienable human dignity. Since this dignity is the basis for all rights and freedoms, and since the law enacted should undoubtedly correspond to these rights and freedoms, it should be all the more consistent with what follows from this dignity. Then it has a chance to be a just law, and thus to give every human being what is due to them.

Interesting observations on the person are formulated by Tatiana Chauvin, indicating that the law tries to combine two very important aspects of human existence, that is, the infinity of the spiritual world and the finiteness of biological experience.[96] Neither of these perspectives can be omitted by the law because it would then be unable to respond properly to the needs of its addressees. Legal regulations refer to the human being in two possible ways: as a person, taking into account their integrity, or as a subject because of certain aspects, usually roles or functions.[97] Public law should specifically focus on the overall picture of a person. All the more so, such a directive can be formulated in the face of criminal law, which—as has already been noted—cannot be considered without an anthropological perspective.

Another direction legitimizing the legal system is anthropological legitimization. However, it does not refer—at least not directly—to philosophical anthropology. Its assumption is that the law has a personal dimension which is realized by constructing tools to ensure the realization of rights of a subjective nature. The legal system is therefore legitimized when it is saturated with subjective rights and, at the same time, with the means to make them effective. As Arthur Kaufmann noted:

> If this whole system of relations, which is the law, is not to disintegrate—that is, if it is not to be possible to call it "law" freely—then there must be an existential phenomenon, not freely manipulable, constituting an identity which is present both within and outside the process of the realisation of the law and which secures the legal process; a phenomenon which must itself be relational in its essence and be processual and historical.[98]

Kaufmann goes on to emphasize that it can be "only a human being, not an empirical human being, but a human being as a person," understood as "a set of relationships in which a human being is to other people or to things."[99] In this concept, "the idea of the law is an idea of a personal human being—or it is nothing."[100]

The special position of the person, his or her role in the implementation of the law, should be taken into account when arguing in favor of the ethical legitimization of criminal law. Marek Piechowiak, interpreting the works of Kaufmann, points out that the goal of the law is to provide man in his historical being with what he deserves. An analysis of Kaufmann's studies on the relationship between law and morality allows us to assume that the task of law is to enable man to achieve personal fulfillment.[101] Therefore, one of the criteria for justifying the law is the criterion of personal treatment of a human being, especially in the context of his or her freedom and the need for self-fulfillment.

In practice, the search for justifications for the legitimization of the law is based on different models—depending on the type of conditions. One of them should be the ethical legitimization of criminal law, which—according to the above division into four strands proposed by M. Stępień—can be qualified as relational legitimacy. Decisions in the area of criminal law are compared to ethical decisions, thus seeking justification for them. The importance of ethics in justifying the law, and thus its legitimacy, may have different generic weights depending on the branch of law to which the norms to be legitimized belong. In the case of criminal law, the relationship between content and ethics or, from the practical point of view, morality, is very strong, which makes it seem natural to seek in ethics the origin of some of the legislator's decisions, inspiration for them or, finally, models allowing the construction of criminal responsibility to be compared with the problems of ethical evaluation of responsibility. This is because criminal law, in its essence, is reactive with regard to the social image of evil and responsibility for it. In other words, criminal law does not create bad behaviors, much less should it transform behaviors judged morally good into legally criminalized behaviors. Thus, criminal law is a kind of matrix imposed on the whole complex of social norms, including moral norms, some of which, as a result of being covered by this matrix, become sanctioned by norms of a criminal law nature.

The relationship between criminal law and ethics described here is legitimized, but not validated. This means that the enforceability of criminal law does not depend on its compliance with moral standards. Formally in the legal system, all standards corresponding to the system of sources of law, adopted in the appropriate procedure and promulgated, are in force. Giving moral decisions a legitimizing power, not a validating one, means that outside the scope of the considerations conducted here, the classic problem of the possibility of refusing to obey a norm, which is in conflict with legal norms, is left out.

The search for justifications, that is, grounds for legitimacy, can be carried out in the area of criminal law, if the codex system is used, in relation to the general and specific parts of criminal law. This process for the specific part takes place within the framework of the criminalization discourse. As it seems, it is not too risky to say that the essence of the proposed theories of criminalization, as well as the discussion on the acceptable scope of criminalization, is precisely the search for justification, or possibly indicating its absence, for the criminalization decisions taken by the legislator. Another space is the issue of legitimizing the issues determining the scope of responsibility, included in the Polish tradition in the framework of the general part of the penal code, which is the subject of the concept of legitimization proposed here.

When considering the issue of ethics in the context of the legitimization of criminal law, it is impossible not to mention the reconstructive concept proposed by Joshua Kleinfeld.[102] He assumes that the form of social life is the embodiment of an ethical life which, following Hegel, can be called *Sittlichkeit*. According to Kleinfeld, the role of normative philosophy is not so much to impose external and abstract ideas on the world as to bring out the values that are already objects in various social relations in a way that shows them better, perhaps more accurately, and allows for their criticism.[103]

The subject of this book is not an analysis or criticism of the assumptions of normative philosophy, whether interpreted by J. Kleinfeld or another researcher, but rather an auxiliary reference to the proposed apparatus in these areas in order to consider the meaning and influence of ethics on the construction of criminal responsibility. However, one might raise doubts about Kleinfeld's philosophical position, his conclusions about the tasks of philosophy, especially ethics, are perfectly consistent with the concept of the ethical legitimization of criminal law. It does not imply the need to discover ethical ideas external to society, which should be imposed on it with the help of instruments proper to criminal law. Ethical legitimization, which appears as the original legitimization of criminal law, consists rather in the search for compatibility between the anthropological and ethical characteristics of man, resulting in a significant part from his dignity, and criminal law, especially the structures contained therein which shape the principles of criminal responsibility.

The main assumption of the reconstructivism referred to here is that criminal law plays a unique role in social life. It is the tool of a community which allows the foundations of moral social order, that is, the principles of moral life of members of a given community, to be reconstructed.[104] Criminal law concerns primarily those rights which are not only violated but also questioned by persons violating the social order. Questioning these rights leads, in consequence, to questioning the social order as such. The reconstructivism of criminal law consists in restoring a disrupted social order, also through the imposition and enforcement of criminal penalties.

In the light of the previous considerations, the concept of a self-governing legal order or sovereignty of law as such must once again be called into question.[105] Even if we assume that the legitimization of a particular legal solution may also take on a legal character, thus seeking justification in accordance with a legal norm, even if placed higher in the hierarchical system of sources of law, this is neither the only, nor even more the definitive, criterion of legitimacy. It only determines the validity of a given solution, which takes the form of a norm or a set of legal norms. The criteria for justifying a rule of law must, for the reasons already set out above, be outside the legal system itself, and that system may indicate them directly or indirectly.

CONCLUSIONS

There seem to be at least three points of reference shaping the perspective of evaluating criminal law: the coherence of the legal system, the will of the legislator, and the virtues of citizens.[106] This does not mean, of course, that it is impossible to indicate other points which would make it possible to assess the solutions adopted in criminal law, but the three points touch on the most frequently mentioned levels in the context of repressive law, which criminal law undoubtedly is.[107]

By the coherence of the legal system, I mean first of all the desire to build criminal law institutions in such a way that they are as close as possible to the legal categories used by other branches of law. Moreover, what may be even more characteristic of this view of criminal law, the perspective of coherence, makes it necessary to strive for the internal coherence of criminal law, and thus to organize its structure in such a way that all its elements fit perfectly together and form a mechanism embedded in the preferred theoretical concept. In this perspective, scientific papers and debates are written which aim above all to consistently apply the previously adopted theoretical concept. This becomes the most important objective of the conducted analyses, in extreme cases detaching the conducted studies from the verification of their effects by any attempt at application and observation of their consequences. This does not mean that maintaining the analysis of criminal law in a coherent paradigm should be viewed negatively. On the contrary, if the theoretical analysis is carried out in order to achieve the guarantee effect, it deserves not only approval but also dissemination. Apart from the intellectual attractiveness of theoretical and dogmatic reflection—building coherent normative structures is undoubtedly a very interesting challenge—it must be concluded that the guarantee aspect is of primary importance.[108] An internally coherent structure allows for a structured analysis of a practical nature, significantly increasing the likelihood of correct and, above all, true conclusions being reached. The analysis of a specific criminal case leads to the conviction that punishment of a person suspected of committing a crime is all the more justified if the premises of the act, illegality, punishment, guilt, and punishment are correctly verified. However, the pursuit of an internal theoretical and dogmatic coherence of criminal law should not be an end in itself.[109]

The second point of reference—the legislator's will or vision—is to be achieved by means of various tools, including criminal law. The issues of the legislator's will as a factor defining the legitimacy of criminal law making and constituting the only perspective for its assessment are related to questions of criminal policy and sometimes also penal populism.[110] It is obvious that the authorities conduct criminal policy.[111] It also consists of shaping, in the direction it chooses, a catalog of principles of responsibility, types of offenses, and sanctions. This reality, however, does not have to translate into a limitation of verification of the lawmaking right only to compare it with the will of the legislator.

Criminal law can and should serve something other than merely sanctioning the will of the legislator. More detailed justifications are needed. As Andrzej Zoll once noted, the norm of criminal law should not boil down to expressing only the will of the legislator that its addressees should act in a specific way. Rather, the norm should be understood in such a way that it expresses both a court that values a given behavior and an order of specific behavior according to the judgment expressed.[112] The use of criminal law is a striking, and sometimes also effective, instrument for responding to social expectations. As with the previous perspective, this one should not be entirely overturned or rejected. After all, criminal law is one of the instruments for exercising state power. However, it is important that the rationale for establishing criminal law norms should not be reduced to voluntaristic arguments alone.

The two previously mentioned paradigms of understanding criminal law evaluation should be subordinated to the principle of the commonweal and the resulting directive to promote the development of virtues by citizens, that is, members of the community whose good is at the heart of our concerns.[113] Independently of other objectives, the state should first and foremost care about the conditions for citizens to achieve their aspirations, ambitions, and develop their personalities. It does not seem particularly controversial to assume that an ideal society is one where people aspire to their perfection, respecting each other's subjectivity expressed in freedoms and rights. In this paradigm, the most important human rights documents have been written, such as the Universal Declaration of Human Rights[114] and the International Covenant on Civil and Political Rights.[115] The constitutions of many countries also refer to these values, expressing them both in the preambles and in their individual chapters. One example of such a constitution is the Constitution of the Republic of Poland, and especially the principle of the commonweal (Art. 1) and the inherent and inalienable dignity of every human being expressed in it (Art. 30).[116]

The goal of the law thus reconstructed, that is, the promotion of the development of human virtues, the creation of conditions for man to be ever better, not only morally but also in terms of developing other types of competence, shows the close relationship between the law and morality.[117] It is not a question of such a relationship which would have a validative character, and thus make the enforceability of the law dependent on the compliance of its content with a moral norm. It is rather a matter of scope and purpose. The scope relationship is unquestionable, which can be seen especially in criminal law. Numerous behaviors described as prohibited in criminal law are also considered immoral in various ethical systems. By purpose relationship, I mean the pursuit of the same goal by the legal system and the ethical system. Both, one and the other, should be aimed at the good and perfection of man, while moral principles usually are going to be based on norms maximally oriented toward this goal, while legal norms—and criminal law norms in particular—on the implementation of the minimum program, while simultaneously encouraging goals close to maximalistic ones to be accomplished. Criminal law has a specific role to play here, since it primarily sanctions behavior that is contrary to what is desirable, and thus indirectly encourages appropriate conduct.

Certain differences, such as a maximalistic ethical approach and a minimalistic approach to criminal law, should not lead to the conclusion that there are no points of contact. Both these systems seek to support man in his quest for perfection, indicate the desired conduct of man, and provide for his responsibility for violating moral or legal norms, respectively. Such a statement should already lead to a conclusion authorizing a joint analysis of ethical and criminal law norms to be conducted. There is, however, at least one more argument in favor of this approach. Ethics are primary in relation to criminal law. In other words, it is a logical, if not chronological, *prius* in relation to positive law, including criminal law. Questions about how to act, how to behave, and for what one can answer are first and foremost ethical questions, and only then legal questions. It seems appropriate to refer to ethics in criminal law research, especially when we are trying to answer fundamental questions about criminal responsibility.[118]

Ethical legitimization can be understood as the authentication of the established criminal law in the light of the ethical norms which in a given legal system are considered relevant. A catalog of these ethical standards must be established in each case by reference to the legal system in question. It also depends on the period during which criminal law standards are analyzed from the perspective of their ethical legitimacy. In view of the pluralistic approach to morality and the dynamic evolution of the various ethical evaluations, it is difficult today to recognize that in all legal systems the ethical authentication process discussed here can be carried out in the light of the same criteria.

It is worth noting that different types of legitimization of criminal law do not have to be mutually exclusive. There is no order to choose one type of legitimization and reject others at the same time. Possible contradictions between them may result only from the content of particular legitimization criteria. It is difficult to imagine that the law in a given legal system would at the same time be ideologically legitimized as belonging to a totalitarian state and would at the same time meet the criteria of international legal legitimacy.

As has been stressed several times above, the criteria for legitimization are not validation criteria, which means that their fulfillment does not determine the validity of a given legal norm.[119] On the other hand, its effectiveness and the ability to achieve much more far-reaching objectives of the legal system, than an objective directly linked to a legal norm, may depend on these criteria and, consequently, on the authentication of the legal norm. This is perfectly expressed by the statement of Z. Ziembiński, who pondered the classic—as he himself noted—dispute within the philosophy of law oscillating around the question of whether a sufficient basis for the law are certain values or a sufficient basis is the lawmaker's will. Even before the development of the argumentation in this respect, the author states that

> it is impossible to construct a system of legal norms capable of functioning without referring to one or another set of assessments and values determined by them, which does not mean, however, that the assessments of some state of affairs by themselves determine that a legal norm ordering such state of affairs to be realised is in force.[120]

Using this thought, one may conclude that it is not possible to construct criminal law, also in terms of the rules governing criminal liability, without referring to a set of values, which does not mean that these values give or take away the validity of the law.

The search for the ethical legitimization of criminal law does not even mean that the norms of this branch of law should cause that human activity bring good exclusively.[121] Such a task is rather to be found in the case of other branches of law. Rather, criminal law is aimed at making individuals accountable for their misappropriation of the values of a political community—values that are so important that they are subject to criminal sanctions. The moral, and therefore ethically legitimized, dimension of criminal law is to correspond to the welfare of the individual concerned, that is, to the welfare of the perpetrator who is called to responsibility and the welfare of the victim. The postulate of seeking the good of the perpetrator should not lead to confusion, which could be caused by a misinterpretation indicating that welfare should be understood as a lenient criminal law aimed primarily at relieving the perpetrator from liability. Criminal law that is good for the offender is a law that consists of principles that correspond to the extent to which human responsibility is permitted. In other words, a good criminal law is a law which takes into account who man is, and therefore his anthropological construction; which understands the decision-making processes taking place in man; which is free from assumptions about man that are not covered by reality. Criminal law should not pursue the goal of developing an ideal human being who meets some or all of the ideological criteria, which are often utopian at the same time. The point is rather that criminal law should be adapted to what man is like, so as to enable him to be held accountable in so far as he can actually be held responsible.

The construction of legal norms in an ethical context, with anthropological and axiological aspects, is so important and characteristic of a state requiring loyalty from its citizens that it can even be presumed.[122] It is important that at least the criterion so outlined is fulfilled in the negative aspect, understood as the absence of contradiction between the state law and the ethical context of social life of a given political community. The actual overthrow of this presumption may even lead, as Ziembiński notes, to an objection which may take the form of passive resistance and civil disobedience, and in extreme cases even to an open rebellion.[123]

Zygmunt Ziembiński also notes that the discussion on the axiological foundations of the legal system usually takes two forms. First, it is conducted on the basis of the philosophy of law, which examines the moral value of law as a social institution. Second, and particularly importantly from the perspective of this study, the axiological justification of individual institutions is also discussed.[124] The concept presented here is not even about axiological evaluation but about verifying the correctness of individual criminal responsibility constructions from the perspective of the principles of ethical responsibility and the findings of philosophical anthropology, based on the convictions of the members of a given political community, acquired in the course of educational processes, and thus also within the framework of various stages of socialization.

It seems that Ziembiński was right when he claimed that the pluralistic character of contemporary societies does not exclude the possibility of finding a common system of values, which is also helped by the knowledge about the correctness of social life. Undoubtedly, it is also helped by the knowledge about the correctness of the individual, aspects of decision-making or his relation to the community.[125] One cannot, moreover, imagine a legal system whose norms would not be derived to some extent from the moral system. As Filip Ciepły rightly states, the legislator decides to introduce a given legal standard into the system precisely because he considers behaviors consistent with its model to be worth protecting, while behaviors contrary to it—to violate social welfare. Legal norms are based on axiological decisions made by the legislator.[126] It is also worth noting that the relevance of the ethical context, which includes axiological and anthropological aspects, is not limited only to the lawmaking stage. Moral assessments, despite their alleged ambiguity and disputability, shape the legal norm in the process of interpreting the regulations. The law enforcement authority may not disregard the moral assessments prevailing in society.[127]

The postulate indicating the validity of the ethical legitimization of criminal law should in no way be interpreted as an attempt to impose a specific concept of morality with the use of legal instruments, in a situation where a given moral and legal issue gives rise to numerous controversies and disputes and therefore is not the subject of consent. In such cases, the ethical legitimization of criminal law does not consist in a simple alignment of the content of established legal norms with any ethical position raised in public debate, even if it is a majority position. Although moral issues, by their very nature, are not subject to verification by the voting method, this is undoubtedly a method appropriate for the lawmaking process. In matters covered by this book, that is, the general principles of criminal responsibility, the space for moral conflict is not as wide as in the case of the issue of the scope of punishment set out in the form of a catalog of types of prohibited acts. However, if such a conflict is identified and at the same time it is determined that the positions presented are internally consistent, meeting the basic requirements for positions presented in public debate, it may be necessary to consider a compromise solution. This does not yet require the introduction of a settlement that reconciles conflicting positions. It may turn out that the polemical position(s) are marginal, and therefore do not have the potential to indicate that they should be included in the final solution. In such a case, it would seem appropriate to provide information on the legal solution adopted in order to confront it with possible moral insights. As has already been noted above, people with moral positions in the obvious minority are usually aware that the majority—which may mean that the legal system as well—takes a different approach to a given issue. It should also be noted that the inclusion in a legislative act of a decision based on a compromise also requires that citizens be reached with information describing the solutions adopted, so as to make them aware of the differences between their moral intuition and legal reality. Compromise, however, has the advantage that it gives a chance for a specific moral understanding of the solutions adopted by a wide range of recipients.[128]

The problem of compromise in relation to the issues of the general part of criminal law is not as important as in the case of the issues covered by the specific part. The concept of ethical legitimization presented here concerns the general part of criminal law, often overlooked in discussions on the moral aspects of criminal responsibility. Michael S. Moore rightly observes that the discourse on criminal law actually involves two different moral judgments.[129] The first concerns the types of behaviors taken up by people. It is about assessing whether these typified behaviors are good or bad. In this area, we are dealing with the abstract assessment of a given type of behavior, referring, among other things, to the moral beliefs present in society. The second concerns the responsibility of a specific person at a specific time for a specific act. That judgment is to determine whether the person concerned has committed an act corresponding to the type and whether guilt can be attributed to him or her. Both of these types of judgments have different moral theories in the background. The first is created in the context of the rules of detailed ethics, indicating good and bad behavior. We are looking for answers to such questions as follows: "Is abortion bad?" "Should aiding and abetting euthanasia be punished?" "Should suicide be legal?"[130] M. S. Moore describes the second theory, which is connected with the second type of judgment, as the morality of honest attribution of guilt. It is a theory of responsibility, indicating when a person is morally responsible for doing evil. We are looking for answers to such questions as follows: "Is sleepwalking a deed?" "Should the perpetrator know in advance (and may even accept) the specific moral norms that he or she is violating in order to be able to attribute responsibility for their violation to him or her?"[131]

However, one cannot agree with the thesis that the theory of responsibility is morally neutral, although it undoubtedly involves a much lower level of moral controversy, and on some issues, this controversy may not even occur at all.[132] This does not mean, however, that the undisputed character of a given issue or disputed to a relatively small extent can be interpreted in terms of its moral neutrality. Ethics, like criminal law, are divided into general ethics and specific ethics, which in itself makes it possible to argue that the content of the theory of responsibility is not morally indifferent. On the grounds of criminal law, the thesis on the ethics of law seems justified.[133]

The findings so far allow us to formulate three theses in favor of the ethical legitimization of criminal law:

1. The task of criminal law is to maintain social order and restore it where it has been disturbed as a result of a committed crime. The social order consists of moral norms that guide the members of the social community when they engage in socially relevant activities. Criminal law cannot effectively perform this task if, in the part concerning the principles of responsibility, it is inconsistent with ethical norms and the provisions of philosophical anthropology adopted and reflected in social attitudes. Possible differences should be communicated and explained to the public.
2. The legitimacy of seeking the rightness of solutions adopted in the general part of the penal code by means of ethical legitimization is also indicated by the historical aspect. Criminal law in our legal culture has developed from canon law and indirectly from moral theology. The changes that took place with the codification of the Enlightenment

period also originated from a specific philosophical reflection, including an ethical one. This allows us to claim that the shape of criminal law institutions, on which reflection is practiced within the framework of the theory of responsibility, is a consequence of philosophical thought, especially anthropological and ethical thought. To the extent that this thought is built into a paradigm of realistic philosophy, its conclusions may reflect the beliefs of citizens and their intuitions about the possibility of criminal responsibility in specific situations. Ethical legitimization therefore consists in searching in philosophical anthropology and ethics for arguments in favor of the legitimization of the legal solutions adopted, and thus also in verifying whether the principles of criminal responsibility are consistent with the idea of the scope of this responsibility, which is available to the members of society.

3. One of the basic principles of the Polish legal system is the principle of inherent and inalienable human dignity expressed in Article 30 of the Constitution of the Republic of Poland. One of its functions is to open the legal system to an ethical context. In order to ensure that the law it lays down complies with the principle of human dignity, the legislator is obliged to determine the content of this system at least to the extent that it follows from the principle of dignity. This means that the ethical legitimization of part of the general criminal law consists in seeking justification for legal constructions in those moral contents which are contained in the principle of human dignity or to which this principle refers. This thesis will be developed further in the later sections of this book.

NOTES

1. D. Priel, *The Place of Legitimization in Legal Theory*, "McGill Law Journal" 2011, vol. 57, no. 1, p. 3.

2. A. Grabowski, *Prawnicze pojęcie obowiązywania prawa stanowionego. Krytyka niepozytywistycznej koncepcji prawa*, Kraków 2009, p. 227.

3. Ibid, pp. 288–365.

4. Z. Ziembiński, *O stanowieniu i obowiązywaniu prawa. Zagadnienia podstawowe*, Warsaw 1995, p. 41. Cf. too K.A. Brożek, *Standardy etyczne w prawie. Próba systematyzacji*, Warsaw 2018, p. 115.

5. Z. Ziembiński, *O stanowieniu. . .* , p. 41.

6. D. Priel, *The Place. . .* , p. 6.

7. Z. Ziembiński, *O stanowieniu. . .* , p. 41.

8. Ibid, p. 43. According to D. Priel, this problem is not ostensible at all, but it can be solved with the help of the category of legitimization. Cf. D. Priel, *The Place. . .* , p. 25.

9. Zygmunt Ziembiński calls it "ideological competence." The word "ideology" is often perceived today as a pejorative term, so it is better to use the term "axiological competence," which equally well, if not better, reflects the intentions presented in this statement. Cf. Z. Ziembiński, *O stanowieniu. . .* , p. 43.

10. Ibid, p. 44.

11. In Z. Ziembiński's opinion, the procedures and norms of the constitution are to limit arbitrariness in lawmaking. Cf. ibid, p. 51.

12. D. Priel, *The Place. . .* , p. 10.

13. W. Jedlecka, *Legitymizacja prawa Unii Europejskiej. Legitymizacja demokratyczna czy cywilizacyjne?*, Łódź 2014, p. 13; W. Sokół, *Legitymizacja polityczna.* In: B. Szmulik, M. Żmigrodzki (ed.), *Wprowadzenie do nauki o państwie i polityce*, Lublin 2006, p. 221.

14. W. Jedlecka, *Legitymizacja prawa. . .* , p. 14. Cf. too W. Sokół, *Legitymizacja polityczna. . .* , p. 221.

15. A. Wierzchowska, *Konceptualizacja pojęcia "legitymizacja."* In: K.A. Wojtaszczyk, *Legitymizacja procesów integracji europejskiej*, Warsaw 2006, pp. 14–15.

16. G. Skąpska, J. Stelmach, *Współczesne problemy i modele legitymizacji prawa*, "Colloquia Communia" 1988–1989, t. 6, no. 41–42, p. 7.

17. Ibid, pp. 7–8. Cf. too W. Jedlecka, *Legitymizacja prawa. . .* , p. 17.

18. D. Priel, *The Place. . .* , p. 6.

19. The importance of historical legitimization of criminal law also emerges from Juliusz Makarewicz's recently resumed work *Polish Criminal Law.* He began researching the history of Polish criminal law in the pre-Partition era, as Adam Redzik notes, as soon as there was a chance of Poland's rebirth, that is, with the outbreak of the Great War in 1914. This allows us to believe that in this way he wanted to prepare, in the area of his interests, the ground for building the reborn Republic of Poland. What else could be the motive for achieving the goal, which, as J. Makarewicz himself noted, was to give an image of Polish criminal law, corresponding to the state at the twilight of the Commonwealth of Poland? Cf. J. Makarewicz, *Polskie prawo karne. Część ogólna*, Warsaw 2017, especially the preface by A. Redzik (ibid., p. 10).

20. Ibid, p. 33. H.J. Berman, *Prawo i rewolucja. Kształtowanie się zachodniej tradycji prawnej*, transl. S. Amsterdamski, Warsaw 1995, p. 33.

21. Ibid, p. 33.

22. Ibid., p. 208.

23. However, the approach he proposes is not universally accepted. David Beetham defines it as an unqualified disaster. In Beetham's opinion, the legitimization of this assessment is determined by the concepts derived later from Weber's proposal. The task of the authorities was to maintain the citizens' conviction that the individual institutions of power were the most suitable for the needs of society. Cf. D. Beetham, *The Legitimation of Power*, Houndmills – London 1991, p. 9.

24. M. Weber, *Trzy typy prawomocnego panowania.* In: W. Derczyński, A. Jasińska-Kania, J. Szacki, *Elementy teorii socjologicznych. Materiały do dziejów współczesnej socjologii zachodniej*, Warsaw 1975, p. 539.

25. Ibid, pp. 540–41.

26. Ibid, pp. 541–42.
27. Ibid, p. 545.
28. T.D. Weldon, *The Vocabulary of Politics*, London 1953, p. 62. Cf. too D. Priel, *The Place. . .* , p. 15.
29. D. Priel, *The Place. . .* , pp. 17–18.
30. G. Skąpska, J. Stelmach, *Współczesne problemy. . .* , p. 6. J. Habermas expressed a similar view, indicating a connection between the research on legitimization and the crisis of legitimization, *Communication and the Evolution of Society*, Boston 1979, as cited in: W. Sokół, *Legitymizacja polityczna. . .* , pp. 223–24.
31. Z. Pulka, *Legitymizacja państwa w prawoznawstwie*, Wrocław 1996, pp. 9–10.
32. M. Stępień, *Legitymizacja prawa w różnych modelach demokracji.* In: A. Preisner (ed.), *Prawowitość czy zgodność z prawem. Legitymizacja władzy w państwach demokratycznych*, Wrocław 2010, pp. 32–33. Cf. too W. Jedlecka, *Legitymizacja prawa. . .* , p. 18.
33. R.H. Fallon, *Legitimization and the Constitution*, "Harvard Law Review" 2005, vol. 118, no. 6, p. 1790.
34. Ibid, p. 1794.
35. According to R. H. Fallon, the legislative authority has a much smaller margin of error. The author does not argue in favor of this thesis, except to refer to a well-known U.S. Supreme Court judgment in the case of *Marbury v. Madison* (5 U.S.) (I Cranch) 137 (1803). Cf. R.H. Fallon, *Legitimacy. . .* , p. 1794.
36. Ibid, p. 1795.
37. Ibid, p. 1796.
38. Ibid, p. 1797.
39. Ibid, pp. 1799–1800.
40. M. Renzo, *State Legitimization and Self*-Defence, "Law and Philosophy" 2011, vol. 30, no. 5, pp. 575–76.
41. Ibid, p. 576.
42. Ibid, p. 578.
43. Ibid, p. 600.
44. G. Skąpska, J. Stelmach, *Współczesne problemy. . .* , p. 6.
45. Ibid, p. 6.
46. H.J. Berman, *Prawo i rewolucja. Kształtowanie się zachodniej tradycji prawnej*, przeł. S. Amsterdamski, Warsaw 1995, p. 30.
47. However, this does not mean that H.J. Berman believes that revolution is a desirable phenomenon. In another part of his book he points out that the revolution "in the historical sense of the term is a rapid, violent, discontinuous change that destroys the bonds of the legal system." Cf. Ibid.
48. Ibid, p. 30.
49. J. Habermas, *Communication. . .* , pp. 223–24. Cf. too W. Jedlecka, *Legitymizacja prawa. . .* , p. 15.
50. D. Beetham, *The Legitimation. . .* , p. 3 et seq.
51. Ibid, pp. 4–5.
52. Ibid, p. 5.

53. S. Vasiliev, *Between International Criminal Justice and Injustice: Theorising Legitimization.* In: C. Bailliet, N. Hayashi (ed.), *The Legitimization of International Criminal Tribunals*, Cambridge 2016, p. 75.

54. Ibid, pp. 75–76.

55. D. Beetham, *The Legitimation. . .* , p. 11. Marian Cieślak noted that "it is desirable for criminal law to be shaped in such a way that it corresponds as far as possible to the moral norms adopted in a given society." The author notes that, among other things, the effectiveness of criminal law depends on this. Cf. M. Cieślak, *Dzieła wybrane. Tom III. Polskie prawo karne. Zarys systemowego ujęcia*, Kraków 2011, p. 24.

56. D. Beetham proposes such a division, ibid, p. 72.

57. The concept of axiological competence refers to the ideological competence described by Z. Ziembiński. Cf. Z. Ziembiński, *O stanowieniu. . .* , p. 43.

58. G. Skąpska, J. Stelmach, *Współczesne problemy. . .* , p. 10. Cf. too M. Zieliński, Z. Ziembiński, *Uzasadnianie twierdzeń, ocen i norm w prawoznawstwie*, Warsaw 1988, pp. 162–63.

59. T.R. Tyler et al., *Legitimization and Criminal Justice: International Perspectives.* In: T.R. Tyler (ed.), *Legitimization and Criminal Justice*, 2007 (no location for printing), p. 10.

60. Cf. D.J. Smith, *The Foundations of Legitimization.* In: T.R. Tyler (ed.), *Legitimacy. . .* , p. 56.

61. I refer to the assumptions and results of the conducted research following: A.V. Papachristos, T.L. Meares, J. Fagan, *Why Do Criminals Obey the Law? The Influence of Legitimization and Social Networks on Active Gun Offenders*, "Journal of Criminal Law and Criminology" 2012, vol. 102, no. 2, p. 397 et seq. The project's research consisted of asking a series of questions to a group of 141 firearms offenders in 52 locations ("neighbourhoods") in Chicago.

62. Ibid, p. 399.

63. J. Jackson, T.R. Tyler, *Future Challenges in the Study of Legitimization and Criminal Justice*, "SSRN Electronic Journal" 2013, March, p. 7.

64. "Social order depends on the widespread belief that the authorities, and their political and legal framework, are legitimate. As long as that belief is widespread, people will largely regulate their own behavior by reference to internalised values that correspond with the law and its underlying principles, and force need only occasionally be used when people get out of line," D.J. Smith, *The Foundations of Legitimization.* In: A. Braga et al. (ed.), *Legitimization and Criminal Justice*, New York 2007, p. 30.

65. At the same time, procedural fairness plays a very important role in the process of legitimizing the actions of the authorities. Cf. J. Jackson, T.R. Tyler, *Future Challenges. . .* , p. 3.

66. Ibid, p. 8.

67. T.R. Tyler, S.L. Blader, *Can Business Effectively Regulate Employee Conduct? The Antecedents of Rule Following in Work Settings*, "The Academy of Management Journal" 2005, vol. 48, no. 6, p. 1145.

68. K.M. Carlsmith, J.M. Darley, P.H. Robinson, *Why Do We Punish? Deterrence and Just Deserts as Motives for Punishment*, "Journal of Personality and Social Psychology" 2002, vol. 83, no. 2, p. 285.

69. K. M. Carlsmith, J. M. Darley, P. H. Robinson, *Why Do We Punish?* p. 286.

70. Ibid, p. 296.

71. Ibid, p. 296.

72. J. Jackson, T.R. Tyler, *Future Challenges. . .*, p. 11.

73. J.M. Darley, K.M. Carlsmith, P.H. Robinson, *The Ex Ante Function of the Criminal Law*, "Law & Society Review" 2001, vol. 35, no. 1, p. 168.

74. Ibid, pp. 170–71.

75. For more on this, see K. Szczucki, *O miłosiernym lekarzu, czyli o moralnych podstawach prawnego obowiązku.* In: B. Namysłowska-Gabrysiak, K. Syroka-Marczewska, A. Walczak-Żochowska (ed.), *Prawo wobec problemów społecznych. Księga Jubileuszowa profesor Eleonory Zielińskiej*, Warsaw 2016, p. 859 et seq.

76. J.M. Darley, K.M. Carlsmith, P.H. Robinson, *The Ex Ante Function. . .*, p. 181.

77. Ibid, p. 182.

78. Especially of note is the work edited by Adam Podgórecki, *Poglądy społeczeństwa polskiego na moralność i prawo*, Warsaw 1971.

79. A. Podgórecki, *Normy prawne a normy moralne.* In: A. Podgórecki (ed.), *Poglądy. . .*, p. 50. However, this relationship does not seem to be universal in the sense that criminalization against the moral convictions of society will imply a negative moral assessment of the criminalized behavior.

80. Ibid.

81. Ibid. pp. 81–82.

82. Ibid. p. 83.

83. Ibid. p. 85.

84. P.H. Robinson, J.M. Darley, *Justice, Responsibility and Blame*, Boulder—San Francisco—Oxford 1995, p. 2.

85. Ibid, p. 7.

86. P.H. Robinson, J.M. Darley, *Justice. . .*, p. 203.

87. The analysis of the empirical research referred to above also shows that the respondents are relatively often in favor of attributing criminal responsibility to the perpetrator and, at the same time, not imposing punishment (P. H. Robinson, J. M. Darley, *Justice. . .*, p. 203). This is not entirely surprising, as such a construction is known to penal systems. In criminal legislation, there are grounds for not imposing a sentence, while at the same time establishing the offender's responsibility for the crime. Such a construction, in some cases desired by society, can also confirm the moral dimension of criminal law. What would be the purpose of convicting someone without serving a punishment, which would not be a conditional withdrawal from serving a punishment, if not moral and simultaneously educative. In such cases, it is a communication issued by the court on behalf of the state—the community—expressing a negative assessment of the offender's behavior, but taking into account the specific circumstances that justify not imposing a sentence.

88. D. Priel, *The Place. . .* , p. 24.

89. By the way, it is worth noting that the problem of the legitimization of the law is very significant in relation to international criminal law, which has been gaining in importance since the end of World War II, and in particular since the period set by the International Military Tribunal in Nuremberg and the International Military Tribunal for the Far East in Tokyo, for example in the creation of the International Criminal Court. According to S. Vasiliev, the international criminal justice system is in a phase of constant legitimization crisis (S. Vasiliev, *Between International. . .* , p. 70). It is pointed out that the institutions belonging to this system are obliged to continuously prove the legitimacy of their existence (D. Luban, *After the Honeymoon: Reflections on the Current State of International Criminal Justice*, "Journal of International Criminal Justice" 2013, vol. 11, no. 3, p. 509). International criminal tribunals, unlike national courts, do not participate in the legitimization given to the entire legal or institutional system in a given state. It is also much easier to establish a certain set of criteria for legitimization within a community designated by the existence of a state and to verify their fulfillment. Thus, states are now, at least for the most part, a typical area of legitimization for authorities, institutions and laws. International law, especially the relatively young ones such as criminal law, does not have such a natural legitimization value. Similar difficulties arise in relation to European criminal law, and undoubtedly the European Union, much more than the international community, provides a stronger axiological context for legitimization (C. Peristeridou, *The Principle of Legality in European Criminal Law*, 2015 (b.w.), p. 221 et seq.). It is worth mentioning that one tries to look for an axiological context of legitimization also for international criminal law and European criminal law. This is particularly evident in the case of the latter system, since the European Union, apart from its purely economic dimension, is also built in the spirit of various values that resound in various legal acts, both primary and secondary. The EU legal order is strongly influenced by the Convention for the Protection of Human Rights and Fundamental Freedoms. The Charter of Fundamental Rights also plays an important role in this respect.

90. G. Skąpska, J. Stelmach, *Współczesne problemy. . .* , p. 14. Cf. too W. Jedlecka, *Legitymizacja prawa. . .* , p. 17. Although M. Peno claims that the influence of natural law on criminal law is historical in nature, it is for this reason that we can claim that the institutions of criminal law that have been formed over the centuries have also drawn from this way of thinking about law, including criminal law. Cf. M. Peno, Philosophical Basics. . . , p. 114 et seq.

91. J. Hervada, *Prawo naturalne*, translated by A. Dorabialska, Kraków 2011, pp. 10–11.

92. Ibid, p. 15.

93. Ibid, p. 15.

94. Ibid, p. 105 et seq.

95. Cf. M. Piechowiak, *W poszukiwaniu ontologicznych podstaw prawa. Arthura Kaufmanna teoria sprawiedliwości*, Warsaw—Poznań 1992, p. 13.

96. T. Chauvin, *Homo iuridicus. Człowiek jako podmiot prawa publicznego*, Warsaw 2014, p. 29.

97. Ibid., p. 39.

98. A. Kaufmann, *Vorüberlegungen zu einer juristischen Logik und Ontologie der Relationen. Grundlegung einer personalen Rechtstheorie*, "Rechtstheorie. Zeitschrift für Logik, Methodenlehre, Kybernetik und Soziologie des Rechts" 1986, vol. 17 no. 3, p. 270, as cited in: M. Piechowiak, *W poszukiwaniu. . .* , p. 79.

99. Ibid, *Problemgeschichte der Rechtsphilosophie.* In: A. Kaufmann, W. Hassemer (ed.), *Einführung in Rechtsphilosophie und Rechtstheorie der Gegenwart*, 1985 (no place of publication), as cited in: M. Piechowiak, *W poszukiwaniu. . .* , p. 79.

100. Ibid, *Vorüberlegungen. . .* , p. 276, as cited in: M. Piechowiak, *W poszukiwaniu. . .* , p. 80.

101. M. Piechowiak, *W poszukiwaniu. . .* , pp. 87–88.

102. J. Kleinfeld, *Reconstructivism: The Place of Criminal Law in Ethical Life*, "Harvard Law Review" 2016, vol. 129, no. 6, p. 1485 et seq.

103. Ibid, p. 1487.

104. Ibid, p. 1489.

105. In the context of the legitimization of European law, J. Helios writes, *Modele legitymizacji prawa europejskiego*, "Zeszyty Naukowe Państwowej Wyższej Szkoły Zawodowej im. Witelona w Legnicy" 2008, no. 3, p. 28. However, one can be critical of the thesis raised by the author: "The role of European Community law is more important than that of the state, since in addition to the competence and procedural requirements for lawmaking, Community law also requires a specific legitimization and substantive justification, some of which relates to the scope of existing legal regulations," ibid. The author does not justify why the role of European Community law is more important or why national law does not require special legal legitimacy. This makes it all the more difficult to find an explanation for the view that national law does not require a substantive justification.

106. Civic virtues are a category of moral virtues that can be defined as the ability of an individual to make wise choices. To the extent that we speak of civic virtues, they will be choices concerning the political community; Cf. J. Finnis, *Human Rights and Common Good. Collected Essays*, vol. III, Oxford 2011, pp. 107–8.

107. In this part of the book I use an excerpt from my article *The relation between ethical and criminal responsibility on the example of the principle of double effect*, "Państwo i Prawo" 2019, no. 3, p. 78 et seq. The text was also published in China: 基于双重效应原则的道德责任与刑事责任的关系 ("Global Law Review" 2018, no. 2). The prospects for the coherence of the legal system and the will of the legislator are undoubtedly familiar to the science of law. Numerous scientific works, including those concerning criminal law, are based on them. The purpose of invoking these perspectives here is primarily to compare them with a third perspective, referring to the virtues of citizens.

108. The guarantee aspect of criminal law is also enshrined in the Constitution, especially in Article 42, paragraph 1; Cf. T. Sroka, *uwagi do art. 42 ust. 1.* In: *Konstytucja RP*, vol. I, *Komentarz do art. 1–86*, ed. L. Bosek, M. Safjan, Warsaw 2016, p. 1033 et seq.

109. Of course, this does not mean that the internal theoretical coherence of criminal law is irrelevant. It has already been noted that its important effect is

the possibility of the guarantee function of criminal law. Coherent theoretical solutions may also foster the correct implementation of the principle of equality in criminal law.

110. Michalina Szafrańska defines penal populism as "a political tactic oriented towards repressive criminal policy. This tactic consists of referring to beliefs or judgements commonly accepted in society—in a real or perceived manner—concerning crime and criminal policy, and proposing corresponding legal, political and organisational solutions. The real effectiveness of these solutions or the existence of criminal-political premises for their implementation is irrelevant. These beliefs or assessments constitute an intrinsic and sufficient justification for the solutions based on them, and irrefutable proof of their validity. This tactic is also distinguished by its specific style of communication (simple, emotional, symbolic), is characterised by the limited role of experts in shaping criminal policy and is based on a symbiotic relationship between politics, media and citizens" (M. Szafrańska, *Penalny populizm a media*, Kraków 2015, p. 39).

111. For more on this topic, see T. Szymanowski, *Przestępczość i polityka karna w Polsce w świetle faktów i opinii społeczeństwa w okresie transformacji*, Warsaw 2012, passim; B. Stańdo-Kawecka, *Polityka karna i penitencjarna między punitywizmem i menedżeryzmem*, Warsaw 2020, passim; W. Jaroch, *Polityka karna - strategia punitywna czy liberalna*, "Studia Prawnoustrojowe" 2012, no. 15, p. 15 et seq. W. Jaroch notes that criminal policy "is one of the elements of criminal policy by which we mean a system of diverse and interlinked state and social measures aimed at preventing, addressing the causes and circumstances of crime and limiting as far as possible, under the circumstances, the possibility of all kinds of criminogenic agents" (W. Jaroch, *Polityka karna. . .* , p. 15).

112. A. Zoll, *O normie prawnej z punktu widzenia prawa karnego*, "Krakowskie Studia Prawnicze" 1990, no. 23, p. 76.

113. As M. Królikowski noted, the theory of criminal law without axiological references "only constitutes a legal—in the pejorative sense of the word—statement referring to the real situation. Moreover, it is powerless if one tries to answer the question about the sense of a given solution in a different way than by juxtaposing formal and logical arguments referring to accepted figures, institutions and constructions. As a rule, this is not the answer most desired by the recipients of a conclusive statement" (M. Królikowski, *Kontekstowa teoria (dogmatyki) prawa karnego*, "Studia Iuridica" 2006, vol. 46, p. 180).

114. UN General Assembly Resolution 217 A (III) adopted and proclaimed on December 10, 1948.

115. Opened for signature in New York on December 16, 1966. (1977 Journal of Laws No. 38, item 167).

116. K. Szczucki, *Wykładnia prokonstytucyjna prawa karnego*, Warsaw 2015, *passim*.

117. The Anglo-Saxon literature indicates that in some cases, researchers of criminal law clearly adopt philosophical positions. This is the case, for example, in the discussion on the subjective elements of the definition of a crime – cf. J. Gardner, H. Jung, *Making Sense of Mens Rea: Antony Duff's Account*, "Oxford Journal of Legal

Studies" 1991, vol. 11, no. 4, p. 559. In Poland, this approach to analyzing these problems is not popular.

118. The acceptability of the act of criminalization must be examined from the perspective of this ethical system, which is the source of the values chosen by the political community as constitutive for it, i.e. this system which ethically legitimizes criminal law.

119. This concerns applicability in the formal sense. Another issue is the possible validity in conscience, which can also be called moral validity. In practice, effectively contesting it does not necessarily mean effectively contesting its formal validity.

120. Z. Ziembiński, *O stanowieniu. . .* , p. 89.

121. This vision of morally good law was presented by Z. Ziembiński. Cf. ibid, p. 93.

122. Ibid, p. 94.

123. Ibid, p. 94.

124. Ibid, p. 95.

125. Z. Ziembiński, *O stanowieniu. . .* , p. 96.

126. F. Ciepły, *Sprawiedliwościowa racjonalizacja wymiaru kary kryminalnej wobec współczesnych tendencji polityki karnej w Polsce*, Lublin 2017, pp. 100–101.

127. Z. Ziembiński, *O stanowieniu. . .* , pp. 94–95.

128. The compromise in question concerns legal solutions, not moral ones, in the sense that working out a legal compromise does not mean giving up differences in moral positions. These differences can be noticed and spoken of. It is a compromise characterized by public awareness of differences. Cf. D. Archard, *Moral Compromise*, "Philosophy" 2012, vol. 87, no. 3, p. 403 et seq.

129. M.S. Moore, *Placing Blame. A Theory of the Criminal Law*, Oxford 2012, p. 31.

130. Ibid, p. 31.

131. Ibid, p. 32.

132. The moral neutrality of this theory is suggested by M.S. Moore, ibid, p. 32.

133. The thesis on the ethics of law as a whole is formulated by K. A. Brożek in the Polish literature. He also proposes the following understanding of ethics: "Ethics are the inner spirit of the law and the spirit of morality, the conviction of harmony, of the uniformity of the law with morality, seemingly separate but united, of a state of harmony between the law and morality, a stable state, resulting not from consensus, but from the natural origin of both from one eternal Lawgiver of the whole order of things. This conviction is conditioned by the existence of an inner disposition which gives the ability to understand the meaning of the law and morality taken together" (*Standardy etyczne w prawie. Próba systematyzacji*, Warsaw 2018, p. 132).

Chapter 2

Human Dignity as the Fundamental Source of Criteria for Ethical Legitimization in Criminal Law

A PRELIMINARY ISSUE

The discussion of the content and function of the principle of human dignity aims to primarily show its importance in the analysis of criminal law, in particular the institutions regulating the principles of criminal responsibility. Dignity is therefore discussed to the extent necessary to consider its relevance to the ethical legitimization of criminal law and thus to the interpretation and reconstruction of the relationship between criminal law and ethics. The thesis will be verified that human dignity is an anthropological category within the philosophical meaning, incorporated into the legal system for a specific purpose. This aim is to orient the legal system toward the rights of man as he is. It is the duty of the legislator to design the solutions in a way that is subordinate to this approach.

Referring to the Kantian approach to philosophical anthropology, and especially to human dignity, it should be noted that dignity is immanently connected with the ability of the individual human to act morally. This ability is inherent in potential and can be updated in a positive or negative way. This means that there is no one whose conscious decisions cannot be morally assessed.[1] As I. U. Dalferth rightly observes, as a moral being, man is capable of orienting his life toward good or evil and, at the same time, is not capable of abandoning the orientation of his life toward good or evil.[2]

Man is not only a living rational being but also a being capable of taking responsibility. This means that not only does he retain the ability to decide about himself, set himself goals and achieve them, but he also has the ability to be accountable to others.[3] Responsibility includes not only the fact of the act or omission itself but also the qualitative aspect, that is, what was the act or under what conditions the omission was committed. All this means that we are members of a community of people who can call us to account for our various acts.[4]

Dignity therefore implies the possibility of holding a person accountable for his or her actions and omissions. Responsibility, as it seems, should not be interpreted as something potential, as an object of possibility, but as an element belonging to the essence of humanity, as dignity itself. The ability and obligation to take responsibility is—as cannot be questioned—a conclusion of fundamental importance for the criminal law, which concentrates precisely on the issue of responsibility. The recognition in man of the capacity to assume responsibility as such, by which pre-lawful and therefore moral responsibility must be understood first and foremost, leads to the possibility of taking further steps toward the recognition of the capacity to bear legal responsibility, including in particular criminal law responsibility.

Moreover, it is not only the mere fact that there is a substantial capacity, or perhaps even a substantial purpose, for responsibility to be incurred that is at issue but also its scope and the fundamental conditions for imputing responsibility. It seems natural that as soon as it is decided that a person is capable of taking responsibility, the question arises as to what this responsibility may look like, its scope, or, to put it another way, its limits. We should therefore consider whether it is possible to derive from dignity at least the basic premises allowing a system of principles guiding human responsibility to be outlined, while at the same time setting the framework for criminal responsibility.

This direction of search in the aspect of human dignity is determined not only by the very fact of the essential connection between human dignity and bearing responsibility. Human dignity also allows—through its anthropological location—something to be said about the individual themselves, their inclinations, characteristics, and thus to point to certain aspects of their being which can be taken into account in the process of constructing postulates in the face of criminal law, especially concerning the principles and scope of the imputed responsibility. What a person is, what they are characterized by, how they make decisions, what role their reason will play, and finally to what extent they are determined by external factors must influence the decision about the possible scope and shape of general constructions regulating criminal responsibility. Human dignity is therefore also a kind of bridge that entitles a lawyer to conduct anthropological deliberations for the purposes of making and applying criminal law.

After all, although for many contemporary jurists this may not make any difference, it seems that the search for coherence between criminal law and what follows from dignity leads to the ethical legitimization of criminal law.

THE CONTENT OF THE PRINCIPLE OF HUMAN DIGNITY

It can already be seen at this point that the principle of human dignity in the context of criminal responsibility seems to have two coherent functions. The first is to interpret dignity as a protected right in itself and as a right in which other rights protected by criminal law are rooted. Within this function of dignity, we can also interpret the directive on the obligation to treat people in a way that respects their subjectivity. Thus, dignity is the plane of reconstruction of protected rights for the purposes of criminalization and the determinant of boundaries in the application of criminal law institutions.[5]

The second function of human dignity in criminal law is to read in human dignity the basis for seeking the ethical legitimization of criminal law. This means that this principle also gains importance in the process of criminal law making—not only in terms of shaping types of prohibited acts but, above all, in terms of establishing the general principles of criminal responsibility, which determine the scope of application of the types of prohibited acts. The principle of human dignity is then used to reconstruct the anthropological vision of man for the needs of the legislator, in order to properly shape the structure and scope of the principles of criminal responsibility. Human dignity is seen here as a platform for understanding between the legislator and a specific anthropological concept of humanity, and in consequence also becomes a plane of relationship between moral responsibility and criminal responsibility.[6]

As the literature points out, human dignity is the subject of academic research undertaken from various perspectives, not only legal but also psychological, political, and bioethical.[7] The principle of human dignity in contemporary constitutionalism gained in importance after World War II, mainly due to the impulse resulting from UN documents, especially the Universal Declaration of Human Rights adopted in 1948. Nowadays, over 160 states refer, in various connotations, to human dignity in their basic laws.[8] Previously, there had been only five countries that referred to human dignity in their constitutions.[9] It is worth noting that only in thirty-seven cases—according to calculations made by Doron Shultziner and Guy E. Carmi—which accounts for 23 percent of the constitutions invoking human dignity, does this principle appear only once. In all other cases, there are at least two references to dignity and in seventeen constitutions at least eight times.[10] Most references to the principle of human dignity can be found in the youngest basic laws.

The principle of subsidiarity, by giving the state a subsidiary role, undoubtedly puts humanity at the top of the hierarchy of actors. Such a conclusion is also justified in the light of the principle of human dignity, often also expressed in the positivist dimension. If the state gains the power to intervene when the individual is unable to achieve their objectives on their own or to protect important rights, it is difficult to question the statement that the individual is the most important.[11]

Difficulties in interpreting the principle of human dignity and indicating its vagueness sometimes lead some researchers to a conclusion suggesting that it is an "empty" concept, the content of which no one is able to determine, or at least indicate the criteria that would bring us closer to a proper interpretation of the meaning of the principle of dignity.[12] However, while reality would not be ingrained, it cannot be overlooked that the category of dignity played an important role in the second half of the twentieth century and seems to still be an important point of reference in international law, in ethical issues, and in the context of other challenges that concern the status of the person.[13]

TWO VIEWS OF DIGNITY

According to Oliver Sensen, the contemporary paradigm of understanding human dignity differs significantly from the understanding of dignity in the traditional archetype, reaching back to antiquity with its roots and lasting at least until the end of the nineteenth century. In the traditional paradigm, according to this author, the principle of dignity would consist of two planes. The first points to the uniqueness of humanity in comparison to all other beings. Humanity is distinguished by its abilities, including above all its reasoning and freedom. The second plane indicates certain moral demands, resulting from the former.[14] The element differentiating the traditional line and the contemporary approach would be the dependence of the attribute of dignity on the characteristics of the subject, for example, social origin, property, or family, which would appear in the traditional approach. Can we really say, however, that it is only the present day that has brought about an interpretation of human dignity as a characteristic of each individual, regardless of his or her resources, background or any other characteristic not relevant to his or her humanity?

Cicero, the ancient artist, wrote about dignity as a characteristic of every human being. When he indicated the features that differentiated man from the animals, which constituted his dignity, he wrote about every individual, regardless of class or origin:

> We must also be aware that nature makes us play two roles. One of them is common to all, which has its source in the fact that we all share reason, as well as this higher nature, with which we dominate over animals, from which all virtue and handsomeness originate and in which we search for tests to know

> the essence of duty. The second is the one that nature has determined for each individual person. Because just like there are great differences among the physical properties of individual people (after all, we know that some people, because of their fleetness of foot, are suitable for running, others are capable of wrestling thanks to their strength, and as far as superficiality is concerned, some are distinguished by the grandeur of their character, others by their beauty), so great and even greater is the diversity of their spiritual characteristics.[15]

In Sensen's interpretation, however, Cicero's position still has a programmatic character for the traditional approach to the principle of human dignity. People are unique in the natural world because of their abilities, especially reason. This entails the need to act in a manner that is appropriate for rational beings.[16]

Oliver Sensen points out that St. Leo the Great was the second groundbreaking thinker who made a significant contribution to the development of the traditional understanding of the principle of human dignity. In one of the most famous fragments of his sermons he stated: "Christians! Know your dignity. You have become a participant of the Divine nature, so abandon the unworthy customs of your past life and do not return to them. Remember to which Head you belong and of which Body you are a member. Remember that you were ripped out of the power of darkness and moved into the light and Kingdom of God."[17] Human dignity has its source in creating it in God's image and likeness. Both Leo the Great and Cicero saw dignity as a quality defined by the characteristics that distinguish humanity from other living beings. Humanity has dignity, which makes it necessary to act properly in a way that corresponds to this attribute.

The famous *Oration on the Dignity of Man* by Giovanni Picco della Mirandola also contains an image of a man unique in the whole of creation. Uniqueness comes from the nature of a person who is characterized by freedom and rationality. The individual human is different from animals in that they can shape their own fate through their choices. Even people living similarly to animals can, unlike animals, decide to change their way of life and try to influence their fate.[18] In one of the excerpts from his treatise, G. P. della Mirandola wrote:

> Who then will not look with wonder upon man, who, not without reason, in the sacred Mosaic and Christian writings, is designated sometimes by the term "all flesh" and sometimes by the term "every creature," because he moulds, fashions and transforms himself into the likeness of all flesh and assumes the characteristic power of every form of life? This is why Evantes the Persian in his exposition of the Chaldean theology, writes that man has no inborn and proper semblance, but many which are extraneous and adventitious: whence the Chaldean saying: *"Enosh hu shinnujim vekammah tebhaoth haf"*—"man is a

> living creature of varied, multiform and ever-changing nature." But what is the purpose of all this? To make us understand that if we are in such a situation that we can be what we want to be, we should take the utmost care for it not to be said of us—when we are in such a respect—that we have become unreasonable animals and beings.[19]

The dignity of the individual, rooted in their uniqueness, is therefore not only a fact but also a commitment.

According to Sensen, Immanuel Kant also inscribed himself in the traditional paradigm of interpreting human dignity.[20] In the interpretation of this author, Kant saw the supremacy of man over other creatures in his possession of free will. The freedom resulting from it is closely connected with the moral law, which is manifested to man in the form of a categorical imperative, the highest moral principle.[21] The requirements of the categorical imperative are properly understood by the individual when the need to perform them is not derived from an external source of obligations, but from a belief in the rightness and legitimization of such conduct. This is what the principle of human dignity is supposed to manifest itself in. Oliver Sensen notes Kant's two-dimensional approach to the principle of human dignity. In one of his works, Kant states: ". . . the responsibilities to himself. They do not consist (. . .) in striving to satisfy his desires and tendencies (. . .). But they rely on his awareness that man has a proper dignity which ennobles him above all other creatures, and it is his duty to act in such a way as not to violate this dignity of humanity in his own person."[22] In his work, too, *Groundwork of the Metaphysics of Morals*, Kant links human dignity to morality. It is only through morality that man can be an end in himself:

> In a target state, everything has either a price or a dignity. Whatever has a price can also be replaced by something else as its equivalent, and what exceeds it at all costs, and therefore does not allow any equivalent, has dignity. Whatever relates to common human inclinations and needs has a market price; whatever needs to correspond to a certain taste, i.e. a taste in the pointless play of our mental authorities, has an emotional price (*Affektionspreis*); what constitutes a condition under which only something can be an end in itself, has not only a relative value, i.e. a price, but an intrinsic value, i.e. dignity. Morality is a condition upon which only depends that a rational being can be an end in itself, because only through it can one be a lawmaking member in a target state. So only morality and humanity, in so far as it is capable of morality, are what has dignity.[23]

The juxtaposition of the perspectives of Cicero, Leo the Great, Picco della Mirandola, and Kant becomes, for Sensen, the basis for the claim that the contemporary understanding of dignity differs in a significant extent from the traditional paradigm adopted in the works of these thinkers. The difference would be that in the traditional sense, dignity: (1) is not perceived as an unrelational human value; (2) is not the basis of rights; (3) is primarily about following a certain standard.[24] It is now appropriate to briefly present these arguments in order to be able to argue with them.

In Sensen's interpretation, dignity in the traditional sense does not constitute an inner value of man but of his features that put him above other creatures. The special position of man in the hierarchy of beings does not result from his independent value but from the possession of qualities and skills that allow him supremacy in relation to animals.[25] It would be a new version of the ancient concept of dignity related to aristocracy, preceding Cicero's works, which justified the special social position of Roman senators. Cicero wanted to universalize the concept of dignity so that it was applied to all people, but its relational pattern remained the same, and it was applied to animals and not—as before—to people of a different state.

A traditional approach to dignity would focus on duties and not on human rights. Rationality and freedom would not be the basis for inferring human rights from others but rather the source of obligations that would imply the proper exercise of the particular qualities with which the individual is endowed.[26] In this interpretation, rights become secondary to duties. They are derived only from further normative premises referring to the principle of human dignity.

The third difference is that dignity is understood as a certain standard of conduct that is intended to lead humanity to perfection. The traditional approach would focus not so much on the dignity of other people as on the dignity of one's own self, which should be aware of itself and strive for the fullness of its humanity, which—as observed above—is its duty. Human dignity is a category that obliges one to improve oneself, not a category that gives priority to the rights of others.

Hannah Arendt questioned the traditional approach to dignity in her works. As John Helis noted, she synthesized the theses of Aristotle, Kant, and Edmund Burke in a way that has resulted in the recognition that the derivation of human rights from the mere fact of human birth is wrong. Human rights are culturally relative and depend on the social context in which they are developed and interpreted. Human dignity is still a permanent, universal element, but it comes down to the right to belong to a political community. This community is necessary for the full development of human potential: "By acting and speaking, people show who they are, actively reveal their unique personal identity, and this is the reason for their manifestation in the human world, while their physical identity appears without any activity of their own, in the unique body shape and sound of their voice."[27] Without community, man could not be realized in action and speaking.

The above differences, identified by Sensen, would, in his opinion, prevent any extraction of content for the principle of dignity from sources covered by the category of the traditional paradigm.[28] It seems, however, that the above interpretation of Sensen can be effectively questioned—in a way that also undermines his conclusion indicated here. A number of doubts arise primarily from the antagonization of the thesis about the inner value of man with the view that man is an exceptional being, characterized by special properties. The contradiction between these theses seems only ostensible or not at all noticeable. If we proclaim the view that man is an exceptional entity, and undoubtedly this assumption accompanies many legal acts and international documents, including the aforementioned Universal Declaration of Human Rights, this is not contradicted by the search for justification for this thesis in the exceptional qualities of man. The very uniqueness or specificity of any features is already relative in its essence, in the sense that it requires an indication of the range of features for which it is exceptional. It is not possible to be special or exceptional unless a set of criteria for such an assessment is identified. Man is unique among all living beings, so the thesis of his uniqueness is relativized to all living beings. There is nothing wrong with this and nothing that would allow us to see the basis for differentiating the traditional approach and the contemporary interpretation of the principle of human dignity.

Human dignity is the basis for inferring not only about human rights but also about human duties. The truth is that different interpreters, in different historical periods, have stressed more the aspect of duties or the aspect of rights deriving from the principle of human dignity. The concept of human dignity, like others, develops with time, gaining new experiences and deepening reflection on a given issue. Oliver Sensen's assessment is correct when he points out that the contemporary discourse on human dignity is primarily of a human rights nature, and therefore focuses on this. In this context, human responsibilities are often overlooked, which also arise from the essence of dignity and from the rights themselves. However, the observation of such a status quo should not constitute a basis for specific cementation of this direction by questioning any continuity of the meaning of the term in question. It is precisely the rooting of dignity in the intellectual tradition, which Sensen also tries to outline, that allows us to grasp its essential aspects, and at the same time does not close the principle of dignity to a later interpretation, emphasizing the role of the resulting rights. It is difficult to find contradictions here. These two views may be complementary.

It does not seem that Sensen has carried out an effective and convincing proof of a break in the continuity between traditional interpretations carried out within the circle of tradition referring to Greek philosophy, Christianity, and Roman law. A sufficiently convincing argument about breaking the continuity of interpretation is certainly not a thesis about orientation of dignity on one's own conduct (in the past) or the conduct of others (in the present). Again, it seems that this is just a matter of different accents.

It is worth noting that in a culture of Judeo-Christian origin, it was not only Christianity that brought in the concept of human dignity. In Judaic philosophy, man has dignity, the source of which is that he was created in the image and likeness of God. In the *Book of Genesis,* there is the statement: "So God created mankind in His own image, in the image of God He created them: male and female He created them."[29] One of the interpreters of this passage from Genesis was Maimonides. He understood this passage as follows: "the soul of every human being is his or her form, which is given to him or her by God; the additional wisdom found in man's soul is also a form of man who is the fullness of his wisdom. The Torah speaks of the form: 'man was created in My image and My likeness.'"[30] The dignity of man in Judaic interpretation determines the sanctity of human life and the equality of people. Human dignity cannot be compromised. This approach to dignity is also reflected in one of the rulings of the Supreme Court of Israel: "The basic element of Judaism is the idea that man was created in the image of God" (*Genesis* 1:27). The Torah thus opens and from this concept of *halakha* (interpretation of the Mosaic Law—author's note) derives certain fundamental principles concerning the value of man—of every human being as such—his equality and love for him. He (R. Akiva) used to say that beloved is the man who was created in the image of God, but it is a sign of even greater love that it was made available to the knowledge of man, that he was created in the image of God, as it is said (*Genesis* 9:6), "because man was created in the image of God" (*Mishnah, Avot 3*, 18). And because of this verse, Noah's sons were forbidden to spill blood even before the Torah was handed over. The difference of opinion between the two main Mishnah scholars in relation to the main value in human relations is very instructive: "you will love your neighbour as yourself" (*Leviticus* 19:18). Akiva claimed that this is the main rule of the Torah. Ben Azai claimed that

> This is the book of Adam's generations (when God created man in the likeness of God he created him—*Genesis* 5:1)—this is the more important rule (*Sifra, Kedoshim* 4:10). According to Akiva, the highest value in human relations is love of one's neighbour; and according to Ben Azai, the highest and preferred value is the equality of people, because every person was created in the image of God. And these two values—equality and love of neighbour—become one in the hands of the Jewish people, together forming the cornerstone of Judaism through its generations and history.[31]

THE UNIVERSAL DECLARATION OF HUMAN RIGHTS AND THE HUMAN RIGHTS INTERPRETATION OF DIGNITY

One of the most important contemporary source documents on the importance of human dignity in today's world is undoubtedly the Universal Declaration of Human Rights adopted on December 10, 1948, at the Third Session of the UN General Assembly. At the beginning of its preamble, the importance of human dignity is pointed out: "Whereas recognition of the inherent dignity and of the equal and inalienable rights of all members of the human family is the foundation of freedom, justice and peace in the world." Later, the preamble reads: "Whereas the peoples of the United Nations have in the Charter reaffirmed their faith in fundamental human rights, in the dignity and worth of the human person and in the equal rights of men and women and have determined to promote social progress and better standards of life in larger freedom." The Universal Declaration of Human Rights developed the reference to the principle of human dignity, which had already appeared in the preamble to the United Nations Charter, where, inter alia, the need to restore faith in human dignity and value was indicated.[32]

The reference to human dignity also appears in three articles of the Universal Declaration of Human Rights:

1) In Article 1, the United Nations declared: "All human beings are born free and equal in dignity and rights. They are endowed with reason and conscience and should act towards one another in a spirit of brotherhood."
2) In Article 22:

> Everyone, as a member of society, has the right to social security and is entitled to realisation, through national effort and international co-operation and in accordance with the organisation and resources of each State, of the economic, social and cultural rights indispensable for his dignity and the free development of his personality.

3) In Article 23(3): "Everyone who works has the right to just and favourable remuneration ensuring for himself and his family an existence worthy of human dignity, and supplemented, if necessary, by other means of social protection."

The problem of the authors of the declaration was the need to provide a basis for the thesis that every human being has certain inalienable rights. The general nature of the freedoms and rights to which the document was intended to refer precluded the possibility of recourse to religious justification.[33] The point was not to relativize the source of these rights by claiming that everyone can derive them from different orders. Even if, in reality, we derive them from different sources, depending on our personal convictions, it was necessary to establish a common moment from which the process of determining the content of these freedoms and rights is already a common process. This common moment, allowing the affirmation of the universality of the freedoms and rights deriving from them, irrespective of personal religious beliefs, is the dignity of man, belonging to each individual by reason of his or her humanity.

The philosopher Glenn Hughes argues that this is how human dignity was understood by three people who had an influence on the final declaration: the Libyan delegate Charles H. Malik, the U.S. delegate Eleanor Roosevelt, and the Chinese delegate Peng Chun Chang.[34] Eleanor Roosevelt believed that the principle of human dignity was not in itself a set of concrete rights. Rather, it is a figure that determines the existence of human rights as such.[35] However, this does not lead to the conclusion that dignity is an empty category, the content of which is determined only by the legislator. We should rather derive from this the thesis that human dignity is the basis of all human rights, and therefore determines that the subjectivity of man must be derived from this, since it requires that each person be treated as a subject rather than as an object of a relationship.

Similar views, at least to some extent, have been expressed by other authors in relation to the issue discussed here. Dignity is understood as a category that aggregates various other freedoms and human rights.[36] Often the principle of dignity is treated ornamentally, more as a metaphorical figure, allowing some important issues to be indicated rather than a category having its own content.[37] Some authors write directly about the very high degree of vagueness of the principle of human dignity. Helga Kuhse believes that human dignity, which is sometimes called for by the opposition participants of the debate, is nothing more than a stenographic expression describing human moral intuition and feelings.[38] Dennis Davis even stated that dignity is "part of a legal Legoland—to be used in any form or shape that is necessary according to the expectations of the judicial designer."[39]

However, one cannot fully agree with the interpretation indicating that the level of abstraction on which the principle of human dignity was constructed does not make it possible to interpret the content of dignity, also by referring to philosophical anthropology.[40] This is a difficult thesis to maintain, especially at the level of the system of state law in which the provisions of the declaration are to be implemented. If the principle of human dignity is to give rise to something more than just a justification for the rights and freedoms indicated in a given document, and if, in practice, it is to be more than just an additional argument and a kind of ornament, it is necessary to refer to its meaningful context, and thus, above all, to individual philosophical concepts, in order to determine its content correctly. It is far from satisfactory to interpret the principle of human dignity as—as G. Hughes wants it—"a symbolic evocation of the majesty and mystery of human existence in a universal and open style, so that it can play an essential role in the expression of values in the liberal and democratic order."[41] I do not want to say that human dignity does not express values that are important for the democratic order. However, it is impossible to interpret norms from any rule—let alone from a rule so vague at the linguistic layer—without anchoring the interpretation in a proper meaningful context. Otherwise, it does not seem possible to interpret even the values that Hughes writes about, and therefore form part of liberal democracy.[42]

In fact, these positions are, to some extent, reconcilable. It can be assumed that human dignity at the universal level should be as open as possible to various cultural contexts, depending, among other things, on the region. Such a thesis is confirmed by the words of Jacques Maritain, one of the co-authors of the Universal Declaration of Human Rights: "How, I asked, can we imagine an agreement of minds between people gathered together to carry out a common intellectual task, people coming from the four corners of the world and belonging not only to different cultures and civilizations, but also to oppositional spiritual associations or schools of thought?"[43]

It cannot be assumed, however, that this openness in meaning implies that it is possible to fulfill the principle of human dignity with any completely free content. Since this principle is the basis for the formulation of the freedoms and rights referred to in the declaration, it means that some of its content allows it—determining the uniqueness of man. The context in which human dignity is to be interpreted can be clarified at national level, where it is no longer necessary to take care of its universal dimension. The political community can draw the principle of human dignity from one or more similar anthropological trends, which does not mean that all members of the community must fully embrace all the demands of this trend. It seems necessary to define the context of the principle of human dignity at the national level in order to be able to agree detailed solutions with the content of this principle. This aspect of the principle of human dignity will be discussed later in the book.

Eventually, G. Hughes himself points to the elements stemming from the principle of human dignity, which are aimed at making its meaning more concrete. According to this author, human dignity indicates the ability—or potential for developing the ability—of a person to consciously ask, imagine, feel, understand, possess knowledge, decide, and act. These processes take place in the consciousness of freedom and are a manifestation of free will. Man is also aware of his responsibility, which is closely linked to his freedom. All these qualities make up the uniqueness of every human being, his or her uniqueness. Human dignity also describes a person's awareness of the possibility of experiencing suffering. This author emphasizes that man lives to know and love and to be an object of knowledge and love.[44]

Linking the principle of human dignity to such attributes as freedom and rationality may create an incorrect belief that this characteristic does not apply to people who, because of their disability, cannot benefit from these attributes. It could be mistakenly thought that a person with a mental illness or intellectual disability is not able to demonstrate rationality to the extent that it could prejudge their dignity. Such a conclusion would contradict the intention of construing the Universal Declaration of Human Rights. It must be remembered that this work took place after the experience of World War II, when it was shown that there was far-reaching contempt for people affected by various dysfunctions. The emphasis on dignity, and therefore the special value of every human being, regardless of his or her health or even his or her moral condition, was the main objective of the declaration.

The category of human dignity is an attempt to express the special value and uniqueness of each individual—not because of his or her merits or condition, but because of his or her human nature, which in itself is unique. Glenn Hughes points first of all to human characteristics such as the irreplaceability of every human being and the susceptibility to suffering. Every person is so unique that they cannot be replaced by others. The author emphasizes that even in people who try to deprive themselves of their humanity through torture, or in people suffering from various diseases or handicaps, it is still possible to experience the existence of an irreplaceable person who suffers.[45]

According to Marek Piechowiak, the proof of a certain concrete concept of a human accompanying the authors of the declaration is provided by its Article 1, which can be interpreted more as a descriptive than a normative text.[46] The declaration that "all human beings are born free and equal in dignity and rights" and that "they are endowed with reason and conscience and should act towards each other in a spirit of brotherhood" is difficult to interpret differently than as a strictly anthropological statement that reveals, at least to some extent, a certain philosophical concept. It may be questionable, however, to what extent this vision of the human being that emerges from the Universal Declaration of Human Rights is concrete and needs no supplementation.

The further-reaching consequences of entrenched legal systems in the principle of human dignity are reflected in the International Covenant on Civil and Political Rights and the International Covenant on Economic, Social, and Cultural Rights of 1966. The preamble attached to these pacts states, among other things: "Considering that, in accordance with the principles proclaimed in the Charter of the United Nations, recognition of the inherent dignity and of the equal and inalienable rights of all members of the human family is the foundation of freedom, justice and peace in the world, recognising that these rights derive from the inherent dignity of the human person."[47] The international community has therefore recognized that human dignity is not a human right but a kind of meta-right which is the source of all other equal and inalienable rights of all members of the human community.

DIGNITY AS A REQUIREMENT OF SUBORDINATION OF THE LAW TO THE WELFARE OF THE PERSON

The indication that human rights are grounded in human dignity leads—in Piechowiak's opinion—to the statement that they are secondary to the person, subordinated to his right.[48] They do not exist independently, without man, from whom they result in dignity. Full protection of human dignity is therefore possible when the law is ultimately subordinated not only to the need to protect human rights themselves but also to the well-being of the person. Against this backdrop, a kind of feedback emerges. Reconstructing an anthropologically correct vision of man allows us to say something about his rights and to formulate postulates concerning the law in general. Also, the rights themselves say something about humanity. It is possible to draw conclusions about the human being from the content of the law insofar as the rights are designed with the well-being of the person and their dignity as the basic reference point.

Dignity should be understood primarily as an objective and intrinsic value of each person. This is what Josef Seifert stressed that the principle of quality is completely different from aesthetic values or intellectual values, because these do not impose any moral imperatives on us. The principle of human dignity, on the other hand, is a principle of moral importance which undoubtedly places certain moral tasks before everyone and imposes an obligation to carry them out.[49] This objective and natural principle makes it possible to infer from it the rights which each person enjoys by reason of the dignity which he or she possesses as a result of his or her humanity. Human dignity is not relativized in the sense that its content does not change depending on external conditions.[50] Everyone has an intrinsic and objective value, every person has dignity, and so everyone is entitled to the obligations arising from this right.

Human dignity is natural. This feature may be misinterpreted as having been inherited from birth. It means, as emphasized by the English term *inherent*, rather something that is an inner property of every human being, revealed with their existence and lasting with them immanently throughout their existence. This dignity has a dimension of personal dignity, for it is due to every human being only by virtue of his or her existence. You do not need to meet any other criteria, represent any other properties than just be a human being to have dignity.[51]

The naturalness of dignity and its constant connection with humanity indicate that equality is a feature of dignity. The dignity of each person in his or her personal dimension is the same, which means that all people, precisely because of their dignity, are equal. Respect for what follows from this human characteristic, which is dignity, is also necessary for the preservation of freedom, justice, and peace. None of the human traits can effectively justify a thesis that deprives someone of their dignity. None of the features can be the basis for the claim that the dignity of individual people can be differentiated. Human dignity is therefore a category serving to express, among other principles, the equality of all people. It is already obvious today that equality is not the same as the postulate of treating everyone the same. It is permissible to vary the terms and conditions according to the circumstances, where justified. However, this does not prejudice the very principle of equality. Differentiation shall cease to be permitted if, on account of its content or the criteria applied, it would violate the principle of human dignity.

In a work devoted to the philosophy of human rights, M. Piechowiak argues in favor of the personalistic establishment of human rights. In his opinion, it is this context of interpretation that allows us for:

(a) the consolidation of the content of the due states of affairs;
(b) the consolidation of the very "due" of these states;
(c) the consolidation of the obligation of the entities realizing the due states of affairs;
(d) the consolidation of the due states of affairs as including elements that are both independent and dependent on free decisions of individuals and communities;
(e) the consolidation of the previously identified characteristics of rights, in particular their naturalness, universality, inviolability, and holistic nature, which from a theoretical point of view requires that the ontological basis of each of the above types of consolidation be found in the rightholder, while it must be both an element which is non-transferable and irreversible throughout the life of the rightholder and an element which "integrates" the other characteristics of man in which the content of the individual rights is grounded.[52]

The aim of this work is not to present and prove the thesis that the personalistic context would be the only one in which it is possible to explain the principle of human dignity. However, if one takes into account the fact that this context, which will be the subject of analysis, plays an important role in the process of designing and establishing Article 30 of the Constitution of the Republic of Poland, as well as in the jurisprudence of the Constitutional Tribunal, it is impossible not to refer to this context at least—in order to better understand the principle under discussion.

It seems that M. Piechowiak is right when he notes that

> the function of the category under discussion is primarily not to refer to conceptual structures or theoretical constructions, but to indicate a certain area of reality which determines the content of postulates concerning both concrete actions and positive law. Dignity is a certain reality which cannot be unambiguously included in legal formulas, but can and is indicated by these formulas and as such must be taken into account—both in the process of lawmaking and its interpretation. In order to indicate these elements of reality, it is not absolutely necessary to have a concept covering all the content that is essential for understanding the law; it is enough, for example, to say that it is about what determines the difference between humans and other beings, and what is the basis for the special treatment of humanity.[53]

Human dignity requires that everyone be guaranteed a suitable area of freedom. The state is obliged to protect the individual from restrictions on their freedom, which could consist of unauthorized interference in the private sphere, either by the state or by other associations.[54] An important aspect of the principle of human dignity is its specific openness. This manifests itself in the fact that the notion of human dignity is not fully defined linguistically, just as the content of a human being is not defined, which also necessarily affects the legal order.[55] The specificity of this openness lies in the fact that it has its limits, determined by the welfare of the person. Already at this stage of the analysis, one can see that human dignity, in terms of its openness, requires the legal order to correspond with the human constitution, that is, with its anthropological vision rooted in this principle.

The importance of human dignity is well reflected in the words of John Paul II:

> The basis and purpose of social order is the human individual as the subject of inalienable rights, which they have not received from outside, but which flow from their nature: nothing and no one can destroy them, for their roots lie in what is most deeply human. It follows from the first and fundamental principle of social order, which preaches that the goal of society is the human, that every society must be organised in such a way as to enable it, moreover, to help them to fulfil their vocation.[56]

Dignity consequently becomes the highest noninstrumental value of the individual, which expresses the necessity of treating it in a manner appropriate to his humanity.[57]

The principle of human dignity also implies an obligation to respect, and therefore to refrain from insulting, humiliating, degrading, or attempting to destroy the humanity of another person.[58] As M. Dubber notes, every person has dignity and enjoys the right to have that dignity respected by other people, whether they are acting on their own behalf, on behalf of the state or on behalf of the justice system.[59] A person's dignity does not derive from their social status, belonging to a particular political community or even from personal achievements. The source of dignity is being a person.[60]

However, the principles of human dignity should not be understood as a basis for individualistic demands. This is visible in the personalistic approach to dignity, which also emphasizes the value of community.[61] Personalism, as opposed to individualism, emphasizes the social nature of the individual, the value of their relationships with other individuals, and even with things.[62] Personalism interprets from human dignity the rights of the human person, whose realization is required by the principle of justice. Justice requires that everyone be given what is necessary for their development and perfection within the limits of the common good.[63] It is worth noting that the requirement to provide everyone, to the extent permitted by the common weal, with a basis for achieving their own ends, all the more so means that each person and the entire community must be protected from such acts as could hamper their progress toward perfection. This process must take account of the principle of subsidiarity, which requires prior verification that a good can be effectively protected without state intervention.

Rooted in the principle of human dignity as the anthropological basis of modern law, in personalistic thought, and thus in the tradition built on ancient philosophy, especially Plato and Aristotle, and the philosophy of St. Thomas Aquinas, allows us to refer to Plato's arguments on justice, especially to the part where he clearly outlines the ethical requirements for the law:

> There was one main point about which we were agreed—that a man's whole energies throughout life should be devoted to the acquisition of the virtue proper to a man, whether this was to be gained by study, or habit, or some mode of acquisition, or desire, or opinion, or knowledge—and this applies equally to men and women, old and young—the aim of all should always be such as I have described; anything which may be an impediment, the good man ought to show that he utterly disregards. And if at last necessity plainly compels him to be an outlaw from his native land, rather than bow his neck to the yoke of slavery and be ruled by inferiors, and he has to fly, an exile he must be and endure all such trials, rather than accept another form of government, which is likely to make men worse. These are our original principles; and do you now, fixing your eyes upon the standard of what a man and a citizen ought or ought not to be, praise and blame the laws—blame those which have not this power of making the

citizen better, but embrace those which have; and with gladness receive and live in them; bidding a long farewell to other institutions which aim at goods, as they are termed, of a different kind.[64]

The above fragment of Plato's *Laws* can be considered in different directions.[65] In the light of the analyses conducted here, the criterion proposed by Plato for assessing rights seems particularly noteworthy. It calls for them to be viewed from the perspective of their function in relation to virtues. Rights must be glorified when they lead a person to virtue and punished when they distance him from virtue. It is not even necessary to find here a postulate allowing to refuse obedience to the law that dissuades man from virtue. It is enough to interpret this passage as indicating the criteria for evaluating the law, that is, at the same time, the criteria for making and applying it. A law can be passed, including a criminal law, which is conducive to human improvement, that is, the acquisition and development of new virtues, and the decisions of the legislator which lead to opposite effects should be criticized. In this context, it is becoming necessary to develop tools that will enable legislation to be made that deserves to be supported.

In interpreting Plato's approach to justice, Piechowiak points to two aspects of justice: the objective and the subjective.[66] The material aspect concerns what can be considered fair because of the relationship of suitability to the addressee of the action. The subjective aspect concerns, however, the evaluation of justice due to the relation of relevance to the subject of action, that is, to the perpetrator. Justice is therefore a relationship of adequacy that is revealed in the relationship between the act and its other end, which may be the perpetrator or addressee of the act. Thus, speaking of the creation or application of fair criminal law, one could speak of the relation between the creation of such a law and its final result in particular in the form of a legal rule interpreted in specific circumstances as applying—to the constituting and applying entity and to the executing entity, including the participants in criminal proceedings. Indeed, justice in its subjective aspect presupposes prior justice in its objective aspect. It is therefore difficult to speak of a just criminal law if the relation of adequacy does not exist in relation to the participants in criminal proceedings.

This adequacy is interestingly explained in Aristotle's works when the Stagirite discusses his concept of the "golden mean." It is not, as is sometimes mistakenly believed, an incentive to establish an equal, abstractly measured, distance to deprivation and excess. Rather, it is a matter of establishing a measure that is appropriate to the entity. As Aristotle stated,

In everything that is continuous and divisible it is possible to take more, less, or an equal amount, and that either in terms of the thing itself or relatively to us; and the equal is an intermediate between excess and defect. By the intermediate in the object I mean that which is equidistant from each of the extremes, which is one and the same for all men.[67]

Aristotle also illustrates his argument with an example:

For instance, if ten is many and two is few, six is the intermediate, taken in terms of the object; for it exceeds and is exceeded by an equal amount; this is intermediate according to arithmetical proportion. But the intermediate relatively to us is not to be taken so; if ten pounds are too much for a particular person to eat and two too little, it does not follow that the trainer will order six pounds; for this also is perhaps too much for the person who is to take it, or too little- too little for Milo, too much for the beginner in athletic exercises.[68]

Therefore, the adequacy relationship means the need to search for what is appropriate for a given subject and does not involve a deficiency or excess. This implies that, while constructing a just penal law, and therefore respecting the principle of human dignity, efforts should be made to create normative constructions which are appropriate for man as such and which retain the ability to take into account certain modifications resulting from some specific characteristics of a given person *in concreto.*

The dignity of man as such, understood not as a feature that distinguishes one man from another on account of his particular characteristics, can be interpreted from the work of St. Thomas Aquinas. One cannot seek to understand human dignity without taking into account the notion of a person in Judeo-Christian culture. The concept of the person understood after Boethius as an individual substance of a rational nature arose in the context of Christological disputes.[69] Undoubtedly, however, it quickly broke away from the strictly theological context and gained an independent philosophical function, including an ethical and anthropological one. This category and its understanding are particularly important in the interpretation of St. Thomas's works because he writes about dignity always in relation to the person. A human being is not only a rational being but also one with dignity.[70]

A human person is characterized by the fact that he or she exists and has a rational nature and dignity. As St. Thomas Aquinas pointed out: "“Person” signifies what is most perfect in all nature—that is, a subsistent individual of a rational nature."[71] Human dignity is therefore presented as a special way of life in this context. However, the basis for dignity is not a single human characteristic that determines his uniqueness. Piechowiak rightly pointed out:

Dignity cannot be identified with any random or proper trait, nor with the sum of traits. Then it would be difficult to explain the "nobility" of the whole being, which is desired not because of an element but because of its entirety. If dignity

> were a feature or sum of features, it could not be said that it is goodness by virtue of itself, since it would exist for its subject as a feature or property.[72]

From the perspective of the relationship between the principle of human dignity and the principles of criminal responsibility, analyzed in this study, it is appropriate to pay special attention to the freedom of man emerging from dignity and his individualization. The individuality of a person is manifested in the decisions they make, in the freedom of their choices. Karol Wojtyła also pointed this out:

> In this dimension, will is not so much seen as an intrinsic property of a deed performed by a person as a property of a person who, therefore, is capable of fulfilling the deed because he has such a property. You can also reverse this relationship and say that it is the person who shows himself through will and not only will through the person and in the person. Every act confirms and concretises this relationship in which will is revealed as a property of the person and the person as a reality in terms of its dynamism, constituted properly by will. This relationship we define as self-determination.[73]

In this context, an extremely important and current issue of human free will arises, its undetermined nature as to specific action or omission. That which determines an individual's actions is their free choice. This was emphasized by St. Thomas: "Man is made master of himself through his free-will: wherefore he can lawfully dispose of himself as to those matters which pertain to this life which is ruled by man's free-will."[74] This issue is developed further in the book.

Dignity is a characteristic to which every human being is entitled and which is unconditionally connected with his or her existence. It can therefore be concluded that if X is human and exists, then X has dignity.[75] Interpreted by Ingolf U. Dalferth, who emphasizes the importance of existence and its strong relationship with dignity, denial of dignity does not necessarily mean denial of humanity. This can be understood as a rejection of perceiving someone as a human being living with us or as a rejection of referring to someone as a person.[76] This means that conduct that violates someone's dignity can be understood as a kind of civil killing of a given person by excluding them from the community of people with whom we have a relationship, recognizing their personal lives.

The principle of human dignity is invoked in different contexts and in different meanings. Problems of mutual understanding in the debate on human dignity may arise not only from fundamentally different philosophical assumptions but also from different aspects of dignity itself. Following Piechowiak, four types of human dignity can be distinguished due to its consolidation: (1) human dignity, established in existence as a human being;

(2) personal dignity, established in the actions of a given person; (3) dignity established in the circumstances of life; and (4) personal dignity, established in the views of other persons.[77]

The category of dignity expressed in Article 30 of the Constitution of the Republic of Poland and in the international documents referred to herein is in the form of personal dignity.[78] It is due to every human being on account of his or her humanity and is inalienable, just as the fact of being human is inalienable. Dignity, as Piechowiak notes, is the basis for the existence of the goal to be achieved by man, this goal is to develop being a person, and thus to achieve the fullness of humanity. Such a state to the highest degree reveals human dignity.[79] Respect for dignity is realized in creating conditions for man to strive for his own perfection, and thus in acting for the common good.

Human dignity is to be understood as the perfection which a person acquires as a result of behavior which complies with moral norms or loses as a result of behavior which does not comply with them.[80] It is not enough just to be a human being—a person. Personal dignity is therefore not inherent and inalienable. Its existence and degree depend on the behavior of a given person.

The dignity established in the circumstances of life is understood, in turn, as an evaluation of the status of a person on the basis of certain conditions, which include some specific abilities of a given person, his position, and the way in which he is treated by others.[81] Depending on these conditions, the degree of dignity may vary from person to person. It is the task of the state to strive to provide its citizens with the best possible conditions for development. However, it cannot be claimed that it is public entities that bear the entire burden of responsibility for the protection of dignity understood in terms of the circumstances of life. After all, as a result of one's own choices, man can lead to a situation in which this dignity is much lower than its desired level. An example is a criminal who is sentenced to prison as a result of his or her conduct. This does not mean that a person deprived of his or her liberty loses dignity so understood. It is the task of the state to protect the personal dignity of every person, including prisoners, but the circumstances of detention do not allow for such dignity, determined by these conditions, which could reach a level similar to that of a person enjoying personal freedom. The dignity established in the circumstances of life is also connected with the category of personal dignity, expressing personal rights, including in particular a good name.

In the light of the analysis carried out so far, it can already be said that it is human dignity that plays a key role in the legal system. The consolidation of the rule of law in the principle of human dignity makes people free from discrimination based on sex, race, descent, or other circumstances. Every human being has the same value as the principle of equality between men and women. Differences in the treatment of people may result from their behavior, and thus from conscious acts for which they may suffer consequences, not only positive but also negative, as moral subjects. The reaction to human behavior is not a threat to human dignity. On the contrary, man as a subject of morality—a person—is fully capable of bearing the consequences of his actions. It is also pointed out that dignity has the advantage of being open to various explanations. Depending on the internal context, that is, that of the state in which it is analyzed, the different religious and philosophical contexts may be indicated as the source of the content of this principle. Human dignity is also described as the highest value, which is the source of other values.

The principle of human dignity should not be interpreted in the direction leading to an individualistic understanding of man, that is, without taking into account the social character of his existence, the significance of human relationships and bonds, or the importance of community for the possibility of individual development. Even if human dignity were only mentioned in the context of the rights that derive from it, it would be quite clear that it is not possible to guarantee it outside a community whose status is also adequately protected. Man functions in various communities in which it is possible to respond to the demands of human dignity. These are the family, the state, and the other groups and associations in which the person lives. Guaranteeing these groups an adequate status, which, as in the case of humans, consists of specific rights and obligations, can guarantee the correct enforcement of human freedoms, rights, and obligations.

An alternative to the personalistic concept, although not entirely different, and certainly more individualistic, is the Kantian interpretation of human dignity.[82] The meaning of dignity adopted in this strand is, as it seems, nowadays more typical for some Western societies than a personalistic interpretation.[83] Dignity is understood in this perspective through the prism of the autonomy of the individual, which consists of the free will of man and his reasonableness. The individual human has the ability unique in the natural world to manage their own behavior, in a way not determined by instinct or external conditions. Furthermore, the understanding of human dignity here is increasingly being detached from the original understanding and interpreted as a right to live according to one's own plan, according to one's own principles, regardless of whether these are justified by reason or morality.[84] It thus ceases to be a guiding moral principle justifying duties toward other people. In Julia Davis's opinion, a return to the Kantian understanding of autonomy, and thus to his concept of human dignity, no longer seems to be possible, for example, because of the lack of consideration for people with disabilities or for other reasons deprived of their ability to exercise freedom or reason.[85]

According to C. McCrudden, the principle of dignity is the basis of an ontological and relational postulate, which summarizes well the findings made at this stage regarding the importance of this principle.[86] The ontological postulate indicates the intrinsic value of every human being. The relational postulate requires that this value be recognized and respected by others, which means the duty of mutual respect for one's humanity. Respect for humanity should take place not only in interpersonal relations but also in relations between the state and man. The fundamental principle governing the conduct of the state toward man should be the principle of dignity.[87]

The principle of human dignity is sometimes invoked as the main argument in the dispute over the death penalty. The Supreme Court of Canada ruling in *Kindler v. Canada* noted that:

> If corporal punishment, lobotomy and castration are no longer accepted, then the death penalty cannot be understood otherwise than as a cruel and unprecedented punishment. It is the highest wickedness for an individual, the highest corporal punishment, final and total lobotomy, and absolute and irreversible castration. As the highest desecration of human dignity, the death penalty in Canada is a clear violation of the protection guaranteed by Article 12 of the Charter [of Canada's Charter of Rights and Freedoms—author's note].[88]

Raising the argument of human dignity in the debate on the death penalty is an expression of the close link between this principle and the value of human life. It is only questionable whether the duty to protect human life stems from the principle of human dignity or whether these principles are equal and together constitute a source of other freedoms and rights.[89]

Establishing an understanding of dignity appropriate to the application of criminal law may require solutions to address perceived difficulties. One of these is the relationship between the category of harm and the category of human dignity. According to J. Davis, in some decisions of American courts, the category of harm is saturated with the content of the principle of human dignity.[90] It also seems necessary to clarify the notion of dignity, first of all in terms of its objectivity, or to accept the relativity of its meaning in relation to the feelings and beliefs of a person. A third difficulty would be that the argument of dignity is double-edged. An illustration of this double-edgedness would be the decision of the United Nations Commission on Human Rights in the case of *Wackenheim v. France*, which concerned so-called dwarf tossing.[91] In this case both sides referred to the argument of human dignity, formulating mutually contradictory theses.[92]

In the above-mentioned case, the applicant indicated that the introduction of a ban on dwarf-tossing entertainment activities, taking into account the fact that he himself was also employed in these activities, violated his dignity and the directly related right to employment. The state and the commission indicated in their decision that human dignity was infringed because of its close connection with public order, which was infringed by the entertainment activities described above. Unfortunately, the Commission on Human Rights did not conduct an in-depth reflection on the content of the principle of human dignity. However, it is only the findings made in this regard that could have allowed a fully justified decision on which of the theses based on the principle of human dignity was formulated correctly.

The vagueness of the principle of human dignity cannot be the basis for a postulate that effectively questions its usefulness and operability. One may wonder that it is not uncommon for the principle discussed here to be rejected precisely because it is out of focus, while at the same time similar demands are not made of other equally or even more vague principles, such as the principle of freedom, equality, or the democratic rule of law. There would be no serious consideration of the need to eliminate any reference to freedom, equality or, even less, the principle of the democratic rule of law from normative texts. Each of these principles has its own permanent place in the constitutional order. Not only a fixed place but also a specific content, or at least the identified main meaning elements, which are the criteria for interpreting the content of these principles. It is also important to note that some of these principles also require an external context, including ethical and anthropological contexts, in order to interpret their essence. How else can we determine, for example, the meaning of human freedom? Moreover, the ethical and anthropological conditions of the principle of human dignity may lead to the conclusion that it is from this that equality between people and their freedom derives.

The vagueness of the principle of dignity, which becomes a problem especially when interpreted in isolation from the appropriate context, also becomes a cause for the emergence of interpretative directions which can be described as reductionist.[93] In these directions of interpretation, reductionism consists in reducing the meaning of dignity to other known and better understood principles of the legal system. One of the human characteristics to which the representatives of these trends most often refer is autonomy.[94]

A certain counterweight to reductionism may be essentialism in the interpretation of dignity.[95] This is an attempt to extract such a content of dignity that points to its essence—it states what dignity is in itself. An example is the view of William Parent, who sees dignity as a negative law that prohibits unjust and discrediting treatment.[96] Christopher McCrudden interprets dignity as the recognition in every human being of his or her inner value.[97]

It is worth noting that Leslie M. Henry's criticism of essentialism as the correct direction for the interpretation of dignity is based, at least in part, on erroneous theoretical and terminological assumptions. If the basis for criticism of this trend is to be the claim that the internal value of each person interferes with the emerging view that some people have greater dignity than others, it is enough to resist it by referring to the systematization of dignity presented above, in particular the division into human dignity and personal dignity. The former refers to the objective, inner value of every human being, independent of his or her social position. Personal dignity, on the other hand, is conditioned by the judgments of other people. The point is, however, that the principle discussed here, which is reproduced in international legal acts and in selected national systems, including Poland and Germany, appears in personal terms, and therefore independently of assessments. Similarly, the argument questioning the reference to the essence of dignity—indicating that dignity may be offended or violated by an act or other act directed against man—is ineffective. Again, the problem lies in terminology and theoretical assumptions. Human dignity in the personal aspect is inviolable and inalienable. This inviolability should be considered in its essential dimension, such as the prohibition on limiting it or conducting activities that would violate it. This does not mean, however, that in practice, sometimes no action is taken against human dignity. They are contrary to it, they harm the individual, but it cannot be said that they restrict the dignity itself in terms of scope.

Human dignity is a principle describing a certain reality, which should be taken into account by the system of law. In this sense, it should not be interpreted as a law but rather as a characteristic of every human being to which the system of law refers, ordering its observance in the process of lawmaking and application. Article 30 of the Constitution of the Republic of Poland of 1997 indicates that dignity is inherent and inalienable. It does not, therefore, come from a decision of one or another body in a particular convention but belongs to the human being by virtue of its very nature. If human dignity is inherent and inalienable, it cannot be a right, especially a right that could be subject to restrictions. Ultimately, the function of human dignity in a given system of law is determined by the meaning given to it, and thus also by the context, as already mentioned above. The reason for the statement indicating that the German approach to the principle of dignity is too far-reaching—at the expense of human rights and freedoms—may be the incorrect identification of the content and meaning of dignity, precisely as a right, and not as a descriptive category in the first place.

The principle of human dignity is not limited to the descriptive dimension, but it should be a starting point in an attempt to interpret this figure. The legislator, whether international or national, does not lay down the principle of human dignity in normative texts but only for descriptive purposes. The law is to be oriented toward the protection of human dignity, and therefore it should be shaped in such a way that it takes into account and respects those features of man which make up his dignity. It can therefore be said that the right to protection of human dignity must be added to the descriptive dimension of that dignity. However, the description of man from the point of view of his dignity is not only a contribution to the interpretation of the right to its protection. It seems to be a certain anthropological description that the legislator should take into account in the lawmaking process, not only to the extent that it could be determined by the law to protect dignity.

The descriptive approach to human dignity is rejected by I. U. Dalferth. He even claims that a number of problems and controversies related to the category of dignity are born out of a constant effort to include it in descriptive frames, characteristic of descriptive categories.[98] This author proposes to explain dignity as an *orienting concept*. Orienting approaches differ from descriptive approaches, in that they cannot be defined because they do not have a semantically fixed meaning. They are pragmatic, with clear rules or grammar of application. Instead of elements characteristic of definitions, they offer orientation schemes, similarly to those that allow us to find ourselves in space or time.[99] One can distinguish the following orienting schemes: spatial (left/right, over/under); temporal (past/future, earlier/later); communication (personal pronouns); moral (good/bad); interpersonal relations (dignity/value). Orientation schemes are characterized by the following characteristics:

1) They allow a person to see what relation he or she has to the world—there is no such thing as "left," "right," "present," "future" without reference to a specific being or a specific object;
2) They do not allow grading or creating exceptions—if something is "on the left," "past," or "over" in a given context, it means that it is "left side," "past," and "over";
3) It is not possible to use one element of a given orienting scheme and reject the others—if we can say that something is "over," then we cannot refuse to say that something is "under"; if I say "I," I cannot not say "you."

The inclusion of human dignity within such an orientation scheme allows I. U. Dalferth to claim that it is not a generalized description or elite concept, but an orientation tool for a concrete practice of human life, namely to relate to others in a moral context and in various forms of social communication.[100] The orienting character of dignity therefore lies in the fact that we treat other people, including strangers and even enemies, in an appropriate way, like a man like us, with respect for his subjectivity. In other words, all people are partners for each other in practicing human dignity.[101]

DIFFERENT CONTEXTS FOR INTERPRETING DIGNITY

Human dignity is interpreted differently from one country to another. In some jurisdictions, it can be a means of expressing the ethical views of a political community.[102] The understanding of human dignity in a given political community reflects the rules that apply to it and that are relevant to interpersonal relations, as well as to the relationship between man and the reality around him. This means that the principle of human dignity beyond a certain universal core, as reflected in the Universal Declaration of Human Rights, can be interpreted differently depending on the legal order of a given state and its dominant ethical tradition.[103] This principle thus establishes certain boundary conditions which set the framework for the legislative activity of individual states. These conditions can be defined as follows: (1) the law is to be person-oriented, regardless of their individual characteristics; (2) the human is a social being, which makes it necessary to shape the law so as to take into account the social dimension of human life; (3) human dignity and the resulting freedoms and rights do not derive their legitimacy from the decisions of the state, since they are natural and inalienable; (4) human rights and freedoms are free from ideology, belonging to man regardless of the ideology chosen by public authority; (5) the values stemming from the principle of human dignity are unchanging, and thus independent of current conditions.[104]

In some jurisdictions, dignity is understood primarily as the basis for the principle of equality. As Judge Kotaro Tanaka noted in a sentence separate from the International Court of Justice ruling in the South-West Africa case, "all people are equal before the law and have equal opportunities, regardless of religion, race, language, gender, or social affiliation. As individuals, they have dignity that requires appropriate treatment. It is the principle of equality, which is one of the fundamental rights and freedoms of man, which are universal for all humankind."[105] A similar view was expressed by Judge Fouad Ammoun:

> (. . .) it is no coincidence that Article 1 of the Universal Declaration of Human Rights expresses the fundamental principle that "All persons shall be born free and equal in dignity and rights." Most rights and freedoms derive from this first principle. Of all human rights, the most important is the right to equal treatment. It is also one of the laws that has long been recognised as a natural law; it could even be said that the doctrine of natural law was developed in antiquity with the principle of the equality of all people as its first element.[106]

In the practice of the functioning of the legal systems of individual states, it turned out that the scope of the universal meaning of dignity is so narrow that it is possible to draw two completely opposite conclusions from this principle. A good example of this phenomenon is the dispute concerning the moral and legal assessment of abortion procedures. In systems that refer more or less directly to the tradition of Christian personalism or Kant's philosophy in the interpretation of dignity, it becomes one of the arguments of those who advocate the right of everyone to life, even in the prenatal phase. The argument in favor of such a position is precisely the dignity—belonging to everyone, regardless of the stage of development, and therefore also to the nasciturus. In the case law of the Polish Constitutional Tribunal, the right to the protection of life is closely related to the principle of dignity:

> Without the need to further broaden the argumentation, it can be stated that the limitation of legal protection of human life in order to protect rights located lower in the constitutional hierarchy, e.g. ownership and other property rights, public morality, environmental protection or even the health of other people, would be definitely unacceptable in a democratic state of law implementing the principles of social justice and protecting life and inalienable human dignity. The condition for limiting the right to legal protection of life is therefore that a situation arises in which it is undoubtedly incompatible with the analogous rights of other persons. This premise can be generally described as a requirement for the symmetry of rights: sacrificed and saved.[107]

In the United States, on the other hand, where individualistic attitudes prevail, dignity is often invoked by supporters of expanding access to abortion. An example is the judgment in *Thornburgh v American College of Obstetricians and Gynaecologists*, in which it was stated that "there are few decisions that are more personal and intimate, or more fundamental to individual dignity and autonomy, than the decision of a woman—taken in consultation with a doctor and within the limits indicated in the judgement in Roe—whether to terminate a pregnancy. The woman's right to freedom in this decision is fundamental."[108]

The philosophical context in which human dignity is interpreted in a given country, and therefore the meaning given to it, is of vital importance for criminal law.[109] Aharon Barak also points this out, indicating that human dignity in a Western country is not the same as human dignity in a country belonging to a different cultural circle. Similarly, the principle of human dignity in one Western state does not have to coincide in substance with the principle of human dignity in another Western state.[110] This dependence of the content of the principle of human dignity on the interpretative context adopted in a given country should not be understood as its relativization in a pejorative sense. The more the principle of human dignity is embedded in a concrete interpretive context, the more precise its content is and the more precise its conclusions for criminal law can be.

Demonstrating that the principle of human dignity is dependent on the context in which it is analyzed does not mean that one has to agree that the principle itself has no content and that its meaning comes entirely from sources external to it. However, it is not necessary—taking into account the assumptions of this work, especially the verification of the hypothesis of the ethical legitimization of criminal law—to search for an objective content of the principle of dignity, independent of particular contexts. On the contrary, these contexts are of particular importance in this work. The principle of human dignity, provided that in a given legal system it is placed sufficiently high in its hierarchy of principles, may serve as a link between the legal system and that particular context, which consists of a specific ethical and anthropological system taken as a starting point.

In this sense, Barak's justified observations pointing to a lack of agreement on the essence of the principle of human dignity, which manifests itself on three levels, that is, on the content of the principle of human dignity, on the justification for human dignity, and on the results to which that principle leads.[111] Each of these problems can be solved in the context in which dignity is embedded in a given legal system. This differentiation should not come as a surprise. If similar problems are solved differently in different legal systems, one of the reasons for this may also be that the system is embedded in a different philosophical and ethical context. Of course, this does not have to be the only reason for the differences, but it is certainly one of the more important ones.

The context from which the principle of human dignity is derived for the needs of the legal system becomes a necessary point of reference in the procedure of interpreting the law. Human dignity is not a general clause which is introduced into the legal system in order to give the body applying the law greater discretion or, as Barak would like, to enable the judge to make the law more appropriate in the light of changing social conditions.[112]

Two concepts of human dignity rooted in moral thinking in Africa are interesting and worth mentioning.[113] The first is based on the principle of vitality, otherwise referred to as life force. According to the second of them, the basis of man's special value is his communal nature. Each of these concepts seeks to justify the idea that man is objectively a good in himself, is equal in relation to others, with the duty to treat each one with due respect and to respect the human rights rooted in that dignity.[114] This does not mean that the Christian and, above all, personalistic approach to dignity has not gained any recognition in some areas of the African continent. However, if we want to point to the specificity of the approach to human dignity that exists there, it is worth getting to know these two concepts more closely.

The first of these concepts refers to the idea of life force, explained as a valuable, spiritual, energy present in material or visible objects.[115] According to this approach, every object in the universe, even inanimate objects, has life force. Living objects undoubtedly have more life force than inanimate objects. Man has more life force than animals and plants. Dead ancestors, who are in the spirit world, and God, who is the source of every life force, have more life force than humans in this concept. Ethics based on the concept of life force gives at least several possibilities for seeking justification for the claim of a particular human value, that is, indicating his dignity. From the perspective of the analysis conducted for the needs of legal sciences, and in this case above all criminal law, it is worth noting an approach that does not refer in its foundations strictly to aspects of the spiritual world, which plays an important role in African philosophy.[116] It can therefore be said that the ethic of vitality emphasizes the vitality of man and his creative abilities.[117] The adoption of this interpretation of human dignity would imply respect for the creative abilities and creativity of every human being.

The concept of understanding dignity which refers to community sees the justification for human dignity in the ability of a person to establish relationships with other people, as well as in his general inclination toward communal life. No one may therefore be killed, taken prisoner or tortured, because that would violate the possibility of realizing a person's social nature. This concept also well justifies freedoms and human rights such as freedom of travel, inter-racial marriage, participation in democratic processes, and the right to make decisions about one's health. This concept also provides the basis for the development of criminal responsibility principles based on the principle of guilt. The concept of community is understood as sharing the way of life with other people and caring for each other's quality of life.[118]

The interpretation of dignity in the context of the ethical interpretations adopted in Africa by Thaddeus Metz seems particularly important precisely because of the emphasized community dimension of human dignity. Progressive individualization in social relations also caused that a significant part of human dignity is presented on the basis of this paradigm. The principle of human dignity is first and foremost read in the key of "freedom from," especially from any interference in the sphere of privacy. This does not mean that dignity does not have such a content; however, it does not seem that it is dignity that determines the basic direction in which this principle was interpreted at the moment when it was included in the acts of international law or in some basic law, such as the Constitution of the Republic of Poland of 1997. Metz's concept shows that human dignity is revealed in a special way when he undertakes various social interactions, thus becoming the foundation of "freedom to" in initiating and shaping social relations. In this context, the thesis that sees human dignity as a basis for claiming the equal value of every human being is justified and is gaining in importance precisely in the context of the community commitment of every human being. In other words, in our social life, we have to treat each other as equals.[119] Any disputes between individuals cannot justify recourse to measures based on fraud or violence.

The resolution of any conflicts should be based on mutual persuasion or even on the *status quo*.[120]

There is no doubt that the figure of human dignity has a relational character, reflecting the social character of man. Man does not function in a vacuum, is not able to realize his intentions on his own, or—using the language of aretalogy—to strive for his perfection. As Barak rightly points out, we cannot talk about the dignity of Robinson Crusoe on an uninhabited island but rather about the dignity of the human being in relation to others.[121] This does not mean that a single person, even one like Robinson Crusoe, does not have the quality of dignity. If dignity is natural and inalienable, then it is also due to a person who has found himself or herself in complete solitude. Under such conditions, however, it cannot be sufficiently manifested. This is confirmed by the thesis that condemning a human being to absolute isolation, making any social interaction impossible, could be interpreted as a solution that unacceptably interferes with their dignity.

THE INTERPRETATION OF *LAS MENINAS* (*THE MAIDS OF HONOUR*)

Dignity, as has already been shown, can be read and understood in different ways. One of them is a rare view of the principle of human dignity through the prism of art in legal literature. According to Christopher McCrudden, a picture that reflects this principle well is *Las Meninas* (*The Maids of Honor*), one of the most important works by Diego Velázquez.[122] Looking through the prism of Velázquez's canvas leads us to point out different perspectives for studying dignity and reading its meaning. It can be analyzed from a historical perspective, its occurrence and understanding over the centuries. The historical perspective also makes it possible to consider the evolutionary consistency of the category under discussion or to consider that the contemporary meaning of this notion is contradictory or to some extent irreconcilable with the understanding available in previous eras. Given that the painting was done in the seventeenth century and directly illustrates an aspect of court life, it provides an opportunity to reflect on the meaning of human dignity in those very circumstances.[123] The painting can also express another argument metaphorically. Just as every epoch interprets a work of art in a different way and draw a different content from it, so it can deal with the category of human dignity.[124] However, if, at least to some extent, the meaning of human creation is universalized in history, and thus connotatively crosses the borders of one era, the principle of human dignity can also be attempted to be interpreted it in a way that gives the potential of being current regardless of time.

The Velázquez painting can also represent human dignity understood as a reflection of a certain social hierarchy that allows for the gradation of dignity, depending on the position held. The work presents people with different positions at the royal court. One can see a woman kneeling in front of the royal couple's daughter, as well as another courtesan who seems to be staring at the royal couple, who wants to determine what action she is to take with regard to the young queen.[125] The dignity of the human being understood in this way is not a reflection of his humanity, the personal nature of his existence, but it is an account of a hierarchical society, ordered according to the criterion of aristocratic origin.

Christopher McCrudden also sees in Velázquez's image a metaphor of the dignity of the profession, which also influences the sense of value of a given person. The painter depicted in the painting, perhaps Velázquez himself, has the Cross of St. James embroidered on his clothes as a symbol of belonging to the Order of St. James. In fact, only those who had an aristocratic background could belong to this order. Excluded were those who came from a family where someone was involved in trade or paid work. This ruled out the possibility that Velázquez himself belonged to this order because he painted the painting for money. This allows us to think that the cross on the painter's clothes means that the author expressed the dignity of his profession, and therefore did not accept his exclusion from the group of worthy people.[126]

An in-depth analysis of the painting allows us to further develop our reflection on dignity. As mentioned earlier, dignity was—and still is—linked to one's social background, profession, or even financial resources. The way in which the royal couple is portrayed also gives rise to another somewhat different interpretation. We see the couple, admittedly, only in the mirror image, as people surrounded by their loved ones, family members, and co-workers, but if one of the interpretations is that the picture shows the process of portraying the royal couple, one might wonder why they are accompanied by their daughter and courtiers. Wouldn't it be easier for the painter and the spouses if they were alone? The process of painting undoubtedly requires peace. However, in the chosen way, their attachment to their daughter, their family character is shown. Christopher McCrudden sees here the adoption of the Erasmian model of the ideal monarch, which he draws not from the royal origin itself but from the virtues of a good ruler.[127] As he rightly observes, from linking dignity to virtues is not far from being linked to the fact of being human as such.[128] Nor can we overlook the way dwarves are portrayed. They are shown in a way that does not distinguish them from other people. This allows us to deduce dignity from the very fact of being human, regardless of different ailments.[129]

However, it seems that McCrudden is not right when in the symbolism of the canvas of *Las Meninas* he finds inspiration to state that dignity is a completely open category, left to be filled.[130] The polemic with such a stance does not concern the inspiration of the work of art itself, but the conclusion in relation to the content of dignity. Although it seems justified to say that dignity can be interpreted in completely different ways, depending on the context adopted by the interpreting community, this does not necessarily mean that it does not have its own content, which could be established even if an appropriate context is needed for this purpose.

HUMAN DIGNITY IN THE JURISPRUDENCE OF COURTS

In the light of the above, an analysis of the understanding of dignity by different courts seems justified. It may result not only in broadening the knowledge about possible connotations of human dignity but above all in verifying the relationship between the independent content of this principle and the content susceptible to the context of interpretation. The findings made on this ground are necessary to verify the thesis on the function of human dignity, which consists in opening criminal law analysis to arguments in the field of ethics and philosophical anthropology, and finally also the thesis on the ethical legitimization of criminal law.

Human Dignity in the Case Law of the Constitutional Court

The articulation of human dignity in Article 30 of the Constitution of the Republic of Poland, which opens the chapter of the Basic Law devoted to the freedoms, rights, and duties of man and citizen, causes this principle to be invoked in proceedings before the Constitutional Tribunal. The judicial context created by the constitutional court may be helpful in the correct interpretation of the meaning of the principle of dignity in which it has been embedded in the Polish legal system. The present study does not include a comprehensive review of all the rulings of the Constitutional Tribunal in which the principle of dignity is invoked. From the perspective of the issues discussed, a choice indicating important features added to the dignity of the constitutional court's jurisprudence seems sufficient.

Human dignity in the jurisprudence of the Constitutional Tribunal is sometimes considered jointly and in connection with the principle of democratic rule of law. Litigation letters addressed to the Constitutional Tribunal indicate that the application of the law in a democratic state governed by the rule of law should be a manifestation of respect for human dignity.[131] Also the tribunal itself stated that Article 30 of the Constitution of the Republic of Poland defines the axiological basis for the rights and freedoms guaranteed therein.[132] In another CT judgment, we read:

> The constitutional control model enshrined in Article 30 of the Constitution recognises inherent and inalienable human dignity as a source of freedom and human and civil rights and proclaims its inviolability, while obliging public authorities to respect and protect it. Pursuant to Article 30 of the Constitution, the notion of human dignity should be assigned the character of a constitutional value of central importance for building an axiology of current constitutional solutions, through the prism of which all other provisions on the rights, freedoms and duties of the individual should be interpreted and applied.[133]

Moreover, the principle of human dignity is, according to the Constitutional Court's ruling, the link between natural law and established law. At the same time, it is the axiological basis and premise of the entire constitutional system.[134]

The objection of unconstitutionality raised in the constitutional complaint against a legislative omission in the Criminal Code is interesting. The subject of the complaint was the limitation of the scope of Article 191 § 1 of the Criminal Code guaranteed by Article 30 of the Constitution for the protection of human freedom and dignity against unlawful attacks. The complaint states that

> The applicant contests not a legislative omission but a narrowing of the protection of its freedom by limiting the scope of criminalisation of the offence of coercion, as provided for in the Criminal Code currently in force. (. . .) However, the applicant does not invoke the principle of the rule of law in relation to the requirements of the sufficient definition of a legal rule as a constitutional model. He accuses Article 191, paragraph 1 of the Criminal Code of violating his dignity and sense of social justice.[135]

The Constitutional Tribunal, disagreeing with the position on the unconstitutionality of the provision, pointed out that dignity may be a benchmark for the assessment of lawmaking omissions:

> It should therefore have been shown that the lack of criminal law reaction to the cutting off of the water supply by the owner of the house undermines the inalienable dignity of the applicant and the principle of justice, since this act is characterised by such a psychological impact that it may undoubtedly lead to a threat to the use of the most important right of the applicant (i.e. life, health, housing . . .), and at the same time is socially assessed as an evil so severe that it requires criminal law reaction. These requirements were not met by the applicant and, as a result, he failed to rebut the presumption of conformity with the Constitution of Article 191(1) of the Criminal Code.[136]

The reference to dignity made by the Constitutional Tribunal in this ruling may raise some doubts. The court's statement, especially in the part where it uses the phrase "the inalienable dignity of the applicant," may indicate that this is an exemplification of dignity understood as a sense of self-esteem, more personal than human, independent of personal feelings. On the other hand, the indication that dignity is inalienable suggests rather its personal character, independent of the sense of the person in whom the dignity is individualized. Most importantly, however, in this ruling, the Constitutional Tribunal *expressis verbis* confirmed that the principle of human dignity may influence the scope of criminalization.

The jurisprudence of the Constitutional Tribunal also indicates that the content of human dignity has not been exhausted by publishing human rights and freedoms in Chapter II of the Constitution of the Republic of Poland: "Article 30 also requires the protection of fundamental human rights which, for one reason or another, are not detailed in specific provisions."[137] Such a finding was made by the tribunal when it pointed out to the applicant that, where the provision complained of infringes a right or a freedom expressed in the Basic Law, a specific right or freedom, possibly in connection with the principle of dignity, should be mentioned among the models without being invoked as an independent standard of control. Dignity may undoubtedly be an independent model of control, but only when its independent content, not being the subject of specification in other provisions of the Basic Law, is relevant in a given case. In another judgment, the Constitutional Tribunal stressed that

> identifying a violation of every right and freedom with a violation of dignity would remove the guarantees contained in Article 30 of the Constitution of its independent field of application. (. . .) It includes the most important values which do not benefit from other, independent constitutional guarantees, and which affect the essence of the individual's position in society, his relation to other persons and to public authority.[138]

In its judgment of March 5, 2003, the tribunal explicitly referred to two aspects of dignity.[139] The first one describes dignity as a transcendent value, original to other rights and freedoms, and being their source. Dignity is inherent and inalienable here, making it impossible to violate it—man always, in all circumstances, retains his dignity. Another aspect of dignity, however, is the law of personality, covering the values of the mental life of each individual, determining the subjective position of the individual in society. Dignity in this latter sense may be subject to infringement. It cannot be taken away, but it is possible to violate it through various actions, primarily aimed at respect for others. It is worth noting that the tribunal's observation that the dignity in its transcendental dimension cannot be violated can be called into question. Undoubtedly, it cannot be diminished or taken away, because it is immanently connected with every human being. However, it is possible to actually undertake such actions which will be incompatible with the principle of human dignity in its normative dimension, although not its necessarily descriptive one. Dignity, as has been mentioned many times before, not only describes certain characteristics of the individual but also requires a certain behavior toward them, even regardless of their perception of that behavior. Behavior that does not comply with these requirements, even if it does not take into account a person's sense of dignity, may give rise to a finding that dignity has been violated.

One of the postulates resulting from human dignity, and therefore manifestations of its normative dimension, is the requirement that "courts and other authorised bodies of public authority should seek to ensure that every moral harm is (as far as possible) repaired and eliminated."[140] The tribunal observes that the dignity of the injured party, for example by infringing their personal rights, does not have to be protected solely by means of measures of a material nature. The manner in which human dignity is protected at the trial stage should be decided by determining the moral and customary standards in force in the society concerned.

In another ruling, the Constitutional Tribunal articulated two other postulates resulting from the principle of dignity. The first is the necessity of the existence of "a certain material minimum, ensuring the individual the possibility of independent functioning in the society and creating opportunities for every person to fully develop his or her personality in the surrounding cultural and civilisation environment." The second postulate concerns the necessity of subjective treatment of every human being. Man cannot be merely an object of action by authority, a "substitutable quantity," and so his role cannot be reduced to a purely instrumental form.[141]

According to the jurisprudence of the Constitutional Tribunal, the violation of human dignity may be an unlawful deprivation of liberty. Unlawful should be understood as such deprivation of liberty which would not be necessary in a democratic state for the protection of one of the values indicated in Article 31(3) of the Constitution of the Republic of Poland.[142] Consequently, unnecessary deprivation of liberty leads to the objectification of the individual by depriving him or her of the freedom to determine his or her conduct. This may also lead to a violation of the personal dignity of the individual deprived of liberty. This is the conclusion reached in the judgment of July 10, 2007. The tribunal presented Article 203(3) of the Code of Criminal Procedure, which in its wording then did not sufficiently protect the individual from prolonged isolation in his or her cell for the purpose of psychiatric observation, as a result of its assessment. In the opinion of the tribunal, this provision violated "the personal dignity of the accused at the same time, because the prolonged need for psychiatric observation combined with social isolation often reduces the subjective position of the individual and his or her self-esteem."[143]

The Constitutional Tribunal has also noted a close link between human dignity and individual privacy. In its view,

> the preservation of human dignity requires respect for his purely personal sphere, where he is not exposed to the need to "be with others" or to share with others experiences of an intimate nature. This does not mean, however, that no state interference in the sphere of privacy is acceptable. However, it is important that such interference is subject to appropriate procedural safeguards and does not lead to a prejudice to the dignity of the person being controlled.[144]

Still more important seems to be the postulate to protect human life, which is based on human dignity. Human dignity and human life are rights that are coupled together in a direct manner. According to the Constitutional Tribunal, the principle of human dignity should be viewed from the perspective of the requirement to protect human life. Consequently, the state should take action to reduce or eliminate hazards to human life. This also implies the human right to personal inviolability, which includes the physical and spiritual integrity of the individual.[145] It is worth noting, however, that the protection of life—in contrast to human dignity—is not absolute. The possibility of restricting the protection of life is extremely narrow, but it does exist:

> Without the need to further broaden the argumentation, it can be stated that the limitation of the legal protection of human life in order to protect rights located lower in the constitutional hierarchy, e.g. property and other material rights, public morality, environmental protection or even the health of other people, would definitely be unacceptable in a democratic state of law implementing the principles of social justice and protecting human life and inalienable human dignity. The condition for limiting the right to legal protection of life is therefore that a situation arises in which it is undoubtedly incompatible with the analogous rights of other persons. This premise can be generally described as a requirement for the symmetry of rights: sacrificed and rescued.[146]

Supreme Court Rulings

Human dignity is also mentioned in the jurisprudence of the Supreme Court. However, this is much less the case in the Supreme Court than in the Constitutional Tribunal. It seems that one of the reasons for such a state of affairs may be another characteristic of the jurisprudence of the Supreme Court, especially in the area of the constitution. In the Supreme Court, the

Basic Law, if at all, is applied in a given proceeding, is co-applied—apart from the provisions that are the direct basis for the ruling. The Constitutional Tribunal, on the other hand, rules primarily on the basis of the Constitution of the Republic of Poland. It should be noted, however, that the Supreme Court has no doubt that respect for human dignity is not only a legal but also a moral obligation.[147]

Human dignity in the jurisprudence of the Supreme Court is presented as a principle having a significant meaning for the issue of the rules of serving sentences: "The guarantee by the State of decent detention conditions is one of the fundamental requirements of a democratic State governed by the rule of law, as reflected in international standards."[148] The duty to protect human dignity should be exercised primarily in those areas where the state operates within its empire. It is worth noting at this point that criminal law is this fragment of state activity that can be characterized as an empire in its pure form. It is therefore an aspect that is particularly sensitive to the impact of human dignity.

Human dignity also determines the need to link criminal responsibility, as well as disciplinary responsibility, which to some extent is modeled on criminal responsibility, with the premise of guilt. This was expressed by the Supreme Court in the context of a disciplinary case:

> Although the Act—Law on the system of common courts does not provide for proper application of the provisions of the Criminal Code in disciplinary proceedings concerning judges, the prohibition on imposing a penalty exceeding the degree of guilt of the perpetrator, contained in Article 53 of the Criminal Code, should be observed in such proceedings, as this prohibition already results from the constitutional principle of respect for human dignity (Article 30 of the Constitution of the Republic of Poland).[149]

Already after this ruling, an amendment was made to the Act—law on the system of common courts, which in Article 128 now states that in cases not regulated in the scope of disciplinary proceedings, the provisions of the Code of Penal Procedure and the general part of the Criminal Code shall apply accordingly, taking into account the differences resulting from the nature of disciplinary proceedings. Nevertheless, the statement that the premise of guilt in criminal law is rooted in Article 30 of the Constitution of the Republic of Poland is still undoubtedly valid.

In some Supreme Court rulings, human dignity is understood more in the sense of personal dignity than human dignity. An example of a decision presenting such a meaning is the decision of February 7, 2007, in which the Supreme Court stated:

> It is undisputed, however, that the free press may become a threat to the rights of dignity, honour and good name. The legislator was obviously aware of this

> fact, which was evidenced by the introduction of a qualified type of defamation in the Criminal Code, namely slander through mass media (Article 212 § 2 of the Criminal Code).[150]

The same meaning of dignity can be found in the case law of the Civil Chamber. Already before the adoption and entry into force of the Constitution of the Republic of Poland in 1997, it was pointed out that human dignity is an important value, expressed in the ability to defend certain recognized values, but it was mainly used in a personal sense.[151]

Case Law of the European Court of Human Rights and the Court of Justice of the European Union

The category of dignity is rarely referred to in the case law of the European Court of Human Rights (ECtHR) and the Court of Justice of the European Union (CJEU). The analysis of case law provides an opportunity to indicate a significant number of judgments in which an appeal to the issue of dignity could be helpful in resolving a case. It also happens that the reference to human dignity appears only in a separate opinion. There are probably many reasons for this. One of them may be the omission of the principle of dignity from the basic text of the convention itself. This does not mean, however, that the issue of human dignity in the jurisprudence of these courts, and in particular that of the ECtHR, is absent in general. It appears in a meaningful sense, that is, when in jurisprudence arguments corresponding to human dignity are invoked, without naming it in this way. It can therefore be assumed that the principle of dignity in terms of content, while less in formal terms, appears in the jurisprudence of the courts. It also happens that it is sometimes directly invoked.

It is worth noting the case of *S.H. and others against Austria*, which concerned an Austrian law regulating the issue of artificial procreation.[152] This is an example of a judgment in which a direct reference to human dignity appears only in a separate opinion. Judge Vincent A. de Gaetano, seeing the need to supplement the grounds for the judgment without questioning the substance of the decision, pointed out that human dignity and the concept of the intrinsic value of human life are at the heart of the Convention for the Protection of Human Rights and Fundamental Freedoms (ECHR) as a whole. Already in the context of the specific factual situation, the judge noted that although the couple's decision to conceive a child is a decision which falls within the sphere of private and family life, Articles 8 and 12 of the ECHR cannot be interpreted as granting the right to conceive a child at any cost. The judge concluded that the desire for a child does not set a superior goal over the dignity of human life. In this case, dignity was interpreted as a value that exposes every human being as a subject and his or her life as a value in itself that needs to be protected. Different desires and aspirations should be subordinate to or at least not interfere with these values. This separate opinion underlines that the recognition of the value and dignity of every person may require the prohibition of certain acts in order to bear witness to the inalienable value and intrinsic dignity of every human being.

As in the case described above, human dignity is referred to in a separate sentence in *VO v. France* concerning the meaning of the term "man" and the scope of protection of human life.[153] Judges Antonella Mularoni and Viera Strážnická submitted a separate opinion in which they pointed out the need to seek appropriate measures for the protection of human rights and human dignity in relation to certain applications of biotechnology and medicine. From this separate opinion emerges a proposal to extend the protection of life at the fetal stage, especially in order to protect human dignity from genetic manipulation and other negative consequences of interference in this period of human life.

The issue of dignity in the context of the prenatal period of human life also arose in the case of *Parillo v. Italy.*[154] In this case, the court noted that dignity is also due to a person before birth. Judge Paulo Pinto de Albuquerque more clearly explained this in his separate opinion. He noted that unborn human life is not fundamentally different from the life of a born person. At each of these stages of life, a human must have the respect that is proper to human dignity. The pursuit of scientific progress cannot justify this treatment of man and his dignity.

Direct or indirect inspiration for the principle of human dignity can also be found in those ECtHR rulings which deal with the issue of degrading treatment of human beings by public authorities or the omissions of public authorities in terms of the prevention of degrading treatment. The decision in *Bouyid v. Belgium*[155] undoubtedly allows such a conclusion. In that regard, the court stressed the intrinsic link between degrading treatment and breach of the obligation to respect human dignity.[156] Human dignity is diminished when public officials use physical force against a given person, in particular in conditions of deprivation of liberty, unless this is strictly necessary in view of the behavior of that person. The court stressed that not only is Article 3 ECHR infringed in such cases but that there is also an infringement of dignity, which affects the very substance of the convention.

Also worth noting is the ruling in the case of *Abdu v. Bulgaria.*[157] In that judgment, the court recognized that Article 3 ECHR protects the dignity and physical integrity of a man.[158] From the perspective of human dignity, it is particularly important that the victim was victimized by racist violence in this case. Judges Paul Mahoney and Krzysztof Wojtyczek, in a separate opinion, supplemented the court's argumentation by pointing out that racist behavior always violates human dignity, is a despicable form of human rights violation, and the state should respond to it appropriately. In another case with a similar context, Judge P. P. de Albuquerque said that freedom of expression, assembly, and association must give way to human dignity and the rights of those whose race, nationality, or ethnic origin is under attack.[159]

Human dignity returns in ECtHR decisions taken on the basis of Article 3 ECHR also in cases concerning deprivation of liberty, that is, various aspects of deprivation of liberty, arrest, and detention. In the court's view, the use of physical force against a person deprived of his liberty, unless it is absolutely necessary as a result of his conduct, is directed against the dignity of the detainee and infringes Article 3 ECHR.[160] The court also reconstructs from the convention the obligation to ensure adequate conditions of detention, which must be compatible with human dignity. It is the responsibility of the public authorities to organize the prison system in such a way as to ensure that the dignity of the detainees is respected. In addition, the lack of measures to ensure appropriate conditions for detainees should mean abandoning strict penal policies and implementing alternative measures.[161] This means that the principle of human dignity is directly translated into the criminal policy of the state. According to the court, the very essence of the convention is respect for human dignity and human freedom.[162]

The principle of human dignity has not been extensively referred to in the judgments of the CJEU. It cannot be ruled out that this trend will be increasingly reversed, particularly in view of Article 1 of the Charter of Fundamental Rights of the European Union, which declares that human dignity is inviolable and must be respected and protected.

Human dignity has appeared in the case law of the CJEU, or rather the European Court of Justice at that time, earlier, before the adoption of the Charter of Fundamental Rights. An example of such a ruling is the judgment of October 5, 2000, concerning Directive 98/44/EC of the European Parliament and of the Council of July 6, 1998, on the protection of biotechnological inventions.[163] The tribunal stated that human dignity was protected in that directive by the prohibition on making the human body, at the various stages of its formation and development, a patentable invention. Human dignity was also protected by the prohibition on patenting human cloning, on modifying the genetic identity of human embryos and on using human embryos for industrial or commercial purposes.

Similar issues have been addressed by the CJEU in the relatively well-known case of *Oliver Brüstle v. Greenpeace eV.*[164] The court noted in that regard that, in that directive, the European Union legislature intended to exclude the possibility of granting a patent whenever it might lead to an infringement of human dignity. At the same time, the court pointed out that a "human embryo" must be understood to mean any human ovum as soon as it is fertilized, since that fertilization may begin the process of development of the human person.

A reference to the problem of dignity also appeared in the case law of the CJEU in connection with the European Union's asylum policy. In this respect, the judgment of December 2, 2014 in the case of *A, B, C v. Staatssecretaris van Veiligheid en Justitie*[165] deserves attention. The submission of the decision requires a brief account of the facts of the case. It concerned the interpretation of Article 4 of Council Directive 2004/83/EC of April 29, 2004, on minimum standards for the qualification and status of third-country nationals or stateless persons as refugees or as persons who otherwise need international protection and the content of the protection granted.[166] Articles 3 and 7 of the Charter of Fundamental Rights of the European Union were also interpreted. In fact, the applicants applied for asylum in the Netherlands, including a temporary residence permit, on the basis of their homosexual orientation. They argued that their sexual orientation could be a source of persecution in their country of origin. The complainants indicated that the Netherlands should have confined itself to their statements, as it was not possible to objectively examine sexual orientation without unduly interfering with human privacy. The court ruled that subjecting a person to verification procedures other than interrogation to obtain evidence, such as video records of sexual activities, may violate human dignity, the respect for which is guaranteed in Article 1 of the Charter of Fundamental Rights.

Supreme Court Rulings in the United States

The principle of human dignity is not a figure often referred to in U.S. court rulings, although, as L. M. Henry pointed out, the importance of this principle, assessed in terms of the number of judgments in which it is referred to, is constantly increasing.[167] The growing popularity of the category of dignity, however, does not require any agreement on the understanding of its content. There are also significant differences in the definition of dignity and in the functions attributed to it in the case law.[168]

In work and discussions on the principle of human dignity, we are usually oriented toward the continental perspective, especially the German one. This approach runs the risk of extrapolating regional arrangements to a much broader geographical scope. The discussion of the content of the principle of dignity, its rootedness in an interpretative context, or finally its significance for the legal order, makes it legitimate to juxtapose and compare the Polish perspective, after all, very similar to the German one, with a completely different tradition, in this case the North American one.

The U.S. Supreme Court refers to the issue of human dignity, above all in the context of the first,[169] fourth,[170] fifth,[171] sixth,[172] eighth,[173] ninth,[174] eleventh,[175] fourteenth,[176] and fifteenth[177] amendments to the U.S. Constitution.[178] The U.S. Supreme Court has invoked the notion of human dignity in more than 900 decisions.[179]

The literature indicates that one of the ground-breaking appeals to the principles of human dignity in the jurisprudence of the Supreme Court of the United States took place in 1946. The argument of dignity was raised in a dissenting opinion as one of the values that the United States shares, belonging to the international community:

> "If we are ever to develop an orderly international community based on the recognition of human dignity, of paramount importance will be the necessity of punishing those guilty of atrocities just as far as possible, free from the ugly stigma of nasty revenge and vindictiveness. Justice must be shaped by compassion rather than the desire for revenge."[180]

However, this was not the first reference to the principle of dignity in U.S. jurisprudence. As early as 1793, the judgment in the case of *Chisholm v. Georgia* stated: "If the dignity of each individual is not diminished, the dignity of all together must be preserved."[181]

The analysis of U.S. Supreme Court jurisprudence by Jordan J. Paust shows that the principle of human dignity is rarely accompanied by any in-depth explanation. The reason for this state of affairs may be the assumption that it is a basic legal figure in the constitutional order of the state, which does not require any particular explanations or supplementing with an appeal to the existing jurisprudence.[182] It is assumed, therefore, that the connotation of the principle of human dignity is relatively well known, and therefore does not require the disclosure of the meaning context in which it is invoked. As has already been noted, the philosophical context, especially ethical and anthropological, is extremely important for determining the content of the principle of human dignity. The universal significance of this principle, as tried to be expressed in the Universal Declaration of Human Rights, is insufficient to allow the principle of human dignity to be operationalized, and thus to enable it to be put into practice in the lawmaking process and in the application of law, including criminal law. If in the legal system of a given country the principle of human dignity is invoked in the vast majority of cases only in one meaningful context, it may seem reasonable to assume that there is no need to explain it each time.

However, only a slight in-depth analysis of the jurisprudence can indicate the various doubts that arise in relation to the category of human dignity. In practice, it is not uncommon for a rule discussed here to be used as a kind of ornament, elevating a given statement, especially if it is a court decision. In other cases, on account of its alleged authority, it is sometimes used, unfortunately sometimes without reflection, as a kind of reinforcement of a given specific right or freedom that is the subject of a judgment.[183] An example of such a generalized use of the principle of human dignity can be found in the dissenting opinion of Judge Felix Frankfurter in the ruling of the U.S. Supreme Court in the *Louisiana ex rel. Francis v. Resweber* case:

> The Fourteenth Amendment did not mean to imprison the States into the limited experience of the eighteenth century. It did mean to withdraw from the States the right to act in ways that are offensive to a decent respect for the dignity of man, and heedless of his freedom. These are very broad terms by which to accommodate freedom and authority. As has been suggested from time to time, they may be too large to serve as the basis for adjudication, in that they allow much room for individual notions of policy. That is not our concern. The fact is that the duty of such adjudication on a basis no less narrow has been committed to this Court.[184]

A more thorough analysis of the jurisprudence of the SCOTUS and the doctrine surrounding it allows us to point to five directional interpretations of human dignity adopted by this court. Dignity is sometimes understood as: (1) institutional status, (2) equality, (3) freedom, (4) personal integrity, (5) collective virtue.[185]

By dignity in institutional terms, the U.S. Supreme Court understands first and foremost the need to protect the position of important state bodies and officials in the most important public functions, such as judges. In the case of *Cooke v. United States*, the Supreme Court, through the mouth of Judge William Taft, pointed out that a properly shaped range of magistrate powers, making up his power, is necessary to maintain the authority and dignity of the court.[186] In this respect, the dignity of other entities of international law was also pointed out. In the case of *Schooner Exchange v. McFaddon*, the court explicitly referred to the need to protect the dignity of other countries.[187] In a number of cases, dignity has appeared as a value justifying the existence of the immunity of foreign states.[188] In another ruling, however, the U.S. Supreme Court stated that "whatever the justification for the immunity of the US government from private trial may be, it is not dignity."[189]

The understanding of dignity as equality developed in the jurisprudence of the U.S. Supreme Court during the Civil Rights Movement. One of the most important judgments of this era was the judgment in the case of *Heart of Atlanta Motel, Inc. v. United States*. The Supreme Court noted that the goal of the Civil Rights Act of 1964 was to confirm that human dignity is violated whenever equal access to public institutions is denied.[190] A number of judgments of the SCOTUS, in which dignity was interpreted through the prism of equality, concerned the issue of unequal treatment on the grounds of race or gender. An example is the ruling in *Powers v. Ohio*, in which the Supreme Court ruled out the possibility of taking into account criteria related to their race in the selection of jury members. As stated in the ruling, "racial discrimination in the qualification or selection of jury members violates the dignity of persons and the integrity of courts."[191]The criterion of gender was assessed in the case of *J.E.B. v. Alabama ex rel. T.B.* in which the Supreme Court found that the selection of members of the jury with regard to sex "is practically a labeling of their inferiority, caused by the law. (. . .) This offends the dignity of the excluded jury member and, from a woman's perspective, restores the history of exclusion from political participation."[192]

In rulings in which the U.S. Supreme Court interpreted human dignity is the key to individual freedom, it became the basis for generating the right to abortion, as well as for recognizing various restrictions on access to abortion as unconstitutional. An example is the 1986 judgment in the *Thornburgh v. American College of Obstetricians and Gynecologists* case, which effectively challenged various government interventions in the process of making decisions about abortion by an individual. The basic argument of the court was the dignity of man understood as his freedom. In Judge Harry Blackmun's judgment: "few decisions are more personal and intimate, more fundamental to individual dignity and autonomy than a woman's decision to terminate her pregnancy. A woman's right to take this decision freely is fundamental."[193] Dignity was also interpreted as freedom in the case of *Lawrence v. Texas* on homosexuality. The Supreme Court, in an opinion written by Judge Anthony Kennedy, accepted that "adults can choose to enter into such a relationship within the limits of their homes and their private lives, and still retain dignity as free persons (. . .). The freedom protected by the Constitution gives homosexuals the right to make such a decision."[194]

Dignity is also sometimes interpreted by the U.S. Supreme Court as personal integrity or a category protecting an individual's personal rights. An example of such an interpretation can be the decision made in the case of *Milkovich v. Lorain Journal Co.* in which the U.S. Supreme Court resolved the tension between freedom of expression and the right to protection of honor. Consequently, by giving priority to the protection of honor, it explained that "the human right to protect one's own honour from unjustified violation and unlawful harm reflects nothing more than our fundamental concept of the essential dignity and value of every human being."[195] In some cases, dignity as personal integrity may also prevail over dignity understood as freedom. This was the case in *Indiana v. Edwards*, where the SCOTUS restricted the autonomy of the individual, in this case a man suffering from mental illness, in the right to represent himself in court.[196] In that case, it was necessary, even though the person concerned had different instructions, to represent him by proxy. Personal integrity as a key to interpreting dignity was also found in the judgment in *Hudson v. Michigan*, whose author was Judge Antonin Scalia.[197] The case concerned the rules for police searches. In the decision it was decided:

> The knock-and-announce rule protects those elements of privacy and dignity that can be destroyed by sudden intrusion. This gives residents the opportunity to prepare for the entry of the police. A short interval between the announcement and entry with a warrant may provide the opportunity for an individual to put on clothes or get out of bed. In other words, it guarantees the opportunity to gather oneself before the door is opened.[198]

The notion of dignity as a collective virtue refers to a communitarian approach, for which moral evaluation depends on current beliefs, practices, and institutions that shape the community at a given time.[199] This context is very important in this case, since it is this context that determines the violation of dignity by the conduct in question. Within this approach, one can find the SCOTUS rulings on the death penalty, in which the possibility to sentence and execute the death penalty is limited to mature and mentally healthy people only. In addition, this also applies to certain decisions in the area of evidence in criminal matters and abortion case law. The case of *Hope v. Pelzer*, in which the eighth amendment to the U.S. Constitution was violated by a guard who, by chaining a prisoner, immobilized him for seven hours, in full sunlight, without a shirt and without access to a bathroom, as a punishment for inappropriate behavior, may be symptomatic of the treatment of dignity that we are discussing here. The court was of the opinion that such proceedings should be prohibited in order to protect individual freedom and human dignity.[200] In another ruling, which also applies to conditions of detention, the court acknowledged that prisoners may be deprived of rights that are fundamental to their freedom, but that they "preserve the essence of human dignity, innate to any person (. . .) which is the reason for the ban under the eighth amendment on cruel and unusual punishment."[201] In the judgment on *Gonzales v. Carhart*, the U.S. Supreme Court found the constitutionality of a law prohibiting partial birth abortion to be unconstitutional.[202] The justification for compliance with the constitution was the statement that the act respects the dignity of human life. At the same time, the SCOTUS challenged its earlier case law construing a woman's right to abortion.

CONCLUSIONS

The debate on the principle of human dignity, which has been conducted so far, allows us to admit that it is a central constitutional value. Aharon Barak notes three functions of the principle of dignity understood in this way:

1) establishing the basis for all human rights,
2) establishing the source of the interpretative context for constitutional norms, and
3) establishing the basis for limiting constitutional human rights.[203]

Even before moving on to discuss these functions of dignity, it is worth noting that such a perspective of interpreting the role of the principle seems to be far from sufficient. It is like this for at least three reasons. First, there is no independent role for the principle of human dignity—which could be translated strictly into any law or freedom that we reconstruct from it. It seems that in the light of previous findings, it is possible to distinguish in the area of dignity independent content, such as, for example, the subjectivity of each person. Dignity is thus not only the source of other freedoms and rights but also has its own content, determining the position of man in the system of law. Second, Barak's interpretation reduces the principle of human dignity to a mere source of rights and freedoms. Meanwhile, it seems that man as a subject, and he is also a subject precisely because of his dignity, has not only rights but also duties. These duties arise in relation to individuals, groups of individuals, or entire communities, especially states. Resignation from noting the obligations resulting from the principle of human dignity leads to depriving people, at least in the narrative layer, of their subjective character. It is obvious that the subject, whether morally or legally, always has not only rights but also obligations. If a person's subjectivity results from his dignity, then it is not only the source of their ability to perform their duties but can also be the source of them. Third, limiting the understanding of the principle of dignity to the way in which all other norms are interpreted may threaten to omit an important anthropological issue. It seems, after all, that the legislator draws on philosophical anthropology when he wants to express his understanding of man with the help of an appropriate category. By doing so in a certain philosophical context, especially if dignity is one of the key concepts in it, it may suggest that it applies the description of man thus expressed to the system order, and that the legal system will organize itself around this description of man.

It therefore seems that dignity constitutes:

1) the basis for all human rights,
2) the source of the interpretative context for constitutional norms,
3) the basis for limiting constitutional human rights,
4) an independent human right,
5) the source of human responsibilities toward other people, their associations, and the state, and
6) the basis for the reconstruction of the anthropological vision of man.

It seems justified to discuss particular functions of dignity, with particular emphasis on the latter, which is the basis for the ethical legitimization of criminal law.

The first of the above-mentioned functions of the principle of human dignity is expressed directly in Article 30 of the Constitution of the Republic of Poland, where it is stated that it is the source of freedom and rights of the individual and citizen. It does not seem that such a dignity can be reduced to a mere statement that it expresses the right to have other rights. It is not so much the source of the right to other rights as these rights derive directly from it.[204] In other words: the value of human dignity determines the range of rights that he or she has. The principle of human dignity is not a normative construct expressing the right to other human rights. Even more so, it is not a construct that draws its validity from the lawmaker's decision, even if he is presented as a legislator, that is, as a qualified lawmaker. The constitution, using the category of human dignity, indicates that the source of his rights is in himself, in his being a person, not in a normative act.[205]

The principle of human dignity plays a key role in the process of interpreting the law, not only constitutional law but also the norms expressed in other branches of law. The Constitutional Tribunal also stressed that the principle of human dignity serves as a determinant of the system and the scope of individual rights and freedoms.[206] At the same time, the principle of dignity becomes a fundamental point of reference in the process of interpreting pro-constitutional criminal law.[207] The values expressed in the Basic Law, as well as in legal acts of a different rank subordinate to the constitution, should be interpreted in such a way as to be as close as possible to the principle of dignity. The third function of dignity, which is to restrict other freedoms and human rights, is also linked to this. In this concept, human dignity is a kind of meta-principle, which allows for a proper interpretation of the hierarchy of other principles, and thus also of the freedoms and rights expressed in them. The better a given principle is rooted, and they can be identified as closer to the principle of dignity, and thus the more closely linked to its essence, the greater the protection it deserves. The principle of dignity can also fulfill this role because it is inherent and inalienable, and therefore not subject to the proportionality test, which means that it cannot be restricted.

The expression of human dignity in the system of law through the use of a formula corresponding to a normative text makes it possible to argue that the principle of human dignity is in itself a subjective right, understood not as the right to possess others but as the right to respect dignity and its protection.[208] As K. Complak noted, "[t]he renewal of the human person's dignity as the highest value of the Polish system would only be fully secured if it enjoyed special legal protection—higher than that which is entitled to any freedom or human right."[209] Human dignity is the most important substantive subjective right enshrined in the constitution and, moreover, bindingly determines human values in the entire legal system.[210] The inviolability of dignity entitles the holder to claim its protection.[211] Distinguishing the subjective right to the protection of dignity should not be understood as agreeing to the thesis of the possibility of disposing of dignity. It is inalienable, and its very inclusion, or in fact one of its aspects, in the formula of subjective law, does not yet make it possible to dispose of it. The right to life and physical integrity, as Leszek Bosek observes, is also a subjective right, which in this case does not mean the admissibility of disposing of these rights.[212]

Interpreting the principle of human dignity as a subjective right should not be understood as giving this right the function of a claim. The subject matter of this right is not a claim to dignity. As already mentioned above, it is natural and nontransferable, and this is how the Polish Constitution sees it in Article 30. Its source is not a decision of any public authority, so that dignity as a subjective right should not be interpreted as a claim for the granting of dignity. Rather, the principle of dignity must be regarded as a right the content of which is to insist on respect for human dignity and for what follows from it, including in particular its subjectivity and freedom.

Human dignity is not only the source of freedom and rights but is also the basis for the duty of every human being. They are characteristic of relations of a horizontal nature, that is, between individuals. Everyone can expect that their dignity will be respected not only vertically, that is, by public authorities, but also by other people. Thus, it can be said that dignity is not only a commitment of the state but also obliges all of us to respect each other. It seems possible to point to another aspect of dignity as a source of duty. If human dignity is the basis for a claim for subjective treatment, then it is at the same time the basis for attributing responsibility for the actions to an individual. Dignity therefore implies an ability to bear responsibility and consequently an obligation to bear responsibility if all the conditions for imputability are met. It also seems legitimate to accept that the obligation to refrain from actions that could then be associated with responsibility, that is, to avoid actions judged to be bad, can be decoded from dignity. Only such an image of dignity, and thus the source of not only rights and freedoms but also of duties, gives a full picture of the functions of humanity.

The principle of human dignity also plays a fundamental role in the ethical legitimization of criminal law. It is a category determining the anthropological vision of man, to which the legislator should adapt the regulations it introduces.[213] This thought becomes even more important in the context of criminal responsibility, which, given the standard of moral accessibility of criminal law, cannot go beyond the scope of human ethical responsibility.[214] First of all, we should consider what allows us to assume that the principle of dignity plays such an important role in the area of the ethical legitimization of criminal law. Then the shape of this anthropological vision determined in the legal system by the principle of dignity should be considered. Finally, it will be possible to work out conclusions that can already be translated into a specific analysis of criminal law constructions.

The previously conducted argument concerning the principle of human dignity—its content—referring to jurisprudence, doctrine, as well as to works in the field of philosophy, allows us to assume that the legal system is not the basis for concluding about the dignity of every human being. It recognizes this quality in man directly or, in other cases, tries to identify and describe those characteristics of man which it recognizes as fundamental to the legal system. The dignity itself or, in other interpretations, these particular qualities of a human being are vested in him or her independently of the will of the legislator. After all, there is no doubt that man is free and rational for reasons other than a normative decision, such as a high-ranking constitution or an international agreement. Human equality before the law is also not based on the goodwill of the legislator but rather on the recognition that the essence of humanity does not give any basis for differentiation in the treatment of citizens by the state in a situation where there are no legitimate and equitable reasons for this. It seems that there are no grounds for claiming that the principle of dignity is introduced in individual states into the basic laws with the conviction that it is a category that is initially empty and which will be filled with content only in practice when the law is made and applied. There is no doubt that the role of the legislator and the judiciary is still important, as will be discussed in more detail further. However, the role of these entities is not to establish the very essence of the principle of dignity.

The role of the public authorities, including first of all the legislative and judicial authorities, is primarily to translate human dignity into normative decisions. The introduction of the principle of human dignity into the legal system means that the system is to be in line with it. If dignity is inherent and inalienable, as well as inviolable, the entire legal system should be oriented toward its protection and updating its potential, and thus obliged to adapt the legal system to what follows from the principle of dignity. This means that the law should not only protect dignity itself but also implement measures that favor it as much as possible.

Within the framework of recognizing and updating the potential of the principle of human dignity, one should first of all note its anthropological significance, based on a certain vision of man, which the legal system—built on respect for dignity—should respect and implement. Philosophical anthropology is understood as "explaining the interpretation of human being, man, and his essentially human action."[215] The most important subject of analysis within philosophical anthropology is the answer to the question concerning the fact of being human and its sources. It is pointed out that anthropology makes an effort to explain "the human fact as seen from the outside."[216] Analyses in this area, in the scope relevant to the issue of ethical legitimization of criminal law, will be conducted in the following chapters. At this point, it should be noted, following the *Universal Encyclopaedia of Philosophy*, that "human fact" gives information on "who a man is, because it reveals his cognition of reason in the construction and use of the tools that are the necessary system of relations; it reveals contemplative, aesthetic and reflective cognition."[217] Philosophical anthropology covers the issue of man's constitution, his cognitive actions, understanding of human freedom, the culture he creates, and finally the social character of man.

The following fragment of the *Universal Encyclopaedia of Philosophy* is particularly worth noting:

> Man, as a conscious and free subject, is a stronger form of existence than the systems of relations that suppose the existence of the subject of these relations. Therefore, the law, as an organisational form of community and the activity of these communities, has essentially one overriding goal, which is the good of man as a personal being. However, the same person, in his biological and vital endowment, is an integrating part of society, and in the aspects of his biological existence, he is necessarily subordinate to a society which has the power to distribute rights (which are in the hands of society) proportionally to its members, according to the measure of justice. Therefore, they cannot get rich and selfishly arrange one at the expense of the other. Areas of social measures should be accessible to all in social proportions, and social proportions are linked to human work, which is an update of human (mainly personal!) potential. Thus, in societies, the human person is sovereign in the order of personal ends—truth, goodness, beauty—and the same person is subject to the sovereignty of society in the field of means of achieving personal ends.[218]

The quoted fragment explaining the social aspect of philosophical anthropology reveals at least two important conclusions for the issues discussed here. The law, which also results from the proverb *hominum causa omne ius constitutum sit*, is to serve exclusively the good of man. The consequence of this assumption will be that the legislator will be obliged to get to know the human being as he is, in order to properly correlate the established law with the human good. The law is not intended to serve man as a product of one or another idealistic concept or ideology but to serve the real man and the rights of such a man. Therefore, if criminal law is to promote the good of man, it must first recognize well who man is and what his good is. This conclusion also leads to the second conclusion. The role of the law is not to set goals for man, but, depending on his anthropological diagnosis, to set goals for himself or to recognize them in his humanity. The task of law is already difficult and ambitious, because it should identify these goals well and enable people to achieve their goals through legal means. At the same time, the law must take into account the common good, and thus model the system in such a way that the means of achieving important goals do not undermine the possibility of achieving other goals—equally important or even more important—at the same time.

NOTES

1. I.U. Dalferth, *Religion . . . , Morality and Being Human: The Controversial Status of Human Dignity*. In: D. Grimm, A. Kemmerer, Ch. Möllers (ed.), *Human Dignity in Context*, Baden-Baden 2018, p. 86.
2. Ibid., p. 87.
3. Ibid. p. 90.
4. Ibid.
5. I have described the issue of dignity in the context of criminalization, K. Szczucki, *Wykładnia prokonstytucyjna prawa karnego*, Warsaw 2015, *passim*.
6. Cf. ibid., *Ethical Legitimacy of Criminal Law*, "International Journal of Law, Crime and Justice" 2018, vol. 53, p. 67 et seq.
7. Cf. eg. O. Kamir, *Honor and Dignity in the Film Unforgiven: Implications for Sociolegal Theory*, "Law and Society Review" 2006, vol. 40, no.1, p. 193 et seq.
8. D. Shulztiner, G.E. Carmi, *Human Dignity in National Constitutions: Functions, Promises and Dangers*, "The American Journal of Comparative Law" 2014, vol. 62, no. 2, p. 461.
9. Constitutions: Mexico, Weimar Republic, Finland, Ireland and Cuba.
10. D. Shulztiner, G.E. Carmi, *Human Dignity. . .* , p. 465.
11. A. Zygmunt, *Zasada pomocniczości w nauczaniu Jana Pawła II*. In: A. Pawłowska, S. Grabowska (ed.), *Zasada pomocniczości. Wymiar europejski, narodowy, regionalny i lokalny*, Rzeszów 2011, p. 43.
12. M. Piechowiak, *Filozofia praw człowieka*, Lublin 1999, p. 87.
13. Cf. I.U. Dalferth, *Religion, Morality and Being Human: The Controversial Status of Human Dignity*. In: D. Grimm, A. Kemmerer, Ch. Möllers (ed.), *Human Dignity in Context*, Baden-Baden 2018. . . , p. 70.
14. O. Sensen, *Human dignity in historical perspective: The contemporary and traditional paradigms*, "European Journal of Political Theory" 2011, vol. 10, p. 75.
15. M.T. Cicero, *O powinnościach*,. In: ibid., *Pisma filozoficzne*, vol. 2, transl. W. Kornatowski, Warsaw 1960, p. 384.
16. O. Sensen, *Human dignity. . .* , pp. 77–78.
17. St. Leo the Great, *Sermones*, 21, 2–3: PL 54, 192 A. Extract as cited in: *Katechizm Kościoła Katolickiego*, pt. 1691. Cf. too O. Sensen, *Human dignity . . .* , p. 78.
18. Ibid., p. 79.
19. G.P. della Mirandola, *Oratio de hominis dignitate. Mowa o godności człowieka*, transl. Z. Nerczuk, M. Olszewski, Warsaw 2010, p. 45.

20. Differently: H.J. Paton, *The Categorical Imperative: A Study in Kant's Moral Philosophy*, London 1947, p. 171; D.W. Ross, *Kant's Ethical Theory; a Commentary on the Grundlegung zur Metaphysik der Sitten*, Oxford 1954, pp. 52–54.

21. O. Sensen, *Human dignity. . .* , p. 81.

22. I. Kant, *Lectures on Pedagogy*, 9: 488; as cited in: I. Kant (1899), *Kant on Education*, transl. A. Churton, London 1899.

23. I. Kant, *Uzasadnienie metafizyki moralności*, transl. M. Wartenberg, Kęty 2013, 435, p. 51.

24. O. Sensen, *Human dignity. . .* , p. 83.

25. Ibid., p. 83.

26. Ibid., p. 83.

27. "In acting and speaking, men show who they are, reveal actively their unique personal identities and thus make their appearance in the human world, while their physical identities appear without any activity of their own in the unique shape of the body and sound of the voice," H. Arendt, *The Human Condition*, Chicago 1958, p. 179.

28. Ibid., p. 85.

29. *Book of Genesis*, 1, 27, King James Version.

30. "the soul of every person is his form, which was given to him by God; and the additional wisdom found in man's soul is the form of a man who is complete in his wisdom. The Torah says about that form: 'man was made in My image and in My likeness.'" Maimonides, *The Code of Maimonides, Book of Knowledge, The Laws of the Fundamental Principles of the Torah*, Chapter Four, Law 8, as cited in: A. Barak, *Human Dignity. The Constitutional Value and the Constitutional Right*, Cambridge 2015, p. 20.

31. "A basic element in Judaism is the idea that man was created in the image of god (Genesis 1:27). The *Torah* so opens, and from the concept the *halakha* derives certain fundamental principles regarding the value of man—every human being as such—his equality and the love of him: He [R. Akiva] used to say, beloved is man in that he was created in the image of God, but it is a mark of a greater love that it was made known to him that he had been created in the image of God, as it is said (*Genesis* 9:6), "For in the image of God He made man" (*Mishna*, *Avot* 3:18). And it was by reason of this verse that the sons of Noah were prohibited from pilling blood, even before the *Torah* was given. Very instructive is the difference of opinion between two leading [mishnaic scholars] as to the crowning value in human relations: "And you shall love your neighbor as yourself" [*Leviticus* 19:18]. R. Akiva said, this is a major rule of the *Torah*. Ben Azai said, "This is the book of the generations of Adam" [on the day God created man He did so in the image of God—*Genesis* 5:1]—this is the greater rule (*Sifra*, *Kedoshim*, 4:10). According to R. Akiva, the supreme value in human relations is love of one's fellow man: and according to Ben Azai, the supreme and preferred value is the equality of man, since every man was created in the image of God. And these two values—equality and love of one's fellow—came together as one at the hands of the Jewish nation, together forming a cornerstone of Judaism throughout its generations and history" (EA 2/84 *Moshe Neiman et al.* v.

Chairman of the Central Elections Committee for the Eleventh Knesset, 8IsrLR 83, 148 (1985), as cited in: A. Barak, *Human Dignity* . . . , p. 21).

32. The debate that took place around Article 1(1) of the Basic Law of the Federal Republic of Germany cannot be overlooked here: "Human dignity shall be inviolable. To respect and protect it shall be the duty of all state authority." ("Die Würde des Menschen ist unantastbar. Sie zu achten und zu schützen ist Verpflichtung aller staatlichen Gewalt," translated into English by Professor Christian Tomuschat, Professor David P. Currie, Professor Donald P. Kommers and Raymond Kerr, in cooperation with the Language Service of the German Bundestag). The formula adopted has from the start been the subject of a number of debates and disputes, also concerning the possible need to define dignity. In the opinion of Carlo Schmid, one of the authors of the Basic Law, dignity should be defined. He understood it as a quality, an attribute that determines the human being and distinguishes them from other creatures. The first German president, Theodor Heuss, was opposed to the normative definition of dignity. He claimed that human dignity must include itself. Its meaning should not be drawn from any governmental position. In the German literature, many opinions interpreting the principle of dignity have been expressed in this context. Attempts have been made to formulate positive and negative concepts that focus more on what may be the cause of a violation of the principle of human dignity. In the context of Article 1 of the Basic Law of Germany the difference between the category "human dignity" and the category "dignity of human beings" was also considered. The former focuses on a certain phenomenon in itself and the latter on one aspect of humanity. The basic difference lies in the fact that dignity itself can be spoken of in complete detachment from the object of that dignity, which may well not exist at all. Dignity as a feature of specific subjects, and thus in the second of the meanings referred to here, is real, dependent on the existence of these human beings. The wording and context of Article 1(1) of the German Basic Law indicate that the object of protection is dignity as an aspect of humanity, and in principle is the human being himself endowed with that dignity (I.U. Dalferth, Religion. . . , pp. 73–75).

33. G. Hughes, *The Concept of Dignity in the Universal Declaration of Human Rights*, "Journal of Religious Ethics" 2011, vol. 39, n. 1, pp. 2–3.

34. Ibid, pp. 3–4.

35. Ibid, p. 5.

36. R. Dworkin, *Three Questions for America*, "The New York Review of Books," 21 September 2006, pp. 24 and 26.

37. W.A. Parent, *Constitutional Values and Human Dignity*. In: M.J. Meyer, W.A. Parent (ed.), *The Constitution of Rights: Human Dignity and American Values*, Ithaca 1992, pp. 47 and 71.

38. H. Kuhse, *Is There a Tension Between Autonomy and Dignity*. In: P. Kemp, J. Rendtorff, N. Mattsson (ed.), *Bioethics and Biolaw*, vol. 2, Copenhagen 2000, pp. 61 and 72.

39. " (. . .) a piece of jurisprudential Legoland—to be used in whatever form and shape is required by the demands of the judicial designer," D.M. Davis, *Equality: The Majesty of Legoland Jurisprudence*, "South African Law Journal" 1993, no. 116, p. 398.

40. This thesis is formulated with reference to the international level. Cf. G. Hughes, *The Concept. . .* , p. 8.

41. Ibid.

42. G. Hughes himself points out that in order to explain the principle of human dignity, it is necessary to resort to philosophical anthropology. Cf. ibid, p. 15.

43. "How, I asked, can we imagine an agreement of minds between men who are gathered together precisely in order to accomplish a common intellectual task, men who come from the four corners of the globe and who not only belong to different cultures and civilisations, but are of antagonistic spiritual associations and schools of thought?", J. Maritain, *Introduction.* In: *Human Rights. Comments and interpretations*, UNESCO, Paris 1948, p. II.

44. G. Hughes, *The Concept. . .* , pp. 9–10. The author points out that human dignity is expressed in freedom, responsibility, irreplaceability, and susceptibility to suffering.

45. Ibid, p. 18.

46. M. Piechowiak, *Filozofia praw. . .* , p. 77.

47. Preamble to the International Covenant on Civil and Political Rights adopted on 16 December 1966 by General Assembly resolution 2200A (XXI).

48. Ibid, p. 78.

49. J. Seifert, *What is Life? The Originality, Irreducibility, and Value of Life*, Amsterdam 1997, p. 97.

50. O. Sensen, *Human Dignity in Historical Perspective: The Contemporary and Traditional Paradigms*, "European Journal of Political Theory" 2011, vol. 10, p. 72.

51. Ibid, p. 80.

52. M. Piechowiak, *Filozofia praw. . .* , p. 225.

53. M. Piechowiak, *Filozofia praw. . .* , p. 87.

54. A. Zygmunt, *Zasada pomocniczości. . .* , p. 44.

55. M. Piechowiak, *Filozofia praw. . .* , p. 88.

56. John Paul II, *Orędzie na XXI Światowy Dzień Pokoju.* In: Paul VI, John Paul II (ed.), *Orędzia papieskie na Światowy Dzień Pokoju*, Rzym–Lublin 1987.

57. T. Metz, *African Conceptions of Human Dignity: Vitality and Community as the Ground of Human Rights*, "Human Rights Review" 2012, vol. 13, p. 19.

58. J.J. Mrozek, *Godność osoby ludzkiej jako źródło praw człowieka i obywatela*, "Civitas et Lex" 2014, no. 1, p. 44.

59. M.D. Dubber, *Toward a Constitutional Law of Crime and Punishment*, "Hasting Law Journal" 2003–2004, no. 55, p. 515.

60. Ibid., p. 515.

61. H. Arendt also pointed out the need to interpret dignity in the context of human social conditions, *The Origins of Totalitarianism*, New York 1951, p. 295. Cf. too J. Helis, *Hannah Arendt and Human Dignity: Theoretical Foundations and Constitutional Protection of Human Rights*, "Journal of Politics and Law" 2008, vol. 1, no. 3, p. 73.

62. International Theological Commission the Dignity and Rights of the Human Person, Vatican 1983, http://www.vatican.va/roman_curia/congregations/cfaith/cti_documents/rc_cti_1983_dignita-diritti_pl.html International Theological

Commission, http://www.vatican.va/roman_curia/congregations/cfaith/cti_documents/rc_cti_1983_dignita-diritti_en.html (accessed 08 June 2020).

63. Ibid.

64. Plato, *The Laws*, 770 c-e, The Project Gutenberg EBook of Laws, by Plato, https://www.gutenberg.org/files/1750/1750-h/1750-h.htm (accessed 28 March 2022).

65. M. Piechowiak derives from it the superiority of the right of the individual over the right of the state. Cf. M. Piechowiak, *Filozofia praw. . .* , p. 230.

66. Ibid, p. 234.

67. Aristotle, *The Nicomachean Ethics*, transl. W. D. Ross, http://classics.mit.edu /Aristotle/nicomachaen.html (accessed 28 March 2022). Cf. M. Piechowiak, *Filozofia praw. . .* , p. 242.

68. Aristotle, *The Nicomachean Ethics*, transl. W. D. Ross, http://classics.mit .edu/nicomachaen.html (accessed 28 March 2022). Cf. M. Piechowiak, *Filozofia praw. . .* , p. 242.

69. M. Piechowiak, *Filozofia praw. . .* , p. 268.

70. In St. Thomas's view: *persona est nomen dignitatis*. Cf. M. Piechowiak, *Filozofia praw. . .* , p. 272.

71. St. Thomas Aquinas, Summa Theologiae I, q. 29, a. 3, Second and Revised Edition, 1920 Literally translated by Fathers of the English Dominican Province, Online Edition 2017.

72. M. Piechowiak, *Filozofia praw. . .* , p. 276.

73. K. Wojtyła, *Osoba i czyn oraz inne studia antropologiczne*, Lublin 2011, p. 151.

74. St. Thomas Aquinas, *Summa theologiae* 2–2, q. 64, a. 5, Second and Revised Edition, 1920 Literally translated by Fathers of the English Dominican Province, Online Edition 2017.

75. Existence as a condition of dignity is strongly emphasized by I.U. Dalferth. Cf. ibid, *Religion. . .* , p. 77. Linking dignity solely to existence allows the author to assert that the dignity of other existing creatures could be claimed without it having to be a dignity of equal importance to that of man., ibid, p. 78.

76. Ibid, p. 79.

77. M. Piechowiak, *Filozofia praw. . .* , p. 343.

78. S. Zieliński, *Rozumienie godności człowieka i jej znaczenie w procesie stanowienia i stosowania prawa. Propozycja testu zgodności regulacji prawnych z zasadą godności człowieka*, "Przegląd Sejmowy" 2019, no. 4(153), pp. 109–15. Cf. too K. Complak, *Uwagi o godności człowieka oraz jej ochrona w świetle nowej Konstytucji*, "Przegląd Sejmowy" 1998, no. 5, p. 43; ibid., *Godność nie jest dobra na wszystko. Propozycja uporządkowania materii*,. In: *Minikomentarz dla maksiprofesora. Księga jubileuszowa profesora Leszka Garlickiego*, ed. M. Zubik, Warsaw 2016, p. 244.

79. M. Piechowiak, *Filozofia praw. . .* , p. 344.

80. Ibid, p. 346. Cf. M. Ossowska, *Normy moralne w obronie godności człowieka*, "Etyka" 1969, no. 5, p. 12. However, not always, as M. Piechowiak emphasizes, is faithfulness to one's beliefs sufficient—as M. Ossowska would like—to gain dignity in the approach presented here. Undoubtedly, one of the sources of moral evaluation

of an act is to convince a given person of the rightness of such or other conduct. However, there are categories of absolutely unacceptable behaviors, which cannot be justified by the thesis that the person committing them could have made a mistake in their assessment. Such acts include behaviors included in the framework of particular types of international crimes.

81. M. Piechowiak, *Filozofia praw. . .* , p. 348.

82. Cf. I. Augsberg, *On Kant's Concept of Human Freedom and Dignity as Auto-Heteronomy*. In: D. Grimm, A. Kemmerer, Ch. Möllers (ed.), *Human Dignity. . .* , p. 67.

83. T. Metz even defines it with the name "Western interpretation." Cf. ibid., *African Conceptions. . .* , pp. 21–22.

84. J. Davis, *Doing Justice to Dignity in Criminal Law*. In: J. Malpas, N. Lickiss (ed.), *Perspectives on Human Dignity. A Conversation*, Dordrecht 2007, p. 172.

85. J. Davis, *Doing Justice. . .* , p. 175. The author also raises the issue of animal rights, which seems to be quite controversial in the context of the principle of human dignity, but remains outside the mainstream of the deliberations conducted here.

86. C. McCrudden, *Human Dignity and Judicial Interpretation of Human Rights*, "The European Journal of International Law" 2008, vol. 19, no 4, p. 679.

87. Andrew Clapham interprets the basic postulates arising from the principle of human dignity differently. He draws attention to four important—in his opinion—aspects: (1) the prohibition of any inhuman or degrading treatment or humiliation of one person by another, (2) the guarantee of freedom of choice and fulfilment for everyone, (3) consideration of the need to protect the human group and cultural affiliation, (4) the creation of the conditions necessary for people to meet their essential needs. Cf. A. Clapham, *Human Rights Obligations of Non-State Actors*, Oxford 2006, pp. 545–46.

88. "If corporal punishment, lobotomy and castration are no longer acceptable and contravene then the death penalty cannot be considered to be anything other than cruel and unusual punishment. It is the supreme indignity to the individual, the ultimate corporal punishment, the final and complete lobotomy and the absolute and irrevocable castration. As the ultimate desecration of human dignity, the imposition of death penalty in Canada is a clear violation of the protection afforded by s. 12 of the Charter," judgment in the case *Kindler v. Canada* (Minister of Justice), [1991] 2 SCR 779, 1991 CanLII 78 (SCC).

89. C. McCrudden, *Human Dignity. . .* , pp. 687–88.

90. Ibid., p. 176.

91. This example is used by J. Davis, ibid., p. 177. Cf. judgement of the UN Commission of Human Rights in the of *Wackenheim v. France* of 26 July 2002, U.N. Doc. CCPR/C/75/D/854/1999, communication No. 854/1999.

92. The case was brought by Manuel Wackenheim, who accused France of several violations of the International Covenant on Civil and Political Rights. Importantly in this case, the applicant was affected by a serious growth deficit. Since 1991, he has been involved in so-called dwarf tossing, organized by a French entertainment company. It was a form of entertainment based on throwing a dwarf—with appropriate protective clothing and not too far away—onto a specially prepared

inflatable mattress. In November 1991, the French Minister of the Interior issued a document in which he instructed the prefects to keep a close watch on the activities of the entertainment industry, with particular emphasis on dwarf tossing. The document indicated that this type of undertaking should be prohibited in view of the standard resulting from Article 3 of the Convention for the Protection of Human Rights and Fundamental Freedoms. Earlier, in October 1991, Manuel Wackenheim filed an application with the administrative court for the annulment of the local mayor's order prohibiting the practice of dwarf tossing, also in local discotheques. The court granted the application, indicating that the practice did not violate public order, peace or public health. The mayor appealed against this ruling to the Council of State. The Council of State overturned the decision of the administrative court, indicating that throwing the dwarf was not in line with the principle of human dignity, respect for which affects the maintenance of public order. The Council of State noted that public order violations could not be allowed even under the principle of freedom of employment and freedom to conduct business. The party concerned appealed again against the order of the mayor. The administrative court overturned the order, not finding a breach of dignity in the project in which the applicant participated. The Council of State again revoked the decision of the administrative court. The applicant pointed out in his application to the Human Rights Commission that the order of the mayor and the decisions of the Council of State made him unemployed, which violated his dignity. He pointed out that the work he was doing did not violate his dignity, as human dignity is reflected in the possibility of his work. The investigation carried out led to the conclusion that the Commission on Human Rights indicated that the prohibition of the activities under assessment was justified on grounds of the protection of public order, which consists of the need to respect human dignity.

93. L.M. Henry, in particular, draws attention to this, *The Jurisprudence of Dignity*, "University of Pennsylvania Law Review" 2011, vol. 160, no. 1, p. 181 et seq.

94. R. Macklin, *Dignity Is a Useless Concept*, "British Medical Journal" 2003, no. 327, p. 1419; S. Pinker, *The Stupidity of Dignity*, "New Republic" 2008, May 28, pp. 28 and 31.

95. This is how L.M. Henry describes the trend. Cf. L.M. Henry, *The Jurisprudence. . .* , p. 182.

96. W.A. Parent, *Constitutional Values. . .* , p. 62.

97. C. McCrudden, *Human Dignity and Judicial Interpretation of Human Rights*, "European Journal of International Law" 2008, no. 19, p. 679.

98. For this reason he also criticizes the idea of F. Fukuyama interpreting dignity as a so-called "Factor X" of humanity. Cf. I.U. Dalferth, *Religion. . .* , p. 72; F. Fukuyama, *Our Posthuman Future: Consequences of the Biotechnology Revolution*, New York 2002, p. 149.

99. I.U. Dalferth, *Religion. . .* , p. 98.

100. Ibid., p. 99.

101. Ibid., p. 101.

102. Ibid., C. McCrudden, *Human Dignity. . .* , p. 675.

103. Clarifying the principle of human dignity at the level of the Universal Declaration of Human Rights could make it impossible to enact it, taking into account how different traditions and philosophical, historical and cultural contexts are represented by different countries at the UN General Assembly. Cf. O. Sensen, *Human dignity. . .* , p. 73.

104. C. McCrudden derives basic human rights characteristics from the principle of human dignity. However, it seems that from this principle there are directives not only concerning human rights, but the legal system as such. Cf. C. McCrudden, Human Dignity. . . , p. 677.

105. "(. . .) all human beings are equal before the law and have equal opportunities without regard to religion, race, language, sex, social groups, etc. As persons they have the dignity to be treated as such. This is the principle of equality which constitutes one of the fundamental human rights and freedoms which are universal to all mankind," sentence ICJ of 18 July 1966, in the case of *Ethiopia v. South Africa* and *Libera v. South Africa* (Second Phase, [1966] ICJ Rep 6, at 308, 312).

106. "It is not by mere chance that in Article 1 of the Universal Declaration of the Rights of Man there stands, so worded, this primordial principle or axiom: 'All human beings are born free and equal in dignity and rights.' From this first principle flow most right and freedoms. Of all human rights, the right to equality is far and away the most important. It is also the one which has been longest recognised as a natural right: it may even be said that the doctrine of natural law was born in ancient times with the concept of human equality as its first element" (Legal Consequences for States of the Continued Presence of South Africa in Namibia (South West Africa) notwithstanding Security Council Resolution 276, Advisory Opinion of June 21, 1971, [1971] ICJ Rep 16, at 77).

107. CT judgment of July 9, 2009, SK 48/05.

108. "(. . .) few decisions are more personal and intimate, more properly private, or more basic to individual dignity and autonomy, than a woman's decision—with the guidance of her physician and within the limits specified in Roe—whether to end her pregnancy. A woman's right to make that choice freely is fundamental," judgment of SCOTUS in the case *Thornburgh v American College of Obstetricians and Gynaecologists*, 476 U.S. 747 (1986). Similar arguments were given in the case of *Planned Parenthood v. Casey*, 505 U.S. 833 (1992).

109. I do not share A. Barak's position in this respect, which postulates that the meaning of the content of human dignity should be sought in isolation from contexts other than the legal system, such as philosophical and theological settings. Indication of the context in which dignity is understood in a given country makes it possible to fill it with content in such a way as to limit excessive judicial discretion. The author himself draws attention to the possible freedom of interpretation applied by judges, but assumes that the rules of interpretation assimilated and applied by judges are a sufficient remedy. Cf. A. Barak, Human Dignity. . . , s. xviii et seq.

110. The author also notes that human dignity is an open concept, acquiring still new content. Cf. ibid., p. 5.

111. A. Barak, *Human Dignity. . .* , p. 10.

112. A. Barak, *Human Dignity. . .* , p. 11 The principle of human dignity can be included in the set of general clauses if we define the general clause as a reference to the extra-legal system of norms. Its function in this case is not to leave the judge free to adapt the interpreted norm to current circumstances. More on general clauses e.g: Z. Ziembiński, *Wstęp do aksjologii dla prawników*, Warsaw 1990, p. 211 et seq.; L. Leszczyński, *Stosowanie generalnych klauzul odsyłających*, Kraków 2001, p. 21 et seq.; T. Spyra, *Granice wykładni prawa. Znaczenie językowe tekstu prawnego jako granica wykładni*, Kraków 2006, p. 218 et seq.

113. They are categorized and described by T. Metz. Cf. ibid., *African Conceptions. . .* , p. 19 et seq.

114. Ibid., p. 21.

115. Ibid., p. 24. Cf. too: N.K. Dzobo, *African Symbols and proverbs as sources of knowledge*. In: K. Wiredu, K. Gyekye (ed.), *Person and Community: Ghanaian Philosophical Studies* I (vol. I), *The Council for Research in Values and Philosophy*, Washington 1992, p. 89 et seq.

116. According to T. Metz, spiritual theories cannot be the basis for analysis by rational legal science at all. Cf. ibid., *African Conceptions. . .* , p. 25.

117. There is an overlapping of parts in this area: the features that make up the dignity in the Kantian view and dignity understood as vitality. Some of the manifestations of the individual's creative abilities will be at the same time a manifestation of their reasonableness and autonomy.

118. T. Metz, *African Conceptions. . .* , p. 35.

119. J. Davis, *Doing Justice. . .* , p. 178.

120. Ibid., p. 180.

121. A. Barak, *Human Dignity. . .* , p. 8.

122. C. McCrudden, *On Portraying Human Dignity*. In: D. Grimm, A. Kemmerer, Ch. Möllers (ed.), *Human Dignity. . .* , p. 26.

123. Ibid., p. 30. The author indicates that similar analyses can be conducted on the basis of literary fiction. Cf. L. Hunt, *Inventing Human Rights. A History*, New York 2008, *passim*; J.R. Slaughter, *Human Rights, Inc. The World Novel, Narrative Form, and International Law*, New York 2007, *passim*.

124. C. McCrudden, *On Portraying. . .* , pp. 30–31.

125. Ibid., p. 32.

126. Ibid., pp. 32–34.

127. Ibid., p. 37.

128. "It is a relatively small step from seeing dignity arising from particular human qualities to seeing dignity arising from the quality of being human, another way in which dignity seems able to escape its boundaries," ibid., p. 37.

129. A similar thesis can be formulated in the context of Juan de Pareja's painting in which Diego Velázquez portrayed his slave, later liberated by himself. The picture shows a proud man who has no attributes of slavery.

130. C. McCrudden, *On Portraying. . .* , p. 54.

131. This was indicated e.g. in the constitutional complaint in the proceedings for the case no. SK 20/98.

132. CT judgment of June 1, 1999, SK 20/98.

133. CT judgment of January 22, 2013, P 46/09.
134. CT judgment of July 9, 2009, SK 48/05.
135. Constitutional complaint in proceedings under no. SK 8/00.
136. CT judgment of December 8, 1999, SK 19/99.
137. CT judgment of February 25, 2002, SK 29/01. Also CT judgment of February 7, 2006, SK 45/04.
138. CT judgment of March 5, 2003, K 7/01.
139. Ibid. The Tribunal based its decision, which is the subject of the judgment, on the understanding of dignity set out in the judgment of October 24, 2006, SK 41/05 and in the judgment of March 7, 2007, K 28/05.
140. CT Judgment of February 7, 2005, SK 49/03. However, it does not seem possible to deduce the limitation of criminalization to the principle of nonmateriality as a principle of human dignity (cf. J. Davis, Doing Justice. . . , p. 181). If one interprets human dignity not only in an individualistic but also in a community dimension, it does not seem justified to make the a priori assumption limiting the scope of criminal law only to conduct that causes harm to individuals. It seems possible to include within the limits of criminal law also those acts which violate the values important for members of a given community—even if their individual goods, in their materialized form, have not been violated. It would be difficult to otherwise justify the criminalization, rather unquestionable, of an act of espionage, that is, participation in the activities of a foreign intelligence service against the Republic of Poland. After all, such activity does not have to involve harm to a particular person. On the other hand, the view which, as a principle of human dignity, leads to an obligation, imposed on the criminal legislator and on the authorities applying the law, of equal treatment, seems justified.
141. CT judgment of March 7, 2007, K 28/05. Cf. also CT judgement of 4 April 2001, K 11/00.
142. CT judgment of July 10, 2007, SK 50/06.
143. Ibid.
144. CT judgment of June 23, 2009, K 54/07.
145. CT judgment of January 22, 2013, P 46/09. Cf. too K. Complak, *Uwagi o godności człowieka oraz jej ochrona w świetle nowej konstytucji*, "Przegląd Sejmowy" 1998, no. 5, p. 45.
146. CT judgment of July 9, 2009, SK 48/05.
147. S.C. judgment of April 11, 2006, I PK 169/05, OSNP 2007, no. 7–8, item 93.
148. S.C. judgment of October 2, 2007, II CSK 269/07, OSNC-ZD 2008, no. 3, item 75.
149. S.C. judgment of May 28, 2008, SNO 34/08, LEX no. 1288868.
150. S.C. resolution of February 7, 2007, III KK 236/06, OSNKW 2007, no. 6, item 50.
151. Cf. S.C. judgment of April 25, 1989, I CR 143/89, LEX no. 5282: "In fact, depriving a man of his rights undermines his dignity. However, not every deprivation of human rights is a recognition of his dignity, justifying the application of civil law measures for the protection of personal rights. It depends on whether, in the general opinion, it constitutes a violation of human dignity or whether the public opinion does

not attach such consequences to it. In this respect, the type and nature of the rights to which a person has been deprived, the manner in which the perpetrator acts and the relationship between other people and the person deprived of those rights are essential for the evaluation."

152. Judgment of the ECtHR of November 3, 2011, in *S.H. and Others v Austria*, no. 57813/00.

153. Judgment of the ECtHR of July 8, 2004, in the case *VO v. France*, no. 53924/00.

154. Judgment of the ECtHR of August 27, 2015, in the case *Parillo v. Italy*, no. 46470/11.

155. Judgment of the ECtHR of September 28, 2015, in the case *Bouyid przeciwko Belgium*, no. 23380/09.

156. Cf. also the previous Judgment of the ECtHR called upon in this case: of October 26, 2000 in the case *Kudła v. Poland*, no. 30210/96; of March 11, 2004, in the case *Yankov v. Bulgaria*, no. 39084/97; of July 17, 2014, in the case *Svinarenko and Slyadnev v. Russia*, no. 32541/08 and 43441/08.

157. Judgment of the ECtHR of March 11, 2014, in the case *Abdu v. Bulgaria*, no. 26827/08.

158. Cf. too judgment of the ECtHR of April 12, 2016, in the case *R.B. v. Hungary*, no. 64602/12.

159. Judgment of the ECtHR of July 9, 2013, in the case *Vona v. Hungary*, no. 35943/10.

160. Judgment of the ECtHR of April 12, 2007, in the case *Dzwonkowski v. Poland*, no. 46702/99.

161. Judgment of the ECtHR of October 22, 2009, in the case *Orchowski v. Poland*, no. 17885/04. Cf. too Judgment of the EctHR: of October 20, 2006, in the case *Muršić v. Croatia*, no. 7334/13 and of September 6, 2016, in the case *W.D. v. Belgium*, no. 73548/13.

162. Judgment of the ECtHR of July 24, 2014, in the case *Al Nashiri v. Poland*, no. 28761/11.

163. C-337/98, ECLI:EU:C:2000:543.

164. Judgment of the CJEU of October 18, 2011, C-34/10, ECLI:EU:C:2011:669.

165. Joined cases C-148/13 to C-150/13, ECLI:EU:C:2014:2406.

166. Journal of Laws Dz.U. L 304, p. 12.

167. L.M. Henry, *The Jurisprudence. . .*, pp. 169–70.

168. Ibid, p. 172.

169. In the *Cohen v. California* ruling on the first amendment, the Supreme Court ruled that, "The constitutional right of free expression . . . is designed and intended to remove governmental restraints from the arena of public discussion . . . in the belief that no other approach would comport with the premise of individual dignity and choice upon which our political system rests," SCOTUS ruling *Cohen v. California*, 403 U.S. 15, 24 (1971).

170. SCOTUS ruling *inter alia* in the cases: *Hudson v. Michigan*, 547 U.S. 586, 594 (2006); *Skinner v. Ry. Labor Execs' Ass'n*, 489 U.S. 602, 613–14 (1989); *Winston v. Lee*, 470 U.S. 753, 760, 766–67 (1985).

171. SCOTUS rulings *inter alia* in the cases: *Heath v. Alabama*, 474 U.S. 82, 88 (1985); *Miranda v. Arizona*, 384 U.S. 436, 460 (1966).

172. SCOTUS ruling *inter alia* in the case of *Indiana* v. *Edwards*, 554 U.S. 164, 176 (2008).

173. SCOTUS rulings *inter alia* in the cases: *Kennedy v. Louisiana*, 554 U.S. 407, 419–20 (2008); *Roper v. Simons*, 543 U.S. 551, 560 (2005).

174. SCOTUS ruling *inter alia* in the case of *Griswold v. Connecticut*, 381 U.S. 479, 482–83 (1965).

175. SCOTUS ruling *inter alia* in the case of *Fed. Mar. Comm'n v. S.C. State Ports Auth.*, 535 U.S. 743, 760 (2002).

176. SCOTUS ruling *inter alia* in the cases: *Lawrence v. Texas*, 539 U.S. 558, 567, 578–79 (2003); *Goldberg v. Kelly*, 397 U.S. 254, 264–65 (1970).

177. SCOTUS ruling *inter alia* in the case of *Rice v. Cayetano*, 528 U.S. 495, 517 (2000).

178. L.M. Henry, *The Jurisprudence. . .* , p. 173.

179. Ibid, p. 178.

180. "If we are ever to develop an orderly international community based upon a recognition of human dignity, it is of the utmost importance that the necessary punishment of those guilty of atrocities be as free as possible from the ugly stigma of revenge and vindictiveness. Justice must be tempered by compassion, rather than by vengeance," SCOTUS ruling in the case of *In re Yamashita*, 327 U.S. 1, 29 (1946). Cf. J.J. Paust, *Human Dignity as a Constitutional Right: A Jurisprudentially Based Inquiry into Criteria and Content*, "Howard Law Journal" 1984, no. 27, pp. 150–51. Jordan J. Paust connects the legacy of the Universal Declaration of Human Rights with those judgments of the Supreme Court of the United States of America, in which the formula of "human dignity" appears directly. He also points out that in the case law, already before the adoption of the Declaration of Human Rights, there were arguments referring to the principles of dignity, human dignity and individual dignity. The findings of J.J. Paust indicating the list of judges of the SCOTUS, who in their opinions, at least in footnotes, referred to dignity are extremely interesting. These are the following judges: (1) William Taft (SCOTUS ruling in the case of *Carroll v. United States*, 267 U.S. 132, 154 (1925)); (2) Felix Frankfurter (*inter alia* SCOTUS rulings in the cases: *De Veau v. Braisted*, 363 U.S. 144, 148 (1960); *Burstyn v. Wilson*, 343 U.S. 250, 263 (1952)); (3) Robert H. Jackson (*inter alia* SCOTUS ruling in the case of *Mandoli v. Acheson*, 344 U.S. 133,139 (1952)); (4) Frank Murphy (*inter alia* SCOTUS ruling in the case of *Homma v. Patterson*, 327 U.S. 759, 761 (1946)); (5) Harold H. Burton (SCOTUS ruling in the case of *Haley v. Ohio*, 332 U.S. 596, 617 (1948)); (6) Hugo Black (*inter alia* SCOTUS ruling in the case of *James v. United States*, 366 U.S. 213, 225 (1961)); (7) William O. Douglas (*inter alia* SCOTUS ruling in the case of *Wolff v. McDonnell*, 418 U.S. 539, 597 (1974)); (8) Tom C. Clark (*inter alia* SCOTUS ruling in the case of *Estes v. Texas*, 381 U.S. 532, 549 (1965)); (9) Earl Warren (*inter alia* SCOTUS ruling in the case of *Wainwright v. City of New Orleans*, 392 U.S. 598, 607 (1968)); (10) John M. Harlan (*inter alia* SCOTUS ruling in the case of *Cohen v. California*, 403 U.S. 15, 24 (1971)); (11) Arthur Goldberg (*inter alia* SCOTUS ruling in the case of *Heart of Atlanta Motel v. United States*, 379

U.S. 241 (1964)); (12) Potter Stewart (*inter alia* SCOTUS ruling in the case of *Gregg v. Georgia*, 428 U.S. 153 (1976)); (13) Byron White (*inter alia* SCOTUS ruling in the case of *Payton v. New York*, 445, U.S. 573, 617–19 (1980)); (14) William J. Brennan (*inter alia* SCOTUS ruling in the case of *Rhodes v. Chapman*, 452 U.S. 337, 359–60 (1981)); (15) Abe Fortas (*inter alia* SCOTUS ruling in the case of *Alderman v. United States*, 394 U.S. 165, 203 (1969)); (16) Warren E. Burger (*inter alia* SCOTUS ruling in the case of *Trammel v. United States*, 445 U.S. 50, 52, 913 (1980)); (17) Thurgood Marshall (*inter alia* SCOTUS ruling in the case of *Rhodes v. Chapman*, 452 U.S. 337, 372 (1981); (18) Lewis F. Powell (*inter alia* SCOTUS ruling in the case of *Board of Educ. Island Trees Union Free School Dist. No. 26 v. Pico* 457 U.S. 430, 462 (1974)); (19) John P. Stevens (*inter alia* SCOTUS ruling in the case of *NAACP v. Claiborne Hardware Co.* 73 L Ed 2d 1215 (1982)); (20) William H. Rehnquist (*inter alia* SCOTUS ruling in the case of *United States v. Ramsey*, 431 U.S. 606, 618 (1977)); (21) Harry Blackmun (*inter alia* SCOTUS ruling in the case of *Bates v. State Bar Arizona*, 433 U.S. 350, 368 (1977)). Cf. J.J. Paust, *Human Dignity. . .* , pp. 157–58.

181. "If the dignity of each singly is undiminished, the dignity of all jointly must be unimpaired," SCOTUS ruling in the case of *Chisholm v. Georgia*, 2 U.S. (2 Dall.) 419 (1793).

182. J.J. Paust, *Human Dignity. . .* , p. 158.

183. Ibid, p. 163.

184. "The Fourteenth Amendment did not mean to imprison the States into the limited experience of the eighteenth century. It did mean to withdraw from the States the right to act in ways that are offensive to a decent respect for the dignity of man, and heedless of his freedom. These are very broad terms by which to accommodate freedom and authority. As has been suggested from time to time, they may be too large to serve as the basis for adjudication, in that they allow much room for individual notions of policy. That is not our concern. The fact is that the duty of such adjudication on a basis no less narrow has been committed to this Court," SCOTUS ruling in the case of *Louisiana ex rel. Francis v. Resweber*, 329 U.S. 459 (1947).

185. L.M. Henry, *The Jurisprudence. . .* , s. 190.

186. 267 U.S. 517, 539 (1925).

187. 11 U.S. (7 Cranch) 116, 135 (1812).

188. SCOTUS ruling in the case of *First National City Bank v. Banco Nacional de Cuba*, 406 U.S. 759, 769 (1972).

189. SCOTUS ruling in the case of *Alden v. Maine*, 527 U.S. 706, 802–3 (1999).

190. 379 U.S. 241 (1964).

191. "(. . .) racial discrimination in the qualification or selection of jurors offends the dignity of persons and the integrity of courts," 499 U.S. 400, 402 (1991).

192. 511 U.S. 127, 142 (1994).

193. "few decisions are more personal and intimate, more properly private, or more basic to individual dignity and autonomy, than a woman's decision (. . .) whether to end her pregnancy. A woman's right to make that choice freely is fundamental," 476 U.S. 747, 772 (1986). Cf. too. L.M. Henry, *The Jurisprudence. . .* , p. 209.

194. "adults may choose to enter upon this relationship in the confines of their homes and their own private lives and still retain their dignity as free persons (. . .).

The liberty protected by the Constitution allows homosexual persons the right to make this choice," 539 U.S. 558, 539 (2003).

195. "the right of a man to the protection of his own reputation from unjustified invasion and wrongful hurt reflects no more than our basic concept of the essential dignity and worth of every human being," 497 U.S. 1, 22 (1990).

196. Cf. 554 U.S. 164, 176 (2008).

197. 547 U.S. 586, 588 (2006).

198. "The knock-and-announce rule protects those elements of privacy and dignity that can be destroyed by a sudden entrance. It gives residents the 'opportunity to prepare themselves for "the entry of the police."' 'The brief interlude between announcement and entry with a warrant may be the opportunity that an individual has to pull on clothes or get out of bed.' In other words, it assures the opportunity to collect oneself before answering the door," 547 U.S. 586, 594 (2006).

199. L.M. Henry, *The Jurisprudence. . .* , p. 222.

200. Cf. 536 U.S. 730, 738 (2002).

201. "(they – aut. note) retain the essence of human dignity inherent in all persons . . . [that] animates the Eighth Amendment prohibition against cruel and unusual punishment," 563 U.S. 493 (2011).

202. 550 U.S. 124, 12 (2007).

203. A. Barak, *Human Dignity. . .* , pp. 103–4.

204. Human dignity also implies the obligation to introduce certain procedural guarantees into the legal system. Cf. A. Sakowicz, *Prawo do milczenia w polskim procesie karnym*, Białystok 2019, pp. 36–37. Dignity also plays an important role in relation to the stage of formation and enforcement of sentence. Cf. E. Hryniewicz-Lach, *Kara kryminalna w świetle Konstytucji RP*, Warsaw 2015, pp. 363–65.

205. In this context, the interpretation described in the following cannot be accepted: C. Enders, *A Right to Have Rights–The German Constitutional Concept of Human Dignity*, "NUJS Law Review" 2010, vol. 3, no. 3, p. 253; A. Barak, *Human Dignity. . .* , p. 105. They would indicate that human dignity is still only a human right originating in a conventional act and not in its very essence.

206. Judgment of the Constitutional Tribunal of October 15, 2002, SK 6/02, OTK-A ZU 2002, no. 5, item 65.

207. This is the subject of my monograph. Cf. K. Szczucki, *Wykładnia prokonstytucyjna*.

208. L. Bosek, *Gwarancje godności ludzkiej i ich wpływ na polskie prawo cywilne*, Warsaw 2012, pp. 151–52; P. Wiliński, *Zasada prawa do obrony w polskim procesie karnym*, Kraków 2006, p. 445; K. Wojtyczek, *Ochrona godności człowieka, wolności i równości przy pomocy skargi konstytucyjnej*. In: K. Complak (ed.), *Godność człowieka jako kategoria prawa*, Wrocław 2001, pp. 203–4; M. Jabłoński, *Klasyfikacja wolności i praw jednostki w Konstytucji RP*,. In: M. Jabłoński (ed.), *Wolności i prawa jednostki w Konstytucji RP*, vol. 1, *Idee i zasady przewodnie konstytucyjnej regulacji wolności i praw jednostki w RP*, Warsaw 2010, p. 87; J. Potrzeszcz, *Godność człowieka w orzecznictwie polskiego Trybunału Konstytucyjnego*, "Roczniki Nauk Prawnych" 2005, vol. 15, no. 1, pp. 27–49. The Constitutional Tribunal also pointed out that human dignity is a subjective right of

the individual. Cf. judgment of the CT of October 15, 2002, SK 6/02, OTK-A ZU 2002, no. 5, item 65.

209. K. Complak, *Uwagi o godności. . .*, p. 47.

210. L. Bosek, *Gwarancje godności. . .*, p. 155.

211. Ibid, p. 157; A. Zieliński, *Pojmowanie godności ludzkiej w świetle praw ekonomicznych i socjalnych*, w: *Godność człowieka a prawa ekonomiczne i socjalne. Księga jubileuszowa wydana w piętnastą rocznicę ustanowienia Rzecznika Praw Obywatelskich*, Warsaw 2003, pp. 48–49.

212. L. Bosek, *Gwarancje godności. . .*, p. 158.

213. Cf. K. Szczucki, *Ethical legitimacy of criminal law*, "International Journal of Law, Crime and Justice" 2018, vol. 53, p. 67 et seq.

214. More about the standard of availability of moral criminal law ibid, *Wykładnia prokonstytucyjna. . .*, *passim*.

215. *Powszechna encyklopedia filozofii*, internet version, heading "philosophical anthropology," dev. M.A. Krąpiec, p. 1, www.ptta.pl/pef/pdf/a/antropologia.pdf (access: 4.12.2018).

216. Ibid, p. 2.

217. Ibid, p. 3.

218. Ibid, p. 8.

Chapter 3

The Ability to Bear Responsibility in the Context of the Dispute over Free Will

PRELIMINARY ISSUES

The previous chapter pointed out that one of the characteristics of the human individual, rooted in their dignity, is their ability for self-determination. It was also indicated that the problem of free will that emerges in this context will be considered later in the book. Before proceeding to further deliberations on the basic ethical categories relating to responsibility and, consequently, to the issue of ethical legitimization in criminal law, it is necessary to clear up a specific foreground and thus to face the issue of disputes about free will. Referring ethical considerations to the issues of criminal law is not possible without paying attention to the anthropological challenges that arise today. After all, these challenges concern not only anthropology or ethics itself but also criminal law, as demonstrated earlier by the link between these areas. The analysis thus undertaken will be conducted to the extent that it seemed necessary from the perspective of the assumptions of the whole work.

One of the fundamental philosophical disputes, with a high degree of relevance to criminal law, is the dispute over free will, which is expressed in tension between indeterministic and deterministic interpretations. This issue has been recognized in philosophical literature for a relatively long time, but it is constantly coming back in new versions. The reason for this is, among other things, the successive achievements of the empirical sciences, especially genetics and neuroscience, which, as a result of expanding the knowledge of biological processes, increasingly often formulate conclusions beyond the scope classically reserved for these sciences. One of the most important is the view that questions free will, indicating that the results of research on the human genome and brain confirm the total determination of human behavior, making it necessary to rethink the responsibility of man, including criminal responsibility as such. The problem of human subjectivity is also closely related to this. The progressive achievements of these sciences provide a fertile ground for reductionist concepts that bring man to a certain conglomerate of biological, physical, and chemical processes that can be interpreted, ordered, described, and perhaps also predicted. Conclusions formulated in this way can be a basis for questioning not only the free will of man but also his subjectivity in general.[1] Free will is sometimes considered to be one of the main factors that constitute human subjectivity.

There are, in fact, many more challenges to human subjectivity. Not without significance here are also all kinds of new technologies that interfere more and more with human life processes, revealing at the same time the tendency of their creators to deeply interfere with the human constitution, perhaps even permanently modifying its nature. These considerations, in principle still outside the mainstream of criminal law doctrine, prove to be crucial to the issue of criminal responsibility. Adam Sulikowski notes that posthumanism, originally perceived as marginal and dissident, is nowadays growing in strength in professional discourses.[2] Therefore, it cannot be ignored in the field of criminal law either.

Subjectivity in law is a topic generally taken up in the context of civil law. This usually involves the problem of subjective rights. This concept originates in natural legal individualism, which proposed to derive rights from who the subject is or, in other words, from the fact that he or she is human.[3] At times, subjective rights even came to the fore, putting the issue of the subject at stake.[4] The problem, however, is that the doctrine of law did not so much try to recognize the characteristics of man, including references to philosophical anthropology, as it began to create a vision of man itself and to tie laws established *a priori* to it. It was not, therefore, the law that was subordinated to who man is, what rights he has, and what he can be responsible for, but it was the subject that was subordinated to the law. So the individual was to become a subject in accordance with the letter of the law.[5] This trend still seems to be noticeable.

Already this short introduction provides sufficient grounds to note the importance of the philosophical findings of the above-mentioned dispute for criminal law. Criminal law is based on the concept of a person capable of bearing responsibility. This is evidenced by the concept of man as the subject of a crime, as the perpetrator of an act, and as the entity to which the guilt can be attributed. Although these constructions would not differ in different legal systems or theoretical concepts, they are—in the prevailing approach of criminal law—built on the conviction of man's ability to shape his own behavior according to his own will and, consequently, his ability to bear criminal responsibility. It is therefore appropriate to consider whether this assumption can indeed be effectively challenged. Finally, it should be considered to what extent the ethical and anthropological findings made earlier, revealing the vision of the human being accompanying the Polish legislator, can be helpful in arrangements concerning the ability of a person to bear responsibility.

THE ISSUE OF FREE WILL: THE TENSION BETWEEN DETERMINISM AND INDETERMINISM

The problems outlined above raise the question of whether free will can still be said to be free or whether it is an illusion, sustained only to justify the existence of a construction of responsibility, including criminal responsibility. It is a popular assumption that free will is a condition for holding anyone responsible for anything.[6] Interesting in this context are Józef Bremer's reflections, which at the same time present the issue of the presumption of guilt in a slightly different light.[7] In addition to the usual justifications that only exceptionally is man not capable of taking responsibility, another reason to support—one might even say expose—this presumption appears there. Thus, the existence of free will is very difficult to demonstrate objectively. Proving guilt in a material law sense must ultimately boil down to proving that a given person had free will during an act. If it is difficult to objectively demonstrate the existence of free will, it is therefore difficult to demonstrate guilt. It is much easier to capture the previously identified and classified characteristics of the perpetrator or act that may indicate a lack of free will.[8]

The problem of free will in the context of criminal law can be reduced to considering the criterion of assessing the perpetrator's behavior as defined by the wording: "he or she could have acted differently."[9] This statement is connected with the possibility of charging the perpetrator and thus attributing guilt to them. The possibility of behaving in a different way is taken into account not only within the scope of the issue of the allegation but also in the examination of the aspects considered as a subjective party. This is particularly evident in the case of the premises of so-called inadvertent unintentionality, which include the requirement to state that it is possible to foresee the consequences of one's deed or omission, and thus also to state that it is possible to behave in a way that avoids these consequences.

At the same time, free will is increasingly often reduced to the category of illusion, while at the same time defending the idea of maintaining it, usually for utilitarian reasons, either because it appropriately models human behavior or because it lies at the basis of the adopted convention of criminal responsibility.[10] The answer to the difficulties arising from the view that free will is an illusion is a view referring to the subject's—the perpetrator's—inner conviction about his freedom and the possibility of doing things differently than he did. If the perpetrator experienced freedom in such a way that the conviction that they could have acted differently was part of this experience, then regardless of the dispute between determinism and indeterminism, it is possible to assign responsibility to him.

The length of the dispute between determinism and indeterminism raises doubts as to whether it can be resolved. John Rogers Searle in his book on the subject of the mind argues that there is still a lot to learn about the functioning of the brain in order to solve the problem of free will.[11] In his opinion, it is therefore possible to point out some reflections, and sometimes only impressions, on the freedom of the will and the resulting conclusions for criminal law. Ultimately, however, the author states: "We don't know why or how evolution has equipped us with an unshakeable belief in the existence of free will. We don't know—to put it briefly— how it would all work. Nevertheless, we know enough to understand that it is impossible to escape the conviction of free will. We cannot act except on the assumption that we are free."[12]

What we are interested in here is the fundamental dispute in philosophy between determinism and indeterminism, that is, between a position—making a certain generalization—assuming that all human behavior is causally conditioned, and a position assuming that man acts in a completely free way, in an extreme form assuming freedom even from internal causes.

Three main approaches to free will and causality are known. The first of them can be described as hard determinism. According to this concept, called incompatibilism, free will is generally impossible—there is a dichotomy between it and determinism. The consequence of such thinking is the rejection of the known principles of human responsibility for their actions.[13] The role of soft determinism is fulfilled by compatibilism, which interprets determinism in such a way that it is reconciled with human responsibility for one's own actions. The third view is indeterminism, which assumes that a person's deed has no cause beyond their will.

Kazimierz Twardowski did not see any difficulties in reconciling the deterministic position with criminal law.[14] On the contrary, he pointed to the tensions arising from the adoption of an indeterministic position. It is worth noting that this author took up the discussed issue long before genetics and neuroscience were created. This philosopher emphasized that when addressing the issue of free will, it is necessary to consider first of all, from what this will is or should be free. After all, the will can be free in physical or philosophical terms. In the former, it means, for example, freedom from bodily restraints, as well as freedom from external coercion; in this sense, it means freedom from obstacles and from external coercion.[15] In the philosophical sense, freedom of will means the attitude in which the action of motives for character, which produces a decision, remains to the law of causality.[16] Causes are those decisions that occur by necessity if there are certain conditions and there is a final cause.[17]

The difference between determinism and indeterminism is well illustrated by the example used by K. Twardowski, namely an official considering applying for leave. The official is already tired, the summer is coming, and she also has health problems. These reasons speak for taking a holiday. The official also notes some negative aspects of such a decision. This may be a fear of a superior's reaction or a colleague's declaration that she needs to take a leave of absence at the same time. It turns out, however, that the doctor recommends going on leave, claiming that a lack of rest may cause a serious deterioration in the official's health. This will convince her to apply for leave. In Twardowski's interpretation, the process described is deterministic in nature, as such a decision had to be made under the circumstances.[18] In the opinion of the indeterminists, the conditions were necessary, but in their opinion, the specific decision did not have to be made at all, because man has free will.

The understanding of man and his nature in this concept is also evidenced by the comparison of the individual to a river, which Twardowski refers to following Arthur Schopenhauer. According to this example, a man standing on the street in the evening, conscious of the possibility of going to the theater, to the cinema, to a restaurant, who ultimately decides to voluntarily return home, is no different from a river he might say: "I can roll huge waves (surely—in the sea when there is a storm), I can flow downstream (surely—in the riverbed), I can fall foaming and humming (surely—in a waterfall), I can freely rise into the air as a stream (surely—in a fountain), ultimately, I can even boil and disappear (probably at 80° Reaumur)—but I won't do any of these, but voluntarily and calmly, and uninhibited, I remain in the glassy lake."[19] Water in a river can do all this if there are good causes for it. It is supposed to be the same with a man. This means that man, like water in a river, is not able to confront the causes, so he is fully susceptible to external conditions, he is determined by them.

Consistent determination does not shirk from accepting the phenomenon of responsibility. Unlike indeterminism, however, it does not accept this as proof of the existence of free will but rather as reflection on one's own character. In this interpretation, man does not so much regret that in a particular situation he could have acted differently, as he regrets his character, which determined him to act this way and not another.[20] There is also the question of responsibility.

According to Twardowski, the deterministic stance does not entail the necessity to assume that any responsibility is impossible. However, it is more a responsibility for character than for the specific act itself. An interesting example in this context is that of torture or other strong influence which, in the indeterministic camp, releases people from responsibility for the behavior caused by them. It is generally accepted that a person is not responsible for behavior resulting from coercion, because the freedom to manifest their will was very limited, even close to complete elimination. This usually leads to the conclusion that, in a deterministic interpretation, the freedom to manifest one's will is always excluded, so that one cannot speak of responsibility. Thus, the deterministic position in the interpretation presented here is strongly opposed to this. Kazimierz Twardowski states that "the essence of the inner compulsion lies in the fact that certain motives usually do not stimulate the will of a given individual to resolve, due to their extraordinary strength they stimulate this will in a direction that does not correspond to his character."[21] The problem of responsibility for character returns.

The perspective of attributing responsibility for character, resulting from the deterministic position presented above, seems interesting, although it is necessary to point to one very important doubt. Does the deterministic position allow for the possibility of shaping one's own character at all? One may wonder whether the nature of the entity is not also determined by external factors over which the entity has no influence. If this were the case, the concept of responsibility for character could turn out to be just as questionable as the proposal of responsibility for deeds.

The concept that free will can be reconciled with a deterministic position is, as mentioned above, called compatiblism or soft determinism.[22] As proposed by the compatibilists, we can still refer to activities as free, but this does not mean that they do not have the preconditions to be causatively sufficient, but with specific characteristics. Human decisions, even the very personal ones, are still determined, but by inner convictions, rational thought processes, and reflections. To define an action in this concept as free is not the opposite of defining an action as conditional, but as forced, imposed, or prescribed. At the same time, however, this approach is accused of failing to answer the most important questions concerning the understanding of actions as the consequences of conditions that are causally sufficient: Are they all like that? Are these conditions somehow essentially differentiated?[23]

The compatiblist position was proposed by Harry Frankfurt, among others, who presented the theory of hierarchical mesh.[24] This theory assumes that the desired behavior has its origin in some kind of wish. This means that the subject acts freely as long as his or her desire meshes with other circumstances—second-order desires. First-order desire is directed toward a particular deed, while second-order desire is interpreted in this concept as the desire of other desires. From the point of view of the issue discussed here, however, another thesis of this concept is important. It indicates space for free will, which can be seen in the juxtaposition of behavior interpreted as free with other behavior that does not meet this characteristic, for example, in an alcoholic or drug addict. Even if we take it for granted that all human behavior is causally determined, based on certain biological processes, there is still a difference between behavior that is the result of addiction and behavior that is considered free.[25] The desires that direct us to an object may be more or less sensible or reflective.

An interpretation of determinism that allows it to be reconciled with criminal responsibility, without the need to reduce its justification to utilitarian assumptions, was also presented by Michael S. Moore.[26] At the outset of his deliberations on this subject, he states that determinism seems likely to him, which is already a sufficient basis to verify the basic principles of criminal responsibility. According to this author, the argumentation suggesting the impossibility of attributing responsibility, at least in its classical sense, as a result of adopting the deterministic variant is *reductio ad absurdum*. In order to understand the further interpretation proposed by M. S. Moore, it is necessary to quote four points, with the help of which he presents the formal structure of this argumentation leading *ad absurdum*:

1. All human behavior is caused by factors beyond the control of a given entity (deterministic rationale).
2. If the behavior or choice is caused by factors beyond the control of the subject, the behavior or choice is morally excluded from responsibility (moral version of the causal theory of exclusion of responsibility).
3. If the behavior or choice is morally excluded from responsibility, the specific behavior should not be punishable by law (punishment theory indicating that moral guilt is a necessary condition for legal responsibility).

   In view of the above:

   No behavior or choice can result in a lawful penalty.[27]

Questioning these theses, assuming a deterministic interpretation of reality, seems difficult. Certainly in this approach the first thesis, which is the essence of determinism, is indisputable. The author, in proposing a retributive approach to the punishment, is also of the opinion that it is unjustified to reduce the justification of the criminal law only to utilitarianist approaches. A number of other arguments, which have been put forward above, support the claim that there is an important relationship between criminal law and morality. If so, the third thesis cannot be challenged.

Michael S. Moore distinguishes four views of determinism, which their supporters believe can be reconciled with the classic concept of criminal responsibility: (1) gradual determinism, (2) ignorance determinism, (3) selective determinism, (4) dualistic determinism.[28]

Gradual determinism assumes that human behavior is not entirely determined. From the moment the cause is determined by the action to the moment of the event, the space for freedom stretches. The reality of human behavior is somewhere between extreme moments, one of which is determined by a thesis of full determination, and the other by a complete lack of it. Therefore, the main focus should be on the deMarchtion line, behind which the space starts, which is entirely causally dependent and therefore excluded from the responsibility of the subject.[29] According to M. S. Moore, the thesis of gradual determination has a similar value to the claim that you are partially pregnant.[30] According to this author, we are either free in our choices or not.

The concept of predisposing causality is a variant of gradual determinism. According to this, external causes do not determine a person's behavior but make them predisposed to a certain behavior. In other words, these reasons are not a necessary and sufficient condition for such behavior. Responsibility is excluded only if the causes are so strong that in principle they become sufficient to commit a prohibited act.[31] According to Michael S. Moore, the thesis of predisposition, replacing the thesis of determination, comes from ignorance or incomplete knowledge of human behavior and its causes. It is more a lack of knowledge of the causes than a lack of the causes themselves. It also appears necessary to demonstrate the legitimization of attributing predisposition to certain circumstances, while at the same time taking away that predisposition from others. One may wonder why mental illness should be more predisposed to and thus excluded from responsibility than morbid greed, which, at least as generally accepted, should not lead to exclusion of responsibility.[32]

The concept of determinism of ignorance refers to the state of knowledge about sufficient and necessary reasons. Exclusion of responsibility will occur in those cases where science, especially social sciences, shows a very strong influence of external factors on the behavior of the perpetrator, for example, bringing up a child in a criminal environment.[33] The fundamental problem that emerges from this theory is the relativization of responsibility to the state of knowledge. From the point of view of a just understanding of punishment, it is difficult to judge someone's responsibility with conviction knowing that it is based only on a lack of knowledge of the reasons that determine this behavior.

Selective determinism is the basic deterministic position according to which everything has a necessary and sufficient cause. At the same time, a selective determinist is distinguished by the fact that he does not consider all of these reasons as grounds for exclusion of responsibility. According to him, only some of the reasons lead to such consequences. As M. S. Moore argues, accepting this theory basically means abandoning the understanding of circumstances that exclude responsibility as a determining reason for behavior. The factor excluding responsibility is no longer the cause but a feature of quality which is intended to make it possible to consider the cause as sufficient to exclude liability.[34]

The last of the above-mentioned varieties of determinism, trying to respond to the challenges of criminal responsibility presented as *reductio ad absurdum*, is dualistic determinism. There are two types of factitive relationships in this concept. The former consist of necessary causes that occur in the natural world. The second is made up of reasons that induce, but do not prejudge, a given event. The latter type of relationship concerns most human behavior and choices.[35] In M. S. Moore's opinion, dualistic determinism is no different from gradual determinism.

Another solution found in the literature is a kind of ignoring of determinism, however accepted, for the purpose of creating the structures and principles of criminal responsibility. This is seen as a concept of "as if"—as if a man has free will and his behavior is not determined. The authors proposing the "as if" interpretation in their scientific assumptions adopt a dualism consisting in the fact that deterministic positions refer only to natural sciences, while in the area of social sciences, which includes the law, including the issue of criminal responsibility, they adopt—as a certain convention—freedom of choice and the related ability to be responsible for their own behavior and choices. The words of Herbert Packer seem significant: "The idea of free will in relation to behaviour is not a statement of fact in the legal system, but rather a preference for values, having very little to do with the metaphysics of determinism or free will (. . .). Very simply, the law treats human behaviour as autonomous and desirable not because it is, but because it is desirable to act as if it were."[36]

The view referring to the "as if" formula raises fundamental doubts. These include problems characteristic of various dualisms in philosophy. However, another accusation seems more important for the subject discussed in this book. Acceptance of the arguments raised in this concept would mean that criminal responsibility is nothing more than a certain convention, to a significant extent shaped without any connection to the knowledge of the person and the processes in which he or she participates. For if we are still working in the deterministic approach, how else can we evaluate the postulate to ignore its basic assumptions in the area of criminal responsibility and behave as if a person had free will and freedom of choice? This is far from those interpretations of punishment which considered it to be the community's response to selected, according to various criteria, immoral behaviors. Issues as important as human freedom would be decided on the basis of a fiction permeating the foundations of criminal law. Already for these reasons, this is a difficult concept to accept.

The above-described failure to reconcile the deterministic interpretation of the world with the concept of criminal responsibility still accepted today leads to recognizing the proposal for solving this problem by M. S. Moore. This author attempts to question the theory of causality as such. Primarily, he attempts to demonstrate that the causality theory is not applicable to circumstances excluding responsibility.[37] One of the circumstances that exclude responsibility is action under duress.[38] He invokes this very circumstance, since decision-making under conditions of determinism can be interpreted as if they were conditions that meet the characteristics of duress. However, as it turns out, the difference between cause and coercion is significant. Coercion understood, as previously indicated, as physical or mental, significantly limits the action, and in extreme cases inflicts rape on practical reason and human will. Man acts then, or allows omission, not because of his own choice but because of this external influence. Causality, on the other hand, builds the context of a given person's behavior, without, however, depriving them of the space of freedom to make decisions. Upbringing in a pathological environment or character traits or certain inclinations do not take away a person's sense of self-agency. In such circumstances, elements of rationality and volitiveness are involved to a greater or lesser extent in the act.

Referring to the above-mentioned difference between causality and coercion, M. S. Moore can ask a further question about the relationship between causality and the deed in general. It is worth considering whether causality understood in deterministic terms may lead to the conclusion that the act did not exist at all. Looking at this problem from a slightly different angle, one can consider whether the act itself is somehow different in identity from its cause. It seems, however, that even opting for a deterministic stance should not lead to the recognition that the causes in their entirety constitute a specific effect, so that the behavior cannot be separated as an independent ontological category. In the case of rational subjects such as man, we would say, for example, that a given subject raises his hand up rather than that his hand raises itself. Even in the deterministic paradigm, we do not give up certain signs of human self-agency, due to the fact that causes are processed by humans.

The above allows, as M. S. Moore points out, the thesis about the incompatibility of determinism and the principles of an individual's responsibility for their deeds to be rejected. In the light of the findings made above, human behavior may be an act even though it is preceded by specific causes. Furthermore, the circumstances excluding responsibility are not based on contribution, but derive justification from interference with an area reserved for practical reason.

It is hard to disagree with the opinion of Peter van Inwagen, who notes that the attitude to the possibility of combining deterministic beliefs and free will depends on the understanding of determinism itself, while at the same time, the author points out that determinism in his proposed understanding is not reconcilable with free will.[39] He defines determinism as the conjunction of the following two theses:

1) at any point in time there is a statement expressing the state of the world at this point and
2) if *A* and *B* are statements expressing the state of the world at some moments, then the conjunction of *A* with the laws of physics entails *B*—the author understands the laws of physics in a broad sense, referring more to the category of laws of nature, excluding voluntary behaviour of rational subjects.[40]

At the same time, the same author explains that by free will he understands the power or ability of the subject to do differently than he did in reality. In other words, denying free will is tantamount to admitting that what a man has done fully overlaps in scope with what he could have done.[41]

A phenomenon from the natural world that is often referred to in literature on free will—usually by authors taking or describing an indeterministic position—is the fission of the atomic nucleus, which occurs at random.[42] Which atom will be fissioned is in no way externally determined. This is also what Edward Jonathan Lowe refers to in his considerations—who divides the authorities of individual substances according to two different criteria. According to the former, these authorities can be divided into factitive and non-factitive. The second criterion distinguishes between active and passive authorities. However, they all individualize themselves by the way they manifest themselves, that is, by the characteristic types of behavior that are associated with them.[43] In this arrangement, active and at the same time non-factitive power must seem particularly interesting in the context of the issue in question. Its active nature would mean that it is not caused by any substance affecting its disponent. Its non-factitivity means that it is not a consequence of some kind of influence of its disponent on another substance. The author describes it as spontaneous power. Apart from the fact that such authorities exist in nature, such as the above-mentioned nuclear fission, free will also seems to fulfill this description. At the same time, however, E. J. Lowe makes the reservation that free will is an authority in at least two aspects different from other spontaneous authorities. It has a two-way character: It is the power of wanting and not wanting. Besides, its specificity is that it is implemented rationally, that is, in a reasonable manner.[44]

The similarity between free will and atomic fission lies in the fact that both can be defined as active and at the same time non-factitive authorities, that is, spontaneous authorities. Wanting precedes the change that a man causes in other substances, but not the change itself.[45] The act of wanting does not make any change, because it is necessary to start various processes, for example, body movement, in order for a given change to occur. The author uses here an example of the relationship between the will to raise a hand and the activity of raising a hand. He indicates that, by wanting to, an entity can actualize the possibility of raising a hand, but the very possibility of wanting to raise a hand is something other than this possibility. Whether or not you eventually manage to raise your hand depends on the existence of an appropriate passive power that can be influenced by the will of the person concerned. In other words, it is necessary to have adequate physical capabilities that will allow the act of will to materialize in the act of raising a hand.[46] It was characteristic of E. J. Lowe to say that the manifestation of power, which is will, is manifested in the desire to do something, not in the act of doing it.[47]

However, this does not mean that there is no difference between the power of free will and the spontaneous power of atomic fission. This difference lies in the already mentioned two-way power in the case of free will. Thus, a man with such power may want something, but he may also refrain from wanting it. This is different for an atom that cannot stop its core from fissioning. If such fission does not occur, it is not as a result of any power of the atom but as a result of a case inherent in nature in the process.

The second difference mentioned is the reasonableness of the power of free will—reasonableness that certainly does not characterize the atom. This means that free will is an authority susceptible to arguments and to reasonable analysis and evaluation. Given this aspect, free will can be described as a power whose decisions can be rationally explained.[48] This is not an "external" explanation of the processes taking place in a substance, as in the case of a decaying atom, but an explanation of the entity that has decided to actualize its power in this or that way. It is obvious that the atom has no such possibility.

The thesis that free will is not factitive is acceptable if one accepts a certain ontological and at the same time anthropological solution which assumes that there is no hierarchical relationship between man and his free will—he does not have to have power over it, because free will is his very power.[49] This is also why it is not at all possible to take control of someone's will. It is possible to take control of someone's body, and it is possible to influence someone's will very intensely, but its shape is always ultimately determined by the individual themselves. Otherwise, we cannot talk about an act of will.

Edward J. Lowe claims that rejection of the thesis that man has the power of free will would not only be inconsistent with the assumptions of metaphysics but also irrational or even logically impossible.[50] If the deterministic position were true, it would mean that everything that appears in our consciousness, as well as everything that is the content of our decisions, would be a consequence of the factitive laws that guide the creation of these states of consciousness and decisions. However, these processes, in this sense, are not able to create new decisions, opinions, and judgments. They come down, because of their deterministic background, only to reproducing certain reasoning. This means that the decision reached in such a process does not have the merit of rationality, even if the findings thus established are true. Moreover, the existence of such a process has also not been confirmed empirically, as the above-mentioned author claims. Participation in the debate of rational thinkers with their substantive arguments is only possible if they are able to respond to the objections of their opponents using rational arguments. This can only happen if they are not reduced to the role of a tube of factitive laws, which—because of their determination—they use without any reflection.[51]

In the context of the problem of free will, it is still worth looking at the statement already referred to above, which defines free will in the shortest way—as the possibility of behaving differently from the subject in given circumstances. First of all, it should be noted that—as may be obvious—this possibility means that something was within the scope of power of a given entity. This should not be equated with a moral evaluation. Something may be in man's power, but from the perspective of moral principles, perhaps he should not or, on the contrary, should do so.[52] Besides, the issue of free will is not only about moral evaluation of a given behavior but also about any other. By saying that a man could have acted differently, we understand that it was in his power. The assessment of this possibility already addresses other issues. Nor can the possibility of alternative behavior be identified with awareness of such a possibility. When we find that there was behavior in the power of a given entity other than that which it exercised, we do not assume that it was aware of that possibility in the circumstances. We only notice that in the scope of his power it was possible to behave differently, assuming at the same time that—naturally—an appropriate shape of consciousness would be necessary to realize it.

Roderick M. Chisholm, in a manner characteristic of analytical philosophy, concentrates the issue of free will on considering the word "could" as consisting of the phrase "could have behaved differently." According to this author, the correct understanding of the word "could" is a condition for properly explaining the issue of free will and determining whether it exists and how it is connected with the subject's self-agency. He defines and at the same time points out the weaknesses of five possible explanations of this problematic word, which allows him to develop his own interpretation. This does not mean that rejected interpretations are always considered to be incorrect, but it is possible to identify cases where they lead to incorrect decisions. This is the case with a logical understanding that is too broad, since it allows those behaviors that were actually impossible to implement to be covered. Similarly, referring to epistemic understanding is not always accurate, because in a given case, we may not have the knowledge to conclude that a person may have undoubtedly acted differently at a given time. The interpretation referring to the definition of possibility through the prism of the perpetrator's will also seems unreliable, because the perpetrator's unconsciousness or possible mistake could cause him not to behave differently even if he wanted to.[53] This is also not just about a physical possibility. Such an understanding of possibility would be very broad in relation to our experience. Finally, the author also rejects a factitive interpretation. He refers to the case of a human being who is able to control and influence another person's decisions by implanting a suitable implant.[54] In such a case, to find that there were no particular factitive obstacles to taking certain actions at a given time is not tantamount to assuming that, at that time, that entity, having been implanted, could actually have behaved differently.[55]

In his proposed solution, R. M. Chisholm reaches for three concepts explaining the phrase "could have behaved differently," that is, to a physical necessity, a factitive contribution, and to the will of the perpetrator, trying to synthesize them in such a way that they would explain the phrase correctly, and thus try to explain the issue of free will. Finally, the author proposes three definitions: the first one, which explains what the freedom of the subject to undertake a specific activity is; the second one, which explains what it means that a specific state of affairs is directly within the scope of the subject's authority; the third one, which refers to the understanding that something is within the scope of someone's authority also indirectly. The third of these definitions is intended to clarify the phrase "could have behaved differently" by assuming that "behaving otherwise was within his sphere of power."[56]

In accordance with the first of the above definitions, an entity is free to undertake a specific conduct at a given time if, for some time before that moment and during that time, there is no circumstance that would be factitively sufficient for that entity to undertake the specific conduct or to abandon it. In this way, R. M. Chisholm refers to the statement of St. Thomas Aquinas, who faced the question of human choice, considering whether it is necessary or free. The Aquinata claimed:

> Man does not choose of necessity. And this is because that which is possible not to be, is not of necessity. Now the reason why it is possible not to choose, or to choose, may be gathered from a twofold power in man. For man can will and not will, act and not act; again, he can will this or that, and do this or that. The reason of this is seated in the very power of the reason. For the will can tend to whatever the reason can apprehend as good. Now the reason can apprehend as good, not only this, viz. "to will" or "to act," but also this, viz. "not to will" or "not to act." (. . .) Therefore man chooses not of necessity, but freely.[57]

The second definition, concerning the direct power of an entity, indicates that a given state of affairs *p* is directly within the power of the entity if the following conditions are met:

1. there is a state of affairs *q* which a given entity can realize at a given time, and
2. realizing *p* means realizing *q*,
3. or, there is such a state of affairs *r* physically necessary at a given moment in time, in the sense that if this state of affairs happens and at the same time the entity undertakes state of affairs *q*, then the entity contributes factitively to the state of affairs *p*.[58]

The above definition touches upon the problem of consciousness of the subject, who may have, within the scope of his or her power, certain behavior, may even contribute to it without even being aware of it. By taking certain actions, we can contribute to the creation of a certain result, without embracing it with awareness, focusing only on the action taken directly.

Finally, the third definition concerns what is within the scope of human power but not directly. Thus, in some cases, it is only possible to commit a certain act after committing another act. In other words, a certain action becomes possible only when another action has been taken. Consequently, R. M. Chisholm assumes that a particular state of affairs falls within the scope of the power of the entity concerned if that state of affairs belongs to a chain of states of affairs constituting a kind of domino effect, that is to say, a chain in which each successive element appears within the scope of the entity's power thanks to the preceding one.[59] However, if an entity does not carry out one of these behaviors, it will not be able to carry out the next one, which is the next element in the chain.

An indeterministic position, which includes a person as a free subject or having free will, does not necessarily imply that the subject is not under the influence or even pressure of other subjects or external circumstances. However, this does not mean that such influence deprives him of any possibility of action or inaction. Even if this happens, for example, as a result of coercion, the area of freedom is opened up to respond to the effects of the action taken following coercion. The influence of external circumstances on an entity's behavior may consist, among other things, in limiting the scope of its possibilities to act. However, the opposite situation is also possible, that is, when external circumstances make the range of possible behaviors broader. Moreover, by taking further actions or making omissions, we create new opportunities for ourselves, while eliminating others.

One of the accusations that arises against the indeterministic arguments referred to here concerns the necessary cause of specific human behavior, which becomes the cause of a specific event. One could get the impression that this behavior has no cause. The allegation is misplaced to the extent that a person decides to do something. This can be seen in the diagram of the human act described in the next chapter, especially in this aspect, which concerns the role of reason and will.

Man contributes factitively not only to various actions but also to omissions. In analytical terms, this is described as follows. We can assume that subject *s* at a certain point *t* contributes factitively to a state of affairs *p*, if there is such a state *q*, which:

1. taken by *s* at time *t* contributes factitively to the state of affairs *p*, or
2. *s* voluntary abandons the state of affairs *q* in time *t* and *p* is the state of affairs that results from voluntary abandonment of the state of affairs *q*.[60]

CRIMINAL RESPONSIBILITY AND NEUROSCIENCE

As regards the findings of empirical sciences that may affect the understanding of free will, it is worth pointing out the findings made in the area of neuroscience. This research area is not the first, nor probably the last, which has become the basis for the formulation of postulates not only for changes in relation to the issue of responsibility but also for a far-reaching transformation in philosophical anthropology, resulting in a reductionist approach. However, it has been noted in the literature that research on the brain shows features that particularly predestine it for this role.[61] As M. S. Moore points out, neuroscience is a much more rigorous research discipline than Burrhus F. Skinner's behaviorism or Sigmund Freud's or Karl Menninger's psychoanalytical theories. Research on the brain can also give hope for a complete explanation of the principles of the "human machine." Finally, neuroscience addresses the direct causes of human behavior. This creates a space to try to fully and mechanistically explain such states as desire, intention, and will.

Studies on the brain indicate clear links between abnormalities in its structure and violent or otherwise abnormal behavior. In his work on the subject, David Eagleman argues that tumors formed in the brain in the area of the amygdala, responsible for emotional reactions, can cause the affected person to react more aggressively, reaching for violence more often.[62] Tumors formed in the prefrontal cortex, on the other hand, carry the risk of susceptibility to various sexual deviations, including pedophilic behavior.[63] The author maintains that "the more we find out, the more the seemingly simple theory of culpability becomes complicated, and the more the foundations of the legal system are tightened."[64]

He points out that consistent consideration of these studies should influence the design of criminal responsibility. This does not only concern the issue of genetic changes or neuroscience but also other factors significantly influencing the human decision-making process. The conditions in which a person grew up and was brought up are also important. This is well expressed by Judge David Bazelon: "It is unacceptable to me that people already crippled by a basically hopeless cycle of poverty, ignorance and drugs should continue to be burdened with the stigma of guilt, not because they are capable of guilt, but only because we cannot treat them as if they are not capable of it."[65] The literature has also repeatedly called for an end to the treatment of perpetrators as entities with free will.[66]

The analysis of the issue of free will and its significance for the concept of responsibility must take into account the tension between legal decisions and the image of man emerging from modern neuroscience.[67] If one accepts the theses that indicate the mechanics of the human mind and the possibility of explaining the processes that take place in it by external persons, one may have doubts as to the validity of maintaining in the system the decisions based on the assumption of free will. As Łukasz Kurek noted, this results "from the various ways of explaining behavior on the grounds of law and the experimental sciences."[68] However, this author does not draw conclusions that go so far as to doubt the correctness of the classical approach to responsibility in criminal law. He claims that the perceived tension results from other assumptions and objectives of experimental sciences and criminal law. The former tries to notice, abstract, and describe various processes taking place in man, in the sphere of his functioning, including making decisions. Criminal law, on the other hand, aims to determine whether the perpetrator is criminally responsible for a given act. Criminal law is geared toward the interpretation of human behavior, since it is essentially about assigning appropriate meaning to it.[69]

It is possible to reconstruct three views on the impact of cognitive science arrangements on criminal law. The first is called eliminationism, the second can be described as a moderate position, and the third as a position indicating the autonomy of criminal law. Eliminativists formulate a postulate to give up such categories as guilt, and even criminal responsibility in general. They indicate that the findings of the experimental sciences contradict the theses formulated in the context of the aforementioned criminal law institutions.[70] Their view can be reduced to implications: lack of free will means no criminal responsibility. The moderate position, on the other hand, allows for the influence of neuroscience on criminal law, although it does not in any way postulate a radical break with the existing pattern of understanding and attributing criminal responsibility. The conclusions of the experimental sciences would make us rethink the meaning of certain concepts and possibly modify their scope.[71] This view also seems to be acceptable to supporters of the thesis about the autonomy of criminal law in relation to the empirical sciences.[72] This is because there is no mechanical obligation to transpose research findings into criminal law. Instead, it seems appropriate to reflect on the structures of criminal responsibility that are adopted, taking into account the achievements of other sciences. However, a radically empirical position can also be distinguished. According to this, it is claimed that the idea of free will in law should not be interpreted as a statement of fact but rather as a value having little to do with philosophical concepts. As Herbert Packer points out, the law treats a person as an autonomous and free entity, not because he is, but because it is desirable to act as if he were.[73] Free will then becomes the basic assumption. It can be said, referring to the previous findings, that it is presumed.

Writing about empirical sciences, whose findings should undoubtedly resonate somehow in the area of criminal law research, at least as a provocation for some reflection, genetics has also been indicated.[74] If one accepts, as some of the theses contained in scientific publications indicate, that the genetic conditions of individual people may influence their life choices, and thus also their possible criminal activities, it may significantly influence the understanding of free will and thus also guilt. In some respect, such findings must lead to the consideration of the anthropological theory formulated by Cesare Lombroso. The literature indicates that the first relationships between the genetic code and the propensity for certain criminal behaviors were already noticed in the 1960s. It was found that there were a disproportionate number of men with an XYY chromosome in high-security prisons.[75] Subsequent scientific studies have shown that the gene responsible for higher levels of aggression (MAOA) is responsible for the metabolism of selected neurotransmitters. People with this gene had particular difficulty in coping with stress.[76] Although the results of these studies have raised some controversy about overly universal conclusions, the relationship between the genetic code and behaviors perceived as criminal in social life has been increasingly rarely questioned. This should not be interpreted as an opportunity to isolate a "criminal gene" but as a statement of the existence of such a gene system which predestines man to react more impulsively to certain stimuli.[77] This means that a comparison of the situation of an entity that carries a given gene with the situation of an entity whose genetic code does not contain such a gene allows the similarity of these entities in terms of free will to be questioned. In other words, the will of the genetically burdened entity does not appear to be as free as the will of an entity without such a burden. However, the question is whether the scientific discoveries, described here in selected aspects, allow us to determine that free will does not exist, and that all human behavior—including pathological—is conditioned by specific neuronal or genetic processes.

Some deterministic theses, including those referring to neuroscience and genetics, not only question the existence of free will as such, but go further undermining the subjectivity of man as expressed in the possibility of doing, and therefore of self-agency. Responsibility may therefore prove to be unfounded not only because of the lack of free will but above all because of the lack of self-agency—the subjectivity of the person. The consequences of the thesis on the lack of subjectivity go much further than the problem of criminal responsibility, but—due to the subject matter of this book—it is here that we should focus on this aspect.

The increasingly accepted mechanistic interpretation of a man's behavior is conducive to taking away his self-agency. It is not so much that a man kills, but his finger, caused by certain processes in the brain and neuronal impulses, pulls the trigger, which results in a gunshot.[78] There are visions in the literature that predict the construction of such devices, which will be able to accurately depict the processes taking place in the human brain to show that all actions taken are nothing more than some neuronal activities.[79] The dispute oscillates around the problem of reductionism, that is, the sometimes expressed tendency to understand the human individual only through the prism of their brain or their genome, taking away other, no longer exclusively biological dimensions.[80] Reductionism manifests itself in the fact that instead of the categories presented today in the literature under the slogan of *folk psychology*, that is, reasonableness, intentionality, and causality, there appear categories of neuroscience, that is, synapses, neurons, brain activity, and so on, which are to replace them completely.[81]

In the literature, four basic groups of arguments can be distinguished, which are supposed to confirm the validity of the thesis about the absence of self-agency, and thus also about the non-subjectivity of the human individual.[82] First of all, it is noted that a great deal of human activity originates in circumstances that they are not even aware of. Second, research shows that more human behavior occurs when the individual's consciousness is limited. Third, laboratory tests show that people can be misled as to their contribution to certain behavior. Fourth, studies have noted that some psychological processes are reflected in the activity of certain parts of the brain.

The reductionist arguments, as S. J. Morse rightly points out, are not strong enough to determine the validity of the thesis on which they are based.[83] Undoubtedly, as acting entities, we are not aware of all the circumstances that are relevant for making a decision about a specific action or omission. However, it cannot be deduced from this conclusion that a person does not act consciously as a result of his or her intentions. Even if they are not aware of all the circumstances that contribute to a particular intention, this does not mean that they are not acting consciously and intentionally. Moreover, this does not mean that the entity is not able to indicate the rationale for its act or omission.

Sometimes it happens that a person takes some action in conditions of limited consciousness or even in the absence thereof. However, it is not possible to draw a general conclusion from this that this is so in every case. It is also worth noting, as has already been analyzed in the previous chapter, that exclusion or limitation of consciousness is the basis for exclusion of responsibility in ethical theories and in criminal law. The possibility of such circumstances is by no means a contemporary discovery. Similarly, no general conclusions should be drawn from the thesis indicating possible manipulation, even experimental, of an operating entity, creating an illusion of taking intentional action. The fact that the possibility of such manipulation exists does not mean that all human activities correspond to this pattern.

The error of overinterpretation of conclusions from brain research findings results from an attempt to describe the whole human and their behavior with the help of tools appropriate to detailed science, which in essence only describes a certain aspect of the individual. In this case, the tools available to biology and medicine try to explain the scope of human activity beyond biology and medicine. Human beings, as has been pointed out earlier, cannot be explained only by the apparatus of the empirical sciences. Perhaps even all manifestations of human activity are linked to the activities of individual parts of the brain or cause-specific reactions in it. This does not yet mean that cerebral processes are the cause of them or that knowledge of these processes will help to explain human behavior or to know the path leading to a particular behavior. The activity of individual parts of the brain does not yet constitute a basis for the statement that man does not act consciously and intentionally.

Reductionists, that is, proponents of drawing far-reaching conclusions from the findings of brain research, going far beyond the mere description of biological processes taking place, seem to identify man with his brain. They claim, as Dennis Patterson notes, that a man's conviction of his free will comes only from ignorance of the processes taking place in his own brain.[84] The natural consequence of such a view is the conviction that appropriately advanced technologies, capable of reading the processes taking place in the human brain, allow for a complete exploration of the mind, which opens up very wide possibilities for their use, also in the area of criminal trials.[85] It goes without saying that the adoption of reductionist assumptions should consequently lead to a revision of the principles of criminal responsibility.[86]

Reductionism is based primarily on the concept of monism, rejecting the dualistic approach, which in the description of man draws attention to two spheres of his nature, that is, what is physical, but also the spiritual area, especially self-agency and the world of spiritual experience.[87] Dualism starts from the assumption that a human act has at the beginning a human cause conditioned by the will of the subject. Spiritual experience is, above all, the experience of self-awareness and the experience of intentions and desires in relation to other objects, even nonexistent ones.[88] Monism, also referred to as physicalism, rejects the existence of any areas that are not part of the physical world.

Physicalism, also called naturalism, is based on three assumptions:

1) everything that exists is found in nature;
2) there is nothing supernatural; and
3) all phenomena can and should be explained using methods specific to the hard sciences.[89]

This physicalism in the approach presented here means that all human behavior, everything, whatever he does, and all his omissions can be reduced to processes involving his nerve cells. In reality, however, the proponents of reductionism, arguing from the position of the empirical sciences, are making philosophical theses, which by their very nature go beyond the methodology and scope of the empirical sciences. Reductionist theses, although their justification would be sought in the empirical sciences, cannot be confirmed in this way. Undoubtedly, neuroscience can determine the occurrence of certain processes in the human brain under the influence of certain factors, reproducible under similar conditions. However, drawing conclusions about the nature of human activity from this, that is, the interpretation of research conducted in comparison with human behavior, is already a philosophical interpretation, especially an anthropological one.

According to D. Patterson, the issue requires attention to be paid to the difference between cause and reason. The determination of a person for specific causes, independent of his or her will, does not occur in those situations where his or her behavior depends to a degree conscious of the specific reasons. This can be seen perfectly well when a person, when asked about the legitimization of his or her behavior, is able to recall certain reasons that were at the basis of one decision and not another. Only those areas of human life that can be explained by mentioning the reasons, and not exclusively the causes of specific behaviors, are and can be normative.[90]

According to Katrina Sifferd, physicalism does not by definition have to reject the category of human responsibility for his actions. She points out that the position presented by non-eliminative reductionism is compatible with this responsibility.[91] This author assumes that maintaining the existing principles of responsibility, and even the responsibility itself, would not be possible if the findings concerning the psychological attitude of the perpetrator to the deed or what in the Polish doctrine of criminal law is referred to as a subjective party were effectively questioned.[92] For if it is not possible to link human actions to the states of consciousness and will, and thus to interpret his actions as being covered by his intention, responsibility, at least as we know it, could not be accepted.

Katrina Sifferd argues that there are other approaches to physicalism that are irreconcilable with such a view of the subjective party. If we assume the assumptions of eliminationism, then we may as well decide on someone's responsibility on the basis of trial by fire or water instead of conducting a criminal trial.[93] Rejecting mental states, such as intention, is tantamount to rejecting the attribution of any responsibility. If it would be reasonable—as the author argues—to claim that there is no such thing as thirst, then why can we assume with a very high probability that a thirsty person will get a drink. In other words, the issue of the subjective party or, more broadly, of folk psychology, although criticized, works quite well in practice.[94] There are also positions that indicate that the states included in the category of folk psychology are reflected in human brain activity.[95]

Although eliminationism in such an extreme form is no longer widely accepted today, another version of it has emerged, quite popular, oriented toward free will. The supporters of this concept are convinced that brain research contradicts the existence of free will. It is worth noting that free will and responsibility for actions are not based on the phenomenological experience of freedom or the sense of freedom.[96] It is sufficient to analyze the circumstances excluding criminal responsibility. After all, a person acting in error, an insane person, or a child can function in the belief of their freedom, and yet they will not be held responsible. At the same time, it is possible that a person acting under great pressure from various circumstances, in his or her experience far from feeling free, will be held criminally responsible for his or her act.

Katrina Sifferd indicates two versions of nonexclusive reductionism. The first refers to the theory of Donald Davidson.[97] This is a concept assuming the supervenience of mentality over physicality. Every change in the mental area involves some change in the human body, a physical change. The opposite, however, is not necessarily true. This view is also called an anomalous monism. Its author claims that the same mental states in different situations and people can manifest themselves differently in the human body. In his opinion, it is impossible to show a constant relationship between a certain mental state and a certain process taking place in the human brain. If this is the case, however, then—which is a weakness of this theory—it turns out that mental states do not really play a causal role. Removing the mental state from the analysis of the causal chain does not cause the causal relationship to be disturbed.[98] This means that the brain and its processes play a fundamental role. It is therefore appropriate to agree with K. Sifferd that D. Davidson's theory does not maintain criminal responsibility in its classical version.[99]

Another approach was proposed by J. R. Searle, who maintains the thesis of mental causality.[100] In his interpretation, states of consciousness or mental states are linked to specific biological processes. This means that the mental causal property is identical to the physical causal property that realizes it. At the same time, the author does not accept the ontological rejection of consciousness as a mental state that we subjectively experience.[101]

K. Sifferd believes that it is necessary to pay attention to the different understandings of causality, especially the difference between macrobehavioral and microlevel understanding. The significance of this difference is well illustrated by the analogy to the relationship between water and H_2O. On the macrobehavioral level, one can use terms defined as folk psychology, while on the micro level one can analyze specific processes in the human nervous system. The relationship between these levels is crucial and also problematic. However, this does not change the fact that it is ultimately possible to maintain most of the main categories we use in assessing responsibility, including criminal responsibility, in this view. This is because this view assumes that what is mental is real and physical, with physical causal characteristics. Finally, K. Sifferd states: "Generally speaking, it seems that, for the purposes of assessing responsibility, folk explanations of human behaviour are better placed than scientific explanations."

TOWARD "NEURO-MODESTY"

Conclusions drawn from the findings of neuroscience and genetics seem too far-reaching or over-interpreted. Of course, the point is not to argue with the findings of researchers confirmed by experiments or other methods appropriate to empirical research. Discussions can naturally be undertaken, but legal science does not have the appropriate tools for this. However, one may wonder about the validity of the conclusions drawn from the results of these studies for the purpose of considering the principles governing criminal responsibility. Thus, it does not seem legitimate to claim that it is necessary to abandon the concept of culpability and focus only on categories of a prospective nature.[102] Such a solution would only be valid if it was proved that all human behaviors, or at least those that are included in the framework of criminal acts, are determined by neurological processes or by the genome of the person concerned, and thus remain independent of the will of the doer. In other words, it would be necessary to show that two people with the same structure and the same properties of their brains must take the same decision. Otherwise, the findings of genetics and neurology should be taken into account primarily on the basis of circumstances excluding responsibility. Moreover, the literature indicates that some methodological deficiencies in brain activity studies may contribute to limiting the significance of the conclusions of these studies in criminal law.[103]

In the literature of criminal law, there is a strong criticism of the theses calling for the construction of criminal law anew, basically referring to the assumptions of compatibility. It is based on the claim that substantive criminal law has no inherent connection with scientific criticism of free will.[104] Stephen Morse even calls for "neuro-modesty," claiming that neuroscience is another science, after psychology, sociology, and others, that would allegedly revolutionize law, including criminal law. Just as a particular revolution did not take place after a thorough description of the human genome in 2001, it should not, according to this author, be expected as a result of the achievements of brain research.[105] In his opinion, crimes are committed by people, not by their brains or their genomes.[106] The starting point of Morse's critical approach to excessive expectations or concerns about the influence of neuroscience on the law is the view of Robin Feldman, which he cited, making criminal law an accusation of the adopted strategy of internalization and externalization of the criteria of the empirical sciences. The internalization strategy consists in incorporating into the law, for example, in the premises of responsibility in criminal law, criteria derived from empirical findings. The strategy of externalization consists in using expertise in order to take a decision on a specific case, for example, to forensic specialists. According to R. Feldman, law does not so much use the legacy of other sciences too little as it does often, not to say too often.[107] Interesting and noteworthy seems to be the conviction of S. Morse, who, in his admiration for brain research in the context of criminal law, sees mainly the need to find arguments to finally reject retributionism and adopt a utilitarian approach to criminal law, especially to punishment. The author even writes about the desire for the legal system to be oriented toward preventive social control based on consequentialism. This system would be run by "kings—neuro-scientists."[108]

In the Anglo-American literature, in the context of responsibility and the associated beliefs, including moral ones, there appears the already mentioned category of folk psychology. The definition of this term should be interpreted descriptively, not in terms of assessments. The Stanford Encyclopedia of Philosophy gives three possible explanations of the concept referred to here. Folk psychology can be understood as: (1) a specific arrangement of cognitive abilities which takes into account—not exhaustively—the ability to predict and explain behavior; (2) a theory of behavior reflected in brain activity; and (3) a psychological theory consisting of beliefs about the mind which ordinary people are willing to express.[109] In the context of Morse's theory and work on the subject of free will, the third understanding of this folk psychology, according to which it is a set of popular beliefs usually used to describe human behavior, seems to be correct in criminal law.[110]

According to S. Morse, there is no other option but to build legal structures, including the principles of responsibility, on the resources of folk psychology, that is, on the conviction that a person is an aware and potentially self-aware being who shapes his or her behavior in relation to the intentions resulting from his or her specific mental states. The author claims that we are beings who are able to behave intelligently and respond to what comes from reason.[111] The law can therefore only treat a person as an entity acting in connection with his or her intentions, and thus in response to the influence of reason and will.[112] The problem in the relationship between neuroscience and the law referring to the category of folk psychology is that neuroscience, unlike folk psychology, is based on the paradigm of a mechanistic approach to human behavior.[113]

Stephen Morse argues that causality, rooted even in neuronal processes or genetics, should not be understood as a circumstance that deprives man of any opportunity to respond to these dynamics. In other words, these processes do not make the human being an automaton, which has no influence on the inclinations that are revealed in him.[114] On the contrary, there are a number of possibilities, including therapeutic ones, which do not allow such a person to expect that any evil done by him or her will be understood and forgiven, thus—translating it into the language of criminal law—excluding his or her responsibility on one or other grounds.

When considering the need for a reform of criminal law triggered by brain research findings, regardless of its scope, it is appropriate to consider to what extent the knowledge derived from this research brings something new to the area of knowledge set out in the criminal law framework. Stephen Morse notes that "we knew with conviction that some people exhibit behavioural abnormalities, such as psychosis, long before psychological or neurological tests to confirm these abnormalities appeared."[115] In less obvious cases, the tools available to neuroscience may also prove insufficient.[116] Since the criteria for criminal responsibility are behavioral in nature, it seems interesting that behavior speaks louder than images.[117] The behaviorality of these criteria allows us to claim that they are not empirical manifestations of specific brain activity. If even a full correlation between brain behavior and brain activity is established, it should rather be claimed that it is the brain's observed activity that proves certain behavioral processes.[118]

This compatiblist concept emphasizes that free will arrangements are not legally relevant to criminal responsibility arrangements. Free will is understood as the power of action, the cause of which is nothing but an acting individual.[119] At the same time, the criminal law refers to the categories that are sometimes included in the framework of free will, that is, awareness, intention, ability to understand one's own behavior, and compulsion. The law treats us as beings who act in a reasonable manner, and therefore the principles of responsibility should correspond to such an anthropological assumption.[120] With this assumption, it is possible to say that the law affects the practical reason of the human being.

The adoption of a deterministic understanding of reality does not exclude the possibility of recognizing that a person can shape his behavior under the influence of a legal norm. Otherwise, it would make no sense to regulate human behavior in this way. The thesis about determinism cannot be identified with a mechanistic approach to human behavior. It is not without reason that we attribute to human behavior such features which cannot be related to the activities carried out by various types of devices or to the effects of these activities.[121]

According to S. J. Morse, the category of free will is abused in criminal law by referring to it in order to justify those circumstances and institutions which can be justified by using other notions not related to such significant controversies. According to this author, even the concept of insanity does not need to refer to free will, because it is sufficient to reach into such categories as consciousness, intentionality, or purpose.[122]

SUMMARY

It is clear that the results of scientific research, including those carried out on the brain, can and should be used in criminal law, especially in individual criminal cases, when the ability of a particular offender to bear criminal responsibility is analyzed. The tools at the disposal of neuroscience make it possible to detect such deformities in the structure of the brain that would justify the exclusion of the reproachability of a given act, that is, the assumption that the act was both conscious and voluntary. An example cited in the doctrine is alien limb syndrome. It manifests itself in sudden movements of limbs, uncontrolled by a given person. It happens that this person is aware of these movements but has no influence on them. The detection of such an abnormality may be grounds for releasing its host from responsibility, as the movements of a given limb, and thus its effects, were not voluntary, even if the subject was fully aware of them.[123]

This kind of use of scientific knowledge is no longer in doubt today. If responsibility has a retrospective dimension and therefore corresponds to an act committed by the perpetrator, which is at the same time a retaliation for that act, it is clear that it cannot be attributed to a person who, by reason of his or her own circumstances, has no influence on refraining from posing a particular threat to others. At the same time, however, a space is opened up for prospective actions, that is, actions which aim—if possible—to cure a given person, to limit the effects of their illness or even in some cases to isolate them. Isolation is then directed toward the protection of the person's rights and those of others, not toward the retribution for the evil done. This is particularly evident in the difference between the punishment criteria and the criteria for determining the length of time spent in a closed psychiatric treatment center.

One can safely admit that the concept presented above of using brain research results in criminal law is rather modest. The literature on the subject proposes an interpretation that goes much further. It has already been mentioned several times above that the results of brain research, referred to as neuroscience, are sometimes invoked as an argument for radical changes in the area of criminal law. The main thesis is the need to renounce criminal responsibility based on guilt. For, if, somewhat generalizing, human acts are considered to be completely determined by neural processes over which we have no control, it is not possible to make the perpetrator of a particular act of accusation, because he could not have behaved differently under the given circumstances. Such a situation would be nothing more than a complete determination of a person to a certain action or omission. Then only our brain could be responsible, not man as a subject. In principle—in an extreme interpretation—one could argue that human behavior is a kind of unconditional reflex, although we think it is the result of a conscious and free choice. This would mean that the guilt paradigm in criminal law would have to be abandoned. It is hard not to disagree with Lars Hertzberg, who points out that the consequence of such an abandonment would be not only a world without punishment but also a world devoid of the essential elements that constitute forms of institutional behavior, including learning and language.[124] All these forms, like the whole human community, are permeated by categories of responsibility and culpability. Blame also involves calling on a given person to correct his or her behavior by adapting it to certain social norms, some of which may be of a criminal law nature. The entity to which the guilt is attributed may try not to accept this, judging the attribution as unfounded. However, if the blame takes place within a specific formal framework—identified by the whole organizational structure established within the framework of social life—failure to comply with the expectations associated with blame means for that person to be unable to function normally within the structure or institution concerned.[125] In the case of criminal law, regardless of whether or not a given assessment is accepted or not, the consequence of the culpability may be that a specific penalty must be observed.

In this context, the experiment conducted by Benjamin Libet is often referred to.[126] This researcher and his team have established that conscious human activity is preceded by activity in specific brain centers. This activity was observed about 350 milliseconds before individual participants reported their intention to appear in their consciousness.[127] The attribution of a function in the brain to these processes, which would lead to the conclusion that man is not able to undertake voluntary and at the same time conscious acts, seems, however, to be a manifestation of certain over-interpretations, trying to contradict the thesis of neuro-modesty. After all, the fact that a given area of the brain is activated before something appears in the human consciousness does not necessarily mean that the very decision about a certain course of action, or the lack of it, takes place in human consciousness. This is what makes a healthy person different from a person suffering from serious handicaps or dysfunctions, that he or she is aware of and at the same time able to control his or her own behavior.

The findings concerning the possibility of applying the achievements of neuroscience to the issues of the subject party, and in particular the determination of its form, that is, the necessary stage of attributing criminal responsibility, also seem interesting. Similarly to the findings described above, also in the case of a subjective party, it seems least problematic to apply these achievements to the examination of a person's ability to manifest intentions.[128] Damage to individual centers in the brain or impairments of any other kind can be the basis for determining that a person could not act with intent because they did not have the competence to acquire such a degree of consciousness or to direct the will in such a way that their intent, either direct or consequential, would manifest itself.

The controversy, however, is aroused by the claim that brain research can be used to determine the content of intentions or to investigate the psychological attitude of the perpetrator to the act in general. The problem—important, but not the most important—is the inability to investigate the processes taking place in the offender's brain while committing a prohibited act.[129] One of the tasks of the criminal trial is to establish the intentional or unintentional behavior of the offender at the time of committing the criminal act. To this end, various pieces of evidence are produced in order to describe as accurately as possible the conduct of the offender. The material aspects of his conduct make it possible to attempt to establish the subjective aspects, including the form of intention or lack of intention at the time of committing the act. It is not known what role would be played by an investigation aimed at establishing the existence of an intention after a given act has been committed.

Another thing, much more serious, is the doubt that it is possible to establish intent by investigating the processes taking place in the brain, even in an examination carried out in parallel to the act of the subject. Accepting such a possibility is tantamount to recognizing that acts of intellect and will are only results of the nervous system activity. According to Michael S. Pardo and D. Patterson, intention is neither a process taking place in the brain, nor some kind of inner feeling, nor neuronal activity preceding any inner process or feeling. It is not the brain, but the human being who can intend something.[130] Knowledge, which is, after all, one of the elements that make it possible to determine the existence of intentions in the perpetrator and its form, cannot be reduced to a specific state of the brain either. The cited researchers maintain that knowledge is a possibility, not a condition located in a particular part of the brain.[131]

Contemporary challenges to the issue of deed and culpability, that is, the most important categories taken into account in the process of determining criminal responsibility, originate not only in the achievements of neuroscience or genetics. The deterministic concepts discussed above do not refer only to these contexts, although they are undoubtedly very important. It has been noted that in this context, the issue of various social burdens acquired in the socialization process also arises, including those particularly pathological, which may affect a person's propensity to act in a manner that does not comply with norms, including legal norms. Here, we can also ask about the possibility of holding a given person responsible, and thus also accusing him/her of committing a given act, if the inclination to commit a given act had originated in factors external to this person.

Undoubtedly, life experiences, especially during childhood and adolescence, play an important role in a given person's mental structure, and thus may also translate into their various inclinations. However, this does not necessarily mean that the person concerned is not responsible. We can expect some level of critical reflection from an individual, who is, after all, intelligent by nature, in relation to the positions he or she takes or the attitudes he or she presents. It is typical for human being to analyze their own behavior. This is sometimes referred to as a follow-up conscience, that is, a shattering act already committed. However, it is difficult to determine the level of critical reflection that we may require of a given person.[132] No universal criterion can be established in this respect. A different standard is formulated for professional entities and yet still different for other persons. Michael Philips proposed the following steps in the procedure for determining the level of reasonableness necessary in the circumstances:

1) to determine the degree and type of verification of beliefs by an entity in the specified circumstances,
2) to verify that the entity has verified its conviction sufficiently and using appropriate methods, and
3) if, as a result of the verification, the entity has acquired the belief that its view requires rejection, to verify whether there has been an abandonment

> of an act or omission consistent with that view and to take action to counteract the consequences of that view in the future.[133]

This problem may be analyzed in the context of an error of law and its possible justification. One can imagine a situation where a person who—due to different external conditions, for example, environment and educational methods—has a seriously distorted perspective of acts considered good and evil. Due to life experience, they may treat the use of violence as one of the methods of dispute resolution. The above-mentioned procedures of the level of reasonableness of the beliefs in question will be analyzed in such a situation as to determine whether the unconsciousness of the unlawfulness—assuming that an act was committed in this state of consciousness—was justified.

However, it is not always the case that the circumstances that may in a way determine a person's behavior cause them to be unaware of their illegality. A tendency to use violence resulting from a person's experience does not necessarily mean that the person is convinced that using it is legal. It is worth noting that consciousness is cognitive, it refers to reason, and the ability to act according to the state of one's own consciousness should be studied primarily in relation to the will. If the will is impaired for some reason, due to a mental illness or other disruption, responsibility is excluded. In any other case, a person who violates penal sanctioned norms will face responsibility, which can, however, be measured due to the personal circumstances of the perpetrator.

The problem of tension between determinism and indeterminism in its consequences goes far beyond the application of the construction of an error of law in a particular case. As already noted above, especially in the context of the postulates built upon the findings of brain research, things can boil down to questioning criminal responsibility as such.

In the theory of criminal law, the notion of an act is the subject of disputes mainly due to controversies concerning its place in the dogmatic structure of a crime.[134] The approach, which can be described as classic, assumes that the deed is included as a subject of assessment. The deed is then considered to be subject to valuation. The first thing to do is to verify the existence of the deed, and only then to verify whether it fulfills the characteristics of the type of deed specified in the Act.[135] According to a different view, the deed, or in fact the type of forbidden deed, is a postulative model for a class of behaviors. The deed becomes one of the normative criteria used in the analysis of criminal responsibility of the perpetrator.[136] A standpoint alternative to the classic approach is well reflected in the statement by Piotr Kardas:

> In an alternative approach, clearly gaining in popularity in the Polish criminal literature of recent years, it is disputed that it is substantially incorrect and

methodologically incorrect to treat an act as a prenormative basis for criminal law evaluation, referring to a concept that includes an act as a postulative model, expressing premises (criteria, attributes of human behaviour) that reflect the current cultural paradigm, whose occurrence justifies the qualification of the behaviour as an act, and then enables the analysis in the context of other premises of crime provided for in the Law. In this approach it is consistently assumed that a deed constitutes the first normative criterion of valuation, defined (coded) in a specific way in the Criminal Law, relating to human behaviour, which is considered in this approach as a pre-normative basis for criminal law valuation.[137]

The problem mentioned here, concerning the nature of the act in the context of criminal law analysis, that is, its normative or pre-normative nature, is important, but it is nevertheless secondary to the fundamental issue that emerges from the earlier analysis. Whether we speak of the act as an ontological and pre-normative category, or whether we speak of human behavior, which is then judged from the perspective of the criteria postulated by using the category of a forbidden act, we will not avoid doubts as to whether human behavior, or the act of a person, can be considered as an object of responsibility. In other words, the question is whether human activity can be subject to any evaluation at all.

At the level of the deed, important issues of responsibility are resolved in criminal law. The decision on whether any behavior meets the criteria of the deed determines the possibility of considering the responsibility of the perpetrator of that behavior. However, the recognition that certain conduct did not meet these criteria is the same as excluding the possibility of holding a person responsible. In a way, these criteria also apply to the dispute between the supporters of postulate modeling of the conditions allowing human behavior to be considered as an act with the supporters of reconstructive modeling.[138] The first of these positions presupposes the need to adopt certain axiology which would make certain behaviors unsuitable for criminal law evaluation. Usually the catalogue of these behaviors includes unconditional reflexes and acting under the influence of absolute compulsion.[139]

Other authors note, however, that the reconstruction of normative criteria is not a space to include axiology but rather to reconstruct what exists in reality, that is, to refer to knowledge about man.[140] However, it seems to be a mistake to interpret too narrowly the context in which one can look for the basis of knowledge about man to reconstruct the premises of an act. When writing about the increasing knowledge of man, authors tend to keep hard science in mind, especially brain research, while ignoring or limiting the importance of ethics and philosophical anthropology.[141] It is difficult to interpret Przemysław Konieczniak's statement differently, in which he states that:

> there is a significant difference between the modern "model of deed" and, for example, the purely causal "model of deed" used in early mediaeval law—namely, that we are able to justify this model with something more than some unclear intuitions. To exclude "unwanted" behaviours from this notion is not an axiom for the science of law, but a result of reasoning. (. . .) When we consider the "law of deed" to be the proper model of criminal responsibility today, it is not, I believe, a function of views on what is good, bad or neutral, but rather of the fact that this model seems rational to us based on what we know about the world and man.[142]

One can gain the impression that such a position is based on the understanding of rationality in the Enlightenment-positivist paradigm, where only those positions that are supported by empirical sciences are rational. Otherwise, it would be unreasonable to argue that views of what is good, bad, or neutral cannot in themselves form a rational pattern. The attribution of unclear intuitions to mediaeval science hides a thesis of rejecting philosophical and ethical considerations as a possible basis for creating rational solutions in the area of criminal law. As already mentioned here, it seems that this is not a valid view.

The deed and its role cannot be discussed in criminal law without reference to philosophical analyses, especially ethical and anthropological ones. Even if the definition of a crime does not understand the deed as an ontological category, rather interpreting from this concept a set of demands, it is still necessary to draw on the achievements of other sciences, including those indicated here, in order to establish the basic requirements for human behavior, the fulfillment of which makes it possible to consider his responsibility. Whether we are trying to define an act or to establish a set of normative criteria, we are still considering the minimum conditions that human behavior must meet in order to be valued.

This means that the concept of a deed adopted in criminal law, regardless of the nature of the essence of this category, is open to a process which in this book has been described as the ethical legitimization of criminal law. As has been demonstrated, the focal point of this legitimization is human dignity, which not only introduces a certain ethical content into the legal system but is also the basis for the requirement that the law be shaped with a human concept anchored in the category of dignity.

If it follows from this concept that a person has the ability to decide about himself, to set goals for himself, to achieve them, and thus also to bear responsibility, then it follows that he can shape his behavior so freely that it can be considered his own behavior. As an exception to this general principle, an excessive restriction of this freedom will be interpreted as a premise justifying exclusion of responsibility.

Thus, at the heart of the legal order lies an anthropological conviction that man is able to undertake voluntary acts, that is, conscious and free. He chooses the good to be pursued and determines the appropriate means of achieving it. Free will determines the executive authorities to undertake the selected measures, and thus to achieve the objective. In each of these stages of making decisions and committing an act, there may be some restriction of human freedom. Depending on the degree of limitation, this may affect the exclusion or limitation of responsibility. However, this does not change the fact that the recognition of dignity in a person confirms that he or she is an actor in the area of freedom, depending on the smaller or greater circumstances.[143]

The successive achievements in the field of neurobiology are the cause of a recurring and growing discussion on the validity of the principles of criminal responsibility. This challenge may not yet have sounded enough in the Polish literature on the subject, but it undoubtedly also applies to the Polish criminal law system. It is universal, just as human nature is universal, in this aspect not differentiated by origin, race, or life experience. The legislator, in building criminal law, cooperating with experts, faces the need to make a number of philosophical choices, including in particular those relating to the vision of the human being, which also includes the assessment of his or her undertaking of free acts, that is, those with which we are used to being criminally responsible. The adopted anthropological concept determines the shape of the principles of criminal responsibility, including the development of the so-called criminal law of an act in which the principle of guilt plays an important role.

Making the dignity of the human being—in the previously decoded sense—the foundation of the legal system means that, within this system, all legal decisions should be aligned with the concept of the human being whose dignity it is intended to characterize. In this light, there can be no doubt not only about the ability but also about the duty of the individual to bear responsibility for their actions and omission. The legislator, taking human dignity as an anthropological starting point, determines that the legal system perceives the human being as an entity capable of taking responsibility for voluntary acts, made aware by the causative subject. Responsibility can only be assumed for acts that are subject to rational evaluation and therefore result from relevant rational processes. In other cases, responsibility is excluded. Such an understanding of man—based on the findings of realistic philosophy, referring to human experience—corresponds to what the Anglo-Saxon authors described above as folk psychology. These categories are, in fact, apparently widely shared. The ethical and anthropological context, which allows for the legitimization of criminal law, provides a strong basis for the claim that criminal responsibility can and should be based on the principle of guilt.

In this context, it is still necessary to consider which interpretation should be taken into account in constructing the principles of criminal responsibility—deterministic or indeterministic. In the light of the findings so far, it would be virtually unfounded to opt for the concept of hard determinism, assuming that a person's behavior is entirely conditioned by circumstances beyond his or her control. Assuming that man, like other animated or even inanimate beings, is only an element of processes independent of him, would result in the necessity to take away his dignity, as well as to reformulate and, in principle, even reject the concept of criminal responsibility for his own actions. This would mean a move away from the criminal law of the deed, albeit with individualizing elements, toward the criminal law of the case or the criminal law of the social danger of the perpetrator.

The rejection of hard determinism makes the choice between soft determinism (compatibilism) and indeterminism less significant for the lawyer, especially as each of them maintains a category of responsibility for the deed. It seems particularly important to assume that there are areas in the life of a person that can be explained and are explained by them by invoking reasons, and thus undergo a certain rationalization. Since we can demand an explanation, we could also expect different behavior. One can therefore call upon such a person to be responsible, who, after all, in their essence is accountable for certain behavior in the process of dialogue with the political community. The community receives explanations for the reasons for a given behavior, indicates its lack of acceptance, and explains the reasons for such a decision. This process is based on treating the perpetrator of an act as an entity capable of participating in the process of communication, not reductive only to a conglomerate of organs and tissues, acting according to the laws of biology, physics, and chemistry.

NOTES

1. F. Ciepły, *Sprawiedliwościowa racjonalizacja wymiaru kary kryminalnej wobec współczesnych tendencji polityki karnej w Polsce*, Lublin 2017, p. 113.
2. A. Sulikowski, *Posthumanizm a prawoznawstwo*, Opole 2013, p. 9.
3. Adam Sulikowski even writes of "natural individualism in its modern form." Cf. too, p. 75.
4. Ibid, p. 75.
5. Ibid, p. 77.
6. J. Bremer, *Czy wolna wola jest wolna?*, Kraków 2013, p. 283.
7. For more on this presumption cf. W. Wróbel, *O domniemaniach w zakresie przesłanek odpowiedzialności karnej*, "Prace Instytutu Prawa Własności Intelektualnej UJ" 2006, z. 96, pp. 246–49. Cf. too A. Jezusek, *"Domniemanie*

winy" w prawie karnym materialnym a procesowe domniemanie niewinności, "Ruch Prawniczy, Ekonomiczny i Socjologiczny" 2016, vol. 78, no. 2, p. 175 et seq.

8. J. Bremer, *Czy wolna wola. . .* , pp. 284–85.

9. Ibid, p. 301.

10. Ibid, pp. 301–2. Cf. too. S. Smilansky, *Free Will and Illusion*, Oxford 2000, p. 93.

11. J.R. Searle, *Umysł. Krótkie wprowadzenie*, transl. J. Karłowski, Poznań 2010, p. 217.

12. Ibid, p. 236.

13. S.J. Morse, *Determinism and the Death of Folk Psychology: Two Challenges to Responsibility from Neuroscience*, "Minnesota Journal of Law of Science and Technology" 2008, vol. 9, no. 1, p. 16.

14. This is how K. Twardowski's views are interpreted by Izydora Dąmbska, who prepared the author's lectures for print. Cf. K. Twardowski, *Etyka i prawo karne wobec zagadnienia wolności woli*, "Etyka" 1983, no. 20, p. 123.

15. Ibid, p. 132.

16. Ibid, p. 141.

17. Ibid, p. 143.

18. Ibid, pp. 143–44.

19. Ibid, p. 147.

20. Ibid, p. 150.

21. Ibid, p. 151.

22. J.R. Searle, Umysł. . . , p. 221; E.H. Atiq, *How Folk Beliefs about Free Will Influence Sentencing: A New Target for the Neuro-Determinist Critics of Criminal Law*, "New Criminal Law Review: An International and Interdisciplinary Journal" 2013, vol. 16, no. 3, p. 461.

23. J.R. Searle argues that the failure of the Compatibilists to answer this question is primarily due to the fact that their aim is to maintain the basis for attributing responsibility for a person's actions: "Above all, they want to show that people like Hitler will not avoid moral responsibility even if we prove that their behaviour was entirely determined," J.R. Searle, *Umysł. . .* , p. 224.

24. In the Anglo-American subject literature this theory is known as the *hierarchical mesh theory of free will.*

25. E.H. Atiq, *How Folk. . .* , p. 462.

26. Cf. M.S. Moore, *Placing Blame. A Theory of the Criminal Law*, Oxford 2012, p. 504 et seq.

27. Ibid, pp. 504–5.

28. Ibid, pp. 506–14.

29. Ibid, p. 506. Cf. too N. Morris, *Madness and The Criminal Law*, Chicago 1982, pp. 61–62.

30. M.S. Moore, *Placing Blame. . .* , p. 508.

31. Ibid, p. 509. Cf. too S. Morse, *Failed Explanations and Criminal Responsibility: Experts and the Unconscious*, "Virginia Law Review" 1982, vol. 68, no. 5, p. 1031.

32. M.S. Moore, *Placing Blame. . .* , pp. 510–11.

33. Ibid, p. 511.

34. Ibid, p. 513.

35. Ibid, p. 513.

36. "The idea of free will in relation to conduct is not, in the legal system, a statement of fact, but rather a value preference having very little to do with the metaphysics of determinism or free will . . . Very simply, the law treats man's conduct as autonomous and willed, not because it is, but because it is desirable to proceed as if it were," H. Packer, *The Limits of the Criminal Sanction*, Stanford 1968, pp. 74–75. Cf. too F. Alexander, H. Staub, *The Criminal, the Judge, and the Public: A Psychological Analysis*, London 1931, pp. 72–73; J. Hall, *General Principles of Criminal Law*, Indianapolis 1960, p. 455; M.S. Moore, *Placing Blame. . .* , pp. 514–15. This argument comes from: I. Kant, *Critique of Practical Reason*, trans. F. Kierski, Lviv 1911, p. 44 et seq.

37. The Anglo-Saxon doctrine does not attach as much importance as the Polish doctrine to the division into circumstances excluding unlawfulness and circumstances excluding guilt. For this reason, wherever a distinction is not necessary, I write about circumstances excluding responsibility without nuances.

38. Polish criminal law in its normative layer does not distinguish this circumstance directly as excluding criminal responsibility. However, this does not mean that coercion does not affect the criminal responsibility of a person who, under its influence, has fulfilled the characteristics of a forbidden act. The analysis of coercion and its effects should be carried out on the basis of the issue of the act (even in the aspect of absolute coercion), the state of higher necessity, or finally the possibility of attributing guilt.

39. P. van Inwagen, *The Incompatibility of Free Will and Determinism*, "Philosophical Studies" 1975, vol. 27, no. 3, p. 185.

40. Ibid, p. 186.

41. Ibid, p. 188.

42. Cf. e.g. E.J. Lowe, *Substance Causation, Powers, and Human Agency*. In: S.C. Gibb, E.J. Lowe, R.D. Ingthorsson (ed.), *Mental Causation and Ontology*, Oxford 2013, p. 153; J.R. Searle, *Umysł. . .* , p. 232 et seq.; M. Poręba, *Wolność i metafizyka. Eseje z filozofii pierwszej*, Warsaw 2017, p. 113.

43. E.J. Lowe, *Substance Causation. . .* , p. 153.

44. Ibid, p. 154.

45. Ibid, p. 161.

46. Ibid, p. 161.

47. Ibid, p. 162.

48. Ibid, p. 165.

49. Ibid, p. 167.

50. Ibid, p. 170.

51. Ibid, p. 171.

52. R.M. Chisholm, *Person and Object. A Metaphysical Study*, La Salle 1979, p. 53.

53. This concept is sometimes modified by reducing this understanding to determining whether the perpetrator may have at least tried to behave differently. Cf. ibid, p. 57.

54. This case, in the nature of a thought experiment, is sometimes presented in various philosophical works. It makes us think about how we would react to another person's behavior if we knew that it is—without their knowledge and will—controlled and inspired by scientists who once implanted a special device into his brain during a seemingly routine procedure. This case is the background to a number of conclusions in the specialist literature. Cf. i.a. H. Frankfurt, *An Alleged Asymmetry between Actions and Omissions*, "Ethics" 1994, vol. 104, no. 3, p. 620.

55. R.M Chisholm, *Person and Object. . .* , p. 59.

56. Ibid, p. 62.

57. St. Thomas Aquinas, Summa Theologiae I-II, q. 13, a. 6, Second and Revised Edition, 1920 Literally translated by Fathers of the English Dominican Province, Online Edition 2017.

58. R.M. Chisholm, *Person and Object. . .* , p. 63.

59. Ibid, p. 64.

60. Ibid, p. 73.

61. M.S. Moore, *"Nothing but a Pack of Neurons": The Moral Responsibility of the Human Machine*. In: B. Donnelly-Lazarov, *Neurolaw and Responsibility for Action. Concepts, Crimes and Courts*, Cambridge 2018, p. 29.

62. D. Eagleman begins his considerations with the story of Charles Whitman, who in 1966 killed many people, shooting from a viewpoint in a tower of the University of Texas in Austin. In the suicide note he made the evening before the assassination attempt, he wrote: "I don't really understand myself these days. I am supposed to be an average reasonable and intelligent young man. However, lately (I can't recall when it started) I have been a victim of many unusual and irrational thoughts. It was after much thought that I decided to kill my wife, Kathy, tonight . . . I love her dearly, and she has been as fine a wife to me as any man could ever hope to have. I cannot rationally pinpoint any specific reason for doing this." As cited in: D. Eagleman, *The Brain on Trial*, Atlantic Monthly, July 2011, https://www.theatlantic.com/magazine/archive/2011/07/the-brain-on-trial/308520/ (accessed 5.8.2019). Interestingly, the author indicates that Charles Whitman was a model citizen previously. The autopsy revealed that Whitman had a brain tumor located in the amygdala.

63. D. Eagleman, *The Brain* . . . An example is the case of a man convicted of pedophile crimes who, as it turned out during his imprisonment, had a brain tumor in the orbital cortex. After removing the tumor, the man's sexual behavior returned to normal. Cf. too E.H. Atiq, *How Folk. . .* , p. 455.

64. D. Eagleman, *The Brain . . .*

65. Dissenting opinion of Judge D. Bazelon in the case *United States* v. *Carter*, 436 F.2d 200, 210 (D.C. Cir. 1970).

66. E.H. Atiq, *How Folk. . .* , p. 460; L.E. Chiesa, *Punishing Without Free Will*, "Utah Law Review" 2011, p. 1403 and note; D. Eagleman, *The Brain . . .*

67. In fact, this is still a debate that has been going on for decades, if not centuries, about free will. Cf. S.J. Morse, *Determinism. . .* , pp. 14–15.

68. Ł. Kurek, *Obraz człowieka w prawie karnym a nauki kognitywne*, https://www.academia.edu/32533446/Obraz_cz%C5%82owieka_w_prawie_karnym_a_nauki_kognitywne (accessed 16.7.2019), p. 9.

69. Ł. Kurek, *Obraz człowieka. . .*, pp. 9–10.

70. J. Greene, J. Cohen, *For the Law, Neuroscience Changes Nothing and Everything*, "Philosophical Transactions of the Royal Society of London" 2004, no. 359 (1451), passim. Cf. Ł. Kurek, *Obraz człowieka. . .*, pp. 11–12. Cf. too D. Eagleman, *The Brain . . .*

71. As an example, differentiating the meanings of criminal responsibility into *accountability* and *answerability* is indicated. Cf. D. Shoemaker, *Attributability, Answerability and Accountability: Toward a Wider Theory of Moral Responsibility*, "Ethics" 2011, vol. 121, no. 3, pp. 602–32. Emad H. Atiq notes that the influence of empirical sciences on normative decisions in the area of criminal law is already significant, as it leads to measuring decisions based on the paradigm of free will. Cf. E.H. Atiq, *How Folk. . .*, p. 452.

72. The autonomous concept is well reflected in the U.S. Supreme Court ruling in the case of *Morissette* v. *United States*, 342 U.S. 246, 250 (1952): "belief in freedom of the human will and a consequent ability and duty of the normal individual to choose between good and wrong [is a belief that is] universal and persistent in mature systems of law."

73. H. Packer, *The Limits. . .*, pp. 74–75.

74. M. Jones, *Overcoming the Myth of Free Will in Criminal Law: The True Impact of the Genetic Revolution*, "Duke Law Journal" 2003, vol. 52, no. 5, p. 1031.

75. H.A. Witkin et al., *Criminality in XYY and XXY Men*, "Science" 1976, vol. 193, no. 4253, pp. 547–55. Cf. too M. Jones, *Overcoming the Myth. . .*, pp. 1039–40.

76. V. Morell, *Evidence Found for a Possible 'Aggression Gene,'* "Science" 1993, vol. 260, no. 51155, pp. 1722–23. Cf. too E.H. Atiq, *How Folk. . .*, p. 456.

77. M. Jones, *Overcoming the Myth. . .*, p. 1041.

78. S.J. Morse, *Determinism. . .*, p. 21.

79. J. Greene, J. Cohen, *For the Law. . .*, p. 1781.

80. B. Donnelly-Lazarov, *Introduction*. In: B. Donnelly-Lazarov, *Neurolaw. . .*, pp. 2–3.

81. D. Patterson, *Neuroscience and the Explanation of Human Action*. In: B. Donnelly-Lazarov, *Neurolaw. . .*, p. 11.

82. S.J. Morse, *Determinism. . .*, p. 26.

83. S.J. Morse, *Determinism. . .*, p. 26.

84. D. Patterson, *Neuroscience. . .*, p. 12. Cf. too J. Green, J. Cohen, *For the Law. . .*, p. 1781.

85. M.S. Pardo, D. Patterson, *Minds, Brains, and Law*, Oxford 2013, p. 26.

86. As an advocate of extreme reductionism noted: "Developments in the biological sciences give rise to difficult but important issues concerning the possible revision and improvement of particular legal practices, especially in the criminal law," P.S Churchland, *Moral Decision-Making and the Brain*. In: J. Illes (ed.), *Neuroethics: Defining the Issues in Theory, Practice, and Policy*, Oxford 2006, p. 15.

87. M.S. Moore, *"Nothing but a Pack of Neurons."* pp. 32–33. As this author notes, not all versions of physicalism are simultaneously reductionist.

88. Ibid, p. 33.

89. D. Patterson, *Neuroscience. . .* , p. 14.
90. D. Patterson, *Neuroscience. . .* , p. 23.
91. K. Sifferd, *Non-Eliminative Reductionism: Not the Theory of Mind Some Responsibility Theorists Want, but the One They Need.* In: B. Donnelly-Lazarov, *Neurolaw. . .* , p. 71.
92. The author conceives it as *mental causation*. Cf. ibid, p. 75.
93. The philosophers Paul and Patricia Churchland are considered by K. Sifferd as the main promoters of this version of eliminationism. Cf. incl. P. Churchland, *Moralność mózgu. Co neuronauka mówi o moralności*, transl. M. Hohol, N. Marek, Kraków 2013, *passim*.
94. K. Sifferd, *Non-Eliminative Reductionism. . .* , p. 79. Cf. too J. Fodor, *Psychosemantics. The Problem of Meaning in the Philosophy of Mind*, Cambridge 1987, pp. 3–4.
95. "Insofar as there is progress in neuroscience, this progress is made via discovering the referents of commonsense mental concepts," K. Sifferd, *Non-Eliminative Reductionism. . .* , p. 79.
96. Cf. the criticism of Greg Caruso and Derk Pereboom's views by K. Sifferd, *Non-Eliminative Reductionism. . .* , p. 83. Cf. too G. Caruso, *Free Will Eliminativism: Reference, Error, and Phenomenology*, "Philosophical Studies" 2015, vol. 172, no. 10, pp. 2823–33.
97. Cf. D. Davidson, *Essay on Actions and Events*, Oxford 1980, *passim*.
98. K. Sifferd, *Non-Eliminative Reductionism. . .* , pp. 91–92. Cf. too J. Kim, *The Myth of Nonreductive Materialism*. In: P.K. Moser, J.D. Trout (ed.), *Contemporary Materialism*, New York 1995, p. 136.
99. K. Sifferd, *Non-Eliminative Reductionism. . .* , p. 92.
100. J.R. Searle, *Umysł. . .* , pp. 38–39 Cf. too K. Sifferd, *Non-Eliminative Reductionism. . .* , p. 93.
101. The author is accused of a number of ontological inaccuracies. Cf. K. Sifferd, *Non-Eliminative Reductionism. . .* , p. 94.
102. This is what D. Eagleman called for, *The Brain . . .*
103. S. Morse raises, among other things, the following doubts: a small number of subjects under research, conducting research mainly on students, incompatibility of the situation of those surveyed with experiences from the real world. Cf. S.J. Morse, *Avoiding Irrational NeuroLaw Exuberance: A Plea for Neuromodesty*, "Mercer Law Review" 2011, vol. 62, p. 850.
104. E.H. Atiq, *How Folk. . .* , p. 463. Cf. too S.J. Morse, *Avoiding. . .* , p. 837 et seq.
105. Ibid, p. 837. In another of his articles, the author diagnoses a phenomenon he describes as *Brain Overclaim Syndrome*. Cf. S.J. Morse, *Brain Overclaim Syndrome and Criminal Responsibility: A Diagnostic Note*, "Ohio State Journal of Criminal Law" 2006, no. 3, p. 397.
106. Ibid, p. 397; S.J. Morse, *Genetics and criminal responsibility*, "Public Law and Legal Theory. Research Paper Series. Research Paper No. 11–34," p. 2.
107. R. Feldman, *The Role of Science in Law*, Oxford 2009, *passim*. Cf. S.J. Morse, *Avoiding. . .* , pp. 838–39.

108. Ibid, p. 839.

109. The headword "Folk Psychology as a Theory" in the *Stanford Encyclopedia of Philosophy*, plato.stanford.edu/entries/folkpsych-theory/#PlatSensFolkPsyc (accessed 9.8.2019).

110. D. Patterson, *Neuroscience*. . . , p. 11.

111. S.J. Morse, *Avoiding*. . . , p. 840.

112. In the case of persons who, exceptionally, because of various ailments or strong external influences, do not have such power, it is necessary to apply specific rules providing for a different response to their behavior.

113. S.J. Morse, *Avoiding*. . . , p. 843.

114. Ibid, p. 848.

115. Ibid, p. 852.

116. Ibid, p. 854.

117. An example would be to exclude or limit the responsibility of children and young people. The findings of neuroscience were not necessary in order to come to the conclusion that the age of the offender is relevant to responsibility and ability to serve the sentence. Cf. the U.S. Supreme Court ruling in the case *Roper* v. *Simmons*, 543 U.S. 551 (2005).

118. S.J. Morse, *Brain*. . . , p. 405.

119. S.J. Morse, *Determinism*. . . , p. 3.

120. Ibid, p. 5.

121. Ibid, p. 6.

122. Ibid, p. 12.

123. M.S. Pardo, D. Patterson, *Minds*. . . , pp. 124–25.

124. L. Hertzberg, *Blame and Causality*, "Mind. New Series" 1975, vol. 84, no. 336, p. 501.

125. Ibid, pp. 503–4.

126. Cf. incl. B. Libet, *Are the Mental Experiences of Will and Self-Control Significant for the Performance of a Voluntary Act?*, "Behavioral and Brain Sciences" 1987, vol. 10, no. 4, p. 783 et seq.

127. M.S. Pardo, D. Patterson, *Minds*. . . , p. 126.

128. Ibid, p. 134.

129. H. Mayberg, *Does Neuroscience Give Us New Insights into Criminal Responsibility?*. In: M.S. Gazzaniga, J.S. Rakoff (ed.), *A Judge's Guide to Neuroscience: A Concise Introduction*, Santa Barbara 2010, pp. 37–38.

130. M.S. Pardo, D. Patterson, *Minds*. . . , pp. 137–38.

131. Ibid, p. 139. It is difficult to say to what extent, when writing about possibility, the authors consciously referred to the well-known classical metaphysics of the division into possibility and act, already proposed by Aristotle. Cf. M.A. Krąpiec, *Akt i możność*. In: *Powszechna encyklopedia filozofii*, ptta.pl/pef/pdf/a/akt im.pdf (accessed 6.9.2019).

132. This is noted by M. Philips, *Rationality, Responsibility and Blame*, "Canadian Journal of Philosophy" 1987, vol. 17, no. 1, p. 147.

133. Ibid, pp. 147–48.

134. Ł. Pohl, *Czyn w prawie karnym*. In: R. Dębski (ed.), *Nauka o przestępstwie. Zasady odpowiedzialności*, System Prawa Karnego, vol. 3, Warsaw 2013, p. 204.

135. A. Zoll, *O wartościowaniu czynu w prawie karnym*, "Państwo i Prawo" 1983, no. 4, p. 112; A. Wąsek, *Recenzja książki J. Majewskiego, "Prawnokarne przypisywanie skutku przy zaniechaniu. Zagadnienia węzłowe, Wydawnictwo Księgarnia Akademicka," Kraków 1997*, "Państwo i Prawo" 1999, z. 3, p. 83; Ł. Pohl, *Czyn w prawie*. . . , pp. 204–5.

136. Ł. Pohl, *Czyn w prawie karnym*. . . , pp. 206–7. It is worth recalling at this point the statement that "contrary to what is often claimed, also in a traditionally oriented system of criminal law, the act is not subject to valuation. This object is the existence of a concrete human being, who constitutes a certain continuum and manifests themselves in various characters and forms. On the other hand, the concept of an act is already one of the normative criteria used in criminal law analysis (generally considered primary)," J. Majewski, *Prawnokarne przypisywanie skutku przy zaniechaniu. Zagadnienia węzłowe*, Kraków 1997, pp. 31–32. Cf. too M. Rodzynkiewicz, *Modelowanie pojęć w prawie karnym*, Kraków 1998, pp. 28–29.

137. P. Kardas, *Zbieg przepisów ustawy w prawie karnym. Analiza teoretyczna*, Warsaw 2011, pp. 51–52. This extract is also referred to by Ł. Pohl, *Czyn w prawie karnym*. . . , p. 207.

138. Ł. Pohl, *Czyn w prawie karnym*. . . , p. 217.

139. M. Rodzynkiewicz, *Modelowanie pojęć*. . . , pp. 31–33.

140. T. Kaczmarek, *Metodologiczne aspekty sporów wokół pojęcia czynu w polskim prawie karnym*. In: tenże, *Rozważania o przestępstwie i karze. Wybór prac z okresu 40-lecia naukowej twórczości*, Warsaw 2006, pp. 42–43.

141. Władysław Mącior made extensive references to these studies as early as in 1990 in his work, but he unequivocally pointed to the need for philosophical interpretation of neurophysiological data. Cf. op cit, *Czyn ludzki i jego znaczenie w prawie karnym. Zagadnienia podstawowe*, Warsaw 1990, pp. 61–62.

142. P. Konieczniak, *Czyn jako podstawa odpowiedzialności w prawie karnym*, Warsaw 2002, pp. 47–48.

143. History shows that even in conditions of extreme deprivation of liberty, a person can maintain the ability to act according to his or her beliefs.

Chapter 4

Issues of Anthropological-Ethical Analysis of Behavior

THE LEGITIMACY OF REFERRING TO A PHILOSOPHY

Responsibility is not a term reserved for the legal sciences. In fact, it seems that the legal dimension of responsibility, although very important, is not fundamental. Legal responsibility, including criminal responsibility, is part of the perspective on responsibility that a person comes into contact with on a daily basis. It is worth quoting here *in extenso* a statement by Jacek Filek from years ago, in which he called for action to face the category of responsibility, addressing his appeal mainly to philosophers:

> After all, it is we, philosophers, who are responsible for the fact that the man who is required to be responsible does not know what responsibility is. (. . .) Today, a measure of inappropriate phraseology of responsibility has changed. We do not want to join the group of mentors orating against the scandalous irresponsibility of modern man. We are philosophers. We see how, rootedly and in various ways, the problem of responsibility stormed philosophical thinking; how it lurks at its very basis. It is time to recognise this situation and to face the problem, reaching deeper than a moralist or jurist, deeper than a philosopher who succumbs to the self-explanatory concept.[1]

I do not interpret Filek's deliberations as a call to limit the conduct of considerations on responsibility solely to philosophy. Rather, it concludes that philosophy, including mainly ethics, is primarily responsible for the correct interpretation of the concept of responsibility by grasping its essence. Other sciences are concerned with learning its selected aspects, or different ways of understanding it, including criminal law. The task of the doctrine of criminal law, which is the subject of this study, is to draw on these philosophical findings for the purposes of the theory and dogma of criminal law. The philosophical understanding of the concept of responsibility is strongly linked to the vision of man as recognized by philosophical anthropology, which determines a number of ethical structures. Therefore, even regardless of the chronological composition of the principles of responsibility, it seems necessary to consider the issue of responsibility from its ethical perspective.[2]

The subject matter of this study does not allow for an in-depth and comprehensive discussion of the phenomenon of responsibility. In fact, this is not the topic here. The aim of the analysis is to indicate the basic principles of moral responsibility, resulting from the reflection on responsibility as such and, above all, on responsibility in the light of ethics. In this context, an idea may arise of the basic principles of moral responsibility. Although in the abovementioned statements, Filek points out that moral responsibility, as well as legal responsibility, is secondary to responsibility in general, we may only stop with this statement in works on the theoretical aspects of the phenomenon of responsibility. In a treatise written for the purposes of criminal law, stopping at such a stage would not be feasible. The philosophical theory of morality (ethics) becomes a relevant reference point. At this point, it is worth recalling the thesis contained in the introduction to this book. The legislator is obliged to shape the criminal law in such a way that the rules of criminal responsibility do not exceed the limits set by the rules of moral responsibility. At the same time, they may also set the scope narrower than the principles of moral responsibility. In other words, criminal law should not lead to the attribution of responsibility to a person who has committed a morally neutral or, even less so, morally good act. However, this does not mean that all immoral behavior should be criminalized and included in criminal law.

It is not the case that lawyers are obliged to uncritically transfer philosophical interpretations to criminal law. Modifications, especially those that narrow the scope of philosophically interpreted responsibility, are permitted but should be made with particular care. An acceptable narrowing down is undoubtedly the understanding of the law of responsibility through the prism of concrete deeds committed by man. In philosophy, especially in the twentieth century, responsibility is understood broadly, without limiting it to a specific act.

Criminal law is therefore a unique branch of the law, as the assessments made on its basis are often confronted in parallel with moral assessments. In the case of more serious moral misconduct, those concerned may have a reasonable suspicion that this behavior also fulfills the characteristics of a criminal act as defined in criminal law. This suspicion usually results not only from a superficial knowledge of criminal law but also from the conviction that what is highly reprehensible morally, which also has a dimension that goes beyond individual relationships, is probably also illegal and punishable.

Criminal law fully implementing the standard of moral transparency would consider it unacceptable to criminalize behavior which would not be at the same time behavior that violates moral norms.[3] For the purposes of the system of law, it can be assumed that the moral position of the community, also referred to as public morality, is expressed in the Basic Law, which is a source of knowledge about rights requiring protection.[4]

The thesis formulated here is not to claim that the theory of criminal law in its terminology should use only the findings made in philosophy. Undoubtedly, criminal law, like other branches of law, retains its autonomy, justified by, for example, a separate origin. As far as the law is concerned, it is important that the legislator has a relatively large degree of freedom in terms of shaping the scope of responsibility.

It seems justified to draw on philosophical, sociological, or psychological works on morality in the process of shaping the principles of criminal responsibility.[5] The extra-legal context, in this case philosophical, sociological, and psychological, can determine the extent of responsibility in the way it is understood and accepted in a given community. Criminal law, like other branches of law, is a certain convention in the rules collected in one, or usually more, legal acts. In this sense, the law as such does not provide us with criteria to guide us in determining the principles and scope of criminal responsibility.[6] Even if these criteria are present in the legal system, it is not because they are intrinsically linked to it, but because it has been decided to introduce them because of a different system, for example, natural law, or as a result of other events (without reference to the sources of a given criterion), such as accession to an international agreement. This problem is well illustrated by the following case. Let's imagine that the next great world war resulted in a nuclear conflict. The consequences were so dramatic that only a few hundred people managed to survive, who managed to escape to an island that was not reached by nuclear explosives. Quite quickly, the survivors realized that they had to organize their lives on this island again. Among many other issues that need to be resolved urgently, there is also the problem of shaping and adopting legal norms that will regulate the most important areas of social life on the island. The daily functioning of the survivors also quickly proved that it was necessary to enact norms of criminal law, as not all of them behaved in the way desired by the newly emerging society. The survivors came from different countries. Only some of them were lawyers, and this was not helpful because they were educated in different legal systems. What can the inhabitants of this island have recourse to in order to enact criminal law? What arguments can be used to find the right solutions? What should criminal responsibility look like? The cited case is only a literary fiction.[7] It is intended to make us reflect on criminal law in a more distanced way from the current normative context.

The likelihood of finding oneself faced with the need to reshape the legal system is negligible. However, the likelihood of reconstructing the rules of criminal responsibility increases considerably. Once in a while, states reform their criminal responsibility systems. These are usually changes to some parts of the existing regulations. However, it is also the case that the existing regulations are repealed in their entirety and replaced by new ones. The reasons for such decisions may be different, for example, the belief that the current system is completely ineffective or the regime change of the state. The current decline of classical criminal law and the shift toward preventive instruments, as discussed in more detail in the next chapter, must not be overlooked either. Reaching for philosophical considerations, including above all philosophical anthropology and ethics, and thus seeking the meaning of responsibility appropriate to who a person is and how they function in the social community, can significantly increase the chances that criminal law will be understood and observed by its addressees.[8] This may not be because there will be a significant increase in interest in the content of penal legislation, but because it will coincide with the moral intuitions acquired in the process of socialization, as life experience grows. The more the penal law realizes the standard of moral transparency, and thus the more it is consistent with moral convictions, the greater the chance of obeying it. The scope of the postulates arising from this standard should be considered. At the same time, this does not mean that the law is only a system that passively takes into account the moral positions prevailing in the political community. At the specific level, that is, concerning the catalogue of forbidden acts, it is possible with the help of legal tools to shape desirable moral attitudes or to disseminate them. This requires appropriate efforts on the part of state authorities and involves the risk of misunderstanding and rejection. However, the legislator cannot shape the principles of responsibility—above all, but not exclusively, at a general level—in such a way that they are incompatible with the principle of human dignity and the human understanding emerging from it.

Already at this point, it is worth noting that the postulate of treating the philosophy of morality as a point of reference in shaping the principles of criminal responsibility does not mean that entire categories with the meanings established there should be directly transferred to criminal law. However, it is necessary to discover, where possible, the relevant ontological categories. However, this does not mean that individual structures cannot gain a degree of independence under criminal law. Theoretical findings of criminal law, including the structure of crime, are primarily of a guaranteed and orderly nature. The reference to ontological categories, on the other hand, is particularly important in order to ensure that the scope of responsibility, as laid down in criminal law, and thus as a consequence of the structure of the offense, does not go beyond that established on the basis of morality.

The literature points to the risk of falling into the trap of essentialism, consisting in the search for the essence of the phenomenon of responsibility, in this case criminal responsibility, or even the individual categories of criminal law in general, under pain of depriving the attribute of legitimization of either philosophical findings or findings on the basis of criminal law theory. Regardless of whether such a trap actually exists, there is no need to abandon research on the borderline between criminal law and philosophy. The aim of this work is to limit the research intentions to the paradigms of responsibility created on the basis of philosophy and criminal law.[9]

The problem of the relationship between the concepts of responsibility in philosophy and in law has for years been the subject of deliberations undertaken in Anglo-Saxon doctrine. This is primarily due to the specificity of the common law, where the importance of case law makes it not so important to construct general and abstract rules as to seek a rational solution in a specific case. This also promotes the consideration of ethical reflection.[10] The importance of the relationship between responsibility in the moral and legal sense was stressed by Joel Feinberg, among others. He put this problem primarily retrospectively. The analysis concerns the situation when the event has already taken place, everything related to it has taken place, and the court proceedings begin, in which the fundamental question is asked: Who is responsible for the event?[11] It is impossible not to call up Robin A. Duff, with his modest version of moralism, or Michael S. Moore.[12]

The combination of ethical and legal understanding of responsibility immediately shows the specificity of the legal understanding of responsibility. The process of appealing to responsibility in legal terms is imbued with a number of practical aspects, more or less veiled. This includes, for example, compensation for damage by the offender or the imposition of a criminal sanction on the offender. Responsibility in the legal sense is also characterized by a specific way of responding to problems arising from the lack of clarity of its rationale. Usually in such cases, the courts apply arbitrary rules developed in case law. An example is the case law on the difference between causing serious damage to health, ending in a person's death, and murder.[13] Arbitrary ways of resolving such ambiguities are not, moreover, the exclusive domain of case law. Similar solutions, often necessary due to the guarantee aspects of criminal law, are already applied at the lawmaking stage, for example, determining the difference between mild and moderate damage to health.[14] Responsibility in the legal sense also retains a certain degree of relativity to various types of objectives, conflicts of interest, and policies. This means that it is not always about discovering responsibility, but deciding on it.[15] There is a reason why criminal law talks about attributing responsibility. For various reasons, it may ultimately be restricted in a legal sense, which does not necessarily result in a limitation in a moral sense. A limitation may also result from certain rules in the legal system, in some cases excluding even the possibility of conducting a trial to finally determine and attribute such responsibility. Such a situation on the grounds of criminal responsibility occurs, for example, in the case of the death of the perpetrator, when proceedings should be discontinued, which makes it impossible to pass a judgment indicating the responsibility of the perpetrator.[16]

The above allows us to ask a still valid question after the legal proceedings have been concluded: Was the defendant actually responsible for the harm caused? When we ask such a question, we are actually asking about moral responsibility. This question is justified for at least several reasons. Behind moral judgments, there are no hidden consequences of a state character.[17] Nor do they result in the imposition of specific sanctions or obligations. Moral responsibility does not accept arbitrary premises setting the limits of responsibility. Moral judgments should also be free from ongoing goals, undertakings, and policies. They cannot be derived from the good or bad luck of the perpetrator. Joel Feinberg points out, although he does not call it that, that there is a significant difference in criminal law between accomplishment and attempt, which may or may not always be reflected in the sanction ultimately imposed. The reason for the nonexistence of an accomplishment, that is, it stops at the attempt, may be an event completely independent of the perpetrator, even accidental.[18] The intention of the perpetrator, which has a much greater share in the final determination of moral responsibility than in the case of legal responsibility, plays a much greater role in moral responsibility. These differences may sometimes even mean that the determination of moral responsibility is much more difficult than the assignment of legal responsibility. The main difference, however, is, as Joel Feinberg puts it, different jurisdictions. Moral judgment is the matter of the *forum internum*, in which the tribunal is above all the conscience of man.[19] Legal judgment is made for the needs of the community, which claims the right to regulate and evaluate a given section of human behavior.

The interpenetration of law and morality, in particular criminal law and morality, is also visible in the sphere of language. In everyday language, when describing various events from a moral perspective, we often use terminology primarily considered to be legal or legal terminology. Even if these languages are not the source of the term, they may constitute its basic meaningful context. An example of such a term is "crime," a word with a strict meaning in criminal law, often used in various contexts in everyday life, including for moral purposes.[20] Individual languages, including Polish, know much more about similar examples. It is not completely indifferent to the analysis of the relationship between morality and criminal law. Rightly, J. Feinberg postulates confronting the meanings of individual concepts with each other—depending on their use for talking about moral norms or legal norms.[21] Although the aforementioned author addresses these recommendations primarily to philosophers, it would be difficult to prove that this method is not also useful for lawyers. Comparing concepts can show the relationships and differences between morality and criminal law. Furthermore, from the perspective of the previously mentioned standard of moral transparency of legal norms, it can also be a basis for verifying whether the autonomous understanding of a legal concept has not become too far removed from the meaning adopted on the grounds of morality.

Sensitivity to the relationship between criminal law and morality, which also manifests itself in the study of the use of particular concepts in each of these systems, cannot consist in the thoughtless transfer of particular constructions from one system to another. This is particularly true of the tendency, perhaps manifested by some, to transfer legal assessments to morality.[22] However, this does not mean that such comparative studies are not justified, especially from a criminal law perspective. Again, it is not a matter of transferring moral assessments to legal assessments without any thought, especially since, as a rule, the scope of behavior covered by criminal law assessments is narrower than that of behavior covered by moral assessments.[23] However, it is worth bearing in mind whether a given behavior, which according to legal norms should be considered unlawful and, consequently, criminal, is also assessed negatively from a moral perspective. Indeed, if an act is considered admissible, and even more so if it is considered advisable, the legitimacy of maintaining it in the catalogue of prohibited acts can be very doubtful. This problem does not only concern the catalogue of types of criminal acts understood as a specific part of criminal law. The difficulty may arise because of a general construction, that is, because of what we can—using the language of mathematics—put before brackets. The reason for criminalizing too broad from a moral perspective may be one of the forms of criminal interaction, for example, formally understood incitement, or the acceptance of the admissibility of the intersection of stadial forms and forms of criminal interaction, that is, allowing responsibility for the attempted incitement, especially when the incitement would be included without effect.

Although it is difficult not to be aware today of the differences in moral evaluations, which occasionally sounds particularly intense in social discourse, it is still possible and necessary to speak of a certain canon of public morality, that is, the principles which constitute, among other factors, a social community. It is worth recalling Patrick Devlin's view that the lack of community of thinking about what is good and bad constitutes a simple path to disintegration.[24] There is no requirement for full unanimity on this issue, but agreement on the importance of norms to a certain extent. What seems particularly interesting is what causes less controversy in the public debate, that is, those principles of moral responsibility that determine its scope, but not the content of morally evil behavior itself.

At this point, even before we move on to the reflection on responsibility and its principles, it should be remembered that, in the light of the findings made, the key category for this reflection is the principle of human dignity, which has been introduced into the legal system in order to orientate it toward the good of man as such. Since the legislator should design solutions in a way that is subordinate to this paradigm, it is necessary not only to establish criteria for responsibility but also to analyze the issue of the structure of the human act, without which it is impossible to talk convincingly about responsibility. If "dignity" is the window of penal law on the issue of moral responsibility, it seems necessary to reach for those ethical concepts that best correspond to the human understanding already discussed in depth. The conclusions of the analyses indicate that human dignity, when viewed on an ethical level, shows that not only is he or she a rational being, but he or she is also capable of bearing responsibility. It was also noted that dignity is a testimony to the social importance of man and his behavior. We are members of a community of people who can call us to account for our various acts.

The purpose of this chapter is to establish the principles of accountability and to analyze the related structure of human action. It should be reiterated that "human dignity" is a kind of bridge that entitles a lawyer to conduct anthropological deliberations, performed for the purpose of solving problems of establishing and applying criminal law. Above all, however, it is about creating the conditions for the ethical legitimization of criminal law.

The reflections carried out in this chapter are based on several philosophical trends whose common point is the reference to the human person, their dignity, and the focus on human action, its principles, and the responsibility that goes with it. Undoubtedly, the common thesis of the philosophical currents referred to here is also the recognition of human action as the result of processes based on the interaction of reason and will.[25] As a consequence, it seems that these concepts not only do not contradict but are also compatible with human dignity—a central category for the ethical legitimization of criminal law. Such an approach justifies referring to the views of Aristotle, St. Thomas Aquinas, Roman Ingarden, and Karol Wojtyla. The deliberations also include selected works written in the Anglo-Saxon analytical philosophy, including in particular such authors as John M. Fischer and Mark Ravizza.

THE ISSUE OF THE FOUNDATIONS OF MORAL RESPONSIBILITY

Responsibility is something specifically personal.[26] It is what distinguishes human beings from other creatures, because only a person can be responsible for what they do.[27] On this dividing line, there is a distinction between responsibility and being solely the cause of a given event. Any living creature can cause certain consequences, for example, a dog can bite someone or cause another change in the outside world. In such a case, there can be no responsibility whatsoever, only contributing to a specific effect.[28] The difference between exclusive causality and responsibility is not only noticeable in the context of holding someone responsible, that is, in the situation of acts considered reprehensible. Responsibility, which will be analyzed in greater depth, may also include positive aspects. After all, you can be responsible for the good you do. Here, too, we will evaluate human behavior differently than the behavior of another living being or the forces of nature in general.[29] John M. Fischer and Mark Ravizza argue for the theses indicated here with the help of a simple thought experiment involving certain technical possibilities. It is enough to consider how we would react to the behavior of another human being, if we know that they are—without their knowledge and will—controlled and inspired by scientists, who had implanted a special device into his or her brain during a seemingly routine procedure. Would our reactions to this person still be similar to those that arise in ordinary situations on a daily basis? Would we show respect, disapproval, anger, gratitude, condemnation, etc.? It seems not. Rather, one should expect feelings of empathy toward this person and possibly transfer other emotions to those who direct his or her behavior.[30]

The subject of responsibility can be understood in at least two ways. First of all, responsibility is a certain permanent feature of human life. It is constant, and not necessarily updated only in case of irregularities in the performance of various types of duties.[31] We are constantly being called upon to be responsible. The second understanding, which is closest to a legal viewpoint, sees responsibility in the context of various shortcomings. These two understandings are linked. The first is a call for good decisions; it has a positive dimension. The reliable exercise of this responsibility should effectively prevent the second meaning of this responsibility, which is characterized by a retrospective approach, from becoming apparent, with a negative impact. Responsibility may relate to a human behavior itself or to its outcome. Human behavior is understood as a certain activity. A behavior that can become the basis of responsibility is not passively enduring something that happens to a given person. However, it is not the case that this passive endurance will always be free of responsibility. For if it is shown that a given person had a duty to resist what happens to him or her, then a possible failure to do so may be associated with responsibility.

One of the more influential and well-known approaches to responsibility in contemporary Anglo-American literature is also the one proposed by Peter F. Strawson, who explained the phenomenon of moral responsibility as a set of social practices. In this sense, it is indicated that whenever members of a given community treat someone as a responsible subject, they demonstrate this by reacting to that person, who may be grateful, outraged, offended, loved, respected, or forgiven.[32] The behavior of a being who does not have the ability to bear responsibility can cause anger or a sense of disappointment or frustration in us. These will not, however, be a reaction of offense, outrage, or forgiveness.[33]

Referring to this thought, R. Jay Wallace viewed moral responsibility through the prism of holding someone responsible. In his opinion, guilt, offense, or indignation are justified by the belief that the moral expectation of a given person is violated.[34] In other words, the recognition of responsibility is justified in the belief that there is a breach of a moral obligation. This gives rise to the conclusion that the subject is morally responsible as long as it is fair to hold him or her accountable, even if we do not ultimately express appropriate feelings toward the perpetrator and hold him or her responsible.[35]

Christopher Cowley describes the process of determining responsibility as a "blame game." This is a game because it involves the participation of a number of people based on predetermined rules. He notes that in moral practice, this scheme is similar to the one we know as a scheme of legal responsibility.[36] The space in which we recognize the principles of responsibility and learn them is the family and first friendships.[37]

Responsibility appears in different meanings and contexts. Responsibility can be understood as: (1) bearing responsibility for something, (2) taking responsibility for something, (3) being held responsible, and (4) acting responsibly.[38] It is worth noting that the first three meanings are related. It even seems that they are actually desirable. Whoever is responsible for something should at the same time be prepared to take responsibility for it and to be held accountable for the actions taken or for the failure to act. It can thus already be noted at this point that the rules on responsibility should be designed in such a way as to make it possible to identify the person responsible and to verify whether he or she has taken up the relevant responsibility, whether he or she should have taken up the responsibility, and whether he or she can and should have borne responsibility for their own conduct. As it is not difficult to notice, these forms of responsibility are only seemingly independent from each other.[39]

The incurring of responsibility is a condition arising in parallel with the fulfillment of a specific act. Responsibility is born where perpetration takes place. Acceptance of responsibility does not depend on the will of the perpetrator, so it is indicated that it is passive in nature. This does not in any way mean that the act is independent of the subject's will. Rather, this passivity should be understood as an acceptance of responsibility as an inevitable consequence of the act. In some cases, however, it is possible to dispense with responsibility by committing another act planned for this purpose.[40] But taking responsibility is an act. It does not have to be an external act. It is sufficient that it takes the form of a mental experience.

Holding someone responsible is already part of the processes undertaken by external entities toward the perpetrator. It is behavior concerning the perpetrator, directed at him, to bring about a certain change in him. This behavior is not causally linked to the act of the perpetrator, but it is this act that entitles the relevant entity to hold the perpetrator responsible.[41] As R. Ingarden pointed out: "A legitimate 'call to account' presupposes that the act was actually done and by the perpetrator himself. It therefore requires a prior examination of the actual facts and circumstances. This may either relieve the perpetrator of responsibility or establish its existence and lead to 'accountability.'"[42] On this basis, the sequence of actions leading to responsibility can be reconstructed:

1. the actual commission of the act,
2. identifying the subject—perpetrator, and
3. determining the circumstances of the subject and subject matter deciding the existence of responsibility.

The issue of the grounds for responsibility is still not sufficiently defined. We should think about the content of these circumstances that determine the possibility of holding the perpetrator responsible for the act committed by him or her. To this end, it is worth quoting the six conditions, following R. Ingarden, on which it is possible to consider that a fact has moral value.[43]

1. Only such events can be valued morally which are realized by an aware subject who understands the meaning of their own conduct and are therefore able to direct their own conduct.
2. The behavior of an entity is evaluated. From a lawyer's perspective, those behaviors which are externalized by an entity seem particularly relevant.
3. Behavior must have a moral meaning, that is, be connected with some moral value. Some behaviors are morally neutral.
4. It is possible to attribute responsibility for the behavior being assessed to a particular entity.
5. The entity should be free to decide and act. A manifestation of this freedom is the possibility of withdrawing from the further performance of a given activity at any time.

6. The decision about a given behavior and the persistence of this decision during a given behavior is to flow from the deep "self" of a given person, and thus the behavior of the subject "should have its point of attachment in the very centre of his/her entire psychophysical organisation."[44]

As far as the responsibility itself is concerned, within its structure can be distinguished:

1. the subject of responsibility—who is responsible,
2. the object of responsibility—for what (for whom) the entity is responsible,
3. the authority imposing responsibility—what (or who) imposes responsibility,
4. the court of responsibility—to whom the entity is responsible, and
5. the executor of responsibility—who holds the entity to account.[45]

As a rule, it is assumed that only a person can be held responsible.[46] At the same time, this does not exclude the possibility of formulating a question that considers the legitimization of holding a whole community responsible. In the case of human responsibility itself, philosophers consider the problem of fragmentary responsibility, only for the act itself, or, alternatively, responsibility for the whole of one's humanity, or for one's own attitude. However, there is no doubt that one cannot be held responsible for another person, either as a scapegoat or even by inheriting responsibility.[47] Interestingly, it is pointed out that a person's sense of responsibility comes first in relation to understanding him- or herself as the cause of events.[48] The conviction of one's own responsibility was only to lead one to discover agency and the causality that it entails.

In the subjective aspect, the possibility of attributing responsibility for acts that are not the result of human intent should be considered. The intention has to be distinguished from the consciousness and cognition itself, because a volitive aspect is necessary for its occurrence.[49] The scope of consciousness itself may also vary considerably in the case of individual acts, being, on the one hand, sufficient to be held responsible, and, on the other hand, far from being fully aware. It is necessary and, at the same time, very difficult to indicate the lowest level of consciousness that would already allow the responsibility of the perpetrator of the act to be attributed.

As noted above, responsibility is also related to the result of the perpetrator's behavior, its outcome. As in the case of an action itself, the responsibility can be incurred only if the result of the perpetrator's behavior is linked to some positive or negative value, or at least indirectly leads to a valuable factual situation.[50] Behavior and its results, if they are value-neutral, should not be evaluated from the perspective of responsibility. Their value can sometimes only be established after an in-depth study of the context of a human's behavior. This is particularly evident in the case of omissions, which can only be valuable after becoming familiar with the duty of action of a given person.

The figure of omission significantly complicates the problem of responsibility. This is because it introduces the need for a much broader spectrum of analysis when trying to assess the scope of a person's responsibility. There are at least two levels of omissions. First, at the axiological level, where the perpetrator's decision to realize certain values while omitting others gains importance. It is therefore possible to consider this omission on an exclusively axiological level. At the same time, however, an omission can be recognized at another level, taking the form of a specific course of action. This becomes the basis for considering whether the perpetrator's decision to take action in a given direction was justified, and at the same time to abandon another direction of his or her own action. The levels of analysis of the problem of omission indicated here are not neutral to each other. An axiological choice, even if not always fully realized, is usually linked to the choice of a particular course of action. For the assessment of responsibility, it seems particularly important that it cannot be reduced to merely examining the result of the perpetrator's action and the values associated with it. The whole axiological context of a given situation before and after deciding on a given act must be taken into account, as R. Ingarden pointed out.[51]

Another element of fundamental importance for the ethical analysis of the issue of responsibility is the issue of human freedom, that is, the thesis that human behavior is so free from external causes that it can be described as deeds. A deed in essence presupposes some freedom of choice. It need not be freedom unlimited in any way. However, it seems necessary to find some limit, the crossing of which will cause a given human behavior not to bear the name of his or her deed but rather a certain reflex independent of human will. At the same time, the indeterminacy of the deed mentioned here does not mean that it was not caused in any way. As noted in the previous chapter, this does not mean a complete break with the determinants external to man, as long as he or she still has a real possibility to resist them. Undoubtedly, if we were to adopt the assumptions of classical determinism, indicating that each event can be explained by the previous event that caused and decided on it, then at the same time the thesis of moral and legal responsibility of man should be rejected, unless the legitimization of responsibility is acknowledged even in the absence of free will.[52]

In the analysis of the issue of responsibility, the issue of the individual dimension dominates. It must not be forgotten, however, that responsibility is usually exercised in the moral community in which responsibility is established and administered, and in the light of the hierarchy of weals in that community, which influences the moral evaluation of a given deed.[53]

The community dimension of responsibility is already visible in what has been mentioned above, namely the relationship of responsibility. If we state that someone is responsible for something, we may also want to find out before whom this responsibility is being actualized. You can be responsible for a specific deed in the sense that you are the person who committed that deed. If, on the other hand, we want to think of responsibility as an opportunity to react to someone's behavior, which is contrary to certain rights or the norms protecting them, it becomes obvious that it is necessary to identify another entity or entities that could demand an appropriate reaction, determine the scope of responsibility, or finally decide on sanctions.

The fact that a person belongs to a community allows him/her to bear responsibility in relation to other subjects. Belonging to the moral community depends on a number of circumstances, which are related precisely to whether a person retains the ability to bear responsibility when they arise. This is not the same as belonging once and for all, whatever the circumstances. Peter F. Strawson believed that belonging to the moral community may be excluded due to hypnosis, brainwashing, loss of cognitive ability, insanity, young age, or any other reason that temporarily or permanently excludes the ability to be a member of the moral community.[54] Thus, in Strawson's opinion, the moral community includes only people with whom we are able to establish a human relationship, and at the same time able to understand the moral evaluation of our own conduct.[55]

In the literature, you can find a number of criteria for assessing membership of a moral community. First, the ability to enter into human relationships is indicated, which consists of the ability to experience feelings and acts of will, such as resentment, gratitude, forgiveness, anger, or love. Second, such a person must be able to participate in the exchange of reasoning.[56] These criteria make up a concept that is referred to as Moral Reasons-Based Theory (MRBT). This consists of two aspects. It verifies the ability to understand and apply certain moral reasoning, which can be interpreted as the ability to reconstruct and apply moral norms. The second aspect of this theory concentrates on the ability of people to control and regulate their own behaviors in the light of these justifications or moral norms.[57]

The above theory seems interesting, but it has a serious drawback, in that it excludes from the moral community people who are mentally ill and unconscious. These cases obviously cause that these people are sometimes excluded from the group of people who are responsible for their own actions. In this narrow sense, one could consider the legitimization of excluding them from the moral community. It would, however, be inappropriate to understand them in such a way as to deprive them of community ties with people who do not suffer from such a lack of ability and who, moreover, have certain moral obligations toward the sick, which stem from a humanity characterized by dignity, but also by belonging to that community. Classical ethics ultimately recognize that the value of the human person does not lie in the acts he or she performs, but in being a person.

Roman Ingarden pointed out that man has a special feature among his characteristics. Despite the obvious pursuit of one's own good, one can also act solely for the good and happiness of other people, even in some cases deciding to sacrifice one's life to save another.[58]

Another characteristic of the human individual is their sense of responsibility for their own deeds, which, in the case of bad deeds, entails feelings of shame and humiliation in connection with certain behaviors, resulting in the need to repent. In some extreme circumstances, it may even happen that a person chooses to be deprived of their life because of the need to save their own honor.[59] Responsibility does not only apply to individual acts performed by the individual but also to the way of life itself and the directions taken by them within it.

A person usually acts for their own or others' benefit. However, human specificity also includes the creation of works and the initiation of processes that do not have a useful dimension. Their function is rather to enrich culture or, as Ingarden puts it, the specifically human world.[60]

This brief description of the individual shows that their predisposition is to be in contact with the world of good. This world does not always have to create the same values, although it would probably be possible to indicate the most permanent ones. Values can change depending on the historical period, a particular civilization, or culture in which a person functions. From the perspective of human nature, the most important thing in this context is that man has a need to have, to know, and to realize values. Establishing a catalogue of these values is therefore basically something secondary.[61] As Ingarden pointed out:

> Without direct and intuitive contact with values, without the joy that this contact gives him, the individual is deeply unhappy. What makes him happy, however, is to realise the values and succumb to their special charm. This is not—at least in the first place—about values that are relative in relation to the needs of life (such as food) or to pleasure (such as health or delight), but about absolute values in their immanent quality, although their realisation depends on the creative strength of man, in a word: moral and aesthetic values.[62]

According to this concept, values are formed by creating the right conditions for them to exist. The law, including criminal law, undoubtedly has an appropriate role to play in this respect. Another quote from Ingarden also refers to the role of law:

> And, particularly, we ourselves transform ourselves under the influence of the works we have created and with which we are in direct and intuitive contact, and—despite our will and our knowledge—we are reborn and transformed by our very effort to remain at the service of values. We enrich ourselves by giving our best strength to produce human reality in general.[63]

Although the author of these words probably did not refer them, at least not directly, to criminal law, they seem to reflect well the human effort to organize reality according to a given value system, even if it is not always a conscious process.

The moral values that make up the axiological reality of our lives must be recognized not only by each person because of their moral needs but also by the legislator, who should shape the solutions he or she adopts in a way that corresponds to these values and takes them into account. Otherwise, there may be a number of difficulties resulting from a misunderstanding of the principles of criminal responsibility, which are contradictory or only to a limited extent consistent with the values recognized in the social community.

THE STRUCTURE OF HUMAN ACTIVITY

It is impossible to write about human responsibility and its permissible scope without referring to what is essential for the ethical legitimization of criminal law, namely the treatment of man in the light of philosophical anthropology. As Tadeusz Styczeń noted:

> The effective realisation of the intention to affirm the addressee requires, therefore, on the part of the affirmer, in addition to good intentions, sufficient knowledge of human nature and adaptation of his actions to it, in particular the knowledge and acceptance of an objective hierarchy of rights, defined by the structure of the human individual.[64]

This is what the whole of ethics is built on, which, in order to value moral behavior of man, needs to learn from philosophical anthropology who man is, what his characteristics are. This regularity takes place regardless of what ethical, and therefore anthropological, direction a given thinker takes. Statements that any ethical considerations are possible insofar as appropriate anthropological arrangements are made cannot be referred to criminal law—to the extent that normative proposals on criminal responsibility are the subject of analysis. Criminal legal constructions are built on certain established anthropological principles. This relationship exists not only because of the outcome of the findings made here so far. This is already the case because of certain aspects of similarity between ethics and criminal law.

If the intention of a person or institution is to value a person's behavior, be it moral or legal, it is impossible not to consider or assume as a premise such a vision of a person that allows him or her to attribute the behavior in question in such a way that he or she can bear responsibility for it. The legitimization of the ethical construction of criminal responsibility can be sought, in the part of general ethics that deals with the issue of man's moral action, including the structure of his deeds, among other things.

The decision-making process, also referred to as the free choice mechanism and the system of execution of the resulting decision, is complex. Mieczysław Krąpiec distinguishes three parts. The first one covers those stages that relate to the intention itself, the second concerns the choice of a particular good, and the third finally indicates the system of execution of the free decision.[65] Not all of these stages are reflected in the criminal law analysis, but it seems worthwhile to present the free choice mechanism in its entirety, while at the same time making some shortcuts in relation to those issues which do not have a particular legal relevance.

The decision-making scheme presented here is based on a philosophical assumption, which is made clear in its first two parts, that man always acts for the sake of some good, and by his very nature wants good. Even if his behavior, objectively speaking, leads to evil, he chooses it because it appears to him as good, even if only superficially. In their choices, aimed at good, the individual ultimately seeks their happiness. They aim at it by striving for various specific goods, which are concrete in everyday life. The concrete good must somehow present itself to the person. In other words, it must be noticed by them and must be enclosed in some kind of judgment, which then presents itself to the will. This is the moment when a given good can become an object of desire. However, before a decision is made to pursue a particular good, there should be a reflection on that good, focusing primarily on considering whether a person should pursue that good.[66] It is also then that reason considers the means necessary to achieve the recognized good. In this context, the acceptance or rejection of such a good and thus the way in which it is achieved is made in terms of will. A practical thought on how to achieve a certain good ends with an act of decision.

The order of execution of a free decision of a human being consists of the order of its execution given to the intellect. The will then moves the human forces necessary to carry out a given act of decision. The next stage is the stage of deriving satisfaction from the decision that has been realized and then already implemented, ending with the fulfillment of the desire that was at the basis of the whole process discussed here. The moral character and the moral evaluation of a given deed is already decided in principle by the decision itself and by its conditions. For this purpose, it is not even necessary to move to the implementation phase. This is different in the case of legal responsibility, where the transition to the implementation of a decision is a condition for being able to bear responsibility, and this implementation may also consist of an omission.

Roman Ingarden, on the other hand, distinguishes other components of the decision-making process: (1) the initial situation to which the act is a response, (2) human behavior, (3) the effect of the behavior, its consequence.[67] Ingarden notes that not all the effects of a human act can be called its creations. An example he uses is jumping into the water to save a drowning man. Leaving the clothes on the shore by a person jumping into the water is some kind of a consequence of undertaking the act of saving another person. At the same time, however, it cannot be regarded as a "work" of rescue or its "creation."[68] The effect of jumping into the water to save another person may be to save them. The action of a human being, defined above as his behavior, must therefore have some peculiar characteristics expressed in a structure typical of him, allowing him to mediate between the initial situation preceding the act and the consequence of that act.

Tadeusz Ślipko proposed the following decision-making schema:[69]

1. To perceive the truth about goodness through reason and to submit to its will. The will corresponds to the desire for that good, which is an expression of man's willingness to do good as such.
2. The court of reason which assesses the good as being willful and achievable. In the will, the intention to achieve a given good is born.
3. The consideration of reason as a consideration of the means necessary or useful to achieve a given good. The will responds by consenting to the chosen measures.
4. Reason determines which of the available means are the most appropriate—it issues a judgment on the choice. The will makes a choice.
5. Reason presents the subject matter of the choice to the decision of the will, resulting in an act of injunction by the will.
6. An injunction of the will is used by the implementing authority for its execution.

In practice, decision-making and implementation do not always go through all these stages, they can be simplified. The strict division into acts of reason and will is usually not reflected in human consciousness, but it is useful not only in philosophical reflection but also in legal reflection. The participation of acts of reason and acts of will constitutes, for example, an important subject of analysis in the context of criminal law issues of the subject matter.

Action consists of two adjacent planes. The first is the multitude of interrelated experiences, and the second is the multitude of bodily and physical activities that lead to changes in the outside world other than those that are these activities themselves.[70] Human bodily movements are to some extent always aware, and thus marked by experience, constituting an answer to some human intention. It is in these experiences that there is a link between the initial situation and human behavior.

Characteristics of the Human Deed and Criteria for Its Evaluation

The axis that links anthropological issues with responsibility, both ethical and criminal, is the human deed.[71] In it, the nature of man is revealed, and at the same time, it is what man can be responsible for. The deed is experienced by a human being, and thus is an object of awareness of the perpetrator of the deed. Man experiences not only his own work but also the values that are realized by this deed, including the resulting good or evil. The deed and its value are expressed in the subjective and personal trait of the human being.[72] An experience of causality, conditioned by the absence of error, only makes it possible to associate a person with a given deed.[73] This allows us to talk about acting in place of "happening," which does not require an experience of awareness.[74] In the realistic concept of philosophical anthropology and ethics presented, unlike in criminal law, an act is understood as a conscious act.[75] As Karol Wojtyla pointed out: "The deed—and therefore the conscious act—we attribute this 'I' as also the conscious perpetrator, and in such an act there is a moment of will, and therefore of freedom, followed by a moment of responsibility of a moral nature. In this way we also enter into the very essence of human subjectivity."[76]

In the conducted experiential analysis of the side of action, R. Ingarden distinguishes three elements that are part of the deed: (a) gaining knowledge of the states of affairs constituting the initial situation; (b) taking a stance toward the intended state of affairs and the initial situation; (c) experiencing the realization of the new state of affairs.[77] Knowledge of the states of affairs should be experienced as a belief in the actual starting situation. We do not usually act in conditions that we believe are delusional. Yes, we may be uncertain as to the validity of our idea of reality, which may justify experimental action. However, this still requires awareness of reality. Usually this is connected with some idea of the production of our action, the result of the effort we undertake. Cognitive experiences can be reflexive acts, nonreflexive experiences of one's own actions, or they can be cognitive acts directed at objects somehow related to a given action.

Apart from learning about the state of things, a person's deed consists in taking a starting position toward that state. This is the aspect of the deed, which Ingarden calls its subjective side.[78] One such attitude may be to desire a given state of affairs, where the following components can be distinguished:

1. Moment of intent—this determines the direction of desire.
2. A desirous attitude with a special moment of content—it is expressed in the phrase "I want (it is to be) that it should be."
3. The intention is to implement a given state of affairs.
4. Undertaking realization, that is, the moment of transforming the intention into action.
5. Proper implementation, still sustained by the desire for the state of affairs.[79]

The distinction between a desirous attitude and an intention which is actually a decision to implement a given state of affairs seems particularly significant for further analysis. It means that it is possible to decide to implement a given state of affairs without a simultaneous desirous attitude. The absence of this attitude may cause indifference to a certain state of affairs. It also seems interesting that, in R. Ingarden's interpretation, the provision is within the scope of the subject's freedom, and the desire is not subject to voluntary decisions.

It is indicated that subjectivity is expressed in the action of something in a person, but it is undoubtedly a subject also when they act. Happening and acting form a certain dynamic unity in the individual, so it is acceptable to juxtapose subjectivity and causality, that is, to talk about the subject of the perpetrator.[80] The individual is both the perpetrator and the subject.

The morality of a human act is conditioned by human freedom. Freedom—as K. Wojtyła pointed out—can be described as "I can – I want – I don't have to."[81] This is where human desire manifests itself, that is, orientation to a certain activity when it is not the result of some kind of coercion. Will, in its essence free, is the power of man as a person. As it was once stated, *persona est sui iuris*, that is, a person possesses himself and is possessed exclusively by himself.[82] This is defined as human self-determination. Everyone has free will in his or her own abilities, but the right conditions are not always in place to allow it to go into the act. Free will is actualized by those who are capable of self-determination. All the factors that take away these abilities from the human being at the same time deprive him of free will, understood not only as an opportunity itself.

Desire, in K. Wojtyła's view, being a manifestation of free will, is an intentional act consisting in choosing a certain good as a goal.[83] If I am aiming for this good, its means, I can, I want, I don't have to. The desire is determined by the choice of a specific object to lead a person to that value. Man thus determines himself in his desire and the resultant action. Wanting is an intentional act which is then passed into an act of settlement.[84] This means nothing else but that the decision, or act of will, is always the result of some desire. An act of will is understood as "directing an active subject, i.e. power, towards an object, i.e. a value, which is wanted as a goal and thus also constitutes an object of aspiration."[85] Human deeds are only those that have the qualities of awareness and voluntariness.[86] Voluntary activity is also the attribute of the human deed which determines the possibility of holding a person responsible for it.[87]

Each decision is preceded by a motivation, understood by K. Wojtyła as something that directs human will to a particular object. Desire is the pursuit of a certain good, which thus becomes a goal.[88] It is pointed out that the goal, also referred to as a motive, is precisely that which releases desire from passivity and prompts the will to start acting.[89]

The act of an individual is therefore preceded by a judgment and is a response to that judgment.[90] The literature proposes two versions of the understanding of action as a response to the judgment of reason: strong and weak. The strong version is based on the following conditions: if there are sufficient reasons for a particular action, a person recognizes it, selects an action in accordance with it, and takes that action.[91] In this version, it is assumed that the entity will address all the reasons for a specific action.[92] In other words, strong arguments in favor of appropriate action should lead people to act in accordance with those arguments. However, it turns out that each of the conditions is both a space of risk and failure. It may happen that a person does not properly recognize the reasons for a certain action. Failure may also occur at the stage of responding to one's own insights. After all, it is possible that a given entity will not decide to take a specific action, despite even discerning the right reasons. Failure can also be about purely reforging the will to do the right thing. The strong version of the understanding of acting as an answer to the judgment of reason is not able to meet the challenges of reality. In complex situations, each of two actions, mutually irreconcilable, may be prompted by the judgment of reason. Professional commitments may suggest that we need to work longer and analyze documents in depth, while at the same time we can recognize the legitimization and need to engage in an important charity event that takes place at the same time. Each of these activities is good in itself. The obvious disadvantage of this concept is basically the deprivation of the will, contrary to reality, of any autonomy. This interpretation resembles the concept of ethical intellectualism attributed to Socrates.

These difficulties have given rise to another version of the understanding of action as responding to the judgment of reason, described as weak. In this view, it is sufficient to take into account some aspects that induce a particular act or omission. It takes into account that in some possible world the subject would behave differently under the influence of a certain state of knowledge.[93] If, as a result of the analysis of a given factual situation, it turns out that none of the reasons could cause any other behavior from a subject, and thus that there is no possible world in which a given person would behave differently, one should consider the existence of a circumstance that excludes the moral responsibility of a given subject. As John M. Fischer and Mark Ravizza point out, "Even an agent who acts against good reasons can be responsive to some reasons."[94] For example, if someone takes the opportunity to go to a match, knowing that someone else will use his absence to rob his house, one can have serious doubts that one can investigate whether his decision was really free.[95] If it was not, the agent should not be morally responsible for his act.

The aforementioned authors proposed another, third, approach to the issue of the structure of human activity, primarily in the area of the relationship between reason and will. The third path to understanding these relationships is described as a modest approach to action understood as responding to the judgment of reason.[96] The weakness of the strong approach has already been described above. The problem with the weak approach is that it does not introduce a kind of causal relationship between the reason for different behavior and that different behavior in a possible world. It does not require, in other words, checking whether it is possible to behave differently in a possible world for that very reason, which indicates the validity of the other behavior. Moreover, it cannot be ignored that the assessment of moral responsibility does not only take into account the mere existence of a reason which, at least in a possible world, becomes the raison d'être for changing or abandoning the behavior. This is because in some cases, it may turn out that it does not change our moral evaluation of an act, if, for example, this reason would be absurd, or would itself be subjected to a critical moral evaluation. What is more, it is not only a matter of determining whether such a reason was possible, which would lead to refraining from a certain action, but whether the perpetrator recognized the whole context of this reason, as well as the hierarchy of values and qualitative relationships between different reasons.[97]

The two basic versions of this theory do not sufficiently take into account the distinction between reason and will, or, as J. M. Fischer and M. Ravizza write, the difference between the ability to know specific causes of action (receptivity) and the ability to react to them by taking action in accordance with them (reactivity).[98] As already noted in this part of the study, reason does not determine the will in such a way that it leaves no room for freedom. It is not without reason that the weakness of the will is often pointed out in the situation of people who know well how to behave in a given situation, and ultimately take a different course of action. The focus of this distinction allows for the conclusion that moral responsibility is possible when the subject is aware of the reasons for taking or not taking a specific action, and there is a possible world where that reason would make the subject act in accordance with it.[99] It should be added that these reasons, which are to be recognized and taken into account, should be of a moral nature, as it is ultimately a question of a moral assessment of an act or omission.

The resulting scope of moral responsibility may be graded, and thus should not be considered on a zero-one basis. A good example is the moral responsibility of children, which appears at some point to a very limited extent, and increases with the child's ability to recognize and formulate moral judgments and act in accordance with them.[100] The concept of a modest approach to action understood as responding to the judgment of reason presented here makes it possible to construct the following pattern of human behavior.[101] All behaviors that may be subject to responsibility that may also be legal in nature must be externalized, and thus rely on some kind of human body movement (action) or lack of movement when the movement should occur (omission).

The movement mentioned above can be either intentional or unintentional.[102] The former are, for example, various kinds of unconditional reflexes, for which, of course, the individual bears no moral responsibility. Intentional movements are divided into two types. The first includes those that are intentional but do not correspond to the causes given by reason. This group includes the movements of people acting in a state of insanity or under the influence of very strong agitation. The second type of intentional movements includes those that constitute a reaction to specific causes indicated by reason. This type of movement is also divided into two more. This is because one can only undertake actions that are in response to reasons other than those of a moral nature. This includes some psychopaths, as well as children. Behaviors that correspond to moral reasons are divided into those that are carried out under duress and those that are free from duress. Duress is understood here as a strong motivational impact but does not exclude the possibility to decide on the reactive measures to be taken. Persons acting in such circumstances cannot be found guilty. Moral responsibility, in turn surely a full responsibility, may concern those who act in response to moral reasons and who are free from duress.

Desire, both for things and directly for the value itself, concerns what is given to a person in the form of some kind of judgment, and so it seems to him somehow rational. The literature on anthropology and ethics points out that reason has to present some content to the will, because it is not capable of cognition in itself. One cannot want something that would somehow be not previously known.[103] The decision-making process therefore combines the aspect of knowledge and the aspect of choice. As M. A. Krąpiec noticed:

> As the culmination of typically human activities, these two directions seem to be at their peak: the power of rational cognition and the power of free desire.

> And they are assigned to each other, they are to be intertwined at the peak of the moment into one act of free human action—into an act of decision, which is a conscious (rational) and voluntary act, that is, a human act as human.[104]

Both of these authorities contribute to each other. Reason is the model cause of acts of will, and will is the causative root of acts of reason.

A person's ability to respond by the will to know good is the basic factor determining his responsibility. This ability, as K. Wojtyla said,

> presupposes truthfulness—a relation to truth, in which the duty as the normative power of truth takes root. It should be this mature form of responding to the values to which responsibility is most closely linked. Responsibility includes something of an obligating reference to values. It outlines the system "I should—I respond": duty—responsibility.[105]

He goes on to emphasize: "Duty determines responsibility, and at the same time responsibility is somehow already present in the constitution of duty."[106] In the case of legal responsibility, which will be discussed later, the obligation is the result of responding to the values expressed by legal norms. The legislator should, however, strive for such a state in which there is no inconsistency between the outcome of this process of duty on the grounds of morality and on the grounds of law.

Factors such as biological processes that remain in the sphere of unconsciousness, emotional attitudes, images, ideas, and judgments may, in certain situations that precede a particular human decision, point to mutually contradictory solutions. Such a state of affairs can usually be realized when someone is experiencing an internal tear, a dilemma, a difficulty in deciding on the right behavior in the given circumstances. In the end, there is usually nothing left to do but to follow that judgment which presents itself to us as the strongest.[107] The strength of a given motive can be determined by very different factors.

Cognitive acts of reason, also referred to in simplified form as acts of consciousness, are which a person knows or predicts at the time of making a decision. Reason is responsible for showing the will of the truth about the good, for presenting its aspects. Will, however, is the deciding factor. Will without indicating reason is not able to determine itself to act because it does not have an image of the potential object of desire.[108] Therefore, when analyzing the act of a man, it is impossible not to take into account both acts of his reason (consciousness) and acts of his will (desire, freedom). Any disruption in these areas, caused by external factors, may significantly influence the evaluation of a given decision and in some cases even decide to take away its conscious and free character. The act of choice is necessary in order for an act to be considered as a moral act, and thus as one that can be subject to moral and, consequently, legal evaluation.[109]

In turn, an act of will can be simple or complex. A simple act of will is revealed when a certain motivation causes the will to be presented to only one object. In other words, in a simple act of will, only one good is visible. Many more problems are related to complex acts, in which a person decides by choosing, even stuck in a multifaceted motivational process. The decision is then preceded by an analysis of the motives. Each of them is associated with some value that can be addressed by human will. K. Wojtyla describes the choice of will as "leaving other objects or other possible values to one object, one value. It is also an offset of other potential desires to the current one."[110] Coming back to the analyses of freedom, one can say that they who retain the possibility of choice are free. It follows that the decision-making process leading to a certain behavior is in fact a transition from a state of determination to self-determination. By determination, one should understand the willingness to want one of the objects, not yet specified. Motivation is what determines and allows self-determination.[111] It is also worth noting that motivation, or rather the related state of human consciousness, is essential in the moral evaluation of a human act. If someone is convinced that he or she is encouraging his or her loved one to swallow a medicine, he or she is not committing a reprehensible act, even if it turns out that—as a result of a third party—a poison tablet was to be found in the box instead of a medicine.

There is still the problem of omission as an act to be discussed. R. Ingarden's considerations on ethical failure to act indicate an important element of intent in the responsibility for failure to act. In his opinion, only an omission that is the realization of an intention can be considered an act. If, on the other hand, the failure to act was due to forgetting or another reason that cannot be interpreted as a form of intent on the part of the perpetrator, it does not constitute an act, which makes it difficult to recognize that reason as the basis for responsibility.[112] However, this is not a dominant position in ethics.

Saint Thomas Aquinas addressed the issue of the difference between doing and not doing on the grounds of sin, but he did so in a way that was suitable for transferring his conclusions to the grounds of ethics. The author pointed out the material genre difference between doing and not doing, but at the same time, he pointed out that in formal terms

> there is no genre difference between these sins, because they are aimed at the same goal and come from the same motive. A miserly person, for example, in order to collect money, takes it away from others and does not give what he should give. Likewise, a glutton, to feed his gluttony, overdoes it and does not keep the prescribed fasts. Similarly with other sins. For always denial is based

on some kind of claim, which is in a way a reason for denial. Therefore in nature for the same reason fire warms and does not cool.[113]

Thus, responsibility becomes possible both for action and for omission. Material genre diversity does not affect the moral evaluation of the omission itself. As the translator of the passage of the *Summa Theologiae* remarked, the neglect of the good that should be realized and the realization of the opposite evil usually comes from the same motive.[114]

Omission, like action, can cause negative moral judgments.[115] Evil caused by action and omission can be qualitatively equally serious. The specificity of omission, that is, failure to act, makes it much more difficult to grasp within the framework of responsibility. From the perspective of an external observer, the action can be seen relatively easily. Noting someone's failure to act is possible only in connection with establishing additional premises.[116] The basis is, of course, to determine the duty to act. Another premise is the possibility of action and prevention of certain effects. In other words, where a person is unable to act effectively under given circumstances, he cannot be held responsible for the omission.[117] If, while strolling by the sea, we notice a drowning man, knowing that we can't swim, we won't be responsible for not jumping into the water to save him. It is our responsibility to call for help, if possible, by telephone or by calling other people capable of providing direct assistance. The prerequisites for responsibility for an omission also include determining whether the entity was able to predict that the act of omission would result in bad consequences.

In order to determine the scope of responsibility for omissions, taking into account the related moral intuitions, it is worth referring to the case study in which an outstanding neurologist, with the help of technologies available to him, has the possibility of interfering in the decision-making processes of subject A, which subject A himself does not know.[118] Imagine that it is subject A walking along the coastline. This neurologist knows this, and for a reason he only knows, he decides that he will influence the decision-making process of subject A in such a way that he will not help a person who might need it. Subject A notices a drowning person during the walk. However, because he is in a hurry to meet someone, he decides—alone, without the intervention of the neurologist—not to help. Although subject A is not in a position—which he is unaware of—to provide assistance, the majority who wonder about the assessment of his behavior probably have no doubt that he should bear responsibility for the failure to act. It is true that a given effect would have been unavoidable anyway, but the omissioner undoubtedly exercised executive control over his conduct and chose not to act within this control.

When analyzing the problem of responsibility for omissions, it is worth recalling the requirement of executive control, which has already been pointed out above as an important premise of responsibility. It will be met if the criteria resulting from the theory of a modest approach to rational action in response to a judgment of reason allow it. If there is a possible world in which a person would behave differently, taking into account the circumstances known to him, we can speak of responsibility. Within the framework of these circumstances, it must of course be considered whether the entity had any obligation at all to take the action whose omission we wish to attribute to him.

There are other possible problems in assessing responsibility for failure to act. If the effect that the omitted action was supposed to prevent is not achieved anyway, even if it is not due to an accident or an act of natural forces, the question of the possibility of attributing responsibility will still be relevant, not so much for the effect itself as for the omission itself.[119]

An important element of consideration on the responsibility of man for his actions, conducted on the grounds of ethics, should be the issue of evaluating the act. Responsibility involves a moral evaluation of the deed, the recognition of it as a good or bad deed. Above all, we think of responsibility when an act is considered reprehensible. The possibility of establishing such an assessment requires appropriate premises. This is not just a detailed standard, indicating a specific way of dealing with a given good. This is, of course, a very important element in the process of evaluating the act. However, this would not have been possible without identifying the aspects of the human act that need to be taken into account and without which it would not have been possible to establish a breach of the norm. The assessment of the deed, as it is indicated in classical terms, should take into account: the object of the deed, the intention accompanying the deed, and the circumstances of the deed.[120]

It may be problematic to establish the relationship between the object of the deed and the aim of the actor, in terms of moral evaluation of the deed. At least three solutions are possible. The first would assume that the subject matter of the action has a more general scope, overarching the action's objective.[121] It is also possible to adopt the opposite reasoning, attributing an overriding character to the aim of the act.[122] The contradiction between these concepts seems to be reduced in the following manner:

> Where an object is not itself related to the objective, the genre difference that relates to the object does not itself determine the genre resulting from the objective, nor vice versa. Thus, one of these genres is not subordinate to the other, but the moral act falls under the two genres separately. For example, we say that someone who steals, in order to commit adultery, commits double evil in one action.[123]

However, the concept of dual-genre membership raises other doubts. These appear when the object and purpose deserve different moral judgments, for example, the acceptance of a financial benefit in order to use the funds thus obtained to save another person's life.[124] It can be assumed, therefore, that in addition to the deeds that are generally good and generally bad, there are also deeds that are partly good and partly bad. For it does not seem reasonable to assume that any element of evil immediately causes a whole evil. Włodzimierz Galewicz proposes to distinguish between the evil of moral imperfection and the evil of moral inadmissibility. The category of evil moral imperfection presupposes the existence of moral evil in some aspect of an act, and this determines not so much the evil of the whole act, as about its moral imperfection. The category of evil moral inadmissibility should rather be understood as determining that any element of moral evil decides about evil and inadmissibility of the entire act as such.[125] Actions may be evil because of their abstract subject matter, but they are nevertheless acceptable—and therefore good—in specific circumstances.[126] It should also be remembered that apart from good and bad deeds, there are also morally neutral deeds.[127] The moral evaluation of an act is determined both by its object and the intention accompanying the act and the circumstances of the act. It is only when all these aspects are taken into account that it is possible to determine whether an act, understood as the result of the interaction of reason and will, is good, bad, or morally neutral.[128] Ethics also distinguish between the moral goodness of an act and the moral rightness of an act. Moral rightness can be spoken of in the light of the object and circumstances of a given act. The recognition of a rightful act as a good deed is made after considering the intentions of the perpetrator.[129]

The Effects of a Deed and the Problem of Responsibility

Until now, the considerations have been conducted primarily around the responsibility for action or omission, and thus for human behavior. However, it cannot be overlooked that moral judgments are sometimes formulated under the influence of knowledge of the effects that have been caused by a deed. In some cases, yes, we do attribute responsibility solely for the act or omission, but in others, the consequences of that act or omission will determine the final judgment. This state of affairs makes it necessary to consider the prerequisites for responsibility for the effect and the extent to which the effect can be linked to a deed or omission by a given entity.

Responsibility for the effect is closely linked to the responsibility for the deed or omission that caused the effect. The imputation of responsibility will not always even be precluded by a finding that in some cases the effect would also occur if the perpetrator had refrained from his action or carried out a rejected action. Responsibility in such cases depends on whether a given effect can be linked to the behavior of the perpetrator, for which he can be held responsible. This problem can be illustrated with the help of two factual states.[130]

In the first, subject A intends to launch a rocket toward a big city. His goal is to cause a major disaster, kill many people, and destroy property. In this state of affairs, however, we also know that even if subject A does not decide to launch the rocket, it will be done by subject B, who is carefully watching the conduct of subject A. If subject A launches the rocket and causes the catastrophe described above, in principle, we will have no doubt concerning whether he can be held responsible, even knowing the intentions of subject B.

In the second state of affairs, a driver is driving a train. During the journey, the brakes fail. If the failure was not caused by the driver, he will not be held responsible for the consequences of having to brake the train in an emergency or, in the absence of appropriate emergency procedures, for an accident. The driver's responsibility could only be considered if it was the driver who contributed to the brake failure or if he reacted inappropriately to that failure.

In this context, the view that responsibility for the effects requires a prior determination of responsibility for the behavior, and then verification that the specific effects were caused by the behavior under consideration, seems justified. The authors already cited, J. M. Fischer and M. Ravizza, when analyzing the attribution of responsibility, refer to the theory of the modest approach to action understood as responding to the judgment of reason, indicating that in the case of responsibility for the effect, it is necessary to distinguish two stages of reasoning. This is because not only should the process leading to a given behavior be a result of such a mechanism but also what happens after a given behavior is finished. The analysis of these authors' proposals leads to the conclusion that there must be a causal relationship between the deed of the subject and the effect for which the responsibility should be linked.[131] They point to the need to compare two possible worlds, which differ only in the fact that in one subject A commits his act and in the other not. All other circumstances and conditions are the same. Thus, if in the former world, the effect under consideration occurs, and in the latter not, it is possible to link this effect to the act of subject A. It is also necessary to determine whether this effect is a consequence of a violation of a moral norm by a given subject. If an entity acted within the limits of the norm, and thus their behavior was assessed positively or at least as neutral, it seems unjustified to attribute responsibility, understood negatively, for a given effect, to him. The responsibility for the effect is also conditional on whether the entity could have foreseen that their behavior would produce a certain effect.[132]

In ethics, especially in its classical version, a distinction is made between the natural effect and the side effect of a human deed. The natural effect, also referred to as "purpose of the deed" or "subject of the deed," is covered by an intention accompanying the deed or by its internal purpose. The intention to carry out a given action is equivalent to the intention to cause a certain effect. Side effects are not covered by this intention but can be realized by the external factor system in the circumstances.[133] A side effect may but need not be covered by the agent's goal.[134] The collateral nature of the effect may be the result of a specific link between the externalities of a given act and the act itself. The following types of relationship that may cause a side effect can be indicated following T. Ślipko:

1. the convergence of two or more causes, for example, a person rushing to the rescue of someone becomes a victim of the same attacker himself;
2. the direct or indirect consequence of two (or more) causes, for example, a person cuts down a tree which then crushes him and he dies (direct consequence); a person cuts down a tree which falls on the road and somebody else, while going down that road, crashes into that tree and dies as a result of the injuries suffered.[135]

A side effect, in the strict sense, occurs when it is caused by a cause external to the perpetrator of the principal act which is covered by natural effect. A person can respond to an expected side effect in two ways. First, he can cover it with his desire.[136] He can also, in his attitude of will, turn only toward the natural effect, while the side effect can only be tolerated.[137]

It is indicated that classifying a given effect as a side effect transfers the moral evaluation of a given action to the plane of another effect, which is qualified as a natural effect, covered by the intention. According to Barbara Chyrowicz, the occurrence of a side effect in an action should not be a reason for moral dilemmas, but it may be a reason for a decision to reject a given action due to the fact that another action, not causing such side effects, is better.[138] It appears that when an agent has a choice between two courses of action, one of which may cause a negative side effect, it can be considered that he should opt for the course of action that does not cause the side effect.

In the literature, there is also a random effect distinguished. This is characterized by the fact that its relationship with the agent's act is only causal. A random effect is not intended or anticipated by the agent. In anticipation, there is a major difference between random and side effects. As indicated above, the side effect, unlike the random effect, is predicted by the perpetrator. The problem of the random effect is nowadays discussed in the context of the moral luck issue, which will be addressed later in this book.[139]

The distinction between natural and side effects involves a distinction between deeds that are acts of direct intention and acts of indirect intention. An act of direct intention is understood to mean "any conscious act in which a person intends a specific object in itself, that is to say, independently of any ad hoc arrangement of external factors, on the basis that it is either the natural effect of the act, or a direct external effect, or the object of a specific intention on the part of the acting person, even though it is only a side effect in the structure of the act."[140] An act of indirect intent is understood to mean "any conscious act in which a person knows that, through the interaction of an external cause, another side effect, no longer intended by him, but only permitted and tolerated by valid reasons, is connected with a specific action and its natural effect, which he directly intends to achieve."[141]

It is noted that there is another group of deeds which do not directly qualify for either of the two previously mentioned. This is because such a state of facts may appear in which someone plans an action and predicts that the consequence of a given action may be some bad consequences, for example, someone leads a social life until late at night, knowing that this may result in sleeping in for work. For such acts, it is proposed to include them in the framework of a direct intention, provided that they have already become apparent at the stage of the original intention.

In classical ethics, another distinction is also made, namely, three types of intentional acts: current, virtual, and habitual. The concept of an intended act corresponds best to the intended act currently. The performance of the activity is accompanied in such a case by an awareness of the intention. In the case of virtual intentional acts, it is indicated that the intention is at the beginning of the act, but it is not realized when subsequent acts, for example, frequently repeated acts, are carried out as a result of a certain routine.[142] Habitual intention is understood in ethics as a decision made in the past, which is no longer remembered by the subject, so it no longer affects their actions. However, it is mentioned because, according to T. Ślipko, due to the fact that it exists and has not been called off, it can have some effects.[143]

It is also impossible not to discuss the issue of double effect here. This principle is derived from the concept of necessary defense proposed by St. Thomas Aquinas. When asked whether it is possible to kill a man in his own defense, he answers in the affirmative, explaining that the same action can have two effects, one intentional and the other unintentional: "Nothing hinders one act from having two effects, only one of which is intended, while the other is beside the intention. Now moral acts take their species according to what is intended, and not according to what is beside the intention, since this is accidental as explained above"[144] Next, the author points out the prerequisites for the admissibility of necessary defense, which are also prerequisites for the principle of double effect, because it is on this figure that the whole structure of necessary defense is based. Deeds performed with good intentions should be commensurate with the goal. If, therefore, the force used to repel an attack is disproportionate, it can be assumed that the person invoking the necessary defense is not defending themselves at all but, on the contrary, is attacking. Commensurality is not the only indication of the boundary of necessary defense. The intention of defending oneself is very important in this concept. According to Thomas Aquinas,

> but as it is unlawful to take a man's life, except for the public authority acting for the common good, as stated above, it is not lawful for a man to intend killing a man in self-defense, except for such as have public authority, who while intending to kill a man in self-defense, refer this to the public good, as in the case of a soldier fighting against the foe, and in the minister of the judge struggling with robbers, although even these sin if they be moved by private animosity.[145]

On this basis, four conditions for the principle of double effect were developed:[146]

1. an act should not be objectively morally evil,
2. the intention of the actor should be good,
3. the good result should be at least as direct as the bad result, and
4. a relatively serious rationale for action is required.

Taking into account the need to adapt the means to the end, as is apparent from the above-mentioned passage of Thomas's statement, allows the conditions of double effect to be reduced to three:[147]

1. the fairness of the measure,
2. the goodness of the purpose, and
3. the proportion of the means in relation to the end.

Coming back to the starting point for the principle of double effect, that is, the approach to necessary defense, it is worth noting that the content of an intention, that is, the goal of the actor, cannot be to kill the aggressor.[148] The consequence of the death of the aggressor is *praeter intentionem.*[149] Although this effect is not intended, it does not mean that it was not covered by the consciousness of the actor. This does not mean, of course, that the defender does not foresee the possibility of killing the aggressor. It is not difficult to predict that you will kill someone if you use a knife or firearm to defend yourself. The mere fact of foreseeing does not necessarily mean that its subject is covered by the intention. At the same time, an act *praeter intentionem* should not be understood as behavior *per accidens*, that is, as a result of an unexpected accident.[150]

In view of the above, it must be assumed that the mere awareness, that is, the predictability of a reprehensible effect—predictable but unintended—does not yet result in behavior being regarded as wrong. It is worth noting that the principle of double effect in Thomistic and neo-Thomistic interpretations, as well as contemporary advocates, is defended against accusations of being assigned to the group of principles resulting from consequentialism. As B. Chyrowicz emphasizes, the category *indirectum* can only be applied to such situations when the means chosen to achieve an end are directed toward the good of a person, that is, they emphasize his/her value. Undoubted awareness of the likelihood of bad consequences does not mean that they are intended as the objective of the actor. The condition for the final positive assessment of subject's performance is the proportionality of the chosen measure and its fairness, as mentioned earlier. Therefore, there can be no intention to have a bad effect but only to tolerate or allow it.[151]

The principle of double effect has met with wide interest in the Anglo-Saxon literature, especially, as it is pointed out, because of its potential to resolve various moral dilemmas.[152] At this point, it is worth recalling the concept that Philippa Foot proposed in the context of the considerations on the principle of double effect. She introduced a division of human acts into those of action and those of admission, which does not overlap with the division into action and omission. Admission refers to a sequence of events that have already begun; the subject could change their course, but does not do so, and can be considered to be admitting them. Omission, on the other hand, is abstention from action, whereas admission may not only be passive but also active in some sense.[153]

Another important problem raised in the context of this principle is the so-called proximity problem, which comes down to distinguishing between intention and expectancy.[154] As noted earlier, St. Thomas claimed that it was ethically acceptable to undertake a defense that would result in the death of the attacker, but it is not acceptable to undertake a defense in conjunction with the intention of killing the attacker. At the same time, the defender, having knowledge of the causal course, can expect his resistance to kill the attacker. The key to understanding this subtle difference is the division between intention and expectancy. Thomas A. Cavanaugh proposes the following approach to the differences between something that is intended and something that is expected and is a causal consequence of what someone intended:

1. intention, which is a voluntary commitment to an action plan, is a reason for action, or even forces it;
2. intention causes consideration and subsequent intentions related to the expected effect, but not anticipation;
3. The intention to use certain measures is the result of prior consideration of the goal to be achieved and the necessary measures, whereas such a complex process is not linked to expectancy;
4. Intent is a manifestation of practical reason, while expectancy of theoretical reason— this means that intent is verified in terms of success or failure, while expectancy is verified in terms of truth or falsehood;

5. intention, in a way, defines the act being committed, even allows it to be named, while the fact of expectancy does not affect the definition of the act.[155]

It is a question of whether a given means was intended to have a good or bad effect. Recognition of the subject's intentions is possible by observing the course of action. In the case of defense, if someone uses blows beyond the need to defend, he stops defending himself and starts attacking.[156] In such a case, it can be assumed that the intention was to have a bad effect.

The principle of double effect has not only ethical but also criminal law potential. Indeed, if one assumes, as is justified from the perspective of the ethical legitimacy of criminal law, that the recognition of a given deed, or type of deed, as morally good should at least lead to consideration of the legitimacy of their criminal law sanction, then behaviors justified in the light of the principle of double effect could be exempted from such a sanction.[157]

Exclusion of Responsibility for a Deed

The issue of free will as a condition for committing a deed by a human being who can be the subject of responsibility is also revealed in an interesting aspect, when situations excluding it are indicated. A rational and free act is only one in which the will is not constrained by external factors.[158] Voluntary activity cannot be spoken of in situations of coercion or in cases of unconsciousness.[159] In the literature, it is even noted that these conditions, also known as negative conditions of responsibility, are universal and thus apply to all possible situations in which there is the question of responsibility.[160] It is worth noting at this point that external factors that negatively influence the voluntariness of an act will not always lead to its complete exclusion, but to its limitation.[161] Also, the limitation of voluntariness undoubtedly influences the moral evaluation of a given act, in a different degree to its complete exclusion.

The literature distinguishes between current and habitual obstacles to the voluntariness of the human deed.[162] Current obstacles are understood as those which appear at a certain point in time, occur for some time, and are transient. It is indicated that these include compulsion, ignorance, and feelings, and among them especially the feeling of fear, as particularly paralyzing mental faculties.[163] On the other hand, habitual obstacles are those which permanently accompany a given person and are an element of his psychophysical structure. These include mental illness, mental disability, false opinions, and addictions.[164]

In his *Nicomachaean Ethics*, Aristotle presented the following understanding of compulsion: "Forced is what the cause is outside the subject, and is such that the one who is the subject or object of a given action, does not contribute to it at all, e.g. if somebody has been carried somewhere by the wind, or people in whose power it lies."[165] The premise of coercion is that the cause of the coercion should be entirely outside the agent. Nor can this entity contribute in any way to the appearance of this coercion.[166] It is also particularly important, which does not resonate directly from the cited fragment of Aristotle's work, that coercion does not exist if the desired behavior is in accordance with the will of the subject affected by this external factor. This is how St. Thomas Aquinas clarified the problem: "In like manner an act is said to be voluntary in two ways. First, in regard to action, for instance, when one wishes to be passive to another. Hence when action is brought to bear on something, by an extrinsic agent, as long as the will to suffer that action remains in the passive subject, there is not violence simply: for although the patient does nothing by way of action, he does something by being willing to suffer."[167] The coercion causes that not only is the goal imposed from the outside but also its realization is forced by external factors.[168] Man is then an enslaved instrument of action, not an autonomous entity whose action can be the object of responsibility. Acts imposed by external factors may not at the same time be voluntary. After all, we cannot order voluntary desire.

The above does not mean that Aristotle did not notice other possibilities of influencing human will, which are not of the nature of physical coercion, and thus similar to what is sometimes called fear.[169] However, he was not necessarily prepared to accept that, like physical coercion, they exclude voluntariness. This is the case when coercion is not so much about forcing a certain activity or passivity but rather about taking the very act of choice. The philosopher gave two examples:

> But with regard to the things that are done from fear of greater evils or for some noble object (e.g. if a tyrant were to order one to do something base, having one's parents and children in his power, and if one did the action they were to be saved, but otherwise would be put to death), it may be debated whether such actions are involuntary or voluntary. Something of the sort happens also with regard to the throwing of goods overboard in a storm.[170]

Ultimately, however, he concludes that these acts tend to come closer to a category of willful acts, that is, voluntary acts. This is because the decision is taken by the agent himself, acting obviously under certain conditions, which may even consist of a threat from an external agent or a risk related to natural forces.[171] This can be seen well with an example. If an attacker demands valuables from us, threatening to harm us, then by choosing to give him these things we do not want it in the sense that we would prefer not to give him the valuables. A choice that tends to protect oneself from harm, for example, from serious damage to one's health, at the cost of giving the attacker our own precious objects, is our own choice, and thus an act of desire. It can therefore be said to be, after all, more voluntary than involuntary.[172]

Interesting, also from the perspective of criminal law, are Aristotle's reflections on coercion caused by an intrinsic cause, namely, by extremely strong emotions. In his reflections, it turns out that compulsive actions are sometimes performed under emotional duress.[173] It seems that this view was not shared by Aquinas, who distinguished between fear, which can be a sign of compulsion, and desire, also caused by violent and strong emotions. An individual who is in fear may commit an act against their own will, while desire causes a redirection of the human will which excludes the possibility of establishing the existence of external coercion.[174]

The involuntariness of an act can also be led to by unconsciousness or lack of knowledge about a given subject.[175] A person is the cause *per se* of a given action, if it corresponds to their consciousness according to the state immediately preceding the action. Only in such a situation may they bear responsibility.[176] However, not every lack of knowledge should lead to the exclusion of responsibility for a given act. In this context, one can speak of culpable and unintentional or insurmountable and surmountable ignorance. Ignorance will not lead to the exclusion of responsibility for an act when it is culpable, that is, when its cause lies with the perpetrator himself.

Unintentional ignorance is divided in turn into physical and moral unintentional ignorance. We are dealing with the first kind of unintentionality when there is no reasonable suspicion in the perpetrator's mind that he may be wrong. Moral unintentionality, on the other hand, occurs when the perpetrator has a well-founded fear that he may be mistaken, but to confirm this would require extremely great difficulties to be overcome.[177] Ignorance that is unintentional or excusable causes man to act involuntarily to the extent determined by this ignorance.

Interestingly, Aristotle also includes in the category of unjustified ignorance cases of acts committed by drunken people. He said:

> but the term 'involuntary' tends to be used not if a man is ignorant of what is to his advantage- for it is not mistaken purpose that causes involuntary action (it leads rather to wickedness), nor ignorance of the universal (for that men are blamed), but ignorance of particulars, i.e. of the circumstances of the action and the objects with which it is concerned. For it is on these that both pity and pardon depend, since the person who is ignorant of any of these acts involuntarily..[178]

Such ignorance, which he committed through his own fault, will not relieve an individual of their responsibility. In some cases, one can even speak of voluntary and deliberate ignorance. In other, similarly reprehensible cases, ignorance is not so much desired as the result of omissions that a man could and should have prevented.[179] They can be caused by some bad habit or negligence in gaining knowledge. Thomas Aquinas also includes in the latter the ignorance of universal law, which everyone should know.[180]

An important factor indicating that an act was a consequence of an error in a given case is also the way the perpetrator reacts when he realizes his error. An apology, regret, repentance, or attempt to remedy possible damage may be evidence of the involuntary nature of the act.[181] An absence of similar reactions may indicate that the perpetrator would have committed a given act also if their action were free from error. In each of the cases indicated here, there is a certain degree of involuntary activity, but not so serious as to determine the involuntary nature of the whole act as such, that is, the release of the person concerned from guilt.[182]

The abovementioned problem was described by Thomas Aquinas as follows:

> Ignorance is "antecedent" to the act of the will, when it is not voluntary, and yet is the cause of man's willing what he would not will otherwise. Thus a man may be ignorant of some circumstance of his act, which he was not bound to know, the result being that he does that which he would not do, if he knew of that circumstance.[183]

The author illustrates this problem with the example of a man who wants to kill his enemy, but kills him unconsciously, believing that he is killing a deer.[184] Notwithstanding some reservations regarding the example itself, only qualified ignorance, that is, ignorance that is not encumbered by one of the forms of culpability set out above, can lead to the agent being discharged from responsibility. St. Thomas indicates that the basis for the exclusion of responsibility may be insurmountable ignorance and ignorance of something that the subject is not obliged to know.[185]

Aristotle believed that the cause of involuntary action could only be due to ignorance of individual circumstances:

> But of what he is doing a man might be ignorant, as for instance people say 'it slipped out of their mouths as they were speaking', or 'they did not know it was a secret', as Aeschylus said of the mysteries, or a man might say he 'let it go off when he merely wanted to show its working', as the man did with the catapult. Again, one might think one's son was an enemy, as Merope did, or that a pointed spear had a button on it, or that a stone was pumicestone; or one might give a man a draught to save him, and really kill him; or one might want to touch a man, as people do in sparring, and really wound him. The ignorance may relate, then, to any of these things, i.e. of the circumstances of the action, and the man who was ignorant of any of these is thought to have acted involuntarily,

and especially if he was ignorant on the most important points; and these are thought to be the circumstances of the action and its end. Further, the doing of an act that is called involuntary in virtue of ignorance of this sort must be painful and involve repentance.[186]

Aristotle included the following aspects in the circumstances of the act: who acts, what does he do, in relation to what or in what, by using what, and why. It follows from the passage quoted above that not all of these circumstances may be subject to ignorance.[187] A slightly different catalogue of circumstances can be found in St. Thomas Aquinas.[188] He referred to circumstances previously indicated by Cicero: who, what, where, with what help, why, how, and when.[189]

One of the habitual obstacles, as indicated above, is to remain in the wrong opinion. The habitual nature of this obstacle means that it is permanent, that is, resulting from a long educational process, one's own negligence, or the influence of the environment on the convictions and opinions of the perpetrator. The source of these false opinions may be, for example, the influence of various false ideologies.[190] An obstacle in the moral action having a habitual dimension is also inborn inclinations and behavior under the influence of an addiction. Addictions are understood here as morally negative habits. In the context of addictions, it is very important to distinguish between awareness and unconsciousness of reaching a certain state before the behavior taken under the influence of an addiction, for example, awareness of alcohol consumption and its consequences. In each of these cases, the intelligibility of the act performed in a state of addiction may be limited or even excluded. However, in the case of deliberately moving into a particular state, the rationality of the acts which led the person to the addiction is not in doubt. This rationality may be a sufficient basis for responsibility for an act performed under the influence of addiction. Habitual obstacles also include mental illness and mental handicap.

The findings so far can be well summed up with the statement formulated by T. Ślipko:

> As a result of the existence of many, and extremely varied, obstacles that violate the freedom of this activity, man is the ethical perpetrator of only a certain part of the acts he commits, and of these, a considerable amount of which he performs only imperfectly, partially. It cannot be said that in all manifestations of his activity he is subject to certain determinations. On the other hand, however, it is obvious that the psychophysical constitution of his nature makes him dependent on a whole range of factors that affect the spiritual side of his actions, often eliminating or at least limiting it to some extent. Worse still, many of these factors are invisible to the outside world, as a result of which

the restriction of the freedom of the act can easily escape the attention of the outside observer. All in all, establishing the degree of freedom of an act is not straightforward. The awareness of the complex nature of this side of human action forces the judgements to be very careful.[191]

Responsibility and Its Principles

The Necessary Prerequisites for Human Responsibility

We cannot assign responsibility to everyone. Only those who have committed an act in the right state of consciousness, capable of understanding the situation, can be drawn to it.[192] We only have the right to hold accountable the one who did something.[193] Depending on the understanding of the act, or not, an omission should be treated separately as an independent basis for responsibility. Roman Ingarden linked the possibility of bearing responsibility with the personal status of a person. He pointed out that a person is "the source point of possible decisions based on an understanding of the situation taken in terms of values, and at the same time is also capable of implementing what he or she has decided."[194] In another work, the author points out that an activity, if it is to undergo moral evaluation, requires "the conscious participation of the subject through appropriate cognitive acts, by giving cognitive impulses to certain activities and consciously sustaining the course of this realisation."[195] The personal dimension of man is therefore manifested in the fact that he is capable of making decisions and implementing them. The participation of the conscious subject is a necessary condition for recognizing that behavior may be subject to moral evaluation at all. This participation must be a part of the proceedings. For human behavior is subject to assessment. If there is no behavior, there is no subject of valuation at the same time.[196] Lack of behavior should also be understood here as lack of omission.

An entity, in order to be responsible for its own behavior, must meet three basic conditions: the right intellectual capacity, the right understanding, and the ability to control.[197] The right intellectual ability is understood to be a level of perception and reception of reality that makes it possible to understand the allegations and assess their appropriateness. Moreover, when punished, the perpetrator should retain the ability to understand that the punishment is a reaction to a specific act for which he or she is responsible. Two objective criteria influence the ability discussed here: the age and mental state of the perpetrator. Intellectual ability closely corresponds to another premise of the description of the responsible entity, namely, an appropriate understanding of the situation. However, this is not so much about the very abstract ability to understand but about understanding in the circumstances of a particular case. It is not enough to believe that the perpetrator knew that in a certain way, it was possible to kill a human being, and he understood the moral weight of such an act. This premise will not be met if, in a specific factual situation, the perpetrator was not aware that he was killing a person. A problem can also occur when, in the circumstances of a particular case, he or she did not know that his deed was wrong.[198] The ability to understand and apply certain moral norms means to have an in-depth understanding of the content of a certain moral norm, of the various possibilities for its application, as well as an understanding of the situations leading to a violation of that norm. Therefore, it is not only a matter of theoretical knowledge of a given norm and its justifications, but also of awareness of its practical aspects, that is, the ability to translate it into everyday life.

The third premise concerns the ability to control your own behavior. It is undoubtedly a complex requirement that the moral entity retains the ability to regulate and control their own behavior. It consists of:

1. the ability to critically assess one's own inclinations and drives and evaluate them in the light of moral justifications;
2. the ability to make decisions based on that critical assessment; and
3. the ability to undertake the behaviors resulting from such a decision.[199]

There are two types of control: guidance control and regulative control.[200] Guidance control takes place when we direct our actions and influence other events, for example, when we decide to steer a car right rather than left. Regulative control is the possibility of alternative behavior in a given situation. Regulative control therefore refers to the possibilities offered by guidance control.[201] The differences between these types of control can be seen well in practical driving lessons. The learner is instructed to turn left at the nearest intersection. The instructor assumes that if the learner tries to go in another direction, for example, by mistake or for any other reason, he will press his brake pedal and prevent this from happening. The leaner has guidance control but is deprived of regulatory control because it is not possible for him/her to turn right instead of left.[202] It is pointed out that guidance control is already a sufficient condition for responsibility. It is worth noting that the instructor will not be responsible for the act of turning left alone, as it is not an act committed by them. However, this does not mean that the exercise of regulatory control, even in isolation from guidance control, cannot involve any responsibility. The fact is that it was the instructor who ordered the left turn. It is also possible to attribute responsibility for failure to comply if he does not prevent a turn and should prevent it.

Deprivation of someone's guidance control results in exclusion of their responsibility. If a person acts as a result of an illness that excludes the ability to control behavior is subject to the incapacitating action of natural forces or under the influence of other circumstances that exclude the ability to guide one's own behavior, one cannot be held responsible for behavior committed in a given state. Such circumstances, as well as coercion and error, undermine the very existence of awareness and voluntariness, as discussed below.

The assumption that responsibility is linked to the possibility of exercising control was the basis of the so-called Principle of Alternative Possibilities (PAP). This is formulated as follows: A person is morally responsible for what they have done only if they could have done otherwise.[203] This formula, which corresponds to moral intuitions, has also met with some reservations. There is no doubt that it always leads to a correct conclusion whenever the circumstances preventing the choice of alternative behavior coincide with those leading to the commission of a specific act. This happens, for example, through coercion. However, it has been pointed out that there are imaginable situations in which these circumstances vary. This can be the case when a person voluntarily undertakes an action but does not know that he cannot withdraw from it, even if he wanted to.[204]

It seems, however, that the issue of the alternative possibility has been reduced in an exaggerated way to casuistry, typical of current analytical philosophy.[205] The problem of responsibility can be solved in such situations by taking into account a subjective factor, which, after all, plays an important role in the issue of responsibility. For it seems that when a perpetrator takes a specific action in the awareness that he does not have to take it, and yet directs his will toward a specific goal, it should be possible to assign responsibility to him. After all, it is not anyone else, but the entity in question that decided to act in such a case.

Roman Ingarden points out that an act can be considered as a personal one if it comes directly from the center of a given person's "I," has its origin there and there is also the center for controlling and directing the deed. Mastery, guidance, and thus this overwhelming influence on the deed can come from two possibilities. The first one has its origin in the context external to the perpetrator of the deed or at least to the center of his "I." It is sufficient that the offender agrees on what happened in him due to all kinds of external circumstances, approves it, even though it does not necessarily correspond to the inner constitution of a given individual.[206] The second originates entirely in the "I" of the individual who performs a given action in a strict sense as his own. Such an act is not subject to any circumstances external to the individual.

The possibilities presented above seem to be primarily examples, which means that they should not always be searched for in exactly this form in the decision-making reality of man. Especially the latter model, free of any external conditions, seems to be somewhat idealized. The greatest numbers of deeds in a person's life are those which contain some aspects of both models, differing in the share of each of them. These models, regardless of the probability of their occurrence in their pure form, play an important role in terms of responsibility. The grounds for responsibility are undoubtedly susceptible to the decision-making pattern preceding the act.

The individual human is a being who combines in themself, also in their actions, spiritual and bodily aspects. These processes are mutually coordinated. Even decisions that are strictly internal in nature, and therefore not externalized in the form of any action, involve not only the spiritual aspect of human life but also the body, various physiological processes, not without an impact on mental processes.[207] What has been completely forced by external factors, without any permission from the person concerned, cannot, however, be called the deed of a given person.[208] If there is at least a small element of acquiescence in a given situation, it may be possible to establish that an act has been committed or even to describe the person concerned as the perpetrator. This is not possible when the behavior was entirely coerced. If a person had no freedom of action in any aspect, and thus could not maintain his independence from external factors, his behavior cannot be valued morally.[209]

The above reasoning outlines important limits of human responsibility, at the same time creating space to establish a specific scale of responsibility. The highest level of responsibility can be said to exist when a given behavior is entirely the result of a person's inner self, that is, the result of a conscious and voluntary decision. However, no responsibility will arise if, as already noted above, there is no consent and no voluntariness in the behavior.

As R. Ingarden pointed out, to find the perpetrator responsible means:

1. the guilt of the perpetrator, who has realized a negative value of the actual state of affairs, and thus has himself a negative value, and in the case of positive actions, it means merit through realization of the desired value;
2. If the negative value of the perpetrator is realized, the claim for compensation for the damage and harm and the expression of an act of repentance shall be met; and
3. the perpetrator has a duty to obey the demands made on him in order to be held responsible.[210]

In the case of positively evaluated acts, the obligation toward the persons responsible for them arises primarily on the part of the community or other entities that are the beneficiaries of such behavior.

Responsibility could not exist without reference to values. In fact, every aspect of responsibility can be looked at through the prism of the values that are associated with it. This applies both to the deed that is the subject of responsibility and to the process of being held responsible. The overriding value, though not the only one, is fairness guiding the compensation process under responsibility.[211]

The responsibility lies with the individual until he or she is freed from the deed. Liberation does not take place by the mere termination of the act, as the responsibility sometimes lies with the individual human long after the act is complete.[212] The scope and content of the responsibility are determined by:

1. the nature of the deed and its value,
2. the nature and value of the result of the deed, and
3. the perpetrator's position in relation to his own deed and its outcome.[213]

In this sense, responsibility cannot be changed, as the above factors absolutely determine it. However, it may be known and understood in different ways, by the perpetrator, by other people, or by the community to which the perpetrator belongs. Regardless of whether the responsibility is realized or not, it exists until the perpetrator performs an appropriate act of repentance, which in essence should be preceded by the realization of this responsibility. In this way, R. Ingarden introduces the problem of the identity of the responsible party: "In order for responsibility to be borne by the perpetrator and also removed from them, there must be an identity of the perpetrator, especially his personal existence, despite all the changes that in the meantime take place within him, and it must be preserved until responsibility is removed."[214] Responsibility may therefore not be transferred or inherited. It also cannot be freely transferred from one entity to another. At the same time, it is even possible to conduct proceedings concerning responsibility after the death of the perpetrator.

The problem of identity may come back with a double force in the future, if the interference with the human organism is possible and effective to such an extent that the continuity of existence between man before the intervention and man after it is carried out is questionable. At the present time, it seems that maintaining this continuity may be disturbed by various kinds of illnesses, especially those that interfere to a significant extent with human memory or the ability to understand reality.

Consideration of responsibility as such should also take into account the issue of the entity imposing responsibility and the tribunal to which the person bears responsibility. Depending on the subject of responsibility and other conditions, it may be one entity performing these two functions, or two separate entities. It is hard to imagine responsibility if it were not entrusted to an individual. The figure of responsibility would also be doubtful without an authority to hold a given individual accountable for how he or she deals with it. Three types of responsibility have been indicated: religious, social, and one's own. Within the framework of religious responsibility, one is accountable to God, social responsibility is dealt with by appropriate social institutions, and self-responsibility takes place before the tribunal of one's own conscience.[215]

It is yet worthwhile to look at the question of the relationship between responsibility and guilt. In light of what has been said so far, it seems that J. Filek is right when he stresses that guilt and the sense of guilt are not the same as responsibility and a sense of responsibility.[216] Responsibility is prime with regard to guilt. You cannot be guilty if you were not responsible for something. Moreover, you cannot be capable of guilt if you are not capable of bearing responsibility. Responsibility, as shown above, is in its dominant form a positive and prospective category, thus indicating the specific nature of a given person's relationship with other entities. Guilt is born where responsibility gains a negative dimension, related to a breach of duty, or misappropriation of certain norms.

Moral Luck

When discussing the issue of attribution of responsibility, especially in the case of unintentional acts, it is impossible not to address the problem of luck and its impact on the final shape of the offender's act or its consequences. This category is known in Anglo-American philosophical literature as moral luck. It has been created in this shape in the contemporary literature thanks to the work of Bernard Williams.[217] This author argued in his text that the thesis that any concept of moral luck is completely inconsistent with the concept of morality is false. In other words, morality is not immune to chance. The main doubt boils down primarily to whether this luck can in any way influence the moral evaluation of the act.

This problem was developed in an article by Thomas Nagel.[218] The difficulty of considering moral luck as a circumstance affecting moral judgment originates in the essential independence of luck from the sphere of influence of the perpetrator. In other words, the luck gets out of the perpetrator's control, and this, as noted above, is one of the basic prerequisites for responsibility. It would seem that the premise of guilt is one of the basic principles of responsibility. This would rule out responsibility for the effects of luck, which, by its nature, is not the result of conscious behavior on the part of the perpetrator, but the consequence of a number of other causes, independent of the perpetrator. In practice, however, it may turn out that the behavior evaluated morally was more the result of luck than of a choice that would have been the natural subject of evaluation. Thomas Nagel distinguishes four types of moral luck[219]:

1. Constitutive luck—refers to the character, appearance, personality in so far as the acquisition of these characteristics takes place independently

of the will and commitment of the subject, including characteristics acquired by birth. Although these characteristics, at least to a significant extent, are not dependent on the entity, they are subject to different moral evaluations. Those characteristics which have been, or at least could have been, influenced by the entity should be assessed.

2. Situational luck—referring to the present, leading to the disclosure of different characteristics of the subject, good and bad. A number of decisions, which are later subject to moral evaluation, would not have been made if it were not for a set of events, sometimes completely random, that create conditions for us to do so. If the protagonist of William Styron's novel *Sophie's Choice* had not been in a concentration camp, not by her own choice, she would not have faced such a difficult choice as that which she eventually had to face.
3. Luck related to the causes for action—the impact of the luck on the causes of behavior, including the offender's decision-making process. This aspect of luck can also be a basis for a discussion on free will and its limits, including factors determining the specific behavior of the perpetrator.
4. Luck related to the effects of an action—it is often a coincidence that decides what kind of effects a human action or omission will cause. This is the case, for example, when a pedestrian is hit by a speeding truck driver. Several drivers at the same time could have exceeded the speed limit, and only in his case did the pedestrian appear on the road.

The analysis of the individual variants of moral luck may indicate that the attribution of responsibility in some of these cases comes close to the standard of objective responsibility, that is, devoid of any element of guilt.[220]

The issue discussed here affects the problem of responsibility in various aspects. However, given the subject of this book, which is concerned with the search for the ethical legitimization of criminal law, it is appropriate to focus primarily on those ethical aspects that are important for understanding and evaluating the construction of criminal responsibility.

Moral luck seems to be an important phenomenon, primarily in relation to responsibility for unintentional acts, and especially when responsibility is not only related to the behavior of the perpetrator themselves but is dependent on the occurrence of an effect. It is enough to recall the example of truck drivers who, on the same stretch of road, under the same weather conditions and to the same extent, exceed the permitted speed. Although they are aware of the breach of the safety rules, they want the goods to be delivered quickly to the recipient. They hope they can do it safely and on time. Unfortunately, while one of them was driving the route, a man started crossing the pedestrian crossing. The driver did not manage to stop, hit the pedestrian, and consequently caused his death. The second driver, on the same stretch, driving across the same pedestrian crossings, did not meet any pedestrians. Many would probably say that the degree of responsibility of these drivers varies. After all, only one of them led to the death of a pedestrian. The second supplied his goods not only safely but also on time.

If we adopt such a reasoning, in which the effect—in this case, after all, unintentional—determines more severe responsibility, it turns out that the moral and, consequently, legal assessment of a given event was influenced not only by the consciousness and will of the perpetrator but also by accident, referred to here as luck. It was accidental that the first driver met a pedestrian, while the second did not. Freeing responsibility from moral luck would mean in this case making the degree of responsibility, and thus also the possible sanction, independent from the effect. After all, the level of danger to rights created by each of these drivers is the same.

The problem of moral luck also arises in those states of fact which, under Polish criminal law, qualify as acts committed intentionally, either directly or indirectly. In the case of an effective crime, the responsibility for the execution depends on the realization of the constituent elements of the effect. Otherwise, we can only talk about trying. The sanction, at least from a formal point of view, is imposed within the same limits, but there is no doubt that these are qualitatively different situations. Intention, in comparison to inadvertence, changes the situation to the extent that here the behavior is, in a way, originally directed toward a certain effect. We are not going to say that the effect is a matter of luck. However, it may be a situation when it does not occur, that is, when, due to circumstances beyond the control of the perpetrator, the fulfillment of the effect did not take place, for example, a deviation of action took place or someone else joined the causal course. Again, it is luck that decides the construction which will become the basis for criminal responsibility, and thus also, to a greater or lesser extent, the sanction imposed on the perpetrator.

The problem presented here, both in terms of moral and legal responsibility, can be described with the help of a paradox. This is because we accept—as it seems—two intuitively justified convictions that cannot be reconciled if we want to remain in the paradigm of classical rationality.[221] On the one hand, we assume that responsibility can only relate to those behaviors which have been carried out in a manner consistent with the principle of control, that is, intentionally. On the other hand, we consider it reasonable to make the scope of responsibility dependent on accidental events that are out of the perpetrator's control, although, admittedly, possible for him to predict.

The key to solving the moral luck paradox is, according to T. Nagel, to show its apparentness.[222] Moral theorists have developed a number of different theories, trying to face the challenge of moral luck.[223] From the perspective of the issues discussed here, the theory proposed by Margaret U. Walker seems particularly interesting. She draws attention to the serious risks involved in assuming that an entity can only be responsible for what is within their control. This is contrary not only to the intuition of responsibility but also to the very belief in its rightness. Walker believes:

> It's hard to imagine any kind of reaction on the part of the subject that would not strike us as inappropriate. Given the circumstances of a given situation, it could be disappointing or irritating, shameful or indecent, shocking or scandalous. (. . .) If our indignation were to be met with a mastered reaction from the subject that our position is the result of a misunderstanding of the notions of moral judgement and control, our detachment would, I believe, deepen rather than weaken. We would think that there was something wrong with this subject, something that went deeper than its original offence.[224]

The key to solving the problem is therefore to free oneself from a principled attachment to the premise of responsibility, if it is not only clashing with reality but above all the widely shared conviction of the scope of responsibility.

This means that responsibility for what we cover in the category of moral luck seems necessary, even if it is not always consistent with the principle of control. It seems, however, that the subject matter of luck in these cases is not the risk posed by the perpetrator. It therefore appears that he should be primarily responsible for the risks he causes, but not for the very result that triggers the process of calling for responsibility. In other words, responsibility arises when an unjustified risk is created, and the call for responsibility usually occurs at the moment when the effect is caused, and in some cases, the effect may already be the mere creation of a specific danger that has not yet materialized.

SUMMARY

The analyses carried out in this chapter on the issues of the deed, the structure of the human act, and responsibility allow us to construct theses which can then be used to draw conclusions on the scope of criminal responsibility in the light of the postulate of ethical legitimization of criminal law.

In the light of the above findings, there can in principle be no doubt that man is responsible for voluntary acts, that is, those that were conscious and free.[225] In the ideal schema illustrating the relationship between reason and will in the human act, it can be seen that human action is preceded by the choice of the weal that is the aim of the action and the act of will to achieve that weal. The individual is then accompanied by the thought of choosing the right means to achieve the outlined goal. Ultimately, the will determines the appropriate action of the cognitive authorities in man—to achieve the goal with the means chosen. When assessing the responsibility of a given person, it is necessary to take into account the moment of intent and the attitude of desire that shapes his or her intention. The juxtaposition of the content of this attitude with the finally implemented human act and its consequences is essential to determine responsibility and its degree.

Responsibility may be incurred by persons who act in response to moral reasons, while being free from coercion. This means that one is not responsible for unconditional reflexes, but also for intentional motions that are not or are not a response to the court of reason (e.g., in a state of insanity), or they constitute such a response, but a person's court of reason does not meet the prerequisites for becoming a subject of responsibility (e.g., decisions made by children).

Responsibility for failure to act is possible if the previously indicated criteria of the theory of moderation are met, understood as responding to the court of reason. A necessary requirement is to meet the requirements of guidance control, that is, to recognize that a person may have acted differently. In the case of an omission, it is fundamental to determine whether the entity was obliged to take action. The absence of such an obligation precludes the person concerned from being held responsible.

The individual is not only responsible for the action itself but also for the consequences it causes. First, it is necessary to establish a causal relationship between human behavior and effect. This can be established with the help of the theory of possible worlds. If in a world it is possible that the elimination of the offender's behavior would cause the effect not to occur, it is possible to conclude that a causal relationship exists. This does not yet prejudge responsibility. It needs to be established whether this effect was actually caused by a given entity. Therefore, it is not sufficient to establish the causal course itself. It seems helpful to clarify, looking at the effects in the possible world of transforming ethically reprehensible behavior into ethically correct behavior and to determine the effects that would occur. So we check to see if the pedestrian would be run over, even if the perpetrator was not driving carelessly. In addition, there is a requirement to determine whether an entity could have foreseen that his behavior would have a certain effect.

Responsibility may be incurred not only for the natural effects of an act but also for side effects if they are covered by the entity's wishes or if the entity, being aware of the risk of their occurrence, has not attempted to counteract them. The subject, being aware of the risk of their occurrence, should take action with a lower risk of undesirable side effects.

The responsibility for an accidental effect is different. As already noted, it is neither intended nor foreseen by the subject. It would be incorrect to say that a person will never be held responsible for his or her behavior, which has been the cause of a given accidental effect. This would lead to the conclusion that it is in principle impossible to be held responsible for unintentionally caused consequences. However, responsibility in these cases is not so much a reaction to the effect itself, after all an accidental one, but to the risky behavior of the perpetrator. The subject becomes responsible when excessive risk is caused, but the call for responsibility is usually made after the effect of the risky action has taken place, and in some cases, it is sufficient for the effect to be limited to the specificity of a given hazard.

The recognition of responsibility of a given subject in the negative dimension means their guilt, that is, attributing to them the fact that it has caused a negative state of affairs. From this, there is a basis for the claim for compensation for the damage and harm caused by the perpetrator. Responsibility means the obligation to meet demands made on the offender in response to the act committed by him. Only when all reasonable demands have been fulfilled will the responsibility of the subject in question be discharged.

NOTES

1. J. Filek, *Pytania do odpowiedzialności*, "Znak" 1995, no. 10 (485), s. 20–21. This statement by J. Filek also became a pretext for Mateusz Rodzynkiewicz to address the phenomenon of criminal responsibility. Cf. M. Rodzynkiewicz, *Fenomen odpowiedzialności w refleksji filozoficznej a prawnokarne zasady odpowiedzialności*, "Przegląd Prawa Karnego" 1997, no. 16, p. 5 et seq. Cf. too J. Filek, *Etyka. Reinterpretacja*, Kraków 2014, p. 233 et seq.

2. In some aspects, it is also justified to refer to the achievements of psychology. Cf. i.a., M. Król-Bogomilska, *"Formy winy" w prawie karnym w świetle psychologii*, Warsaw 1991, *passim*; J. Giezek, *Świadomość sprawcy czynu zabronionego*, Warsaw 2013, p. 17 et seq.; M. Budyn-Kulik, *Umyślność w prawie karnym i psychologii. Teoria i praktyka sądowa*, Warsaw 2015, p. 75 et seq.

3. Which does not mean that all immoral behavior should be criminalized. More on the standard of moral transparency K. Szczucki, *Wykładnia prokonstytucyjna prawa karnego*, Warsaw 2015, p. 13.

4. I wrote on this topic: ibid, *passim*; *Prawo karne jako instrument przeciwdziałania zachowaniom niemoralnym*. In: M. Różański, R. Sztychmiler (ed.), *Wychowanie religijne i moralne*, Olsztyn 2015, p. 171 et seq.

5. Michał Peno explicitly notes that "the view about the possibility of developing a universal understanding of responsibility is justified. Responsibility as known by the law and responsibility in morality can be considered on the same level" (M. Peno, *Odpowiedzialność prawna z perspektywy filozofii odpowiedzialności. Rozważania na tle prawa karnego*, Szczecin 2018, p. 69).

6. The criticism of philosophical works carried out by Joel Feinberg is interesting when he observes that philosophers who conduct considerations on human behavior uncritically accept the law as the ultimate determinant of the assessment of the value of human behavior, cf. *Doing and Deserving*, Princeton 1970, p. 3. Also from this perspective, the need to conduct and refer to independent philosophical research is visible.

7. I used a similar case in the article *Ethical Legitimacy of Criminal Law* published in the "International Journal of Law, Crime and Justice" 2018, vol. 53, p. 67 et seq.

8. Reconstructing a vision of a human being cannot be limited only to observations of typical human behavior or general patterns of behavior. Cf. S. Kamiński, *Jak filozofować?*, Lublin 1989, p. 291.

9. J. Woleński, *Analiza i odpowiedzialność*, "Znak" 1995, z. 10, p. 56; M. Rodzynkiewicz, *Fenomen odpowiedzialności. . .* , pp. 7–8.

10. For more on this topic, cf. K. Szczucki, *Wykładnia prokonstytucyjna prawa karnego*, Warsaw 2015, p. 63.

11. J. Feinberg, *Doing and Deserving. Essays in the Theory of Responsibility*, Princeton 1970, p. 25.

12. Cf. i.a. R. A. Duff, *The Realm of Criminal Law*, Oxford 2018; M. S. Moore, *Placing Blame. A Theory of the Criminal Law*, Oxford 2012.

13. In practice, it is extremely difficult to determine whether, in a given case, the offender's behavior consisted of intentionally causing serious damage to health, and the effect in the form of death was actually unintentional, or whether the entire behavior of the offender was aimed at causing death, at least with a possible intention. Cf. i.a.: judgment of the Appellate Court in Lublin of September 7, 2017, II AKa 175/17, LEX no. 2369743; judgment of the Appellate Court in Łódź of October 16, 2014, II AKa 230/14, LEX no. 1649014; judgment of the Appellate Court in Wrocław of March 6, 2014, II AKa 34/14, LEX no. 1451862; judgment of the Appellate Court in Białystok of December 6, 2012, II AKa 210/12, LEX no. 1246605.

14. In the Polish Penal Code, a slight health impairment is understood as one that lasts no longer than 7 days. Average impairment lasts more than 7 days. The Code also distinguishes serious damage to health, which has the following characteristics: "§ 1. who causes serious damage to health in the form of:

1) deprivation of sight, hearing, speech, ability to conceive,
2) other serious disability, serious incurable or long-term illness, a life-threatening illness, permanent mental illness, total or significant permanent inability to work in an occupation or permanent, significant permanent disfigurement or deformity, is punishable by a term of imprisonment of not less than 3 years."

15. J. Feinberg, *Doing. . .* , p. 27.

16. An interesting analysis in this respect was undertaken by the Court of Appeal of England and Wales in the case of *Turk (Deceased) v R.* [2017] EWCA Crim 391 (April 06 2017). The decision concerned the possibility of continuing criminal proceedings in the case in which the accused committed suicide.

17. Such an approach clearly determines the legal nature of disciplinary responsibility. In this connection, it is only possible to consider, by the way, the actual ethical nature of the standards contained in the codes of ethics, which are the basis for disciplinary responsibility. In those types of disciplinary responsibility where there are no codes of ethics, the assessment of the behavior of a given guilty party comes significantly closer to that of moral responsibility.

18. J. Feinberg, *Doing. . .*, p. 32.

19. Ibid, p. 33. This does not mean, however, that morality is also not one of the tools of social control.

20. A similar regularity was noted in English by J. Feinberg, *Doing. . .*, p. 39.

21. Ibid, p. 40.

22. In the view of H. L. A. Hart and A. M. Honore: "we must not impute to ordinary thought all the fine discriminations that could be made and in fact are to be found in a legal system, or an equal willingness to supply answers to complex questions (. . .) Where there is no precise system of punishment, compensation, or reward to administer, ordinary men will not often have faced such questions as whether the injuries suffered by a motorist who collides with another in swerving to avoid a child are consequences attributable to the neglect of the child's parents in allowing it to wander on to the road," H.L.A. Hart, A.M. Honore, *Causation in the Law*, Oxford 1959, p. 71. Joel Feinberg even observes that "in abstraction from all practical questions about punishment, compensation, and the like, there is no rational way of answering such questions," J. Feinberg, *Doing. . .*, p. 41.

23. In this context, it is sometimes pointed out that the catalogue of types of prohibited acts also includes types included in the "mala prohibita" collection, which criminalize morally neutral behavior. However, the thesis of moral neutrality of these types does not seem to be justified. Violation of workers' rights, traffic rules or even tax regulations, that is, committing behavior which is usually included in the "mala prohibita" group, leads to a state of at least threatening important goods, if not even to their infringement. There are no grounds to indicate the moral neutrality of such acts. Cf. R.A. Duff, *Perversions and Subversions of Criminal Law*. In: idem et al. (ed.), *The Boundaries of the Criminal Law*, Oxford 2010, pp. 89–94. In such cases, criminal law contributes to the moral justification of criminalization. See K. Szczucki, *Wykładnia. . .*, p. 91.

24. P. Devlin, *The Enforcement of Morals*, London–New York 1965, p. 10.

25. It is worth noting that psychological analyses rather do not use the term "will," they replace it with the terms "motivation," "decision making," "conflict resolution." See more on this subject: M. Budyn-Kulik, *Umyślność. . .*, pp. 247–48.

26. For the genesis of the term "responsibility" cf. M. Peno, *Odpowiedzialność. . .*, pp. 30–32.

27. J.M. Fischer, M. Ravizza, *Responsibility. . ., and Control. A Theory of Moral Responsibility*, Cambridge 2008, p. 1.

28. I deliberately reject the terminology of dividing causality into causal and moral responsibility, because it could lead to confusion about the role of causality in moral responsibility. Cf. ibid., pp. 1–2.

29. Ibid, p. 2.

30. The problem of emotional response to the second one in the context of the problem of responsibility was stressed by P.F. Strawson. This view is discussed later in this chapter. See: P.F. Strawson, *Freedom and Resentment*, "Proceedings of the British Academy" 1962, vol. 48, pp. 187–211; J.M. Fischer, M. Ravizza, *Responsibility. . .*, p. 3.

31. J. Filek, *Ontologizacja odpowiedzialności*, Kraków 1996, pp. 30–31. Cf. too J.M. Fischer, M. Ravizza, *Responsibility. . .* , pp. 2–3.

32. P.F. Strawson, *Freedom. . .* , p. 194. Cf. too J.M. Fischer, *Recent work on Moral Responsibility*, "Ethics" 1999, vol. 110, no. 1, pp. 93–94.

33. J.M. Fischer, M. Ravizza, *Responsibility. . .* , p. 6.

34. R.J. Wallace, *Responsibility and the Moral Sentiments*, Cambridge 1994, p. 38.

35. Ibid, p. 76. Cf. too J.M. Fischer, *Recent work. . .* , p. 95.

36. C. Cowley, *Moral Responsibility*, Durham 2014, pp. 25–26.

37. G. Williams, *Sharing Responsibility and Holding Responsible*, "Journal of Applied Philosophy" 2013, vol. 30, no. 4, p. 351 et seq.

38. R. Ingarden, *Książeczka o człowieku*, Kraków 1987, pp. 73–74. Cf. too M. Peno, *Odpowiedzialność. . .* , pp. 48–50.

39. Ibid, p. 74.

40. Ibid, p. 75.

41. Ibid, p. 76.

42. Ibid, p. 76.

43. R. Ingarden, *Wykłady z etyki. . .* , Warsaw 1989, pp. 303–4.

44. Ibid, p. 304.

45. J. Filek, *Ontologizacja. . .* , p. 21. Cf. too H.M. Kallen, *Responsibility*, "Ethics" 1942, vol. 52, no. 3, p. 359.

46. The stories about the legal responsibility of animals are anecdotal nowadays, such as the one from the 18th century, when in Brazil the Order of Friars Minor sued ants who fed on flour from religious warehouses. They were sentenced to eviction. Cf. J. Filek, *Ontologizacja. . .* , pp. 2–23.

47. Ibid, p. 23. The author rightly points out that even in biblical sources he can In those days they shall say no more, The fathers have eaten a sour grape, and the children's teeth are set on edge. But every one shall die for his own iniquity: every man that eateth the sour grape, his teeth shall be set on edge. (Jr 31, 29–30). The prophet Ezekiel instructed the people as follows: "Yet say ye, Why? doth not the son bear the iniquity of the father? When the son hath done that which is lawful and right, and hath kept all my statutes, and hath done them, he shall surely live. The soul that sinneth, it shall die. The son shall not bear the iniquity of the father, neither shall the father bear the iniquity of the son: the righteousness of the righteous shall be upon him, and the wickedness of the wicked shall be upon him." (Ez 18, 19–20). Cf. also Plato, *Laws*, Kęty 2017, pt. 855 A. It is worth noting at this point, however, that although in the case of individual responsibility, one cannot speak of its inheritance, this phenomenon is revealed in the context of the over-generational responsibility of nations. This is because metaphysical guilt is inherited.

48. J. Filek, *Ontologizacja. . .* , pp. 24–25. Cf. too P. Ricoeur, *Symbolika zła*, transl. S. Cichowicz, M. Ochab, Warsaw 1986, p. 98; W. Jaeger, *Paideia*, vol. I, transl. M. Plezia, Warsaw 1962, p. 186.

49. R. Ingarden, *Książeczka*. . . , pp. 78–79.
50. Ibid, p. 81.
51. Ibid, p. 82.
52. J.M. Fischer, M. Ravizza, *Responsibility*. . . , p. 16.
53. D. Shoemaker, *Moral Address, Moral Responsibility, and the Boundaries of the Moral Community*, "Ethics" 2007, vol. 118, no. 1, p. 70.
54. P.F. Strawson, *Freedom*. . . , p. 82.
55. D. Shoemaker, *Moral Address*. . . , p. 74.
56. P.F. Strawson, *Freedom*. . . , p. 79; D. Shoemaker, *Moral Address*. . . , p. 74.
57. D. Shoemaker, *Moral Address*. . . , p. 75.
58. R. Ingarden, *Książeczka*. . . , p. 22.
59. Ibid, p. 22.
60. Ibid.
61. Ibid, pp. 22–23.
62. Ibid, p. 23.
63. Ibid, p. 24.
64. T. Styczeń, *Etyka*, s. 13. In: *Powszechna encyklopedia filozofii*, ptta.pl/pef/pdf /e/etyka.pdf (accessed 8.10.2019).
65. I'm using M.A. Krąpiec's analysis of the decision-making act. Cf. ibid., *Ludzka wolność i jej granice*, Lublin 2008, p. 69.
66. Cf. M.A. Krąpiec, *Ludzka wolność i jej granice*, Lublin 2008, pp. 143–44.
67. R. Ingarden, *Wykłady z etyki*. . . , p. 100.
68. Ibid, p. 100.
69. Cf. T. Ślipko, *Zarys etyki ogólnej*, Kraków 2004, p. 83.
70. R. Ingarden, *Wykłady z etyki*. . . , p. 101.
71. A deed can take two forms: doing something or not doing something, that is, omissions (R. Ingarden, *Wykład z etyki*. . . , p. 115). Roman Ingarden uses a slightly different terminology in his description of acting and omission than we know from criminal law. This may lead to a certain confusion, so it is worth paying attention to it at this point. In criminal law, a deed is an overriding category, it may consist of an act or an omission. Ingarden, on the other hand, uses the concept of deed and the concept of action equally. What we understand by action in criminal law theory is sometimes referred to as deed in the cited works on ethics.
72. K. Wojtyła, *Osoba i czyn oraz inne studia antropologiczne*, Lublin 2011, p. 98.
73. Human performance is also subject to psychological research. Józef Kozielecki pointed out that "the human individual is above all the perpetrator, they undertake a variety of purposeful actions, the course of which is sometimes regulated by knowledge encoded in the mind and information coming from the environment." (J. Kozielecki, *Koncepcje psychologiczne człowieka*, Warsaw 1995, p. 234).
74. K. Wojtyła, *Osoba i czyn*. . . , p. 116.
75. K. Wojtyła, *Osoba: podmiot i wspólnota*. In: tenże, *Osoba i czyn*. . . , p. 381. More on the topic of philosophical anthropology and its tasks, cf. S. Kamiński, *Jak filozofować?* p. 282 et seq.
76. K. Wojtyła, *Osoba: podmiot*. . . , p. 384.

77. R. Ingarden, *Wykłady z etyki. . .* , p. 102.
78. R. Ingarden, *Wykłady z etyki. . .* , p. 106.
79. Ibid, p. 107.
80. K. Wojtyła, *Osoba i czyn. . .* , p. 121.
81. Ibid, p. 148.
82. Ibid, p. 152.
83. Ibid, p. 165.
84. Ibid, p. 171.
85. K. Wojtyła, *Osobowa struktura samostanowienia*. In: ibid., *Osoba i czyn. . .* , p. 427.
86. M.A. Krąpiec indicates that this characteristic of the human deed, being a conscious and voluntary action, is a direct conclusion from the reflection on the fact that "man acts." It does not require any ethical theory to be applied. Cf. ibid., *Ludzka wolność. . .* , pp. 139–40. As J. Woroniecki pointed out: "A characteristic feature of those human deeds which belong to the scope of moral conduct is that they are voluntary, i.e. that they deliberately pursue a known and intended goal, and that goal is always linked to this or that degree of development and improvement of the acting person himself, by the fact that it is linked to the primary goal of human life as a whole, to the goal of man as such," ibid., *Etyka*. In: *Zarys filozofii. Praca zbiorowa*, vol. 2, Lublin 1929, pp. 181–82.
87. J. Woroniecki indicated *expressis verbis* that: "From this attribute of moral behavior, which we call a voluntariness, immediately comes the second, called responsibility. Since our actions are voluntary, they are in our power, we are their masters and are responsible for them. It is up to us to what extent they respond to the purpose of our life and the principles on which its development is based. This relationship is governed by two basic notions of the moral field, the notions of duty and authority," ibid., *Etyka. . .* , p. 182. Cf. too R. Polak, *Człowiek i moralność w myśli Jacka Woronieckiego OP. Filozoficzne podstawy katolickiej etyki wychowawcza i jej zasady*, Warsaw 2017, p. 212.
88. K. Wojtyła, *Osoba i czyn. . .* , p. 174.
89. M.A. Krąpiec, *Ludzka wolność. . .* , p. 141.
90. In the English literature, this is known as *reasons-responsiveness*. Cf. J.M. Fischer, M. Ravizza, *Responsibility. . .* , p. 41.
91. Ibid, p. 41.
92. D. Zimmerman, *Reasons-Responsiveness and Ownership-of-Agency: Fischer and Ravizza's Historicist Theory of Responsibility*, "The Journal of Ethics" 2002, vol. 6, no. 3, p. 199 et seq.
93. J.M. Fischer, M. Ravizza, *Responsibility. . .* , p. 44.
94. Ibid, p. 45.
95. Ibid, p. 43.
96. Ibid, pp. 62–63.
97. Ibid, pp. 70–71. In this context the authors give a number of interesting examples illustrating the issue discussed here. One can imagine that someone is going to a match of their favorite sports team. The only reason that could dissuade him from it would be the cost of a ticket in the amount of 1000 PLN. Therefore, one can say that

there is such a possible reason that would lead a given entity to resign from watching the match. However, if it turned out that the resignation would be caused only by the price of 1000 PLN, and already 2000 or 3000 PLN not, we would have doubts as to the legitimacy of considering moral responsibility for a given act. It seems that if the price of PLN 1,000 is a good reason to resign from the match, then the price of PLN 2,000 is even more so.

98. J.M. Fischer, M. Ravizza, *Responsibility. . .* , p. 81.

99. J.M. Fischer and M. Ravizza indicate that this is a combination of what they call regular reasons-receptivity and weak reasons-responsiveness. Cf. ibid. p. 81.

100. Ibid, p. 80.

101. Cf. ibid., p. 83.

102. Similar to the presented division is the division into rational and irrational acts, but these divisions do not overlap in their entirety. For rational acts are to be interpreted as intentional acts originating from reason. Irrational acts seem to be intentional acts that do not originate from reason and unintentional acts. See T. Slipko, *Zarys etyki. . .* , p. 75. As T. Slipko notes, irrational acts do not have much significance for ethics.

103. M.A. Krąpiec, *Ludzka wolność. . .* , pp. 15–16.

104. Ibid, p. 38, It is worth noting that St. Thomas, in his treatise on human action, deals only with action that is voluntary, that is, in a sense dependent on the will. Cf W. Galewicz, Translator's Introduction. In: St. Thomas of Aquinas, *Treatise on Human Action*, transl. W. Galewicz, Kęty 2013, p. 10.

105. K. Wojtyła, *Osoba i czyn. . .* , p. 213.

106. Ibid, p. 213.

107. M.A. Krąpiec, *Ludzka wolność. . .* , pp. 38–39.

108. Ibid, p. 50.

109. Ibid, p. 61.

110. K. Wojtyła, *Osoba i czyn. . .* , p. 176.

111. Ibid, p. 185.

112. R. Ingarden, *Wykłady z etyki. . .* , p. 115.

113. St. Thomas Aquinas, Summa Theologiae I-II, q. 72 a. 6, Second and Revised Edition, 1920 Literally translated by Fathers of the English Dominican Province, Online Edition 2017.

114. F. W. Bednarski, *Objaśnienia tłumacza.* In: St. Thomas Aquinas, *Suma Teologiczna,* vol. 12, trans. F. W. Bednarski, London 1963, p. 172.

115. Omission on the grounds of ethics raises a number of doubts. It is even postulated to abandon the use of this category. Cf. B. Gert, Ch.M. Culver, K.D. Clouser, *Bioetyka. Ujęcie systematyczne*, Gdańsk 2009, p. 421; M. Ferdynus, *O działaniu, zaniechaniu i dopuszczeniu do śmierci*, "Colloquia Theologica Ottoniana 2013, no. 1, p. 207.

116. T. Ślipko, *Zarys etyki ogólnej*, Kraków 2004, p. 421.

117. J.M. Fischer, M. Ravizza, *Responsibility. . .* , p. 127.

118. This type of example refers to the method of H. Frankfurt. Cf. ibid., *An Alleged Asymmetry between Actions and Omissions*, "Ethics" 1994, vol. 104, no. 3, p. 620.

119. J.M. Fischer and M. Ravizza seem to overlook the possibility of being held responsible for an omission even if it has had no effect. Cf. J.M. Fischer, M. Ravizza,

Responsibility. . . , pp. 134–36. The problem of randomness in the determination of responsibility will be addressed once again in the further part of the book, in the context of the so-called moral luck.

120. W. Galewicz, *Wstęp tłumacza. . .* , p. 173 et seq.

121. This is how St. Thomas put it in his *Commentary on the Sentence of Peter Lombard*: "just as a genus is specified by the genre, so too is the good by genus specified by the good that arises from the purpose and from other circumstances; and therefore this good arising from the purpose and circumstances refers to the good by genus just as genre to genus, taking over the terms belonging to the latter; so, for example, to feed the hungry in honour of God is to feed the hungry, but not the other way around," Saint Thomas Aquinas, *Super Sent.*, lib. 2 d. 36 q. 1 a. 5 ad 3, as cited in: W. Galewicz, *Wstęp tłumacza. . .* , p. 40.

122. "The vices take their genre from the nearest goal, but the target is the genus and the cause. Thus, in the case of someone who commits adultery for the purpose of theft, here we have a genre of adultery that is derived from a direct purpose and object, but from the ultimate purpose it is evident that adultery is born of theft and contains itself as an effect in the cause or as a genre of the genus," St. Thomas Aquinas, *Summa Theologiae* II-II, q. 11a. 1 ad 2, as cited in: W. Galewicz, *Wstęp tłumacza. . .* , p. 41.

123. St. Thomas Aquinas, Summa Theologiae I-II q. 18 a. 7 co., Second and Revised Edition, 1920 Literally translated by Fathers of the English Dominican Province, Online Edition 2017.

124. Cf. W. Galewicz, *Wstęp tłumacza. . .* , p. 42.

125. Ibid, p. 44.

126. Ibid, p. 47. The interpretation adopted here does not contradict the concept of intrinsically evil acts adopted within the framework of moral absolutism. More on this subject: ibid., pp. 48–51.

127. According to Aquinas, "of the genre of any deed is its object, and of the genre of human deeds, called moral deeds, the object referring to the principle of human deeds, which is reason. Therefore, if the object of a deed contains something that is in accordance with the order of reason, the deed is good because of its genre, such as the support of a person in need. If, on the other hand, the act contains something that is contrary to the order of reason, the act is evil because of its genre, such as theft, which is the appropriation of someone else's property. However, it happens that the object of a deed does not contain anything that is connected with the order of reason, such as lifting a blade of grass from the ground, going out into the field, etc. And such acts are neutral because of their genre," St. Thomas Aquinas, *Treatise on Human Action. . .* , pp. 192–93 (ST I-II q. 18 a. 8 co.). Cf. also R. McInerny, *Aquinas. . . , on Human Action. A Theory of Practice*, Washington 2012, pp. 86–89.

128. R. McInerny, *Aquinas. . .* , p. 89.

129. T. Styczeń, *Etyka. . .* , p. 13. In: *Powszechna encyklopedia filozofii*, ptta.pl/pef/pdf/e/etyka.pdf (accessed 8.10.2019).

130. I give the factual states following: J.M. Fischer, M. Ravizza, *Responsibility. . .* , pp. 93–94.

131. Cf. ibid., p. 112.

132. Ibid, p. 121.

133. T. Ślipko, *Zarys etyki. . .* , p. 423.
134. Ibid, p. 177.
135. T. Ślipko, *Zarys etyki. . .* , pp. 423–24.
136. B. Chyrowicz illustrates this with an example of a person who takes painkillers not because of their main effect, but counting on intoxication, which is indicated in the leaflet as a possible side effect. Cf. B. Chyrowicz, *O sytuacjach bez wyjścia w etyce*, Kraków 2008, p. 302.
137. T. Ślipko, *Zarys etyki. . .* , pp. 426–27.
138. B. Chyrowicz, *O sytuacjach. . .* , p. 304.
139. Ibid, p. 302.
140. T. Ślipko, *Zarys etyki. . .* , p. 427.
141. Ibid, p. 427.
142. Where there is doubt about the actual existence of the intention in the subconscious of the actor, account should be taken of the time that has elapsed since the intention was taken up, as well as the actor's ease of referencing. Thus, T. Slipko, Zarys etyki . . . 4, p. 81.
143. Ibid, p. 81.
144. St. Thomas Aquinas, *Summa Theologiae* II-II, q. 64 a. 7, Second and Revised Edition, 1920 Literally translated by Fathers of the English Dominican Province, Online Edition 2017.
145. Ibid.
146. Following: B. Chyrowicz, *O sytuacjach. . .* , p. 307.
147. Ibid, p. 308.
148. B. Chyrowicz, *Zamiar i skutki. Filozoficzna analiza zasady podwójnego skutku*, Lublin 1997, pp. 35–36.
149. T. Ślipko, *Zarys etyki. . .* , pp. 423–24.
150. T.A. Cavanaugh, *Double-Effect Reasoning: Doing Good and Avoiding Evil*, Oxford 2017, pp. 7–8.
151. Actually, T.A. Cavanaugh writes about this directly, attempting to establish the difference between action praeter intention and per accidens. Cf. ibid., *Double-Effect. . .* , p. 11.
152. B. Chyrowicz, *O sytuacjach. . .* , p. 310. Cf. P. Foot, *The Problem of Abortion and the Doctrine of the Double Effect*. In: J.M. Fischer, M. Ravizza, *Ethics. Problems and Principles*, Fort Worth 1992, p. 59 et seq.; P. Foot, *Morality, Action, and Outcome*,. In: P.A. Woodward, *The Doctrine of Double Effect. Philosophers Debate a Controversial Moral Principle*, Notre Dame 2000, p. 67 et seq.
153. P. Foot, Morality. . . , p. 68. Cf. too B. Chyrowicz, O sytuacjach. . . , p. 315.
154. T. A. Cavanaugh, *Double-Effect. . .* , p. 85.
155. T.A. Cavanaugh, *Double-Effect. . .* , pp. 106–7.
156. B. Chyrowicz, *O sytuacjach. . .* , p. 325.
157. Cf. K. Szczucki, *Relacja między odpowiedzialnością etyczną i karną na przykładzie zasady podwójnego skutku*, "Państwo i Prawo" 2019, no. 3, p. 78 et seq.
158. T. Ślipko defined the free act of reason as follows: "A free act is thus understood to mean an act in which the will, not constrained by external obstacles, nor subjected to the compulsion to act according to the laws of nature, possibly the strongest

motive, chooses a certain good from among several known possibilities of action," ibid., *Zarys etyki. . .* , p. 77.

159. W. Galewicz, *Wstęp tłumacza. . .* , p. 11.

160. J.M. Fischer, M. Ravizza, *Responsibility. . .* , p. 12.

161. In this way, I refer to the described category of partially conscious acts. See T. Ślipko, *Zarys etyki. . .* , p. 80.

162. Ibid, p. 84.

163. Ibid, pp. 87–88.

164. Although T. Ślipko does not indicate mental handicap among habitual obstacles, it can undoubtedly be such an obstacle, and it cannot be classified as a set of mental illnesses. Cf. ibid., p. 85.

165. Aristotle, *Nicomachaean Ethics*, Warsaw 2011, trans. D. Gromska, p. 122 (III, 1, 1110a 2).

166. Cf. W. Galewicz, *Wstęp tłumacza. . .* , p. 11. This author uses an example which well reflects the premises of the existence of coercion invoked here. A sailor whose ship is being blown by the wind cannot claim to be subject to compulsion because with the help of sails and rudder he can change the course of his boat. If he does not do so, he also—this time by his omission—contributes to the course.

167. St. Thomas Aquinas, ST, I-II, q. 6 a. 5 ad 2, Second and Revised Edition, 1920 Literally translated by Fathers of the English Dominican Province, Online Edition 2017. Cf. too St. Thomas Aquinas, *Commentary on Aristotle's Nicomachean Ethics*, Notre Dame 1993, trans. C.J. Litzinger, pp. 128–29.

168. M.A. Krąpiec, *Ludzka wolność. . .* , p. 46.

169. According to T. Ślipko, fear should be understood as "a state of anxiety felt by the sensual faculties of man, and caused by the threat to him by an evil difficult to avoid," ibid., *Zarys etyki. . .* , p. 88.

170. Aristotle, *Nicomachaean Ethics*, III, 1, 1110a 4–5, http://classics.mit.edu/Aristotle/nicomachaen.html, transl. W. D. Ross (accessed 28 March 2022). Cf. W. Galewicz, *Wstęp tłumacza. . .* , p. 14.

171. St. Thomas Aquinas, *Commentary. . .* , p. 130.

172. R. McInerny, *Aquinas. . .* , p. 23.

173. W. Galewicz, *Wstęp tłumacza. . .* , p. 20.

174. St. Thomas Aquinas, *Summa Theologiae I-II q. 6 a. 7 ad 2*. In: St. Thomas Aquinas (ed.), *Treatise on Human Action. . .* , p. 71.

175. W. Galewicz, *Wstęp tłumacza. . .* , p. 22. Cf. too R. McInerny, Aquinas. . . , p. 14.

176. R. McInerny, *Aquinas. . .* , p. 17.

177. T. Ślipko, *Zarys etyki. . .* , p. 85.

178. Aristotle, *Nicomachaean Ethics*,III, 1, 1111a 3, http://classics.mit.edu/Aristotle/nicomachaen.html, transl. W. D. Ross (accessed 28 March 2022).

179. W. Galewicz, *Wstęp tłumacza. . .* , pp. 25–26.

180. St. Thomas Aquinas, *Summa Theologiae* I-II q. 6 a. 8 co, Second and Revised Edition, 1920 Literally translated by Fathers of the English Dominican Province, Online Edition 2017.

181. St. Thomas Aquinas, *Commentary. . .* , p. 136.

182. W. Galewicz, *Wstęp tłumacza. . .* , p. 24.

183. St. Thomas Aquinas, *Summa Theologiae* I-II q. 6 a. 8 co., Second and Revised Edition, 1920 Literally translated by Fathers of the English Dominican Province, Online Edition 2017.

184. According to W. Galewicz, the example quoted by St. Thomas is imperfect because it is not known whether in a given case the hunter would have executed his intention, even if he could. A better example, according to this author, may be the case of a man who seduces a young girl, not knowing how old she is, but would seduce her, even if he knew her age. Cf. W. Galewicz, *Wstęp tłumacza. . .* , p. 25. It is worth noting at this point that similar cases are qualified in criminal law as pseudo-eventual intention. Cf. I. Andreyev, *Ustawowe znamiona czynu. Typizacja i kwalifikacja przestępstw*, Warsaw 1978, p. 205.

185. W. Galewicz, *Wstęp tłumacza. . .* , p. 26.

186. Aristotle, *Nicomachaean Ethics*, III, 1, 1111a), http://classics.mit.edu/Aristotle/nicomachaen.html, transl. W. D. Ross (accessed 28 March 2022).

187. W. Galewicz, *Wstęp tłumacza. . .* , p. 27.

188. On the reasons for this difference: W. Galewicz, *Wstęp tłumacza. . .* , pp. 28–30.

189. Ibid, p. 28.

190. Cf. T. Biesaga, *Spór o normę moralności*, Kraków 1998, pp. 70–71. Cf. too T. Ślipko, *Zarys etyki. . .* , p. 90.

191. T. Ślipko, *Zarys etyki. . .* , p. 93.

192. Karol Wojtyła pointed out directly that only conscious action deserves to be described as a deed. Cf. K. Wojtyła, *Osoba i czyn. . .* , p. 73. According to R. McInerny, responsibility for deeds is possible because they are fulfilled in a conscious and free way. Cf. R. McInerny, *Aquinas. . .* , p. 8.

193. R. Ingarden, *Wykłady z etyki. . .* , p. 290.

194. Idem, *Książeczka. . .* , pp. 77–78.

195. R. Ingarden, *Wykłady z etyki. . .* , p. 290.

196. Ibid., p. 292. Ingarden understands conduct in ethics very broadly, including purely mental positions. Cf. ibid., p. 292.

197. C. Cowley, *Moral Responsibility. . .* , p. 26.

198. Ibid, p. 27.

199. D. Shoemaker, *Moral Address. . .* , pp. 75–76.

200. J.M. Fischer, M. Ravizza, *Responsibility. . .* , p. 31. Cf. too P. Łuków, *Metafizyka wolności i odpowiedzialności*. In: S. Kołodziejczyk (ed.), *Przewodnik po metafizyce*, Kraków 2011, pp. 506–7.

201. J.M. Fischer, M. Ravizza, *Responsibility. . .* , p. 31.

202. Ibid, p. 32.

203. H. Frankfurt, *Alternate Possibilities and Moral Responsibility*, "Journal of Philosophy" 1969, vol. 66, no. 23, p. 829. Cf. too D.P. Hunt, *Moral Responsibility and Unavoidable Action*, "Philosophical Studies" 2000, vol. 97, no. 2, p. 195; J.M. Fischer, *Recent work. . .* , p. 99.

204. H. Frankfurt constructed a case study to illustrate such a possibility, but it is more of a science fiction one. In this case study Smith decides to kill Jones. He does

not know that Black cares very much about Smith committing this very deed. Black has a device that allows him to control and influence Smith's thoughts. He programs the device so that it will only intervene in Smith's intention if he withdraws from his own intention to kill Jones. Cf. H. Frankfurt, *Alternate Possibilities. . .* , p. 835.

205. Cf. the analysis conducted by D.P. Hunt in: idem, *Moral Responsibility. . .* , p. 196 et seq.

206. R. Ingarden, *Książeczka. . .* , p. 85.

207. Ibid, pp. 89–90.

208. Ibid, p. 92.

209. Idem, *Wykłady z etyki. . .* , p. 301.

210. Idem, *Książeczka. . .* , p. 93.

211. Ibid, p. 100. The author states explicitly: "It is clear: if none of the above mentioned values were applicable to the relevant objects and ways of proceeding, there would be no liability for anything. Then it would be completely irrelevant how you act and what you cause by your actions. The mere act—even if fully proven—of a deed and its outcome would not yet provide any basis for accountability. Nor would there be any power to hold someone responsible, if the deed did not cause anything good or anything bad. Any criminal prosecution or recognition of merit would be completely senseless," (ibid. p. 102).

212. Ibid, pp. 110–11.

213. Ibid, p. 111.

214. Ibid, p. 112. idem, *Wykłady z etyki. . .* , p. 297.

215. J. Filek, *Ontologizacja. . .* , p. 38.

216. Ibid, p. 42.

217. B.A.O. Williams, *Moral Luck*, "Proceedings of the Aristotelian Society, Supplementary Volumes" 1976, vol. 50, p. 115 et seq.

218. T. Nagel, *Moral Luck*, "Proceedings of the Aristotelian Society, Supplementary Volumes" 1976, vol. 50, p. 137 et seq.

219. T. Nagel, *Moral Luck. . .* , pp. 140–41. Cf. too Ch. Cowley, *Moral Responsibility. . .* , pp. 114–16.

220. T. Nagel, *Moral Luck. . .* , p. 143.

221. M. Juzaszek, *Paradoks trafu prawnego. Studium filozoficznoprawne*, unpublished doctoral thesis written under the supervision of promoter Prof. dr. hab. Tomasz Gizbert-Studnicki and assistant promotor Dr. Adam Dyrda, Kraków 2017, p. 20, available at the library of the Faculty of Law and Administration at the Jagiellonian University.

222. T. Nagel, *Moral Luck. . .* , pp. 142–43. Por. też M. Juzaszek, *Paradoks trafu. . .* , p. 44.

223. The most important of these are described by M. Juzaszek, *Paradoks trafu. . .* , pp. 45–64.

224. M.U. Walker, *Moral Luck and the Virtues of Impure Agency*. In: D. Statman (ed.), *Moral Luck*, 1993 (no place of publication.), p. 240, as cited in: M. Juzaszek, *Paradoks trafu. . .* , pp. 59–60.

225. T. Ślipko, *Zarys etyki . . .* 4, p. 429.

Chapter 5

Ethical Legitimization of Selected Criminal Law Structures

PRELIMINARY REMARKS

The previous chapters focused on methodological considerations on legitimization. The principle of human dignity, which is a source of reconstructing the vision of man, taken for the purposes of the law from philosophical anthropology, and thus being the axis of reflection on the ethical legitimization of criminal law, was also discussed. The challenges facing ethics and criminal law in the context of the human capacity to bear responsibility were considered, and finally the basic principles of responsibility in classical ethics were discussed. The aim of this chapter is to take into account these reflections directly in criminal law. A specific application of previous findings to criminal law will be made here, that is, to three selected theoretical constructions, two of which are constructions that make up the shape of criminal responsibility, that is, omission and necessary defense, and the third—criminal law of enemies—is a certain theoretical phenomenon that is gaining ground increasingly.

It is not possible, due to the framework of this study, to discuss all theoretical constructions in the context of ethical legitimization. Rather, the monograph is intended to provide tools to help those interested in making an independent analysis of the individual solutions either contained in criminal law or just proposed. It thus shows another aspect that can be taken into account in the process of analysis carried out both *de lege lata* and *de lege ferenda*. At the same time, it is neither possible nor necessary to make a comprehensive dogmatic analysis of the above structures. This is the subject of separate studies available in Polish and foreign literature. Only those aspects that are relevant from the perspective of ethical legitimization are addressed here.

In the light of the analysis described in the previous chapters, criteria of general responsibility can be identified which the criminal legislator needs to take into account:

1. The generality and equality of responsibility. The dignity of the human being gives the capability to hold someone accountable—this gives the state the capability to hold him/her criminally accountable and at the same time imposes an obligation to establish principles that correspond not only to dignity as an independent category but also to the anthropological and ethical criteria to which it refers. At the same time, the rooting of responsibility in human dignity means that the criteria of this responsibility should not be differentiated according to the characteristics of individual perpetrators. Since every human being has dignity, he or she retains the same capacity for responsibility and should answer on the same principles. The only exceptions are people who, for reasons beyond their control, show limitations in terms of awareness or voluntariness.
2. The deed. The basis for human responsibility may be his/her deed or, depending on the adopted ontology of omission, its absence. Through a deed, an individual expresses his or her own responsibility. The deed reflects the interaction of reason and will and executive authorities. Each deed is directed toward a goal whose object is perceived as a good. The interaction between reason and will is the basis for the statement that a deed is conscious and voluntary. The absence of one of these characteristics excludes the possibility of responsibility. Responsibility is possible when a person is aware of the reasons for taking or failing to take a specific action. Consequently, the one who commits an act in response to causes indicated by reason may be responsible in a situation of freedom from compulsion. It is problematic to understand omission as a deed. However, there is no doubt as to the possibility of being responsible for an omission. It is permissible when a person is able to act effectively in given circumstances. The intention and state of consciousness of the perpetrator are important in assessing a deed.
3. Criteria for assessing a deed. The evaluation of a deed should be made from the perspective of the subject of the deed, the intention accompanying the deed, and the circumstances of the deed.
4. Responsibility for the effect. Responsibility for the result is possible when there is a causal relationship between the deed of an entity and the effect with which responsibility is to be associated. It is also necessary to determine whether the effect is a consequence of an entity's breach of a norm, moral, or legal, respectively. Responsibility for the effect should not occur if the deed was committed in accordance with a norm. The

individual is responsible not only for the effects which are acts of direct intent but also for those which are acts of indirect intent, that is, not only intended but also conscious and tolerated effects.

5. The ability to bear responsibility. In order to be able to bear responsibility, the entity should meet three conditions: it should have the right intellectual capacity, proper understanding, and ability to control. This means that the perpetrator should have a level of perception and reception of reality that allows him/her to understand the allegations and assess their appropriateness. Responsibility can only be assumed by a person who retains the ability to regulate and control their own behavior.
6. Exclusion of responsibility. As already noted with regard to the category of the deed itself, the deed itself, and thus also responsibility, will not arise due to a lack of voluntariness, when the behavior was committed under duress or as a result of unawareness. These circumstances are described as negative conditions of responsibility. The compulsion must be external to the actor. It must be understood not only as an externally imposed objective but also as the extortion by external factors of the concrete realization of a given objective, without leaving the decision-making space to the subject and actor. Physical coercion meets these criteria. With regard to the issue of ignorance, it should be noted that the reason for exclusion of responsibility can only be ignorance that is not guilty or unfeasible. It is indicated that the reason for an involuntary action can only be ignorance of individual circumstances. In ethics, it is noted that the exclusion of responsibility may also occur as a result of the double effect principle. The subject should not be held responsible for a result *praeter intentionem*, as long as the criteria of the fairness of the measure, the goodness of the aim, and the proportion of the measure to the aim are met.
7. Scope and content of responsibility. Responsibility for a given deed is not fluid, subject to dynamic changes in its content or scope. Responsibility is determined by: the nature of the deed and its value, the nature and value of the result of the deed, and by the position of the perpetrator toward his own deed and its result.
8. "Neuro-modesty." The findings of brain research, as well as those relating to the human genome, do not translate directly into the need to substantially correct the rules of criminal responsibility. Even a deterministic understanding of reality does not preclude the possibility of recognizing that a person can shape their behavior under the influence of a legal norm.

These criteria, as noted earlier, are formulated at a fairly high level of generality. The detailed application of the analyses conducted so far will be shown on the example of two constructions known to Polish criminal law, that is, the issue of responsibility for omission and necessary defense.

Before proceeding to discuss these constructions in the context of ethical legitimization, it is worth noting that the deliberations conducted here are not aimed at simply transferring ethical constructions to criminal law. For various reasons, this would be very difficult or impossible. The role of the ethical considerations in this case is rather to inspire the legislator, to indicate prudent solutions, and to set limits of responsibility that the legislator should take into account when deciding on the scope of criminal responsibility. If we assume, as shown in this book, that criminal law should not criminalize morally good behavior, then we consider that ethics sets this impassable limit for criminal law. The ethical legitimization of criminal law may lead to agreeing, at least to some extent, to legal decisions with the moral convictions of members of a political community, and thus bringing the law closer to the standard of moral accessibility.[1]

RESPONSIBILITY FOR OMISSION

In the doctrine of criminal law, the issue of responsibility for omission is entangled in serious disputes, determined by basic theoretical assumptions concerning this branch of law. In foreign literature there are arguments in favor of excluding or limiting responsibility for omissions.[2] In Poland, during the interwar period, W. Wolter noted that "the problem of crimes of omission is one of the most contentious issues of criminal law. Everything, beginning from the issue of omission as a deed, through the link of causation, of unlawfulness, to an attempt at aiding and abetting, is questionable here."[3] The attitude to the omission, its relation to the deed, the basis of responsibility, is directly connected with the concept of the crime adopted by a given author and a number of other theoretical assumptions approved by him. The basic doubt is whether an omission can be classified as a deed. In other words, whether it is a material object, that is, an externalized behavior that can also simultaneously be the object of valuation.[4] Although this is not an argument prejudging the theory of criminal law, the current criminal code has been constructed on the basis of a deed understood not only as an action but also as an omission.

Perhaps the best known Polish opponent of the recognition of an omission as a deed is Władysław Mącior. He stated in the strongest possible terms that an omission is not a real phenomenon in the external world.[5] Just as there exists no denial of existence, so the denial of action is not real. To make the opposite assumption, according to this author, would lead to the assumption that everything that someone does not do at a given time, that is, everything that was in his capacity, not even updated at all, is real. Moreover, the author argued that this omission differs from action, and thus also from the deed, in that it is not perceived. However, it is concluded.[6]

Also Przemysław Konieczniak's stance is counted among the camp that opposes the recognition of the omission as actually existing, that is, as an equivalent to an action in the form of the deed. He clearly stated that an omission is not part of the physical world. It also does not affect the environment either energetically, nor informatively.[7] This author, referring to the view of R. Ingarden—who considered negative states of things to be intentional, although not purely mental—stated *expressis verbis* that an omission does not exist in reality. Its real existential foundation is a complementary reality, not an omission itself.[8] The author further states that

> regardless of the philosophical stance adhered to, the so-called negative phenomena are only a form of description of positive reality, that is, something that has a linguistic nature, not a real one, and which belongs to the scope of human cognition rather than ontology. (. . .) (. . .) Therefore, it is difficult to consider an omission as a phenomenon "objectively existing"; it is at most something intersubjectively stated.[9]

Leszek Kubicki unambiguously spoke out in favor of the ontologically equal status of omission and action.[10] This author stated that the constitutive element for an omission is an unassessed observation, showing a lack of activity in a specific direction. He wrote about directional inactivity, as real as action in a specific direction.[11] This observation is free from evaluation, because in order to make it, it is not necessary to take into account whether the subject was obliged to undertake a specific activity. This thought was also continued by Tomasz Kaczmarek, who assessed that the mistake of concepts negating the causality of an omission is to assume that it is not any element of reality.[12] Similarly, Leon Tyszkiewicz pointed out that an omission which is a negation of an activity is not a fiction, just as hunger or lack of knowledge in a student during an examination is not. Therefore, he considered it too simplistic to refuse the attribute of reality to omission.[13]

Jarosław Majewski, considering the problem of causality of omission, stressed that the reality of omission does not have to be considered only on the ontological plane but also on the epistemic plane. In the latter sense, we speak out when we acknowledge a certain fact, referring to the scheme "X has omitted the act C." We consider it to be a true sentence, describing a fragment of reality. This reality is not as strong as in the case of action. If one considers that an omission is always associated with not manifesting a certain state of affairs, then "reality" gains an ontological dimension, which makes it impossible to relate it to action as much as to an omission.[14]

An indirect position was also taken by Władysław Wolter, who noted that certainly omission is not as real as action. For in the case of an omission, only the real complementing reality determined by the absence of a certain expected action is real.[15] At the same time, however, this author stated that refraining from action, taking place within a person, is important for objective reality, because it forms it negatively, allowing it to shape itself differently than we would expect.[16] Another author, Witold Świda, considered that even assuming that inaction is only a judgment of inactivity is still real because it is in the mind of the observer, who is in reality. By this, omission becomes objectively a part of this reality.[17]

The decision on the reality or just conceptuality of omission does not appear to be at all necessary to decide not only whether responsibility for omission is possible, but even whether omission can be recognized as a deed under criminal law. The conclusion of the ethical analysis can already be signaled here. From the perspective of the issue of ethical legitimization, the most important thing is not whether criminal law, both in theory and legal norms, can classify an omission as a deed. What seems to be much more important is whether one can be held responsible for omission at all and to what extent. This is what A. Zoll believed, who—without referring to the problem of ethics—claimed that the essence of a deed cannot be reduced to an ontological category, and thus one can speak of committing an act by omission, even if an attempt to prove the ontological nature of the omission cannot be successful.[18]

The conclusion outlined in this way corresponds to the view of M. Rodzynkiewicz, who argued that no object or phenomenon corresponds to the concept of the deed. According to this author, from the point of view of logic, the word "deed" is a name-forming functor, and not a name. This makes it impossible to speak of a classic definition of deed. Consequently, M. Rodzynkiewicz notes that: "In order to decide whether a particular behavior constituted a deed, we refer to a previously created model, which is postulatory in nature, i.e. it does not reproduce any 'essence of things,' but creates a certain template. The content of this template is not fixed, but is a function of views on what can be subject to criminal law valuation."[19] This assertion is related to this author's initial assumption that research in the field of criminal law theory, which also involves giving content to legal concepts, such as the concept of deed, is not the discovery of objective objects but the creation of cultural objects.[20]

W. Mącior, who was looking for an understanding of the deed as a certain universal ontological category, would certainly not agree with such a view. Universal in the sense that it would correspond to the deed as such, and thus be analyzed not only by criminal law but also by other fields of knowledge, including primarily philosophy. He noted that the deed is not an instinctive reaction to a stimulus but a conscious and deliberate act. This character of a deed results from the human being's ability to think and the ability to make a sensible self-determination. As a result, the author decided that the problem of the deed is primarily of a philosophical nature.[21] Therefore, the author not only rejects the recognition that an omission is an ontological category but also the possibility of considering an omission as a deed. The deed is "only such human behaviour which was created under the influence of the active role of consciousness and, as its product, went through the stage of a decision taken for a specific purpose, and then manifested itself in the form of an action."[22]

W. Patryas does not consider omission as a deed, mainly for grammatical reasons. The definition of omission proposed by this author is particularly interesting. It is based on the fact that subject X in period t omitted a deed C, if and only if subject X in period t was able to perform the deed C and subject X in period t did not perform the deed C.[23] This author did not include in the definition of omission the duty of a specific act. This method of analysis met with significant criticism, undermining the adopted method in particular. It was pointed out that linguistic and grammatical analyses cannot be compelling for the theory of criminal law.[24]

In view of the previous argument, it is difficult to consider that an omission can be regarded as a deed in ontological terms. Even if it is assumed, following J. Śliwowski, that a properly directed inaction manifests itself in an omission, it is necessary to define this obligation to the act in a given direction, out of the infinite number of variants of inaction of every person in every unit of time.[25] It is therefore necessary to take into account the norm of this obligation. Otherwise, we would have to say that a person is subject to many omissions at all times. Such a statement does not yet preclude criminal responsibility for an omission, or even recognition as a deed, for the purposes of the dogma of criminal law.

It follows from the considerations in the previous chapter on the basic categories of responsibility in ethics that an omission relevant to responsibility should be accompanied by intention. An omission resulting from forgetting or for any other reason cannot be included in the category of deed, and, consequently, should not give rise to responsibility.[26] To transpose such a conclusion into criminal law could mean that it would be inappropriate to introduce responsibility for an omission committed unintentionally, that is, where the perpetrator, without having had an intention to commit it, nevertheless committed it as a result of failure to observe the prudence required in a given set of circumstances, even though he or she anticipated or could have anticipated the possibility of committing that deed. Omission would then become a weaker form of deed, in the sense that it would allow a narrower scope of responsibility than in the case of action. Adopting this interpretation in criminal law would lead to a narrowing of responsibility too far. For it would not be easy to justify the failure of a parent who, in a state of unconscious unintentionality, is allowed to fail to look after a small child, and the child falls out of an open window. However, not always, and not in every relationship, will the moral intuition regarding responsibility for unintentional negligence be equally strong in demanding the responsibility of the perpetrator.

Ontological findings do not seem to have to be ethically translated in this case. This would mean for the theory of criminal law that also this or that other ontological understanding of the deed need not translate into the same understanding of the deed for the purpose of determining criminal responsibility. For if an omission can be as bad as an act, then there is no obstacle to putting both of these categories within the framework of the deed, if this is the term used by the law to establish the principles of responsibility. Aquinas noted that responsibility can be caused by both doing and not doing, that is, by turning away from the required good by not doing it.[27] The acceptance of responsibility for an omission does not yet resolve the difficulty that was indicated in the context of R. Ingarden's statement. The question remains whether responsibility for an unintentional or unconscious omission is admissible. On the one hand, intuition tells us, as in the above example of the mother, that such responsibility cannot be ruled out, while, on the other hand, it is difficult not to have the feeling that an omission, especially in the case of unintentional acts, can be a weaker form of deed, even if it leads to the same result. Thus, to equate the principles of responsibility for action and omission does not therefore seem entirely obvious.

Thomas Aquinas approved of the responsibility for unintentional evil. In his considerations about murder, this author came to the conclusion that one can also be responsible for a murder if it is done unintentionally:

> This happens in two ways: first when a man causes another's death through occupying himself with unlawful things which he ought to avoid: secondly, when he does not take sufficient care. Hence, according to jurists, if a man pursue a lawful occupation and take due care, the result being that a person loses his life, he is not guilty of that person's death: whereas if he be occupied with something unlawful, or even with something lawful, but without due care, he does not escape being guilty of murder, if his action results in someone's death.[28]

Moreover, the author also clearly stresses that the perpetrator's error cannot always be justified. Even if someone claims to have killed a man by mistake, it is necessary to check whether he took sufficient care to avoid this mistake.[29]

In modern ethics, views on moral responsibility for unintentional omission vary. There are different arguments and justifications to demonstrate the validity of attributing responsibility in such cases. The views most relevant to the analysis of criminal law are presented below.

George Sher notes three possible scenarios of omission.[30] In the first, the perpetrator does not intend to commit an omission, but at the same time he intends to act in such a way as to cause a simultaneous omission, for example, the subject of the perpetrator's intention is to write a scientific article on a given day, so that they are allowed to fail to teach that day. The subject in this scenario does not lead to a bad effect with his or her action, but allows and accepts it, knowing that it must happen.[31] It is therefore questionable whether there is any moral difference between causing evil by action and causing evil by omission, accompanied by the certainty that it is necessary to cause this passivity of a certain effect. Translating this into the language of criminal law, such a situation is more like a direct intention than a resultant one. The perpetrator knows that staying at home means that he will avoid the lessons. If he decides to stay at home with such knowledge, it is legitimate to claim that he wants to avoid them.

In the second scenario, the perpetrator does not seem to be failing, but at the same time—despite the doubts that have arisen—he does not decide to verify his opinion.[32] Coming back to the example of the researcher, it seems to him that classes start only in the following week and—despite some doubt—this conviction is so strong that he does not decide to look at the academic year calendar on the university's website. The responsibility in this case is connected with the fact that the perpetrator takes the risk, so he does not decide to take any actions that may protect him from omission. Using the categories of the subjective party known to Polish criminal law, this example should be placed in the structure of conscious unawareness. Precise, if possible, determination of the form of the subjective party would require more thorough verification of the state of knowledge and will of the perpetrator.

In the third scenario, the perpetrator is not at all aware that an omission is being or may be committed. There are no doubts that would make him verify his knowledge. George Sher points out that it is precisely such cases that pose the greatest difficulties in the moral assessment of an omission.[33]

The author notes that one of the possible explanations for the legitimacy of attributing responsibility for such an omission is an attempt to create a standard which would result in the obligation to take certain actions to prevent the perpetrator from committing the omission. However, if the perpetrator had never before experienced a similar situation, had no reason to doubt his memory or other circumstances relevant to a given event, it is difficult to find in his behavior an attitude, some moment of desire, with which responsibility could be associated.[34] However, the problem may look different if we give up the assumption, accepted by some ethicists, that the source of responsibility should always be sought in some attitude of will.[35]

Another possibility comes not so much from an appeal to the will as from the assumption that the perpetrator may be responsible for their actions if and only if they express what is important or constitute a response to their judgment. These judgments need not be consciously invoked. Those who support this explanation note that beliefs and judgments have a significant impact on our cognitive abilities.[36] Unintentional omission may involve responsibility, according to this explanation, as long as the neglect to know the obligation to act is explained by indicating the lack of validity of this fact for a given perpetrator.[37] For if a given thing was important enough for the perpetrator, they would certainly be more careful in checking it and would maintain appropriate control.

George Sher finally accepts a slightly different explanation, however, referring to the two above. Responsibility for an omission can be attributed to a given person if they retain the ability to react wisely to surrounding stimuli. If such an ability is not excluded for some reason, the subject can be held responsible for all their omissions. This interpretation assumes that a given entity takes full responsibility for all of itself, all of its processes, including the inability of its cognitive centers to recognize the necessity of action and the associated risk of omission.[38]

The above is linked to the premise of responsibility for failure to act, which requires that the possibility of action and prevention of certain consequences be established. In the previous chapter, the concept of so-called managerial control was indicated. If a person is not able to act effectively in given circumstances, they should not be liable for an omission.[39] At the same time, it is not the objective possibility that should be examined but the perpetrator's idea of what can be done. One can also talk about moral responsibility when the perpetrator objectively could not act, but in their conviction, he saw such an opportunity and—despite this—refrained from acting. According to G. Sher, the perpetrator will also be responsible if they have maintained managerial control, and yet have not noticed any circumstances indicating an obligation to act.

Angela M. Smith interprets the issue of responsibility for an omission, which she describes as an unconscious omission, somewhat differently.[40] She criticizes the concept of a specific omission in the foreground, which is that moral responsibility for an unconscious omission can be attributed when we are able to associate it with some previous voluntary and conscious action or omission.[41] At the same time, she proposes another solution, referring to the concept presented by Patricia Smith.[42] In this concept, responsibility for an unconscious omission can be attributed if one could require the subject to undertake such an action that would prevent their unconsciousness and, consequently, the omission itself. The responsibility comes from a standard of conduct that was not followed by a given individual.[43]

The standard of defined conduct should be understood as meaning that a given person should have been expected to behave in a certain way because:

1) A could have, under normal circumstances, or should have, done s and knew it; and should have known it; and
2) s is likely to be behavior for A or for people in a similar situation—you usually do s in such a situation; or
3) s is behavior appropriate for A (or persons in their situation) because of their particular duties, moral obligation, or other responsibility to do s.[44]

One of the comments raised against this concept is the vagueness of the phrase "it is reasonable to expect subject A to behave as s in the given circumstances." This is the wording of the standard properly presented above. The phrase can be understood descriptively and normatively. A descriptive understanding is anchored in some experience related to a given situation and reflects a certain regularity that usually occurs in such a factual context. A normative understanding, on the other hand, refers not to past observations but to obligations, that is, to a norm that obliges a given entity to perform a certain behavior.[45] With a descriptive understanding, which can also be described as epistemic, the problem is that from a certain habit, practice, repeated observations, it is not necessarily possible to derive a legitimate expectation that a person should once again behave according to a certain regularity. In other words, we cannot accuse someone of omission when someone—consciously or not—deviates from a given regularity.[46] For this reason, the second premise mentioned above, referring precisely to probability, that is, to the descriptive layer, can be questioned.

According to A. M. Smith, although P. Smith's approach is largely accurate, it is impossible to give up looking for a subjective element. However, it is not so much this element that we should look for in the time before the omission itself, but afterward, that is, when the perpetrator makes an *a posteriori* evaluation of their conduct.[47] The determination that some non-activity can be qualified as an omission does not mean condemning it. Whether a given omission is accusable or should be a cause for praise depends on the context. Therefore, the author proposes other criteria of omission. In her interpretation, it is reasonable to assess the omission A in the implementation of an action s, because:

1) A under normal circumstances could or should have done s, and A should have known this, and

2) there was a standard in force which, under the circumstances, gave A reason to believe that a given action was preferred or required, and A knew or should have known this.[48]

In the light of the ethical concepts cited, it is reasonable to recognize that unintentional omission may not only occur but may also give rise to responsibility. This is also possible in the case of unintentional negligence, that is, when the perpetrator was unaware of their duty to act and unknowingly violated the precautionary principle with their action. In the Polish doctrine of criminal law, it is noted that the lack of awareness of the fact that the signs of the type of a forbidden act are realized is a result of "lack of knowledge or inability to extract it from the so-called permanent memory."[49]

In the search for ethical legitimization for such solutions, it is helpful to look at the views of A. M. Smith presented above. Responsibility for an omission committed in unintentional thoughtlessness is therefore possible when:

1) the perpetrator was able to fulfill his duty, according to the rules of prudence, and knew this or should have known it, and
2) there was a legal norm imposing a legal obligation on A to act, and the entity knew it or should have known it.[50]

This criminal law paraphrase of the ethical formula proposed by A. M. Smith uses the category of legal norm and legal obligation, because criminal law does not explicitly sanction ethical norms. Criminal law sanction refers only to those obligations that are included in the scope of legal norms. Other obligations are subject to other, nonlegal sanctions.

The standards referred to in the ethical analysis have been reflected here with the help of the precautionary principle category. Under criminal law, in the case of unintentional acts, it is precisely the precautionary rules that reflect the standard of proper behavior. The precautionary rules are understood as rules of conduct with the good, the observance of which is supposed to prevent a violation of that good.[51] The rules of prudent conduct are established objectively in relation to a given good. Any personal circumstances of the perpetrator are irrelevant here.[52]

The need to be aware of the possibility of fulfilling a duty and the knowledge of the duty itself is not as objective as the proponents of a normative guilt theory would like.[53] The claim that the perpetrator should—in the context of an omission—have been aware of the obligation to act and the possibility of acting should not be understood as creating premises of responsibility completely detached from the individual characteristics of the perpetrator, their intellectual capacity, or education. It seems unjustified to assume that every person has the intellectual capacity and awareness at the same level. Although the supporters of the pure normative theory of guilt transfer the necessity of taking into account subjective elements to the stage of investigating the chargeability of an act, it is impossible not to doubt the completely objective interpretation of the possibility of predicting the commission of a prohibited act.

The fact that the possibility of anticipating does not mean that all the circumstances relating to the possibility of recognizing obligations should be taken into account at this stage of the analysis. Rather, the point is that when constructing a model of a reasonable citizen, the model cannot be dissociated from the qualification of the person whose behavior is being analyzed. Distortions occurring at the time of committing a prohibited act do not constitute a pattern according to which we examine the duty of a specific behavior. However, this pattern should take into account the attributes of a given person that go beyond this individual situation, for example, intellectual capabilities. Otherwise, we construct a norm of conduct that comes close to contradicting the principle of *impossibilium nulla obligatio est.*[54] It is necessary to establish, as J. Lachowski notes, the real possibility of predicting the commission of a forbidden act.[55] The thesis of the Supreme Court from more than forty years ago, still referred to in the literature, may be helpful in this:

> The necessity and possibility of anticipating the consequences of the perpetrator's action cannot be assessed in isolation from the specific situation. They should be assessed taking into account the probability of the consequences resulting from the specific behaviour of the perpetrator, taking into account their life experience. On the other hand, probability should be assessed as something more than just an abstract possibility. The perpetrator may be charged with the duty and ability to predict only normal, typical consequences, and not completely exceptional ones, taking into account the perpetrator's personality, age, life experience, education and intellectual level.[56]

It should also be noted that from the perspective of ethical legitimization, the key factor is the result, that is, the correct assessment of responsibility, and a much less important theoretical solution to the level of this assessment, that is, the choice between the level of unlawfulness or guilt. Michał Królikowski also takes a practical approach to the theoretical controversies:

> The silence of the Code [concerning the determination of the normative concept of guilt—author's note] is in this case fortunate enough to allow it to be more freely placed in a place chosen by the authority applying the law, depending on its possibilities and argumentation needs, as well as to be defined in this way.[57]

The issue of omission in its scope includes at least one more issue that is important for both legal and ethical analysis, that is, worthy of attention when considering the ethical legitimization of criminal liability for omission. To accuse someone of an omission is tantamount to stating that they should have behaved differently, and thus should have taken some action, in many cases also to prevent a specific effect. Omitting the component of the duty to act would mean that every person commits a constantly unlimited number of omissions. If I teach, I do not help my wife at this time, nor do I become involved in the activities of a social organization and do a number of other things. However, this does not mean that I can be held accountable, be it morally or legally.

The link between omission and obligation is also noticeable in individual provisions of the Penal Code relating to omission, for example, in Article 6 § 1 of the Penal Code, which states that: "A prohibited act shall be deemed to have been committed at the time when the perpetrator acted or failed to act as he was obliged to do." Therefore, it is rightly noted that it would be incomplete to understand an omission as the absence of a specific action, as it should be understood as the failure to take the action to which the perpetrator was obliged.[58] This obligation is sometimes defined as "an obligation to take an active action, the social consequence of which is not to violate a given social good, and the legal consequence is to avoid committing an act prohibited by law under penalty (a typified threat to the legal good)".[59]

As we know, the attribution of criminal responsibility for an omission varies depending on the material or formal nature of the offense, that is, whether it is an improper or proper offense of omission.[60] In the case of formal offenses, the attribution of responsibility does not differ from the rules applicable in the case of an act.[61] As W. Wolter pointed out, in the case of formal offenses, which are characterized by the deed itself, it must be clear from the statutory definition of the type whether responsibility is also possible or exclusively for the omission.[62] In offenses with criminal consequences, in which the determination of a deed is made by the description of causing the effect, the law usually does not specify the form of the act, that is, it does not indicate whether it can occur both by action and omission or only by one of these forms of act. This, however, is due to the verbal phrase used, as well as the description of the consequence. What is even more important in the case of an offense with criminal consequences, there appears an additional condition of responsibility, indicated in Article 2 of the Criminal Code: "Only those who were under a legal, special obligation to prevent the effect are criminally responsible for an effective offence committed by omission." Such a person will be described in the doctrine of criminal law as a "guarantor."

The obligations of the guarantors are divided into the duties of paying heed to the legal good, the obligation to control the situation—supervision of the sources of danger, the obligation to protect a specific legal good only against danger of a certain type or danger coming from a specific source.[63] The obligation to prevent an effect may result from the act, but also from the voluntary and actual assumption of the guarantor's function. As Ł. Pohl notes, this may be not only a contract but also a prior action by which a given entity created a danger to the legal good.[64] The statutory obligation in most cases will need to be specified in the contract or in a specific situation.[65]

The principles of liability for offenses with criminal consequences committed by omission are sometimes criticized, as there is a risk that the obligation to act is too broad. In this way, excessive criminalization may occur.[66] Armin Kaufman, for example, pointed this out: "Even if a provision were to be passed tomorrow requiring postal workers to provide assistance to all persons in danger encountered in the course of delivering letters, we should not consider that a postman who failed to do so killed a person in danger if they eventually died as a result of his omission."[67] In such cases, it is not obvious to place a mark of equality between a finding of failure to assist, even if the person was legally obliged to do so, and the attribution of responsibility for the murder or even, depending on the party involved, for committing manslaughter. Even at the level of language, it is difficult to accept the statement that a person committing an omission causes death. It seems that they rather do not prevent it. It is likely that death was caused by other circumstances.

The problems outlined above are side-effects of the convention finally adopted, which requires both action and omission to be treated equally as a deed. These may not be difficulties that make one give up on this assumption, but they cannot be overlooked in reflections on the responsibility for failure to act.

Duties are an obvious element of moral norms.[68] Everyone who is confronted with a given duty is obliged to take actions for its accomplishment and to omit what could be betrayed by this duty. Aquinas had already pointed out the close link between the omission and duty.[69]

The doctrine developed in classical ethics to reconstruct the hierarchy between individual duties also seems to be important for the deliberations conducted here. It interprets the principle of the so-called order of love (*ordo caritatis*), which allows for the proper shaping of the process of fulfilling one's duties, especially when their simultaneous fulfillment is not possible, for various reasons. The doctrine presented here is applicable not only in the case of omissions but also to the interpretation of the so-called collision of duties, which is expressed in Art. 26 § 5 of the Penal Code.[70]

The doctrine of *ordo caritatis* dates back to St. Augustine, who in his work *De doctrina christiana* noted that: "We must all be loved equally, but because we cannot help everyone, we must help those who, because of place, time or other circumstances, are more closely connected to us by fate."[71] The doctrine was developed by Saint Thomas Aquinas, who proposed the following order: love of God, love of ourselves, love of our neighbor, love of our body, love of our neighbor's body; and then love for our parents, love for our children, love for our wife, love for relatives, love for people we know well, love for strangers, love for enemies.[72] Moral values must be considered as superior to material values.

At the same time, Thomas pointed out that the circumstances of the situation are not without significance:

> Now the order of nature is such that every natural agent pours forth its activity first and most of all on the things which are nearest to it: thus fire heats most what is next to it. (. . .) Therefore we ought to be most beneficent towards those who are most closely connected with us. Now one man's connection with another may be measured in reference to the various matters in which men are engaged together; (thus the intercourse of kinsmen is in natural matters, that of fellow-citizens is in civic matters, that of the faithful is in spiritual matters, and so forth): and various benefits should be conferred in various ways according to these various connections, because we ought in preference to bestow on each one such benefits as pertain to the matter in which, speaking simply, he is most closely connected with us. And yet this may vary according to the various requirements of time, place, or matter in hand: because in certain cases one ought, for instance, to succor a stranger, in extreme necessity, rather than one's own father, if he is not in such urgent need.[73]

This means that in terms of ethics, in the classical point of view, the order of assistance should take into account the subjective aspect (ties with the needy),[74] the scale of the need (a person in great need, for example, a life-threatening one, should be helped more than a person experiencing a slight injury) and the type of need (spiritual over material need).

The assumptions of the concept of ethical legitimization of criminal law certainly do not serve to resolve theoretical discussions or academic disputes arising from criminal law. Rather, the task of this concept is to create such a set of tools that will orient the process of creating and applying criminal law toward a realistic understanding of the human being as such and the morally acceptable scope of their responsibility. We will not, therefore, decide, with the help of these tools, whether criminal law should treat omission and action as equivalent forms of deed. This does not mean, however, that it is impossible to formulate certain assessments or guidelines relating to this theoretical tension.

Doubts may arise, in some cases, with regard to the degree of reprisal of omission compared to acting, also because of the stigmatization labels which are linked to criminal law. This problem concerns material crimes. In the case of an action, we have no difficulty in defining the act of the perpetrator as murder, causing death, or causing serious damage to health. The perpetrator then directs their activity in such a way that it actively causes such a consequence. By acting, the perpetrator becomes involved in the causal processes, modifying them in such a way that a specific result is achieved. In the case of omission, however, in many cases, the perpetrator refrains from being included in the causal chain.[75] The equation of omission with action is of value. Differentiation at the level of penalty may not be sufficient.

The outlined difficulty becomes apparent in the case of unintentional omission. The reprehensibility of behavior consisting in an omission depends to a large extent on the detailed characteristics of the obligation which a person is misappropriating. The stronger this obligation is, the more axiologically conditioned it is, the greater the degree of reprimand that is charged to a given omission. Although unawareness is always an omission in some aspect, because it consists in not observing the rules of prudence, it nevertheless seems less reprehensible in the case of an omission than in the case of an action. From the perspective of moral responsibility, it is difficult, in the light of the analyses carried out above, to put a sign of equality between action and omission, although this does not mean that an omission is not subject to responsibility.[76] It is possible to understand the dogmatic solution of considering both forms as deeds, if only to avoid creating two separate dogmas—act and omission.[77] However, it seems appropriate to consider giving normative expression to the difference between these forms, for example, in directives on punishment.

The above ethical category *ordo caritatis* may be helpful in analyzing the extent of this differentiation. Its axiological conditionality will also depend on the position of the obligation in the hierarchy. As a consequence, the failure to fulfill an obligation placed at most in this order, or high enough, will bring the degree of reprehensibility of an omission closer to that known to us from action.

NECESSARY DEFENSE

Necessary defense is one of those concepts that are commonly recognized in criminal law, albeit with many stereotypes. It is also an institution in criminal law about which much has already been written.[78] However, it seems worthwhile to look at how the possibility of repelling an attack attempt, even reaching the point of depriving another person of their life, relates to ethics, especially those currents which have been chosen here as the basic point of reference. The reflections conducted in this area can help to shape the limits of necessary defense, especially its premises.

General considerations on how to defend oneself have already been taken up in the previous chapter. Here, it is appropriate to focus primarily on the preconditions for necessary self-defense, which determine its limits.

In ethics, the issue of self-defense is directly linked to the doctrine of double effect. It was on the basis of Aquinas's considerations about necessary defense that the whole concept of the principle of double effect was later built.[79] The problem of necessary defense which Thomas analyzed was not clearly solved at that time. The author himself quotes an excerpt from St. Augustine's statement, which only allowed the killing of someone by a soldier or a person holding public office, but not in their own defense but in the defense of other people and the state. In his opinion, one cannot kill in order not to be killed oneself.[80] Thomas stood in opposition to this view.[81]

The following arguments can be derived from St. Thomas's argument concerning necessary self-defense:

1. two effects may result from one act, one of which is intentional and the other unintentional,[82]
2. in the case of defense, one effect is to defend one's life, the other is to kill the attacker,
3. it is natural to strive to preserve one's own life,
4. a deed committed with good intent becomes unlawful if it is disproportionate to the aim,
5. defense is permissible if it is exercised in moderation, and
6. it is unacceptable for someone to intend to kill a person for their own defense.[83]

From the above, it follows first of all that the action of the one reacting to the attack should be directed directly at their defense; this should be the subject of direct intention. This is clearly emphasized in the premise relating to intention. According to the abovementioned premises, a person who wanted to kill another human being in self-defense cannot be exempted from responsibility, so the two accompanying goals were of a direct nature, and certainly the direct intention was to cause the death of the attacker.[84] The defense is to be undertaken *cum moderamine inculatae tutelae*, that is, as necessary, without committing guilt.[85] If it is possible to defend one's life without killing the attacker, the reaction is to be limited to the means necessary and sufficient to defend.

Another premise is to defend ourselves in moderation. Together with the premise discussed earlier, they indicate that the self-defense should be directed toward neutralizing the attacker, so that they could not continue their intention. The moral responsibility does not come if the killing of the attacker took place in spite of the will. The measures taken should be moderate, and thus not exceed necessity.[86] They should be sufficient to repel the attack. The defender must not use means beyond what is necessary.

In his reflections on the possibility of taking life in self-defense, Thomas does not consider the possibility of killing in defense of someone else, even if they are weaker. Although he explicitly accepts the possibility of actions of soldiers or other state functionaries, he does not refer to what makes the necessary self-defense different from his own, and so the necessary defense absolutely need not be one's own.[87]

In the ethics developed in the classical tradition, which also refers to Thomas' thoughts, a position has emerged which allows for a necessary defense even when the object of the defender's direct intention is to deprive the aggressor of life.[88] According to Tadeusz Ślipko, who considers necessary defense in the context of a threat to human life, both the attack and the defense are, from the point of view of their effect, directly fatal actions. In each of these cases the natural result of the perpetrator's behavior is the death of the other. The only difference, with effective necessary self-defense is that the intended effect was achieved not by the attacker but by the defender.[89] This author is unequivocally opposed to the understanding of the necessary self-defense through the prism of the principle of double effect. In his interpretation, the mere presence of an intrinsically, morally evil act in the structure of a human act, regardless of whether we consider it directly intentional, makes the whole act morally evil.[90] Consequently, he rejects the thesis of merely tolerating the death of the attacker. According to Ślipko, the death of the aggressor directly lies in the purposefulness of the one defending themself.[91]

Before proceeding to further deliberations, it should be noted that, according to the author mentioned above, one can defend not only one's own life but also the lives of others. Therefore, the premises discussed here are not limited to defending one's own life but also the lives of others. A similar view had been previously expressed by J. Woroniecki, indicating that this is especially true of people to whom we have special obligations: spouse, children, parents, wards, but also other kith and kin.[92]

By aggression, T. Slipko means

> a direct killing action by another person (aggressor) directed against the life of a person defending their life. The death of the defending person lies in the structure of the activity of the aggressor as its natural result, and this activity by the aggressor itself was not provoked by an identical action of the defending person, but resulted from his own will.[93]

According to this definition, the object of the intention of a person defending themselves against a deadly attack may be the death of the aggressor. At the same time, it is unacceptable to provoke someone to attack, and thus to contribute to their taking on the role of an aggressor. At the same time, the author adds that the aggression must be of a current, direct nature, so the defense against it cannot anticipate the aggression itself or at least the act revealing a direct readiness to undertake it.[94]

The defense must be necessary. In the opinion of T. Ślipko, it is therefore only admissible if it is the ultimate and only means of defense against aggression. It does not become so when it is possible to escape from the attacker. From this reasoning, it may be concluded that self-defense has a subsidiary character in this sense. If it is possible to avoid an attack without confronting the aggressor, this solution should be chosen.[95]

If we agree with T. Slipko's abovementioned statement that killing is an intrinsically evil act, it is impossible not to notice that self-defense may appear to be a morally inadmissible act, regardless of whether we assume that killing the attacker was the subject of direct or indirect effect. It might seem that in this situation there is a conflict between the right to defend the life of the defender and at the same time the attacker's right to defend their own life. However, such an approach would lead to a violation of human dignity, and thus of the moral order as such. After all, it cannot be claimed that the protection of life, which is directly embedded in the dignity of the human being, can only take place at the expense of protecting the life of another human being. Even if one is the aggressor, they still retain their dignity, which is inborn and inalienable.[96]

The principle of human dignity, which is discussed extensively in chapter 2, assumes, as noted, an equal moral status for all people. Every human being has the same dignity, so everyone should be treated as a moral subject, capable of bearing responsibility. If everyone has dignity, then everyone has the same moral value, so that the value of everyone's life is also the same. The moral value of one person must not be privileged, as this would lead to a diminished value of another.[97]

The above, contrary to appearances, does not exclude the possibility of depriving someone of their life in necessary self-defense. In order to understand this properly, special attention should be paid to the problem of favoring one at the expense of the other. Denying the defender the right to defend their life against an aggressor would at the same time lead to privileging the moral value of the attacker's life. His life would then in an obvious way be more protected than the life of the defender.[98] According to T. Slipko:

> If [the defender—author's note] undertakes this act in order to defend his own life equivalent to the life of the aggressor, but does not cause any other morally reprehensible motives (e.g. desire for revenge or cruelty), then he fulfils an act comprehensively free from the flaw of moral evil and—because of the greatness of the goal—morally acceptable.[99]

Thus, the author introduces the category of a morally intrinsically evil act into his deliberations on necessary self-defense.[100]

The concept of a morally intrinsically evil act is a restrictive one, indicating that there are moral acts consisting of two fixed and unchangeable elements: the essential content of good or evil and the moral neutrality and proper restriction of it.[101] It cannot therefore be claimed that every act falling into this category will, depending on the act, be bad or good. For if it falls within the scope of the restrictions associated with a given act, it will only be morally neutral. An example of such acts can be the following triad: truthfulness (a good act)—a lie (a restrictively bad act)—falsehood when keeping a secret (a neutral act). As for the necessary defense, it appears in this way: the protection of human life (good act)—murder (restrictive bad act)—killing a person in necessary self-defense (neutral act).[102] The introduction of this restriction as a component of moral acts prevents the introduction of this theory of ethics into the field of conflict of laws, and thus leads to the recognition of the moral order as an order characterized by harmony and internal balance.[103]

The question, obvious and necessary, which is revealed in the light of the ethical considerations to date on necessary self-defense, is whether it is possible to defend others' rights than one's own or others' lives against aggression, so as to avoid responsibility. The answer that classical ethics gives us indicates that this is possible while the defense covers goods that are integral to human existence. It is also of a reductive nature, which means that the scale of the means of defense used and of the goods sacrificed by the aggressor depends on the goods threatened by the attack.[104] Deprivation of the aggressor's life is permissible above all in the situation of defending one's own life, or that of another person, against an attack. Is it also acceptable in other cases? In his ethics manual, J. Woroniecki stated that it is possible in two more cases: a woman can kill the aggressor in the case of an attempted rape; it is also possible to kill the aggressor if he deprives someone of an asset necessary for life, unless there is another method of defense.[105]

In modern ethics, attention is drawn to the problem of the attitude not only of the defender but also of the perpetrator of an attack. It is not without significance whether it seems that the perpetrator acts with intent, in error, or accidentally.[106] What if, for example, it turns out that the alleged attack was the legitimate action of a police officer on duty? A possible solution was proposed by R. B. Miller. He notes that the victim of an attack, regardless of whether it is real or to some extent delusional, has the right—in case of doubts that cannot be resolved in time to repulse the attack—to decide to defend his own life.[107] It seems, according to this author, that the perspective of an external observer should be accepted. The limits of necessary self-defense in a specific case become narrower—or indeed the right to necessary self-defense ceases to exist—if it can be concluded in context that in reality the perpetrator's behavior is not a morally reprehensible act.

Nor can it be ruled out that an attack, even one which threatens the life of another person, will be caused by omission. In such a situation, too, it is possible to undertake necessary self-defense, maintaining all the premises which have been discussed in relation to the defense necessary in response to the attack which is an act. Although it is more difficult to imagine such an attack caused by an omission, which would endanger the life of the victim, and in order to repel it, it would be necessary to kill the attacker, if it actually took place, the necessary self-defense will also justify the deprivation of the aggressor of life.[108]

In modern ethics, attention is drawn to the problem of cognitive uncertainty, which is essentially linked to necessary defense. This uncertainty is caused by the anticipatory nature of necessary defense. Necessary self-defense consists of repelling an attack, very often at its initial stage. The defender may not yet know what effects the attack would ultimately lead to, may not be aware of other options of responding to the attack, and may not have full knowledge of the subjective status of the perpetrator, including the circumstances that could determine his responsibility.[109]

In this state of uncertainty, the defender is obliged to observe the necessary self-defense so that their behavior does not become a basis for attributing responsibility to them. The premise of proportionality, necessity, and retreat is discussed in this context.[110] Proportionality presupposes the obligation to choose means of defense proportionate to the degree of infringement of the good that the perpetrator of the attack wants to cause.[111] The premise of necessity is understood as the use by the defender of only such means as are necessary to avoid the attack. Although proportionality and necessity are sometimes the subject of disputes and different interpretations, the most questionable is the premise of retreat. It raises the question whether the defender should first consider the possibility of escaping the attacker as a basic solution, that is, avoiding the attack in such a way that it does not lead to any damage to the attacker's goods.[112] The premise of retreat is oriented on the perpetrator's sacrifice of the good, which is the right to remain in a given place, which is in the hierarchy of goods lower than the life and health of the perpetrator of the attack.[113] It is noted that where it is possible to escape from the aggressor, this should be undertaken instead of deciding to repel an attack that could lead to deprivation of the assailant's life.

The question of the intention accompanying the necessary self-defense is discussed. This is particularly evident in the context of a provocation, that is to say, a behavior that is intended to cause another person to behave aggressively, giving the provocateur a basis for applying necessary self-defense. In such cases, the provocateur acts with the intention of depriving the person they are provoking of life. In the light of the abovementioned grounds for defense proposed by Thomas Aquinas, in such a case, there will be no exclusion of responsibility. A different view on this issue is presented by the contemporary philosopher L. Alexander. He observes that the provoked entity should maintain such a level of self-control that will allow them to refrain from reacting in accordance with the premises of the attack.[114]

One of the ways in which ethics attempts to deal with the problem of intent in self-defense today is to construct this figure using only objective premises.[115] One such theory assumes that killing an attacker is possible when they violate the victim's right to life, and thus lose their right to life.[116] This concept is based on the already commented suspension of the killer's right to life.[117] Another objective theory assumes that necessary defense, both of oneself and another person, is possible within the limits set by the principles of necessity and proportionality, as long as the attack was not justified.[118] The third popular objective theory assumes that it is justified to kill a person whose body movements pose a serious threat to the life of another person. The force used to repel an attack will be justified if it is necessary and proportionate, and the threat caused by the attacker was not justified. At the same time, necessary defense is excluded if the behavior of the defender will lead to the death of neutral persons or attackers whose attack was justified.[119] The objectivization of criteria causes difficulties that can be avoided using subjective criteria.[120]

It follows from the ethical considerations set out above with regard to necessary defense that it is permissible to exclude moral responsibility for an infringement of the attacker's goods by a person who defends himself or another person. It is essential, however, that the defense should be commensurate with the type of attack and that moderate measures should be used. Only exceptionally can an attacker be deprived of their life. In such situations, a decision to retreat is preferable, if it is actually possible. One of the major problems is the issue of subjective premises. First of all, the intention of the defender may be important. The assault should not be provoked by the defender.[121] However, there is no longer any agreement as to whether the defender can include in his or her intention, especially direct intention, to take the assailant's life. It has also been pointed out that necessary defense is not acceptable when the defender's goods are justifiably violated. However, if it is not possible to establish, in sufficient time to allow the defense, that the infringement is justified, the defense will be admissible.

These conclusions must now be confronted with the basic theses concerning necessary defense in Polish criminal law, so as to determine whether they find support in ethics, and thus whether they are ethically legitimized.

The literature of criminal law notes that necessary defense consists in repelling a direct and unlawful attack on any good protected by law.[122] This finds direct empowerment in the wording of Article 25 § 1 of the Penal Code. The name of the discussed category, which in criminal law functions as a legal defense, is explained by indicating that this "necessity" makes it necessary to interpret the premises of the defense through the prism of socially tolerated limits of defense, set by a certain set of axiological conditions.[123] It is noted, for example, that participation in a fight or a previous provocation precludes the possibility of using necessary defense.[124]

The prerequisites for the necessary defense in question include, in criminal law, the necessity of an assault. Violation of the attacker's goods can only take place in a situation where they have caused an attack. What is particularly important, in view of the ethical considerations carried out earlier, is that an attack does not have to be targeted, which means that it does not have to be the subject of the perpetrator's intention. An attack may be caused even by unconscious behavior.[125] In modern ethics, the analysis of the intentions of the perpetrator of an assault is not without significance. It is important above all in those situations where defense is necessary to justify taking the life of the perpetrator of an assault. Although it does not seem justified to require the person whose life is in danger to passively accept the threat simply because the perpetrator of the attack remains inadvertent, in such cases, one may consider abandoning the necessary defense and preferring to retreat. Thus, in such situations, when the victim of an assault is aware, or can and should have been aware, that the perpetrator of the assault is acting unintentionally, they should first—insofar as it is possible—take advantage of the option to escape, that is, to avoid the assault in such a way that it would not cause damage to the goods of the perpetrator of the attack. This modification would be justified especially if the necessary self-defense had to aim at depriving the attacker of their life. However, it may be considered to extend it to the defense necessary against unintentional assaults in general.

An assault can also be caused by omission. A similar conclusion was reached in ethical considerations. In the literature of criminal law, there is also the problem of the duty to provide assistance in the context of necessary defense. One of the problems arises from a case described by J. Kulesza. Person B refuses to consent to the transplantation of his kidney to the body of person A, although the latter is at risk of death due to kidney failure and the transplantation is the only way to prevent the harmful effect. It is also known that the procedure can be performed without exposing the life of the donor to immediate danger.[126] In criminal law terms, the problem is particularly important when this form of assistance is avoided by a person who has a particular legal obligation to prevent the effect and is therefore a guarantor. In the case of a formal offense, described in Article 162 of the Criminal Code, an unlawful assault by omission will not take place, as § 2 excludes the obligation to provide assistance, for which it is necessary to undergo a medical procedure or in conditions in which immediate assistance from an institution or a person appointed for this purpose is possible.[127]

However, the question of the possibility of applying the necessary defense to a father who does not want to consent to the transplantation necessary for the life of his child remains.[128] The parent or other appointed guardian has undoubtedly a duty to act in order to keep their ward alive. This is due to the very nature of the care. It can therefore be considered whether the failure to consent to the kidney transplantation for the child is not unlawful and consequently does not give rise to responsibility for the relevant offense, depending on the subject and the effect that occurred. In the context of necessary defense, it is essential to establish that the action of the guardian is unlawful in such a case and may therefore be regarded as unlawful assault by omission. The possibility of a necessary defense appears difficult to accept. One of the possible justifications for rejecting this solution is an attempt to demonstrate that the current legislation, including the Family and Guardianship Code, we do not find sufficient grounds to derive the parent's obligation to donate their organ for the child.[129] At this point, it is worth considering whether, from an ethical perspective, it would be reasonable to expect the criminal law to release the doctor who took the kidney without the patient's consent to transplant it to that patient's child from responsibility.

First of all, taking into account previous considerations on omissions, it is necessary to consider whether this case is indeed an assault by omission. In this case, it is not the omission that is the source of the danger. The threat to life has previously arisen from an illness that has affected the child's body. In some cases, it is the omission that is the direct source of the violation of a good or the cause of danger. This is the case, for example, in the case of an omission to cross the barrier at a railway crossing. Persistence in the omission is the only source of danger. In the context of the case in question, however, it is doubtful to talk about the guardian's assault on the child's life to the extent that it is possible to talk about it in the case of action.

Another issue is just allowing a kidney to be taken without the consent of the patient who is alive. In such a case, it cannot be claimed that kidney removal against the patient's will is only a matter of indirect intention, as the doctor acts primarily to protect the child. After all, this is not a single act with a double effect, but two separate human acts. One is the removal of the kidney and the other is the implantation of the kidney into the child's body. It is not at all clear whether the two acts would be performed by one and the same person.

The inviolability of the human body and its autonomy as a patient result directly from human dignity. The removal of a kidney from someone for transplantation, without their will, cannot be considered as anything other than the treatment in question, and therefore an insult to the dignity of the human being, which does not allow it to be treated as a means to an end, even if that end is to save another person's life. The right to self-determination and bodily integrity, even if they are moral goods in a restrictive manner, cannot, precisely because of human dignity, be considered to include within the scope of this restriction the right to take an organ from someone without their consent. The restriction may primarily concern the good of the person themselves when they are unable to decide their fate voluntarily and consciously, for example, a life-saving operation may be decided on when the patient is unconscious.[130]

Undoubtedly, in the area of morality, we can consider the moral obligation of a parent to save the life of their child, even at the expense of their own bodily integrity. This does not mean, however, that a morally positive assessment can be made of a situation where a parent is forced to make such a decision or even when someone decides for them. All the more so, the demand for the admissibility of such a scheme of justification should not be formulated in the face of criminal law.

Consideration should be given to the legitimacy of using the phrase "direct, unlawful assault" in Article 25 § 1 of the Criminal Code, which may suggest the exclusion of the possibility of using necessary defense in a situation of direct threat of an assault.[131] Some representatives of the doctrine and judicature allow for the possibility to start defending an attack already at the stage of directly threatening it. This is the so-called "advance defense."[132] The Appelate Court in Lublin noted that:

> Thus, an assault will not only create a threat to a certain legal good, but also the next stage, in case of failure to defend, or inefficiency or ineffectiveness of the defense, i.e. violation of the attacked good. This notion is broad, it covers both the stage of creating a danger of infringing a legal good, as well as the stage of its violation. A denial of the idea of the right of defense would be such a situation, that the attacked person would be forced to "wait" for the stage of violation of their legal good in order to be sure that the attacker really wants to violate this good.[133]

In practice, it can be extremely difficult to determine when the immediate danger of an assault turns into an assault itself, especially for those who feel a serious threat. Such a person cannot be required to give up their preemptive defense and thus seriously risk their goods. At the same time, which can lead to some confusion, the literature indicates that an attack starts, in the case of intentional crimes, when the criminal activity enters the phase of attempted execution.[134] In the case of unintentional offenses, it is necessary to create an immediate danger.[135] This would mean that the immediate danger of an assault precedes the assault that involves the creation of an immediate danger to the good.

Regardless of these difficulties of interpretation, when referring to the problem of preemptive defense, from the perspective of the earlier ethical analysis, it is worth considering giving priority to the obligation to retreat, that is, giving up the self-reliance of necessary defense. This would mean that if the assault has not yet begun, and there is a possibility of escaping from the attacker, this would be the solution. The withdrawal from the defense would then take place when a potential defender noted a threat at the stage that preceded the assault, and thus that preceded the attacker's attempt to carry out or to cause a direct danger. The codex solution does not provide for such a scheme at this point in time, so this conclusion can be seen as a comment *de lege ferenda*.

Nowadays, in the Polish criminal law literature, some doubts have already been raised as to the legitimacy of necessary defense's absolute self-sufficiency.[136] One of the main arguments that appears in the context of a necessary defense resulting in taking the assailant's life is the wording of Article 2 of the Convention for the Protection of Human Rights and Fundamental Freedoms.[137] According to Article 2(2)(a) of the Convention, deprivation of life shall not be considered to be contrary to Article 2(1) if it results from the use of force necessary to defend any person against unlawful violence. The use of force is to be absolutely necessary.[138] If, at the time of the attack, there was a possibility of effective withdrawal, of which the attacker was aware, it cannot be convincingly claimed that it was absolutely necessary to take the life of the attacker. In such a situation, one could consider a statement of intense excess—crossing the boundaries of necessary defense.[139] The case law, including the Supreme Court's ruling of 15 April 2015, allows for any subsidiarity, because of the Conventional requirement invoked, to be applied to the very way in which an attack is repulsed and not to give up the defense by taking flight.[140] According to J. Kulesza, the Conventional standard imposes an obligation to measure the defense, and not to avoid the threat brought about by the assault in any other way than by undertaking the necessary defense.[141]

It is impossible not to notice that—as the Appellate Court in Szczecin put it—"the claim that the accused 'could just stand up and leave, could also repel the attack without a weapon,' is a contradiction of the broad jurisprudence of the Supreme Court and the Appellate Courts of Appeal in terms of necessary defense." However, it seems worth rethinking the dogma of the absolute independence of necessary defense, especially in those aspects highlighted above.

From the perspective of the moral assessment of defense, the aspect of the subjective side is very important, especially the intentions of the defender. It has been noted in the literature of criminal law that one can only speak of necessary defense if the necessary links exist: temporal (directness of the assault) and situational and motivational (awareness of the assault and the will to repel it) between the behavior of the defender and the assault.[142] At the same time, it is pointed out that necessary defense does not take place when the perpetrator acts not with the intention of defending himself, but with the intention of retaliation, revenge, giving a lesson, making self-judgment, or reciprocating for harm or insult.[143] Andrzej Zoll believes that the hallmark of the legal justification of the necessary defense "is based on the awareness of the signs defining the conditions for taking defensive action, the intention to repulse an assault, and thus to sacrifice the good of the attacker for this purpose."[144]

This should be understood as meaning that the defender should not be guided by the intention to kill the attacker or cause other damage to his goods as an end in itself. Instead, they should have the intention of repelling the attempted assault. Any action taken without this very intention does not fulfill the conditions of a necessary defense. It seems that such an understanding of the subjective side corresponds to the views of T. Slipko on ethics presented above. He indicated that it would be improper of the defender, as some continuators Thomas Aquinas's thoughts would like, not to have the intention of harming the attacker's goods, including—in life-threatening situations—even the task of killing them. In this context, the conception of the double effect can be shaken by a certain artificiality, completely different from the typical experience of the perpetrators of the necessary defense in reality. The important thing is that such an intention would probably not have come into being if it had not been for the fact of being attacked by an assailant.

Another important issue is the question of provocation and the possibility of taking the necessary defense afterward. The case law has indicated *expressis verbis* that: "deliberately provoking the injured party to do so, so that the provoked 'assailant' may, under the guise of exercising his defense, then confuse it—denies the possibility of justifying the offender's action in necessary defense."[145] The situation is interpreted differently when the perpetrator does not intentionally, but culpably provoke the other person to react. In such cases, it is possible to invoke necessary defense, especially if the attack was disproportionately intense in relation to the course of the provocation. The admissibility of necessary defense in such cases is fortified by doctrine with a relatively narrow interpretation of the premises that shape the limits of this legal defense.[146]

The view on provocation is essentially based on the ethical analyses mentioned above. However, a different view is presented by L. Alexander.[147] This author believes that the provocateur should retain the ability to analyze their situation and refrain from the assault. After all, despite the provocation, he retains the ability to make a rational assessment of the surrounding reality. A provocation does not reduce a person to an entity that reacts instinctively, without prior reflection. At the same time, L. Alexander compares these situations to provocations used by the police and secret services, which, after all, do not exempt the perpetrator of a crime from responsibility for the behavior resulting from the provocation.

L. Alexander's view deserves to be taken into account. At the same time, it is difficult to pass indifferently by the content of the intention of the provocateur, who undertakes this action only to then damage the goods of the provocateur, under the guise of necessary defense. After all, their intention is not to defend their goods. Therefore, it seems that this view, which limits the provocateur's right to a necessary defense only to those cases in which the provocateur's reaction was excessive in relation to the course of the provocation itself, is justified.

THE CONCEPT OF ENEMY CRIMINAL LAW

Probably no one doubts today that the criminal law of many countries of our legal culture is now in a state of transformation. One of its paradigms is to move away from certain classical solutions and institutions and to introduce those that are supposed to strengthen the preventive dimension of criminal law, thus making it a more effective tool in providing citizens with a sense of security. This is done in the context of threats such as organized crime and terrorism.[148] Increasing globalization often makes these threats cross-border in nature. Criminal law is beginning to point to the twilight of classical criminal law, giving way to preventive solutions. The intellectual sources used to describe this phenomenon are sought in the well-known division into "citizens' criminal law" and "enemy criminal law."

This division was introduced and disseminated by Günther Jakobs. This author originally used these categories merely descriptively, but after some time, he began to postulate the legitimacy of constructing criminal law in such a way that it contained not only "civic" but also "enemy" elements.[149] Citizen's criminal law is, in short, classic criminal law, with all the theoretical and dogmatic baggage we know. Enemy criminal law, also known as preventive criminal law, rejects a number of principles and guarantees of classical criminal law, far ahead of the protection of legal goods.[150] To this end, solutions are introduced that allow for intervention as early as at the stage of preparation for an act violating a protected good, and these changes are encapsulated in the process in such a way that it is possible to apply operational and exploratory measures without any limitations, and—at the stage of criminal proceedings—fewer of the guarantees traditionally associated with repressive law.[151] The structures qualified for enemy criminal law are intended as a response to the behavior of those individuals who not only infringe a protected good but also question the legal order and often the moral order as such. By their actions they place themselves outside the community, which means that they cannot draw on the guarantee standards provided for community members. The solutions applied are aimed at protecting citizens from harm caused to them by the enemies of the community.[152]

The essence of the concept of "enemy criminal law" is that people who show disloyalty or even reject the legal order, such as terrorists or even sex offenders, are excluded from the classic rules of criminal responsibility and are subject to other rules, formulated specifically for such perpetrators, considered enemies of the legal order.[153] This view is based on the premise that the guaranteed norms of substantive and procedural criminal law cannot be extended to those perpetrators who, by their conduct, fundamentally challenge the order that these norms prescribe. The application of other rules to such perpetrators, which are much less stringent, is to be motivated by the need to protect society, and thus public security. The "citizens' criminal law" is addressed to those responsible, who are loyal members of the political community and who are willing to comply with legal norms, including those of criminal law.[154] It is worth noting that preventive criminal law is rooted not only in G. Jakobs concept. At the same time, his concept of an "enemy combatant" was developed by the United States.[155] The problem discussed here reflects well the question formulated in legal journalism: "What is the difference between a criminal and an enemy?"[156]

In constructing the theory discussed here, G. Jakobs refers to a specific understanding of two concepts: compulsion and orientation toward legal institutions.[157] Explaining his understanding of the reference begins with reference to the work of Kant, who noted in his work that freedom, being an innate right, connects the law with the power of coercion.[158] This is coercion against evil to prevent violation of freedom. However, Kant does not explain, according to G. Jakobs, how coercion influences the personal status of an individual. In this respect, the author refers to the works of Paul J. A. R. Feuerbach, who stated that an individual subjected to coercion, although he is an intelligent being, in such conditions is governed by the law of nature, not the law of reason.[159]

Preventive action, influencing the potential perpetrator in such a way as to make them refrain from illegal behavior, and even the process of punishment, is still an expression of the law of reason in this concept. From its scope, the very compulsion, which is covered by the law of nature, escapes. It is therefore legitimate to state that the law of reason allows coercion under the law of nature.[160] This conclusion by G. Jakobs, taken from P. J. A. R. Feuerbach, must be translated into the status of an entity subjected to punishment. After all, there is no doubt that in the process preceding the use of coercion, that is, under the law of reason, the perpetrator had the status of a subject—a human being, a person. However, this changes with the moment of passing under the power of the law of nature. The perpetrator then becomes, in this concept, an individual. The constraint does not affect a person, but an individual, a natural being.[161] According to G. Jakobs, this claim is not undermined by the fact that it is a human being with the status of a person who, by their act, activates the whole machine leading to the use of coercion.[162]

This author, knowing the basic arguments critical of his theory, refers to the accusation that depriving a person, subjected to compulsion, of their status as a person violates their dignity. In response, G. Jakobs, starting from individualistic positions, notes that a human themselves is responsible for bringing themselves to such a state, as it is nothing else but his act, assumedly conscious and voluntary, that triggered the criminal trial leading to punishment. The author states, quite emotionally, that: "A human who questions this responsibility and takes away from the perpetrator of the coercion the ability to downgrade their status as a subject of the law, and ultimately even to waste this status, does not take them seriously as a person. Not a word more about it!"[163]

The role of legal institutions—this issue is dealt with by G. Jakobs under the motto "orientation towards legal institutions"—is to give the citizen a sense of security and a credible belief that they will not become a victim of crime. It is the citizen's responsibility to uphold the law even when others do not. The law must be respected because of its validity alone.[164] A potential offender has a duty to obey the law so that their case does not become real. A potential victim has the right to direct the conviction of potential perpetrators that they will not become actual perpetrators. If this expectation is not confirmed, the victim should know that it was not their belief that was wrong but the offender's behavior. However, it is not only, as G. Jakobs notes, a person having an abstract belief that they should not be killed. Perhaps for an abstract subject, an abstract sense of security is sufficient. A real person needs real certainty that they are safe.[165]

G. Jakobs, who notes that the legal system is built on awareness of its limitations, has an interesting observation. The institution which proves this is necessary defense. The attacked person may still express a normative expectation that they will not be harmed, but the legal system already has a kind of "awareness" that it is not capable of realizing this expectation and therefore allows the attacked person to use other means.[166] As already noted above, G. Jakobs claims that a person who is being coerced loses their status as a person, becoming a natural being. This statement appropriately describes the status of the attacker against whom necessary defense is applied, within its time limits of course. The example with necessary defense is supposed to prove that a community cannot exist only on the basis of abstract normative assumptions. Members of a community do not want to live only with a sense of security belonging to them abstractly. They want to be aware that such security is indeed guaranteed to them.

The two assumptions presented, that is, the connection of each law with coercion and the guarantee of real security by legal institutions, constitute a kind of clearing of the foreground for the justification of "enemy criminal law." Another occurrence which is supposed to confirm the existence of this phenomenon in the legal system is the development of security measures and other preventive mechanisms, which have become increasingly common in criminal law in recent decades.[167] Sometimes these preventive measures are disguised and dressed in the forms known to repressive measures in response to a past act. The very high penalties for certain crimes may lead us to believe that their primary function is to be general prevention rather than a reaction proportionate to the evil done by a given subject. "Enemy criminal law" is saturated primarily with preventive solutions, as opposed to "citizens' criminal law," which is intended to provide an appropriate response to acts already committed.[168] As is evident in these examples, "enemy criminal law" does not only include solutions that are directly related to terrorist, organized or sexual crime. After all, the preventive measures provided for in criminal law are applied not only to perpetrators of crimes belonging to these groups.

The division into "citizens' criminal law" and "enemy criminal law" refers to two types of communication between the state and its citizens. It is possible to communicate based on a personal paradigm or an instrumental paradigm.[169] The personal paradigm consists in the subjective treatment of an individual who is a responsible member of the political community. In criminal law, the types of offenses that are prohibited for violation of a good prevail. This is because we assume that people generally try to comply with the law, and an overly preventive criminal law reaction is not necessary. In the instrumental paradigm, citizens are seen through the prism of those who perceive legal norms as an external source of oppression, seeking only their own pleasure. The only means of influence by the state becomes direct coercion or the threat of its application.

It is noted that the transformations taking place have their origin in the transformation of the relationship between the citizen and the state and the relationship between citizens themselves.[170] This is a sign of a loss or at least a significant reduction in the level of trust both in vertical (state–citizen) and horizontal (between citizens) relations. G. Jakobs's concept of the function of law, especially criminal law is based precisely on trust. This author does not look at criminal law through the prism of the protection of legal goods but rather through the prism of emphasizing and sanctioning the validity of legal norms.[171] The role of the law as such is to create the conditions for individuals to cooperate in those areas where the personal trust in each other of the entities involved in the interaction is not sufficient. The law can fill this gap, but only if society expresses confidence that the validity of the standards is respected. In other words, the law can perform its tasks when its addressees are convinced that, as a matter of principle, the legal norms are respected, and therefore they are loyal to the law. By committing a crime, the perpetrator puts the validity of the law to test. The aim of bringing them to justice and punishing them is to restore the validity and enforceability of the law. The political community thus reminds us that the established norms are still valid.[172]

This indicates, as seems obvious, that crimes are also committed under the "citizens' criminal law." Thus, not every criminal immediately becomes an alien or even an enemy to the community. The role of criminal responsibility is to restore loyalty to the political community of the perpetrator—the citizen.[173] This means that a given offender perceives themselves and is seen by others as a person who is essentially loyal to the community. The crime they have committed is an exception that cannot undermine this rule. The perpetrator themselves in such cases usually perceives their act as reprehensible. The punishment does not exclude them from society, and therefore does not transform their status from a citizen to an enemy.

In some cases, however, it cannot be said that the perpetrator of a crime remains essentially loyal to the political community and its legal order. A crime is then not just an exceptional departure from the rule. The offender may, by their behavior, express not only a lack of loyalty to the law in force but even a complete rejection of this order.[174] Thus, the perpetrator can no longer be seen as having the will and ability to comply with legal norms.[175] The individual by their act expresses a hostile attitude toward the legal order. This characteristic may fit the perpetrators of organized crime, terrorist crimes, or serial sex crimes. By "alien" or "enemy" G. Jakobs understands the perpetrator, who "not only by chance through his attitude (. . .) or professional life (. . .) or membership of an organisation (. . .), but in any case is likely to have permanently turned away from the law and therefore does not guarantee a minimum of safety for their personal behaviours and manifests this deficit in their behaviour."[176]

Enemy criminal law can take various forms. One should rather not expect a separate law codifying, as it were, separate rules for perpetrators questioning the foundations of a given legal system.[177] These are rather individual provisions, sometimes also certain tendencies, that depart from the guarantee solutions adopted in the canon of classic criminal law. In the area of the specific part, this may be criminalization in the form of the performance of behaviors which *de facto* constitute only a preparation for the act that the legislator wants to prevent. In other areas, these may be provisions that increase liability, for example, because the offender's behavior meets the criteria of a terrorist offense.

In the "citizens' criminal law" oriented toward responding to the acts committed, the community establishes a relationship with the perpetrator by sending a message to him: "You have culpably injured us, which gives us grounds for forced compensation."[178] It should be emphasized that society still enters into a relationship with the perpetrator. This is not the case with "enemy criminal law." The perpetrator is treated there as a suspect from whom one must protect oneself. There is no longer any chance of any kind of relationship.[179]

George P. Fletcher presented the difference between citizens' criminal law and enemy criminal law in an interesting way. He notes that citizens' criminal law is aimed at reintegrating the offender into society. By repaying their "debt" to society, they take corrective action, subjecting themselves to a social rehabilitative effect, the citizen rebuilds the shaken relationship and returns to normal life among fellow citizens. Enemy criminal law is directed toward a different goal. The aim is then to get rid of or neutralize the perpetrator.[180]

It has rightly been pointed out in the literature that the division into citizens' criminal law and enemy criminal law may resemble the concept of the genesis of the state referring to the theory of the social contract. It can be argued that the perpetrator—all the more so the perpetrator of a terrorist act that strikes the political, social, and economic order—violates the provisions of the social contract to such an extent that they cease to be a party to it and at the same time become an enemy not only of the state itself but also of all those who try to observe this contract.[181] Some interpretations of Kantian philosophy suggest that anyone who, by their actions, question their belonging to the state must not only be removed from it but also deprived of their status as a person. They are then only entitled to the status of enemy.[182]

The above allows us to assume that at least in some interpretations giving a given perpetrator the attribute of enemy is the same as depriving them of the status of a person and the rights connected with that status. Such reasoning is possible if we assume that a person derives their status from some convention, whether it takes the form of a social contract or certain national or international legal acts. Violation of these norms would result in their status as a person being taken away. Thus, the possibility is ruled out that this status and its consequences are not intrinsically linked to a human being but are subject to verification on the basis of some, one or other, discretionary criteria. The personal character of a human being then derives from an institutionalization and can be taken away by these institutions.

The main measure used in the criminal law of the transition period is to criminalize behavior at a stage when it is merely a preparation for a possible infringement of a protected good, or in some cases, even remains completely neutral. The only condition for responsibility is that they are accompanied by criminal intent and sometimes only carelessness, which can result in a violation of a protected good that is important for the state.[183] Apparently, this issue is limited to the problem of criminalization, which is not addressed in this book. This concerns the scope of responsibility, including the relationship between intention and the deed actually committed. There is no doubt that equipping states with effective tools to fight terrorist crime is necessary, but this does not mean that it is possible to reject the vision of a human, which must be at the core of any legal system. Even the most serious act does not take away the status of humanity, which means that institutions of preventive criminal law should also be verified by criteria of ethical legitimacy.

Günther Jakobs points out that, under German criminal law, the main types of detention that are eligible for "enemy criminal law" are: preventive detention (§ 66 StGB), placement in a psychiatric hospital (§ 64 StGB) and the types of offenses relating to the creation and running of criminal and terrorist organizations (§ 129–129b StGB). As can be seen, the author includes in the "enemy criminal law" constructions, which are treated as protective measures in the Polish Criminal Code. One of the constructions that G. Jakobs also qualifies for "enemy criminal law" is preparation.[184] He believes that the punishment for preparation is in fact not a punishment for an evil already committed, but a future evil that is yet to happen. It is therefore a purely preventative construction.

Criticism of the concept of preventive criminal law touches upon various aspects of it. It is equally difficult to discuss it consistently as a presentation of the idea itself, as there are a number of ideas and evaluations concerning this issue in the literature.[185] One of the accusations raised against the concept of enemy criminal law is the claim that it puts loyalty to the state and its laws above such fundamental principles as human dignity. The stigmatizing character of the separation of enemy criminal law is also raised, as well as the risk of a populist, referring to the need to provide citizens with security, excessively broad transformation of criminal law structures into a preventive model. Technologies also provide today an increasingly better recognition of the interests, views, and inclinations of individual citizens. This may intensify the aim of enabling the state to intervene in an appropriate manner in parallel with the consideration of the offender's intention to commit a specific criminal act. There is also concern about the possibility of applying some kind of special preventive behavior to those whose only offense is that their attitudes do not correspond to the pattern adopted by decision-makers.[186]

In Manuel Cancio Melia's opinion, the solutions presented as enemy criminal law are, in their essence, incompatible with the rule of law.[187] A possible justification for this unequivocally critical, not very deep, opinion is to identify these instruments with the events known to us from Guantanamo Bay. Regardless of this connotation, the author believes that anti-terrorist legislation—the issue of preventive criminal law is discussed in this very context—contaminates classical criminal law and at the same time tries to hide the revaluation taking place.[188] The contamination would consist in permeating solutions that were originally exceptional, limited to specific threats, also to other parts of criminal law, in such a way that at some point these solutions would become not exceptional but typical. It considers clearly unconstitutional the Spanish solutions designed for terrorist offenders, such as longer sentences or specific regimes for their execution. At the same time, the author challenges the reasoning that sees a link between increasing criminal responsibility and raising the level of security. According to M. C. Melia, enemy criminal law first generates these enemies itself, in order to be able to fight against them.[189]

In the context of the concept of ethical legitimacy of criminal law described in this book, it seems interesting to see the postulate of actual legitimacy of legal concepts, in this case assumptions postulating the creation of enemy criminal law. It is argued that every normative concept requires actual rooting, so that it is not considered merely theoretical or even illusory. In other words, every normative solution requires cognitive assurance of normative expectations. For this to happen, the society to which the norms are addressed must take the legal system seriously. People should therefore have certain expectations attached to the legal system and be convinced that at least some of them, preferably the most important ones for them, can be fulfilled. Thanks to this relationship between citizens' beliefs and the law, norms are not only objects belonging to the world of ideas.[190] Such reasoning reminds us of the thesis about the need to ensure ethical legitimization for the law. One of the arguments mentioned above in support of this thesis is precisely the necessity of rooting legal norms in the moral convictions of citizens. It seems that this would sufficiently meet the postulate of cognitive assurance of normative expectations, without the need to refer to solutions that are for reasons that are in many aspects risky.

Critical arguments against the concept discussed here include those that indicate the state cannot secure its own existence in this way. By betraying the ideas on which the state is founded, it itself leads directly to annihilation.[191]

The conception presented by G. Jakobs raises a number of doubts, some of which have already been presented. The author, in refuting the charges against him, points to the dualism he has observed. Undoubtedly, all standards and guarantees relating to classical criminal law, as well as its functions and principles, are lofty and important. At the same time, however, in practice they often turn out to be insufficient, or perhaps rather inappropriate, to the situation. Exclusion from the community, that is, the application of solutions from the scope of "enemy criminal law" applies when the perpetrator, especially their attitude, the committed act, and personal circumstances, do not provide any guarantee that they will observe the law in the future. Since they do not present themselves as a credible person, it can be assumed that they will again commit a serious criminal offense in the future.[192]

The role of the law is to strengthen social ties rather than to antagonize community members. Nevertheless, reality, that is, the fact that serious crimes pose a threat to society, may justify practices such as preventive detention, severe penalties, wiretapping, and various types of operational activities. These measures, in the concept of "enemy criminal law" are not aimed at citizens but at the enemies of the community. The state must retain the ability to oppose its enemies.[193]

Although its formula has no precise limits, classical criminal law should not be regarded as a dogma, that is, an inviolable existence that does not allow for any exceptions. The very allegation of violation of the principles of classical criminal law has very limited force, because it would be difficult to prove that it is an ideal that cannot be deviated from. The legislator, also in Poland, very often, in various political arrangements, departs from certain classical canons and, despite criticism from academic circles, it is not uncommon for individual solutions to become part of the criminal law system for longer.[194]

The problem begins when the changes introduced violate not so much the boundaries of some notion of criminal law, even supported by certain theoretical concepts, but the boundaries, whether they are determined by higher order legal acts or—which from the perspective of the subject matter of this book is particularly important—by anthropological and ethical findings. The vision of a person emerging from philosophical anthropology, rooted in his innate and inalienable dignity, and the ethical principles of responsibility associated with it, have no validation dimension. Their violation does not formally call into question the validity of a given legal norm. Instead, it may reduce, or even diminish, the effectiveness of criminal law in maintaining and restoring social order where it has been violated by the crime. Criminal law, disconnected from anthropological and ethical reality, cannot, as has already been shown, effectively perform this task.

It has already been mentioned above that the conclusions drawn from philosophical thought, here especially philosophical anthropology and ethics, if they are consistent with the axiology of a given political community, may reflect the convictions of citizens and their intuitions about the possibility of incurring criminal responsibility in certain situations. Disagreement with these findings can lead to a significant tension between the shape of criminal responsibility and its public perception. Most importantly, however, the vision of a person and their accompanying ethical principles outlined here refers to the principle of natural and inalienable human dignity. The failure of a given construction of criminal responsibility to comply with the conclusions derived from the principle of human dignity may mean that it violates this principle.

It should be noted that enemy criminal law is a certain theoretical phenomenon, combining descriptive and normative dimensions. It is undoubtedly a description of the changes that are taking place in criminal law, in addition in those states that are considered liberal democracies. At the same time, it is also sometimes the case that the introduction of solutions that can be included in the framework of enemy criminal law is postulated, whether by lawyers themselves or politicians. An in-depth analysis carried out within the framework of ethical legitimization would require looking at the individual constructions falling within the scope of criminal law of enemies. Here, an overall assessment of the total concept is made, indicating the specific risks arising from its application as a whole.

First of all, it should be noted that every human being, whether a citizen or an enemy, regardless of the rules for assigning these labels, has a personal dignity that they cannot lose, regardless of their actions. It cannot be given up independently.[195] Dignity, its content and conclusions for criminal law have already been widely discussed earlier. In the perspective of enemy criminal law, one of the most important principles of dignity is the equality of all perpetrators. This means that to the extent that the individual principles of responsibility are rooted in the principle of dignity, it is not possible to modify them depending on the qualification of the perpetrator to the regime of citizens' or enemy criminal law. It is therefore not possible, for example, to construct enemy criminal law without taking into account the principle of guilt, since this principle is rooted in the principle of human dignity.[196] Similarly, reference should be made to other canonical principles of responsibility, such as the principle of responsibility for the deed.

Similarly, the classification of a given deed as a set of typified acts, which entails criminal responsibility, should not depend on the division of the addressees of the standards into citizens and enemies. Only those subjective criteria which we use, due to the specificity of the good and circumstances, when constructing individual types, are acceptable. The reprehensibility of an act should not result from the fact that it was committed by an "enemy." In other words, the same act, committed with the same intention and under the same circumstances, should be punished to the same extent, regardless of whether it was committed by a citizen or an enemy. Undoubtedly, the legislator can provide for directives increasing the level of punishment for repeat offenders, but they apply equally to anyone who finds themselves in such circumstances.

The proposed criminal law, including the fight against the most serious crimes, including terrorism, must not allow for the subjective treatment of human beings. The criminal law response to a deed should be appropriate, first and foremost, to the evil caused by it, that is, to the object of the deed, the intentions of the perpetrator, and the circumstances in which the deed was committed. Other goals that the legislator wants to achieve through punishment are acceptable, but should not lead to establishing responsibility beyond the limits set by the aforementioned premises.

SUMMARY

The analyses of two criminal law dogmatic figures presented above, that is, omission and necessary defense, and the concept of enemy criminal law have shown that it is sufficiently useful to include an ethical analysis, herein presented as an ethical legitimization of criminal law, in the reflection on criminal law, conducted both *de lege lata* and *de lege ferenda*.

The conclusions concerning omission and necessary defense should inspire the legislator, who in subsequent legislative undertakings analyzes and assesses the accuracy of the normative solutions adopted thus far. In the area of omission, it seems particularly important to consider a stronger emphasis on the difference in responsibility for evil caused actively in relation to failure to prevent evil. The problem has emerged primarily in the context of consequential offenses committed by omission. A simple equalization of the punishment of these behaviors with consequential offenses committed by action seems inappropriate in the context discussed.

In the area of necessary defense, one of the main and at the same time doctrinally controversial problems that deserves to be rethought is the absolute independence of this legal defense. Above, those areas have been identified where it may seem justified to consider retreat as the behavior recommended for the defender. This is primarily a necessary defense against unintentional attack, as long as the defender recognizes this state of affairs. Similar conclusions have been reached with respect to the situation where a potential defender is able to predict at a sufficiently early stage that an attack on their good is likely to occur. In such cases, too, retreat may be a justified solution. This argument is reinforced when the goods most important to the individuals involved, including primarily their lives, would be at risk in an assault situation.

The analysis of enemy criminal law issues has shown that the transformation of criminal law, regardless of the chosen direction of change, cannot go beyond the limits set by such principles as human dignity and the anthropological and ethical findings arising from it. This is not a matter of attachment to the solutions found, but of the need to go beyond the usefulness of the approach to criminal law and to carry out an analysis to determine whether it has not broken away from the basic points of reference indicated here.

The analysis also indicates the usefulness of the conclusions resulting from the ethical legitimization of criminal law at the stage of its application. It constitutes another important point of reference in reconstructing the interpretative context appropriate for understanding a given legal norm. Philosophical anthropology and ethics are not in their essence dependent on one or another decision of the legislator or another entity. They are immune to this kind of voluntarism. Rather, they are about a constant need to deepen our reflection on who a person is, how they act, and how they should act. This gives lawyers and the law the perspective of inspiration necessary to establish norms that correspond to the nature of the human being and at the same time remain fit to be observed by them.

NOTES

1. More on this topic, see K. Szczucki, *Wykładnia prokonstytucyjna prawa karnego*, Warszawa 2015, p. 12; J. Gardner, *Offences and Defenses. Selected Essays in the Philosophy of Criminal Law*, Oxford 2007, pp. 43–45.

2. J.-M. Silva Sanchez indicates such views in Spanish criminal law doctrine. See ibid, *Criminal Omissions – Some Relevant Distinctions*, "New Criminal Law Review: An International and Interdisciplinary Journal" 2008, no. 3, p. 455.

3. W. Wolter, *Przestępne przeszkodzenie*, "Czasopismo Prawne i Ekonomiczne" 1939, no. 1/6, p. 18. This citation was later repeated many times by many representatives of Polish criminal law doctrine. Cf J. Kostarczyk-Gryszka, *Podstawy odpowiedzialności za materialne przestępstwa z zaniechania (Uwagi na tle stanowiska Władysława Woltera)*, "Zeszyty Naukowe UJ. Prace Prawnicze," 1977, z. 74, p. 67; M. Rodzynkiewicz, *Pojęcie zaniechania a odpowiedzialność za przestępstwo popełnione przez zaniechanie w projekcie kodeksu karnego*, "Przegląd Prawa Karnego" 1994, no. 11, p. 21; P. Kardas, *Przestępstwo ciągłe w prawie karnym materialnym*, Kraków 1999, p. 53; P. Konieczniak, *Czyn jako podstawa odpowiedzialności w prawie karnym*, Kraków 2002, p. 199; P. Burzyński, *Zaniechanie jako zamach na dobro prawem chronione a obrona konieczna*, "Czasopismo Prawa Karnego i Nauk Penalnych" 2005, no. 2, p. 45; J. Kulesza, *O pojmowaniu zaniechania w polskiej nauce prawa karnego*, "Czasopismo Prawa Karnego i Nauk Penalnych" 2007, z. 2, p. 19.

4. Łukasz Pohl points out that the subject of criminal law valuation is not the deed but concrete human behavior. The only condition, the fulfilment of which is necessary for the behavior to be suitable for such valuation, and thus to be included in the framework of the deed so that it exists materially in an objective reality. This excludes the category of so-called internal deeds, that is to say, intentions that are not external to behavior. Cf. Ł. Pohl, *Czyn w prawie karnym*. In: R. Dębski (ed.), *System Prawa Karnego. Tom 3. Nauka o przestępstwie. Zasady odpowiedzialności*, Warsaw 2013, p. 210.

5. According to W. Mącior, "omission is not a second form of deed because omission as an absence of a specific action is not a real phenomenon in the outside world.

For omission as a denial of action is just as unreal as some 'negative existence' as a denial of existence is unreal. If omission was a real phenomenon, then it would lead to the conclusion that not only what someone is doing at a given moment is real, but also everything that that someone is not doing at a given moment—and that is naturally within their means—regardless of whether the omission is illegal or lawful. After all, there are no rational grounds for claiming that the abandonment of an action ordered by law is real, while the abandonment of only a possible but not ordered action is not real" (W. Mącior, *Czyn ludzki i jego znaczenie w prawie karnym*, Warsaw 1990, pp. 77–78).

6. Ibid, pp. 79–80. Similarly P. Konieczniak, *Czyn. . .* , p. 208.

7. P. Konieczniak, *Czyn. . .* , p. 208.

8. Ibid, p. 216.

9. Ibid, p. 217.

10. P. Konieczniak sees L. Kubicki as "the most determined and consistent advocate of the thesis about the equivalence of action and omission in our literature." (P. Konieczniak, *Czyn. . .* , p. 204). Cf. Ł. Pohl, *Czyn w prawie karnym. . .* , p. 211.

11. L. Kubicki, *Przestępstwo popełnione przez zaniechanie. Zagadnienia podstawowe*, Warsaw 1975, p. 76.

12. T. Kaczmarek noted that "the notion of a deed in criminal law is in fact always a reconstruction of a real event, and which only because it exists in objective reality can then and only then be subject to criminal law evaluation." (T. Kaczmarek, *Spory wokół przyczynowości zaniechania i przypisywania jego skutku*. In: Ł. Pohl (ed.), *Aktualne problemy prawa karnego. Księga pamiątkowa z okazji Jubileuszu 70. urodzin Profesora Andrzeja J. Szwarca,* Poznań 2009, p. 205).

13. L. Tyszkiewicz, *O definicji przestępstwa, jej strukturze i elementach*, "Prace Naukowe Uniwersytetu Śląskiego—Problemy Prawa Karnego" 1995, vol. 21, p. 44.

14. J. Majewski, *Prawnokarne przypisywanie skutku* przy zaniechaniu (zagadnienia węzłowe), Kraków 1997, pp. 29–30.

15. W. Wolter, *Nauka o przestępstwie*, Warsaw 1973, p. 54.

16. Ibid.

17. W. Świda, *Uwagi o przyczynowości zaniechania*, "Państwo i Prawo" 1957, no. 11, p. 841. Cf. too J. Kulesza, *O pojmowaniu. . .* , p. 24.

18. A. Zoll, *Okoliczności wyłączające bezprawność czynu*, Warsaw 1982, pp. 17–18.

19. M. Rodzynkiewicz, *Modelowanie pojęć w prawie karnym*, Kraków 1998, p. 32.

20. M. Rodzynkiewicz, *Treść pojęcia czynu w prawie karnym jako efekt procedury modelowania*. In: Z. Ćwiąkalski et al. (ed.), *Problemy odpowiedzialności karnej. Księga pamiątkowa ku czci profesora Kazimierza Buchały*, Kraków 1994, p. 211 and note.; ibid, *Modelowanie. . .* , pp. 12, 27 and note. Cf. too J. Kulesza, *O pojmowaniu. . .* , p. 21.

21. W. Mącior, *Czyn. . .* , p. 5.

22. Ibid, p. 62.

23. W. Patryas, *Zaniechanie. Próba analizy metodologicznej*, Poznań 1993, pp. 20, 52; ibid, *Odpowiedź na "Uwagi o W. Patryasa koncepcji zaniechania,"* "Ruch Prawniczy, Ekonomiczny i Socjologiczny" 1996, z. 1, pp. 135–36.

24. A. Wąsek, *Recenzja pracy W. Patryasa, "Zaniechanie. Próba analizy metodologicznej," Poznań 1993*, "Ruch Prawniczy, Ekonomiczny i Socjologiczny" 1993, no. 4, p. 174; J. Kulesza, *O pojmowaniu. . .* , p. 34.

25. J. Śliwowski, *Prawo karne*, Warsaw 1979, pp. 74–76.

26. R. Ingarden, *Wykłady z etyki*, Warsaw 1989, p. 115.

27. St. Thomas Aquinas, *Summa Theologiae* II-II, q. 79 a. 3, Second and Revised Edition, 1920 Literally translated by Fathers of the English Dominican Province, Online Edition 2017.

28. St. Thomas Aquinas, *Summa Theologiae* II-II, q. 64 a. 8, Second and Revised Edition, 1920 Literally translated by Fathers of the English Dominican Province, Online Edition 2017.

29. Ibid, p. 159.

30. G. Sher, *Unintentional Omissions*. In: D. K. Nelkin, S. C. Rickless (ed.), *The Ethics and Law of Omissions*, Oxford 2017, pp. 3–4. George Sher begins his article by sharing his own experience of missing classes because of the misconception that the semester did not start until the following week. I think we all have this kind of experience.

31. Tadeusz Ślipko, using the nomenclature of classical ethics, would describe such a situation as an act of direct intention, since missing classes is obviously connected with the realization of the intention, so it cannot be unintentional. The effect of an indirect intent could be said to have the character of a side effect, that is, one that arises due to the inclusion of some external circumstance in the causal system. In the example discussed above, the intended purpose is achieved by an omission. It is not a side effect. Cf. T. Ślipko, *Zarys etyki ogólnej*, Kraków 2004, p. 427.

32. G. Sher, *Unintentional. . .* , p. 4.

33. Ibid, p. 6.

34. Ibid, pp. 6–7.

35. Cf. R. Ingarden, *Wykłady z etyki. . .* , p. 115; G. Rosen, *Culpability and Ignorance*, "Proceedings of the Aristotelian Society" 2003, vol. 103, no. 1, pp. 61–84; M. Zimmerman, *Moral Responsibility and Ignorance*, "Ethics" 1997, vol. 107, no. 3, pp. 410–26.

36. G. Sher, *Unintentional. . .* , pp. 7–8. Cf. too A. Smith, *Responsibility for Attitudes: Activity and Passivity in Mental Life*, "Ethics" 2005, vol. 115, no. 2, p. 236 and note.

37. G. Sher, *Unintentional. . .* , pp. 7–8.

38. Ibid, pp. 11–13.

39. J.M. Fischer, M. Ravizza, *Responsibility and Control. A Theory of Moral Responsibility*, Cambridge p. 127.

40. A. M. Smith, *Unconscious Omissions, Reasonable Expectations, and Responsibility*. In: D. K. Nelkin, S. C. Rickless (ed.), *The Ethics and Law of Omissions*, Oxford 2017, p. 36 and note.

41. Ibid, p. 37. Cf. too R. Jay Wallace, *Responsibility and the Moral Sentiments*, Cambridge (MA) 1998, p. 142; N. Levy, *Culpable Ignorance and Moral Responsibility: A Reply to Fitz Patrick*, "Ethics" 2009, vol. 119, no. 3 p. 729 and note. St. Thomas

Aquinas notes that in such cases, the responsibility only becomes apparent with the omission, nevertheless, due to an earlier cause: "It must therefore be said, rather, that the fault for the omission begins to be borne by someone at the time when he had to fulfil a certain duty, but for an earlier reason, for which the subsequent omission is considered voluntary" (St. Thomas Aquinas, *Summa Theologiae* II-II, q. 79 a. 3, Second and Revised Edition, 1920 Literally translated by Fathers of the English Dominican Province, Online Edition 2017).

42. P. Smith, *Feinberg and the Failure to Act*, "Legal Theory" 2005, no. 11, p. 238.

43. A. M. Smith, *Unconscious Omissions. . .* , p. 39.

44. P. Smith, *Feinberg. . .* , p. 240. Cf. too A. M. Smith, *Unconscious Omissions. . .* , p. 42.

45. A. M. Smith, *Unconscious Omissions. . .* , pp. 45–46.

46. Ibid, pp. 48–49.

47. The division into pre-emptive and post-emptive evaluation was taken from the definition of conscience proposed in: A. Podsiad, Z. Więckowski, *Mały słownik terminów i pojęć filozoficznych,* Warsaw 1983, p. 375.

48. A. M. Smith, *Unconscious Omissions. . .* , p. 52.

49. J. Giezek, T. Kaczmarek, *Przestępstwo z niedbalstwa jako wynik deficytu informacji.* In: *Rozważania o przestępstwie i karze. Wybór prac w okresu 40-lecia naukowej twórczości*, Warsaw 2006, p. 19. Cf. too J. Lachowski, *Strona podmiotowa czynu zabronionego.* In: R. Dębski (ed.), *System Prawa Karnego. Tom 3. Nauka o przestępstwie. Zasady odpowiedzialności*, Warsaw 2013, p. 582.

50. Łukasz Pohl notes that "we only deal with the realisation of the signs of a wrongful crime of omission if:

1. the one who did not prevent the effect was the guarantor of its non-replacement,
2. this effect was foreseeable,
3. the guarantor of the non-repudiation of the effect could have foreseen the occurrence of the effect,
4. the guarantor of non-repudiation of the effect could have prevented that effect,
5. Failure to prevent the effect was socially unacceptable behaviour." (Cf. Ł. Pohl, *Komentarz do art. 2 k.k.*. In: R. Stefański (ed.), *Kodeks karny. Komentarz*, Warsaw 2019, nb. 25).

51. J. Lachowski, *Strona podmiotowa. . .* , p. 570.

52. As A. Zoll stated: "When we take a practical approach to determining whether objective caution has been violated in a particular case, we should ask ourselves how a conscientious driver, pedestrian, machine operator, doctor, for example, would behave in the situation being judged. A certain pattern of conscientious and prudent citizen acting in a specific situation is therefore introduced for comparison." (ibid, *Odpowiedzialność karna lekarza za niepowodzenie w leczeniu*, Warsaw 1988, pp. 44–45). Cf. too M. Rodzynkiewicz, *Modelowanie. . .* , p. 109.

53. Ibid, p. 583. A. Zoll: "In accordance with the adopted assumption consisting in separating the subjective features of a prohibited act from the guilt, the possibility

of foreseeing the commission of a prohibited act referred to in Article 9(2) does not refer to the individual abilities of the perpetrator resulting from his personality, education, state of health, and so on, but is determined according to the abilities of a model citizen with appropriate qualifications for performing a given activity, conscientiously treating his duties and possessing extraordinary information, possibly possessed by the perpetrator. It shall not be a prohibited act to carry out the characteristics of the deed in question in a situation where it is not a normal consequence of the actions taken by the perpetrator" (A. Zoll, *Komentarz do art. 9 k.k.*. In: W. Wróbel, A. Zoll (ed.), *Kodeks karny. Część ogólna. Tom I. Cześć I. Komentarz do art. 1-52*, Kraków 2016, nb. 42).

54. The statement by St. Thomas Aquinas is important in this context: "After all, no one is obliged to do the impossible. Therefore, no one who does not do what he cannot do sins by omission." (St. Thomas Aquinas, *Summa Theologiae* II-II, q. 79 a. 3, Second and Revised Edition, 1920 Literally translated by Fathers of the English Dominican Province, Online Edition 2017).

55. J. Lachowski, *Strona podmiotowa. . .* , p. 584. Cf. too J. Giezek, T. Kaczmarek, *O subiektywnym przypisaniu nieświadomego przestępstwa nieumyślnego*. In: *Teoretyczne problemy odpowiedzialności karnej w polskim oraz niemieckim prawie karnym*, Wrocław 1990, pp. 202–10.

56. Supreme Court judgement of 23.8.1977, VI KRN 180/77, OSNPG 1978, No. 1, item 2. Cf. too M. Królikowski, *Komentarz do art. 9* k.k.. In: M. Królikowski, R. Zawłocki (ed.), *Kodeks karny. Część ogólna. Komentarz do artykułów 1–116*, Warsaw 2017, p. 282.

57. M. Królikowski, *Komentarz do art. 9 k.k. . .* , p. 282.

58. M. Królikowski, R. Zawłocki, *Prawo karne*, Warsaw 2016, p. 199.

59. Ibid, p. 199.

60. Cf. J.-M. Silva Sanchez, *Criminal Omissions. . .* , p. 453.

61. Ibid, p. 199.

62. W. Wolter, *Nauka. . .* , p. 86.

63. M. Królikowski, *Komentarz do art. 2 k.k.*. In: M. Królikowski, R. Zawłocki (ed.), *Kodeks karny. Część ogólna. Komentarz do artykułów 1–116*, Warsaw 2017, p. 158.

64. Ł. Pohl, *Komentarz do art. 2 k.k. . .* , nb. 27.

65. I assume that a generally defined legal obligation does not yet constitute a legal, specific obligation referred to in Article 2 of the Criminal Code. This obligation should be specified in the contract or in a specific situational context. It cannot be claimed that a doctor, wherever they appear, is a guarantor of the health of all persons encountered. See more on this subject: K. Szczucki, *O miłosiernym lekarzu, czyli o moralnych podstawach prawnego obowiązku*. In: *Prawo wobec problemów społecznych. Księga Jubileuszowa profesor Eleonory Zielińskiej*, Warsaw 2016, p. 859 and note.

66. It even points to the original sin which encumbers the idea of responsibility for wrongful crimes committed by omission. Cf. J. D. Gomez-Aller, *Criminal Omissions: A European Perspective*, "New Criminal Law Review: An International and Interdisciplinary Journal" 2008, vol. 11, no. 3, p. 427.

67. A. Kaufmann, *Die Dogmatik der Unterlassungsdelikte*, Göttingen 1988, pp. 284–85, as cited in: J. D. Gomez-Aller, *Criminal Omissions. . .* , p. 427.

68. One of the main duties in morality relating to relationships between people is the duty to respect human life. Cf. T. Ślipko, *Zarys etyki szczegółowej. Tom. 1. Etyka osobowa*, Kraków 2009, p. 221 and note.

69. He stated that "an omission can only concern a good related to a duty that someone has to fulfil." (St. Thomas Aquinas, *Summa Theologiae* II-II, q. 79 a. 3, Second and Revised Edition, 1920 Literally translated by Fathers of the English Dominican Province, Online Edition 2017).

70. More on the so-called conflict of duties in criminal law: J. Majewski, *Tak zwana kolizja obowiązków w prawie karnym*, Warsaw 2002, *passim*. Cf. too J. Giezek, *Tak zwana kolizja obowiązków w prawie karnym, Jarosław Majewski, Warszawa 2002 : [recenzja]*, "Kwartalnik Prawa Publicznego" 2003, no. 1, p. 251 and note.

71. St. Augustine, *De doctrina christiana – O nauce chrześcijańskiej. Tekst łacińsko-polski*, księga pierwsza, XXVIII 29, transl. J. Sulkowski, Warsaw 1989, p. 35. Cf. too A. Bartoszek, *Odpowiedzialność za bliźnich w potrzebie w kontekście kategorii ordo caritatis (z uwzględnieniem problemu migracji)*, "Teologia i Moralność" 2017, vol. 12, no. 1(21), pp. 60–61.

72. I give this order following: A. Bartoszek, *Odpowiedzialność za bliźnich. . .* , s. 61–62. Thomas himself noted doubts appeared concerning this division, especially concerning the hierarchical relation between love for parents and love for children.

73. St. Thomas Aquinas, *Summa Theologiae II-II q. 31, a. 3*, Second and Revised Edition, 1920 Literally translated by Fathers of the English Dominican Province, Online Edition 2017.

74. In this respect, it is worth noting the statement of J. Woroniecki: "A general principle can therefore be formulated that, with equal opportunities to come to the aid of others and with equal needs of love on their part, they should prevail on the side of the one with whom we are more closely related to by the community of blood or custom. Where there is a greater and deeper connection, there is a greater duty of love. It is a recognition of a debt of gratitude to that community, family or nation to which we owe our lives and its greatest spiritual values and to which we repay it by loving its members" (J. Woroniecki, *Katolicka etyka wychowawcza*, vol. II/2, Lublin 1986, p. 19).

75. I reserve the right in the text to refrain from inclusion in the causal chain "in many cases," as some of the facts may be difficult to assess in relation to the causal chain. An example of such a difficulty could be to cause the death of a child by starvation. In criminal law, this would qualify as an omission because the guardian—who is obliged to feed the child—does not fulfil their duty. Claiming that they do not engage in the causal chain would mean that the mechanisms of life lead the child—unable to take care of his or her own needs—to death, while feeding modifies the chain, postponing death. Otherwise, this problem would no longer exist. A doctor who for some reason does not help a person with a gunshot wound. Could it be claimed that the perpetrator of death is the doctor, or is it rather the one who shot that person?

76. This view is supported by the reflections of St. Thomas Aquinas: "The gravity of a sin depends on its remoteness from virtue. Now contrariety is the greatest remoteness, according to Metaph. x [Didot. ed. ix, 4. Wherefore a thing is further removed from its contrary than from its simple negation; thus black is further removed from

white than not-white is, since every black is not-white, but not conversely. Now it is evident that transgression is contrary to an act of virtue, while omission denotes the negation thereof: for instance it is a sin of omission, if one fail to give one's parents due reverence, while it is a sin of transgression to revile them or injure them in any way. Hence it is evident that, simply and absolutely speaking, transgression is a graver sin than omission, although a particular omission may be graver than a particular transgression." (St. Thomas Aquinas, *Summa Theologiae* II-II, q. 79 a. 4, Second and Revised Edition, 1920 Literally translated by Fathers of the English Dominican Province, Online Edition 2017).

77. Cf. K. Indecki, A. Liszewska, *Prawo karne materialne. Nauka o przestępstwie, karze i środkach karnych*, Warsaw 2002, p. 108; K. Buchała, *Prawo karne materialne*, Warsaw 1980, p. 184. Cf. too J. Kulesza, *O pojmowaniu. . .* , p. 32.

78. See i.a. A. Gubiński, *Wyłączenie bezprawności czynu. O okolicznościach uchylających społeczną szkodliwość czynu*, Warsaw 1961; A. Krukowski, *Obrona konieczna na tle prawa polskiego*, Warsaw 1965; J. Majewski, *Okoliczności wyłączające bezprawność czynu a znamiona subiektywne*, Warsaw 2013; A. Marek, *Obrona konieczna w prawie karnym. Teoria i orzecznictwo*, Warsaw 2008; M. Szafraniec, *Przekroczenie granic obrony koniecznej w polskim prawie karnym*, Kraków 2004; A. Zoll, *Okoliczności wyłączające bezprawność czynu (zagadnienia ogólne)*, Warsaw 1982; M. Bielski, *Koncepcja kontratypów jako okoliczności wyłączających karalność*, "Czasopismo Prawa Karnego i Nauk Penalnych" 2010, z. 2, p. 25 and note; J. Błachut, *Wybrane problemy stosowania instytucji obrony koniecznej w prawie karnym*, "Monitor Prawniczy" 2005, no. 4, p. 190 and note; P. Burzyński, *Zaniechanie jako zamach na dobro prawem chronione a obrona konieczna*, "Czasopismo Prawa Karnego i Nauk Penalnych" 2005, no. 2, p. 45 and note; L. Gardocki, *Granice obrony koniecznej. O reformie prawa karnego*, "Palestra" 1993, no. 7–8, p. 57 and note; ibid., *Sprowokowana obrona konieczna i zawiniony stan wyższej konieczności w polskim prawie karnym*, "Studia Prawnicze" 1988, no. 1–2, p. 263 and note; W. Grzeszczyk, *Zamach uzasadniający prawo do obrony koniecznej*, "Prokuratura i Prawo" 2000, no. 5, p. 129 and note; M. Królikowski, *Okoliczności wyłączające bezprawność jako konstrukcja sprawiedliwości korygującej*, "Czasopismo Prawa Karnego i Nauk Penalnych" 2010, z. 2, p. 5 and note.; E. Plebanek, O *obronie koniecznej i innych kontratypach w świetle zasady proporcjonalności*, "Czasopismo Prawa Karnego i Nauk Penalnych" 2006, no. 1, p. 71 and note; M. Szczepaniec, *Przekroczenie granic obrony koniecznej motywowane strachem lub wzburzeniem usprawiedliwionym okolicznościami zamachu*, "Prokuratura i Prawo" 2000, no. 9, p. 12 and note; A. Wąsek, *Problematyka kontratypów przy przestępstwach nieumyślnych*, "Palestra" 1988, no. 10, p. 61 and note; D. Zając, *O obronie koniecznej w przypadku przestępstw abstrakcyjnego narażenia na niebezpieczeństwo*, "Państwo i Prawo" 2016, no. 1, p. 87 and note.

79. Unfortunately, the work of this author and that era is sometimes overlooked in contemporary works on criminal law, including those concerning necessary defense. Cf. eg. M. Peno, *Obrona konieczna – moralne uzasadnienie instytucji oraz jej zakresu – robocza wersja referatu (poszerzona)*, https://www.academia.edu/34223011/obrona_konieczna_a_moralno%C5%9B%C4%87-szkic.pdf (accessed: 8.04.2020).

80. St. Augustine, *Letter to Publicola*. In: św. Augustyn, *Listy*, Pelplin 1991, transl. W. Eborowicz, pp. 312–313. Cf. too St. Thomas Aquinas, *Summa Theologiae*

II-II, q. 64 a. 7, Second and Revised Edition, 1920 Literally translated by Fathers of the English Dominican Province, Online Edition 2017. Thomas also quotes a fragment from the Decretum Gratiani: "Concerning the clerics about whom you have consulted Us, those, namely, who have killed a pagan in self-defense, as to whether, after making amends by repenting, they may return to their former state, or rise to a higher degree; know that in no case is it lawful for them to kill any man under any circumstances whatever."

81. As an argument in the so-called *sed contra*, he cites a fragment from the Book of Exodus: "If a thief be found breaking up, and be smitten that he die, there shall no blood be shed for him." (Exodus 22, 1, as cited in: King James Version, public domain).

82. Such a pattern of effects occurs, among other places, in the so-called torts "qualified by consequence," that is, offenses where the offender's intention is subject to a milder effect, while in reality a more serious effect is committed, which was not the subject of the offender's intention, and certainly not their direct intention. Cf. M. Thompson, *Aquinas, Locke, and Self-Defense*, "University of Pittsbrugh Law Review" 1996, no. 57(3), pp. 680–81.

83. St. Thomas Aquinas, *Summa Theologiae* II-II, q. 64 a. 7, Second and Revised Edition, 1920 Literally translated by Fathers of the English Dominican Province, Online Edition 2017.

84. In this context, the thesis that it is only to the Enlightenment's thought that we owe the exclusion of the possibility of invoking necessary defense when motivated by a desire for revenge is untenable . Cf. M. Peno, *Obrona konieczna. . .* , pp. 3–4.

85. J. Woroniecki, *Katolicka etyka. . .* , p. 159.

86. Fr. F. W. Bednarski, Objaśnienia. In: St. Thomas Aquinas, *Suma teologiczna*, vol. 18, transl. Fr. F. W. Bednarski, London 1966, p. 202.

87. According to M. Peno, the tension between self-defense and necessary defense, and thus also concerning the goods of others, is, in his opinion, the tension between the liberal approach and the communitarian approach. The liberal approach is supposed to limit the defense to the individual's own goods, while the communitarian approach is supposed to include the goods of other people and the community itself. Cf. M. Peno, *Obrona konieczna. . .* , pp. 4–5.

88. T. Ślipko, *Zarys etyki szczegółowej. . .* , p. 229.

89. Ibid., p. 230.

90. Ibid.

91. Ibid, p. 231.

92. J. Woroniecki, *Katolicka etyka. . .* , p. 159.

93. T. Ślipko, *Zarys etyki szczegółowej. . .* , p. 231.

94. Ibid, p. 232.

95. Tadeusz Ślipko says that: "Assuming the real nature of these means of defense, taking a directly lethal action would be an unnecessary defense, which ethics puts beyond the question of possible admissibility against aggression" (Ibid., p. 232).

96. Ibid., p. 233. D. Wasserman also writes about the assailant's right to life. Cf. ibid., *Justifying Self-Defense*, "Philosophy & Public Affairs" 1987, vol. 16, no. 4, p. 361.

97. T. Ślipko, *Zarys etyki szczegółowej. . .* , p. 234.

98. "The elementary reason for equality therefore demands that the moral value of an aggressor's life and the law that emerges from it should have such an objective

normative status that it would tighten their validity and imperative power, putting the situation of aggression beyond their borders. They therefore maintain their objective and intact axiological state to the limit beyond which aggression begins. Aggression is outside this area. Thus, all actions that directly harm a person's life outside of aggression are morally evil and forbidden, but in the act of aggression, even if they are also directly deadly, they are not morally evil. They become morally 'not bad,' in other words they do not show any incompatibility with the objective moral value of the aggressor's life, and do not violate their law. This is because this value and this law do not reach the area of aggression, so they simply 'do not exist' there. It is a situation that is subject to moral restriction." (T. Ślipko, *Etyka szczegółowa. . .* , p. 235).

99. Ibid., p. 235.

100. Tadeusz Biesaga points out that the distinction of intrinsically evil acts restrictively constitutes T. Ślipko's original contribution to ethics. Cf. T. Biesaga, *Wkład ks. T. Ślipki w rozwój etyki tomistycznej*, "Studia Philosophiae Christianae" 1990, vol. 26, no. 2, p. 106.

101. T. Ślipko, *Zarys etyki ogólnej. . .* , p. 242.

102. Ibid.

103. Ibid.

104. T. Ślipko, *Zarys etyki szczegółowej. . .* , p. 237.

105. J. Woroniecki, *Katolicka etyka. . .* , p. 160. T. Ślipko, who limits the admissibility of deprivation of the assailant's life to situations where the life of the defender is in real danger, does not accept such a view. Cf. T. Ślipko, *Zarys etyki szczegółowej. . .* , p. 237.

106. R. B. Miller, *Killing, Self-Defense, and Bad Luck*, "The Journal of Religious Ethics" 2009, vol. 37, no. 1, p. 132. Cf. too D. Wasserman, *Justifying Self-Defense. . .* , pp. 358–59.

107. R.B. Miller, *Killing. . .* , pp. 155–56.

108. In ethics, the issue of assault by omission is highlighted by, among others, D. Wasserman, *Justifying Self-Defense. . .* , p. 372.

109. L. Alexander, *Recipe for a Theory of Self-Defense*. In: C. Coons, M. Weber (ed.), *The Ethics of Self-Defense*, Oxford 2016, p. 20. This author also includes, among the range of epistemic difficulties, ignorance of whether an attack will actually take place. This doubt depends on the accepted limits of necessary defense. If one considers that the repulsion of an assault can only take place when it begins, one can no longer state that the attacker is not yet certain of the start of the attack. However, I do not know what effects this attack may eventually lead to.

110. L. Alexander, *Recipe. . .* , p. 34; C. Coons, M. Weber, *The Current Debate*. In: C. Coons, M. Weber (ed.), *The Ethics. . .* , pp. 3–5.

111. Incidentally, in the context of the proportionality of the defense, it is worth noting that R. Nozick proposed that the pain caused to the perpetrator of the assault as part of the necessary defense should count toward the penalty imposed by the court on that perpetrator (R. Nozick, Philosophical Explanations, 1981, p. 364. Cf. too G. P. Fletcher, Punishment and Self-Defense, "Law and Philosophy" 1989, vol. 8, no. 2, p. 201 and note). If, in the course of an attempted rape, the perpetrator is injured by a knife, then, according to this theory, the penalty for attempted rape should be reduced

in proportion to the severity of the injury. This concept goes against the assumption, not only in ethics, but also in the doctrine of criminal law, that only the court can impose punishment. It should be proportional to the harm done. Thus, it cannot be claimed that the victim's defensive reaction goes in a way toward the punishment to be served. We assume that the sanction applied by the state, that is, state coercion, has priority. It should even rather be stated that the principle is to reserve the use of coercion only to the state, with the exception of the possibility of its use only by individuals. Another assumption in his philosophy of the state was made by R. Nozick. In the state, the individual has priority over collective justice.

112. Larry Alexander qualifies all these grounds as a requirement of proportionality. Cf. L. Alexander, *Recipe. . .* , p. 34.

113. Ibid., p. 35. This doctrine, as the author himself notes, is not generally accepted in individual jurisdictions.

114. The author compares these situations to provocations conducted by the police and other services. Cf. ibid., p. 48.

115. R. Christopher, *Self-Defense and Defense of Others*, "Philosophy & Public Affairs" 1998, vol. 27, no. 2, pp. 123–24; M. Gorr, *Private Defense*, "Law and Philosophy" 1990, no. 9, p. 254.

116. R. Christopher, *Self-Defense. . .* , p. 125.

117. Russell Christopher points out that this theory can lead to a contradiction, especially if the assailant also became the victim of aggression caused by a third party. They would not be able to defend themselves because their right to life would be suspended because of the attack they had caused. Cf. ibid., p. 127.

118. Ibid., p. 129. According to R. Christopher, this theory, like the previous one, leads to a logical contradiction. It is enough to imagine a situation in which subject A threatens to deprive subject B of life. At the same time, subject B threatens to deprive subject C of life. At the same time, subject C threatens to deprive subject A of life. If an assault by subject C is unjustified, then the attempt by B against C—in defense of A—is justified. For this reason, the attack by A against B in defense of C is an unjustified assault. Consequently, attack C on A in defense of B is justified. It turns out, therefore, that assault C is both justified and unjustified. Cf. R. Christopher, *Self-Defense. . .* , p. 129.

119. Ibid., p. 131. The author points out that also in relation to this theory the same contradiction will arise as in the previous one.

120. Cf. too M. Budyn-Kulik, *Zabójstwo tyrana domowego. Studium prawnokarne i wiktymologiczne*, Lublin 2005, s. (sec. 2, r. VII, pt. 4).

121. L. Alexander's different view was mentioned above.

122. W. Zontek, *Komentarz do art. 25 k.k.*. In: M. Królikowski, R. Zawłocki (ed.), *Kodeks karny. Część ogólna. Komentarz do artykułów 1–116*, Warsaw 2017, p. 508.

123. Ibid., p. 509.

124. Cf. in the section covering fights: Judgement of the Appellate Court in Kraków of 26 March 2013, II AKa 27/13, "Krakowskie Zeszyty Sądowe" 2013, no. 6 item 80; Judgement of the Appellate Court in Warsaw of 2 March 2015, II AKa 14/15, Legalis. Cf. in the section covering provocation: L. Gardocki, *Sprowokowana obrona konieczna i zawiniony stan wyższej konieczności w polskim prawie karnym*,

"Studia Prawnicze" 1988, no. 1–2, p. 263 and note.; (Judgement of the Appellate Court in Wrocław of 23 September 2015, II AKa 201/15, Legalis).

125. W. Zontek, *Komentarz do art. 25 k.k. . .* , p. 511; J. Kulesza, *Obrona konieczna. In:* L. K. Paprzycki (ed.), *System Prawa Karnego. Tom 4. Nauka o przestępstwie. Wyłączenie i ograniczenie odpowiedzialności karnej*, Warsaw 2013, p. 175.

126. J. Kulesza, *Obrona konieczna. . .* , p. 178. Cf. too A. Wąsek, *Sporne kwestie stanu wyższej konieczności w prawie karnym*, "Przegląd Prawa Karnego" 1992, no. 7, p. 32; W. Łuniewski, *Stan wyższej konieczności a zasada proporcjonalności dóbr*, "Palestra" 2002, no. 3–4, p. 42; J. Kulesza, *Przestępstwo nieudzielenia pomocy w niebezpieczeństwie: art. 162 k.k. na tle uwag dotyczących § 323c niemieckiego kodeksu karnego*, Łódź 2008, pp. 260–65.

127. The problem would arise if the circumstance described in § 2 were to be considered as a circumstance excluding guilt. Then we would still be dealing with an unlawful attack. Cf. J. Kulesza, *Przestępstwo nieudzielenia pomocy. . .* , p. 238; ibid., *Obrona konieczna. . .* , p. 179.

128. This case can also be considered within the framework of a state of higher necessity. I will avoid this topic.

129. J. Kulesza, *Obrona konieczna. . .* , p. 179; ibid., *Granice obowiązku gwaranta w świetle art. 162 k.k.*, "Prokuratura i Prawo" 2006, no. 7–8, p. 108 and note.

130. Moral controversies will be raised by such medical interventions, which are carried out for the benefit of others rather than the patient themselves, such as chemical castration carried out against their will.

131. J. Lachowski draws attention to this. Cf. ibid., *Komentarz do art. 25 k.k.*. In: V. Konarska-Wrzosek (ed.), *Kodeks karny. Komentarz*, Warsaw 2016, pp. 161–62.

132. W. Zontek, *Komentarz do art. 25 k.k. . .* , pp. 514–15.

133. Judgement of the Appellate Court in Lublin of 26 May 2008, II AKa 93/08, LEX nr 453977.

134. J. Kulesza, *Obrona konieczna. . .* , p. 184.

135. Ibid. Cf. too W. Wolter, *Nauka. . .* , p. 168; J. Warylewski, *Prawo karne. Część ogólna*, Warsaw 2012, p. 258.

136. Cf. W. Zontek, *Komentarz do art. 25 k.k. . .* , p. 523; E. Plebanek, *O obronie koniecznej i innych kontratypach w świetle zasady proporcjonalności*, "Czasopismo Prawa Karnego i Nauk Penalnych" 2005, z. 1, p. 71 and note. Case law stands on the ground of the absolute autonomy of necessary defense. Cf. e.g. Judgement of the Supreme Court of 9 April 2002, V KKN 266/00, LEX nr 52941; Judgement of the Supreme Court of 9 April 2002, IV KKN 289/99, LEX nr 53340; Judgement of the Supreme Court of 12 June 2012, II KK 128/12, LEX nr 1212374; Judgement of the Appellate Court in Łódź of 7 February 2006, II AKa 4/06, Prok. i Pr. – wkł. 2007, no. 5, item 34. For more on this topic, see M. Budyn-Kulik, *Zabójstwo tyrana domowego. Studium prawnokarne i wiktymologiczne*, Lublin 2005, p. (sec. 2, chap. VII, item 3).

137. Thus W. Zontek, *Komentarz do art. 25 k.k. . .* , p. 521.

138. Cf. Z. Jędrzejewski, *Artykuł 2 ust. 2 lit. a Europejskiej Konwencji o Ochronie Praw Człowieka i Podstawowych Wolności a obrona konieczna (art. 25 KK). In:* B.

Bieńkowska, D. Szafrański (ed.), *Europeizacja prawa polskiego – wybrane aspekty*, Warsaw 2007, p. 47 and note.

139. The Supreme Court found that: "Necessary defense, as it follows from the wording of Article 25 § 1 of the Criminal Code, is of an intrinsic nature, and not "relatively intrinsic and subsidiary." Conventional regulations (Article 2(2)(a) of the Convention for the Protection of Human Rights 1 Fundamental Freedoms of 4 November 1950, Journal of Laws of 1993, No. 61, item 284 as amended), however, indicate that the right to effective defense must have limits resulting from axiological and humanistic aspects, since human life is an asset of the highest value, so this regulation of the Convention does not eliminate the independence of necessary defense, since it concerns the issue of proportionality of the manner of defense undertaken with regard to the danger of a specific assault, which in Article 25 § 2 of the Criminal Code is a separate condition of the institution of the necessary defense, included from the negative side" (post. SN of 15 April 2015, IV KK 409/14, OSNKW 2015, no. 9, item 78). This means that the Court sees the implementation of the conventional standard from the negative side in Article 25 § 2 of the Criminal Code.

140. Referring to the nomenclature adopted by W. Zontek, the Supreme Court sees the absence of need for defense in its intrinsic aspect, but does not notice its extrinsic aspect. Cf. W. Zontek, *Komentarz do art. 25 k.k. . . .* , p. 522.

141. J. Kulesza, *Obrona konieczna. . .* , p. 166. cf. too A. Marek, *Obrona konieczna. . .* , p. 97.

142. A. Marek, *Obrona konieczna. . .* , pp. 124–25; J. Kulesza, *Obrona konieczna. . .* , p. 219.

143. J. Kulesza, *Obrona konieczna. . .* , p. 220. Cf. too, the case law: judgement of the Supreme Court of 6 September 1989, II KR 39/89, LEX nr 18000; judgement of the Supreme Court of 19 February 1997, IV KKN 292/96, LEX nr 29547.

144. Unintentional necessary defense is excluded. A. Zoll, *Komentarz do art. 25 k.k.*. In: W. Wróbel, A. Zoll (ed.), *Kodeks karny. Część ogólna. Tom I. Cześć I. Komentarz do art. 1-52*, Kraków 2016, nb 41. Cf. too Judgement of the Appellate Court in Łódź of 20 May 2008, II AKa 79/08, LEX nr 491917.

145. Judgement of the Appellate Court in Lublin of 20 May 1996, II AKa 111/96, LEX nr 30419. Cf. too A. Marek, *Obrona konieczna. . .* , p. 95; J. Kulesza, *Obrona konieczna. . .* , p. 222.

146. J. Kulesza, Obrona konieczna. . . , p. 222; L. Gardocki, Sprowokowana obrona. . . , pp. 269–70; A. Wąsek, Kodeks karny. Komentarz, Gdańsk 1999, pp. 316–17; M. Budyn-Kulik, Zabójstwo tyrana domowego. Studium prawnokarne i wiktymologiczne, Lublin 2005, p. (sec. 2, chap. VII, pt. 2.4).

147. L. Alexander, *Recipe. . .* , p. 48.

148. It is not uncommon for references to the concept of state of emergency presented by C. Schmitt and modified by G. Agamben to appear against this backdrop. Cf. R. De Massol De Rebetz, M. Van Der Woude, *Marianne's liberty in jeopardy? A French analysis on recent counterterrorism legal developments*. In: *Critical Studies on Terrorism*, 10.1080/17539153.2019.1633838, s. 4.

149. F. Golser, *The Concept of a Special Criminal Law as a Weapon Against "Enemies" of the Society*, "Studia Iuridica" 2016, vol. 67, p. 66.

150. The very concept of enemy criminal law rejects the legitimacy of using the category of "legal goods." Cf. D. Gruszecka, *Ochrona dobra prawnego na przedpolu jego naruszenia. Analiza karnistyczna*, Warsaw 2012, p. 208.

151. The European Union has also taken some of these tools. See European Parliament and of the Council Directive 2017/541 of 15 March 2017 on combating terrorism and replacing Council Framework Decision 2002/475/JHA and amending Council Decision 2005/671/JHA (OJ EU L 88/7). In Poland, a tool which seems to correspond to the features of "enemy criminal law" is the Act of 22 November 2013 on Proceedings against persons with mental disorders posing a threat to the life, health or sexual freedom of others (Journal of Laws of (Dz. U.) 2019, item 2203).

152. G. Jakobs, *Bürgerstrafrecht und Feindstrafrecht*, "Höchstrichterliche Rechtsprechung zum Strafrecht" 2004, no. 3, p. 90; F. Golser, *The Concept. . .* , p. 67.

153. Daniel Ohana points out that this application of the theory proposed by G. Jakobs is an expression of a serious change in the views of that German author, who was originally opposed to the introduction of responsibility already in the forefront of violation of a good. Cf. D. Ohana, *Trust, Distrust and Reassurance: Diversion and Preventive Orders Through the Prism of Feindstrafrecht*, "The Modern Law Review" 2010, vol. 73, no. 5, p. 721. Cf. too G. Jakobs, *Selbstverständnis der Strafrechtwissenschaft vor den Herausforderungen der Gegenwart (Kommentar)*. In: A. Eser, W. Hassemer, B. Bukhardt (ed.), *Die Deutsche Strafrechtswissenschaft vor der Jahrtausendwende*, München 2000, p. 47.

154. D. Ohana, *Trust. . .* , p. 722.

155. Cf. D. Moeckli, *The US Supreme Court's 'Enemy Combatant' Decisions: A 'Major Victory for the Rule of Law'?*, "Journal of Conflict & Security Law" 2005, vol. 10, no. 1, p. 75 and note. An interesting problem, although remaining outside the mainstream of the considerations here, is taken up by Carlton F. W. Larson under U.S. law. In one of his articles, he considers the need to classify terrorist crimes as acts of treason, which would entail certain procedural requirements preventing a terrorist from being treated as a hostile fighter. Cf. C. F. W. Larson, *The Forgotten Constitutional Law of Treason and Enemy Combatant Problem*, "University of Pennsylvania Law Review" 2006, vol. 154, no. 4, p. 863 and note.

156. "Legal Times," 22 November 2002. Cf. too C. Gomez-Jara Diez, *Enemy Combatants Versus Enemy Criminal Law: An Introduction to the European Debate Regarding Enemy Criminal Law and Its Relevance to the Anglo-American Discussion on the Legal Status of Unlawful Enemy Combatants*, "New Criminal Law Review. An International and Interdisciplinary Journal" 2008, no. 4, p. 530.

157. G. Jakobs, *On the Theory of Enemy Criminal Law*. In: M. D. Dubber (ed.), *Foundational Texts in Modern Criminal Law*, Oxford 2014, p. 415.

158. I. Kant, *Metafizyka moralności*, Warsaw 2005, transl. E, Nowak, pp. 42–43.

159. The law of nature mentioned here cannot be confused with the natural law in its classical version. Natural law cannot be separated from the law of reason. On the contrary, it is in fact a law of reason. It is enough to recall the definition of the natural law according to St. Thomas Aquinas, who stated that it is "the participation of the eternal law in a rational creation." ("Lex naturalis nihil aliud est quam participatio legis aeternae in rationali creatura"). Cf. J. Salij, *Prawo naturalne i prawa stanowione*

w ujęciu św. Tomasza z Akwinu, "Łódzkie Studia Teologiczne" 2017, no. 2, p. 104. St. Thomas's definition of law as such is also important: "The law is nothing but a certain regulation of reason for the common good, coming from whoever is entrusted with the care of the community, promulgated." Cf. M. Piechowiak, *Prawo naturalne a prawa człowieka*. In: A. Maryniarczyk et. al. (ed.), *Substancja. Natura. Prawo naturalne*, Lublin 2006, p. 394.

160. G. Jakobs, *On the Theory. . .* , p. 416.

161. Ibid.

162. Ibid.

163. Ibid., p. 417.

164. Ibid.

165. Ibid., pp. 417–18.

166. Ibid., p. 418.

167. G. Jakobs describes this phenomenon as the "policization" of criminal law, because prevention is primarily the task of the police. Cf. G. Jakobs, *On the Theory. . .* , pp. 418–19.

168. Ibid, p. 420.

169. G. Jakobs, *Das Strafrecht zwischen Funktionalismus und "altereuropäischem" Prinzipiendenken*, "Zeitschrift für die gesamte Strafrechtwissenschaft" 1995, no. 107, p. 867 and note.; D. Ohana, *Trust. . .* , p. 724.

170. D. Ohana, *Trust. . .* , p. 722.

171. Ibid., p. 723.

172. D. Ohana, *Trust. . .* , p. 725.

173. G. Jakobs, *Das Schuldprinzip*, Opladen 1993, pp. 23–26; D. Ohana, *Trust. . .* , p. 725.

174. M. D. Dubber, *Citizenship and Penal Law*, "New Criminal Law Review" 2010, vol. 13, no. 2, p. 203.

175. G. Jakobs, *Selbstverständnis. . .* , p. 51.

176. G. Jakobs, *On the Theory. . .* , p. 420.

177. But this is the kind of separation G. Jakobs would want. Carlos Gomez-Jara Diez quotes it as follows: "we must separate as clearly as possible the provisions pertaining to enemy criminal law from those belonging to citizen criminal law" (C. Gomez-Jara Diez, *Enemy. . .* , p. 555).

178. G. Jakobs, *On the Theory. . .* , p. 421.

179. Ibid.

180. G. P. Fletcher, *The Grammar of Criminal Law. American, Comparative, and International. Volume One: Foundations*, Oxford 2007, p. 172. It is interesting that the author believes that the death penalty becomes an instrument of enemy criminal law, but only when its purpose is not of a just nature, but utilitarian, consisting in irreversibly neutralizing the perpetrator of the crime.

181. Ibid., p. 539.

182. Ibid., p. 541.

183. A.E. Bozbayindir, *The Advent of Preventive Criminal Law: An Erosion of the Traditional Criminal Law?*, "Criminal Law Forum" 2017, p. 3, doi: 10.1007/s10609-0170-9322-y. Cf. too A. P. Simester, *Prophylactic Crimes*. In: G.R. Sulivan,

I. Dennis (ed.), *Seeking Security: Pre-Empting the Commission of Criminal Harms*, Oxford 2012, pp. 59–61.

184. G. Jakobs, *On the Theory. . .* , p. 422.

185. As an example, we can indicate e.g.: L. Zedner, *Security, the State, and the Citizen: The Changing Architecture of Crime Control*, "New Criminal Law Review: An International and Interdisciplinary Journal" 2010, vol. 13, no. 2, p. 379 and note.; M. D. Dubber, *Citizenship and Penal Law*, "New Criminal Law Review: An International and Interdisciplinary Journal" 2010, vol. 13, no. 2, p. 190 and note.; M. C. Melia, *Terrorism and Criminal Law: The Dream of Prevention, the Nightmare of the Rule of Law*, "New Criminal Law Review: An International and Interdisciplinary Journal" 2011, vol. 14, no. 1, p. 108 and note.; C. Gomez-Jara Diez, *Enemy Combatants Versus Enemy Criminal Law: An Introduction to the European Debate Regarding Enemy Criminal Law and Its Relevance to the Anglo-American Discussion on the Legal Status of Unlawful Enemy Combatants*, "New Criminal Law Review: An International and Interdisciplinary Journal" 2008, vol.11, no. 3, p. 529 and note.

186. D. Ohana, *Trust. . .* , pp. 728–29.

187. M. C. Melia, *Terrorism. . .* , p. 112.

188. The author states: "Thus, if such draconian measures creep into what has typically been considered legitimate and normal criminal laws, they may generate significant changes in which the logic of enemy criminal law slowly but surely contaminates our system of criminal law until it becomes the norm rather than the exception" (ibid., p. 112).

189. M. C. Melia, *Terrorism. . .* , p. 116.

190. C. Gomez-Jara Diez, *Enemy. . .* , pp. 538–39.

191. Ibid, p. 562.

192. G. Jakobs, *On the Theory. . .* , pp. 422–23.

193. Ibid., p. 424.

194. An example is the regulation on the statute of limitations for certain crimes committed to the detriment of minors (Article 101 § 4 of the Penal Code), added in 2008. (Journal of Laws of 2008, No. 214 item 1344), later amended several times, but maintaining the original purpose. Another example is the exclusion of criminal liability for exceeding the limits of the necessary defense (Article 25 § 2a of the Criminal Code), introduced in 2018. (Journal of Laws (Dz. U.) of 2018, item 20).

195. Cf. the above considerations on the dignity of the perpetrator of an attack in the context of necessary defense.

196. M. Królikowski, *Komentarz do art. 1 k.k.*. In: M. Królikowski, R. Zawłocki (ed.), *Kodeks karny. . .* , p. 143; A. Wąsek, *Kodeks karny. Komentarz, t. 1*, Gdańsk 1999, p. 37; A. Zoll, *Komentarz do art. 1 k.k.*. In: W. Wróbel, A. Zoll (ed.), *Kodeks karny. . .* , nb. 45.

Conclusion

So what are the conclusions of this book? Above all, it must be assumed that it is impossible to legislate and apply criminal law reliably and rationally without first recognizing anthropological assumptions. Not only because any law should be made for the sake of man, although this is undoubtedly the most important reason. Another reason is that there is no real possibility of creating norms of criminal law without prior determination and, as far as possible, consent as to who the person is and for what they can be responsible. It is impossible to set boundaries and principles of human responsibility without reflecting on the person.

The reflection on the individual for the purposes of criminal law should go hand in hand with an analysis of the Constitution of the Republic of Poland, especially with regard to the principle of human dignity, which not only indicates the essential elements of human nature but also constitutes a reference to the extra-legal system of judgments and rights on which the political community has founded its existence. Apart from its numerous functions, human dignity has also revealed itself as a basis for the reconstruction of the anthropological vision of humanity. So far, in the area of criminal law, this approach to the category of dignity has not been widespread. This seems to require not only the wording of the Basic Law but also the essence of responsibility, which is not something abstract, but a call on a particular person to report his or her behavior and to sanction him/her for it, if he or she has violated certain norms. The meaning of responsibility will be revealed only if it is tailored to the real person and not functioning only in the imagination or in the utopian imaginations of one or another ideology.

Moreover, the rooting of criminal law content in ethics is not an entirely new and unnoticed issue in the doctrine of criminal law, although the issue of the relationship between ethics and the general principles of criminal law is still awaiting greater attention. Although the situation is slightly better than it was a few decades ago, the view expressed by Andrzej Wąsek, who criticized the lack of interest by the science of criminal law in the results of research in the field of philosophy, including ethics, still seems to be valid. This author noted that ethical issues of criminal law are important for both the science of criminal law and the science of morality.[1] Zbigniew Ziembiński's statement still seems to be equally accurate:

> Lawyers-practitioners and representatives of specific disciplines of jurisprudence often have serious difficulties when in their dogmatic and legal deliberations they have to take into account various types of relations between law and morality; they do not see the complexity of the issues; they lack the mastery of the appropriate conceptual apparatus in this field.[2]

As A. Wąsek, already mentioned, rightly pointed out, the reflection on the relationship between criminal law and ethics does not mean moralizing. Rather, it is about "drawing attention to whether and which aspects of a moral nature are related to this criminal law issue and how they may affect the establishment of the basis and scope of the criminal responsibility of the perpetrator."[3] The same author indicated that the need to refer to ethics in criminal law research is noticeable, especially in such areas as the problem of determinism; tensions between the responsibility for a deed and the responsibility for the danger of the offender; the category of guilt, error, active regret, consent of the possessor of the good; or the very concept of punishment.[4] Undoubtedly, the social harmfulness of an act also belongs to this list.[5]

The space to take into account moral judgments is also visible in the context of such institutions as responsibility for omission, necessary defense, the state of higher necessity, the consent of the possessor of the good, and active regret.[6] The approach to criminal law presented here can be found in North American case law. Already in the 1960s, Judge Thurgood Marshall indicated: "The doctrines of *actus reus*, *mens rea*, insanity, error, justification and duress have historically provided the tools to continuously change the regulation of tension between the evolving aims of the criminal law and changing religious, moral, philosophical and medical views of the nature of man."[7]

The need for ethical legitimization of criminal law is gaining strength today. The transformation of criminal law, which is taking place in many legislations, requires the development of criteria allowing for a reliable assessment of the admissibility of the changes introduced. Criteria developed outside the criminal law itself are particularly important. Criteria derived from criminal law may be not only reproducible but also, by their very nature, defending the existing structures. From an internal viewpoint, it is difficult to allow any change that would call this perspective into question. Therefore, there is a need for evaluation that, without denying the need for change as such, will protect the criminal law against the violation of human dignity and everything that results from it.

The requirement to seek ethical references to criminal law stems from the principle of human dignity. The dignity of the human being is evidence of their ability to be responsible for their action and omission. This ability to bear responsibility should be the starting point for an analysis of the ability to bear responsibility as defined by criminal law. Human dignity has allowed for much more than just the formulation of a thesis about a person's ability to bear responsibility. It also makes it possible, through its anthropological dimension, to reconstruct the concept of man, which through it is rooted in the legal system. This concept should be taken into account in the process of formulating postulates to criminal law, especially regarding the principles and scope of the assigned responsibility.

The thesis that it is necessary to look for a reference to criminal law in ethics, to see its legitimacy there, is also confirmed by other findings. If one assumes that the task of criminal law is to maintain and restore the social order, it cannot disregard the moral norms that have a fundamental influence on the shape of that order. A far-reaching discrepancy between the moral concept of responsibility and its legal equivalent would contribute to the opposite result, that is, to creating and deepening chaos in society and its structures.

The need to take the ethical context into account when shaping the principles of criminal responsibility also has its historical justification. Criminal law in our legal culture was created under the influence of canon law and, indirectly, moral theology. The changes that took place along with the codifications of the Enlightenment also had their source in a specific philosophical reflection, including ethical reflection. This makes it possible to argue that the shape of the criminal law institutions, on which the reflection is observed in the area of the theory of responsibility, remains—at least to some extent—a consequence of philosophical thought, especially ethical thought. To the extent that this thought is built on the basis of realistic philosophy, its conclusions may reflect the convictions of citizens and their intuitions regarding the possibility of incurring criminal responsibility in specific situations. Ethical legitimization therefore consists in seeking, in ethics, arguments in favor of the rightness of the legal solutions adopted, and thus also in verifying whether the principles of criminal responsibility are consistent with the idea of the extent of this responsibility that is available to members of society.

Conducting an analysis at the junction of criminal law and philosophy makes it possible to grasp some important tensions arising in the context of the concept of responsibility. From the point of view of morality, the main goal is to determine the person actually responsible. Usually, a judgment in the case of morality is—as it is defined in ethics—an internal tribunal of conscience that strives for the full truth about the event. The need for moral responsibility will not be met by a kind of legal fiction or a formal judgment that breaks away from the reality it assesses. The moral judgment will continue until a judgment is reached that takes into account all the circumstances and identifies the person responsible for a particular evil. In some cases, the moral responsibility can never be established. In the case of a criminal trial conducted on the basis of rules of positive law, taking into account the norms of substantive criminal law, the truth is still a fundamental principle, but unlike in the area of morality, it does not always win over compromises of a different nature—such as presumptions or consensual modes—among others.

This may make the whole process of attributing criminal responsibility a kind of "game of responsibility" rather than a process similar to the one carried out on the basis of morality.[8] Some elements of this game are probably necessary; they are assigned to implement the guarantee function in criminal law. However, in my opinion, it is worthwhile striving for the criminal law to create not so much the conditions for conducting this game but rather to search for people who are really responsible and who can and should bear the consequences of their behavior.

NOTES

1. A. Wąsek, *Prawo karne – minimum moralności?*, "Annales Universitatis Mariae Curie-Skłodowska. Sectio G. Ius" 1984, vol. 31, p. 36.
2. Z. Ziembiński, *Etyczne problemy prawoznawstwa*, Warsaw 1972, p. 5.
3. A. Wąsek, *Prawo karne. . .* , p. 37.
4. Ibidem, pp. 37–38.
5. R. Zawłocki, *Pojęcie i funkcje społecznej szkodliwości czynu w prawie karnym*, Warsaw 2007, pp. 127–28.
6. In part, similar examples are given by A. Wąsek, *Prawo karne. . .* , p. 38.
7. Extract of the opinion on the case of *Powell v. State of Tex.*, 392 U.S. 514, 536 (1968).
8. M. Rodzynkiewicz, *Fenomen odpowiedzialności w refleksji filozoficznej a prawnokarne zasady odpowiedzialności*, "Przegląd Prawa Karnego" 1997, no. 16, pp. 9–10.

Bibliography

Abelard P. *Etyka, czyli poznaj samego siebie*. In: P. Abelard (ed.) *Rozprawy*, transl. L. Joachimowicz. Warszawa: De Agostini Polska, 2001.

Alexander F., and Staub H. *The Criminal, the Judge, and the Public: A Psychological Analysis*. London: Free Press, 1931.

Andrejew I. *Ustawowe znamiona czynu. Typizacja i kwalifikacja przestępstw*. Warszawa: Wyd. Prawnicze, 1978.

Archard D. "Moral Compromise." *Philosophy* 87, no. 3 (2012): 403.

Arendt H. *The Human Condition*. Chicago: University of Chicago Press, 1958.

Arendt H. *The Origins of Totalitarianism*. New York: Harcourt, Brace and Co., 1951.

Aristotle, *Nicomachean Ethics,* transl. W. D. Ross, http://classics.mit.edu/Aristotle/nicomachaen.html (accessed 28 March 2022).

Ashworth A., and Zedner L. *Preventive Orders: A Problem of Undercriminalization?* In: R. A. Duff, L. Farmer, S. E. Marshall, M. Renzo, and V. Tadros (eds) *The Boundaries of the Criminal Law*. Oxford: Oxford University Press, 2010.

Atiq E. H. "How Folk Beliefs About Free Will Influence Sentencing: A New Target for the Neuro-Determinist Critics of Criminal Law." *New Criminal Law Review: An International and Interdisciplinary Journal* 16, no. 3 (2013): 3–23.

Augsberg I. *On Kant's Concept of Human Freedom and Dignity as Auto-Heteronomy*. In: D. Grimm, A. Kemmerer, and Ch. Möllers (eds) *Human Dignity in Context*. Baden-Baden: Hart Publishing, 2018.

Austin J. L. "A Plea for Excuses: The Presidential Address." *Proceedings of the Aristotelian Society* 57, no. 1 (1956): 1–30.

Baer M. *Eliminating the Divide Between the State and Its Citizens*. In: P. H. Robinson, S. P. Garvey, and K. Kessler-Ferzan (eds) *Criminal Law Conversations*. Oxford: Oxford University Press, 2009.

Barak A. *Human Dignity: The Constitutional Value and the Constitutional Right*. Cambridge: Cambridge University Press, 2015.

Barczak-Oplustil A. "Sporne zagadnienia istoty winy w prawie karnym. Zarys problemu." *Czasopismo Prawa Karnego i Nauk Penalnych* 9, no. 2 (2005): 75–96.

Barczak-Oplustil A. *Zasada koincydencji winy i czynu w Kodeksie karnym*. Kraków: Wyd. Krakowski Instytut Prawa Karnego Fundacja, 2016.
Barmash P. *Homicide in the Biblical World*. Cambridge: Cambridge University Press, 2009.
Beccaria C. *On Crimes and Punishment*. In: J. Grigson (transl.) *The Column of Infamy*. Oxford: Oxford University Press, 1964.
Beetham D. *The Legitimation of Power*. Houndmills-London: Palgrave Macmillan, 1991.
Berman H. J. *Prawo i rewolucja. Kształtowanie się zachodniej tradycji prawnej*, transl. S. Amsterdamski. Warszawa: Wyd. Prawnicze, 1995.
Biesaga T. *Spór o normę moralności*. Kraków: Wyd. Naukowe Papieskiej Akademii Teologicznej, 1998.
Bosek L. *Gwarancje godności ludzkiej i ich wpływ na polskie prawo cywilne*. Warszawa: Wyd. Sejmowe, 2012.
Bourke A. F. G. *Principles of Social Evolution*. New York: Oxford Scholarship, 2011.
Bremer J. *Czy wolna wola jest wolna?* Kraków: Wyd. WAM, 2013.
Brożek K. A. *Standardy etyczne w prawie. Próba systematyzacji*. Warszawa: Oficyna Naukowa, 2018.
Burgh. *Guilt, Punishment and Desert*. In: F. Schoeman (ed.) *Responsibility, Character, and the Emotions: New Essays in Moral Psychology*. Cambridge: Cambridge University Press, 1987.
Carlsmith K. M., Darley J. M., and Robinson P. H. "Why Do We Punish? Deterrence and Just Deserts as Motives for Punishment." *Journal of Personality and Social Psychology* 83, no. 2 (2002): 284.
Caruso G. "Free Will Eliminativism: Reference, Error, and Phenomenology." *Philosophical Studies* 172, no. 10 (2015): 2823–33.
Cavanaugh T. A. *Double-Effect Reasoning: Doing Good and Avoiding Evil*. Oxford: Oxford University Press, 2017.
Chiao V. "Two Conceptions of the Criminal Law." In: C. Flanders and Z. Hoskins (eds) *The New Philosophy of Criminal Law*. London and New York: Rowman & Littlefield International, 2016.
Chiesa L. E. "Punishing Without Free Will." *Utah Law Review* no. 4 (2011): 1403–60.
Chisholm R. M. *Person and Object: A Metaphysical Study*. La Salle: Open Court Publishing Company, 1979.
Churchland P. S. "Moral Decision-Making and the Brain." In: J. Illes (ed.) *Neuroethics: Defining the Issues in Theory, Practice, and Policy*. Oxford: Oxford University Press, 2006.
Churchland P. S. *Moralność mózgu. Co neuronauka mówi o moralności*, transl. M. Hohol, N. Marek. Kraków: Copernicus Center Press, 2013.
Chyrowicz B. *O sytuacjach bez wyjścia w etyce*. Kraków: Wyd. Znak, 2008.
Chyrowicz B. *Zamiar i skutki. Filozoficzna analiza zasady podwójnego skutku*. Lublin: Towarzystwo Naukowe Katolickiego Uniwersytetu Lubelskiego, 1997.
Cicero M. T. "O powinnościach." In: Cicero M. T., *Pisma filozoficzne*, t. 2, transl. W. Kornatowski. Warszawa: Wyd. PWN, 1960.

Ciepły F. *Sprawiedliwościowa racjonalizacja wymiaru kary kryminalnej wobec współczesnych tendencji polityki karnej w Polsce*. Lublin: Wyd. KUL, 2017.

Clapham A. *Human Rights Obligations of Non-State Actors*. Oxford: Oxford University Press, 2006.

Complak K. "Uwagi o godności człowieka oraz jej ochrona w świetle nowej konstytucji." *Przegląd Sejmowy* 5 (1998): 42.

Cowley Ch. *Moral Responsibility*. Durham: Routledge Press, 2014.

Dalferth I. U. "Religion, Morality and Being Human: The Controversial Status of Human Dignity." In: D. Grimm, A. Kemmerer, and Ch. Möllers (eds) *Human Dignity in Context*. Baden-Baden: Hart Publishing, 2018.

Darley J. M., Carlsmith K. M., and Robinson P. H. "The Ex Ante Function of the Criminal Law." *Law & Society Review* 35, no. 1 (2001): 701–26.

Davidson D. *Essay on Actions and Events*. Oxford: Oxford University Press, 1980.

Davis D. M. "Equality: The Majesty of Legoland Jurisprudence." *South African Law Journal* 116 (1993): 398.

Davis J. "Doing Justice to Dignity in Criminal Law." In: J. Malpas and N. Lickiss (eds) *Perspectives on Human Dignity: A Conversation*. Springer, Dordrecht, 2007.

Delong M. "Korporacjonizm i subsydiarność w nauczaniu papieża Piusa XI." In: A. Pawłowska and S. Grabowska (eds) *Zasada pomocniczości. Wymiar europejski, narodowy, regionalny i lokalny*. Rzeszów: Wyd. A. Marszałek, 2011.

Devlin P. *The Enforcement of Morals*. London and New York: Oxford University Press, 1965.

Dubber M. D. "Toward a Constitutional Law of Crime and Punishment." *Hasting Law Journal* 55 (2003–2004): 509–72.

Duff R. A. *Punishment, Communication and Community*. Oxford: Oxford University Press, 2001.

Duff R. A. *The Realm of Criminal Law*. Oxford: Oxford University Press, 2018.

Duff R. A. "Towards a Modest Legal Moralism." *Criminal Law and Philosophy* 8, no. 1 (2014): 217–35.

Duff R. A. *Trials and Punishments*. Cambridge: Cambridge University Press, 1986.

Durkheim E. "Forms of Social Solidarity." In: A. Giddens (ed.) *Emile Durkheim: Selected Writings*, transl. A. Giddens. Cambridge: Cambridge University Press, 1972.

Durkheim E. "Moral Obligation, Duty and Freedom." In: A. Giddens (ed.) *Emile Durkheim: Selected Writings*, transl. A. Giddens. Cambridge: Cambridge University Press, 1972.

Durkheim E. "Religion and Ritual." In: A. Giddens (ed.) *Emile Durkheim: Selected Writings*, transl. A. Giddens. Cambridge: Cambridge University Press, 1972.

Durkheim E. "The Division of Labour and Social Differentiation." In: A. Giddens (ed.) *Emile Durkheim: Selected Writings*, transl. A. Giddens. Cambridge: Cambridge University Press, 1972.

Durkheim E. "The Science of Morality." In: A. Giddens (ed.) *Emile Durkheim: Selected Writings*, transl. A. Giddens. Cambridge: Cambridge University Press, 1972.

Dworkin. "Three Questions for America." *The New York Review of Books*, 21 September 2006.

Dziadzio A. *Powszechna historia prawa*. Warszawa: Wyd. PWN, 2011.

Dzobo N. K. "African Symbols and Proverbs as Sources of Knowledge." In: K. Wiredu and K. Gyekye (eds) *Person and Community: Ghanaian Philosophical Studies* I (t. I), *The Council for Research in Values and Philosophy*. Washington, 1992.

Eagleman D. "The Brain on Trial." *Atlantic Monthly*, Lipiec 2011. https://www.theatlantic.com/magazine/archive/2011/07/the-brain-on-trial/308520/ (dostęp 5.8.2019).

Enders Ch. "A Right to Have Rights – The German Constitutional Concept of Human Dignity." *NUJS Law Review* 3, no. 3 (2010): 262.

Falandysz L. "O koncepcji tzw. przestępstw bez ofiar." *Państwo i Prawo* 8–9 (1978): 105–13.

Fallon R. H. "Legitimization and the Constitution." *Harvard Law Review* 118, no. 6 (2005): 1787–1853.

Feinberg J. *Doing and Deserving: Essays in the Theory of Responsibility*. Princeton: Princeton University Press, 1970.

Feinberg J. *Harm to Others*. Oxford: Oxford University Press, 1984.

Feinberg J. "The Expressive Function of Punishment." In: R. A. Duff and D. Garland (eds) *A Reader on Punishment*. Oxford: Oxford University Press, 1994.

Feldman. *The Role of Science in Law*. Oxford: Oxford University Press, 2009.

Filek J. *Etyka. Reinterpretacja*. Kraków: Wyd. Benedyktynów, 2014.

Filek J. *Ontologizacja odpowiedzialności*. Kraków: Wyd. Baran i Suszczyński, 1996.

Filek J. "Pytania do odpowiedzialności." *Znak* 485, no. 10 (1995): 20–27.

Finnis J. *Human Rights and Common Good: Collected Essays*, vol. III. Oxford: Oxford University Press, 2011.

Fischer J. M. "Recent Work on Moral Responsibility." *Ethics* 110, no. 1 (1999): 93–139.

Fischer J. M., and Ravizza M. *Responsibility and Control: A Theory of Moral Responsibility*. Cambridge: Cambridge University Press, 2008.

Fodor J. *Psychosemantics: The Problem of Meaning in the Philosophy of Mind*. Cambridge: Cambridge University Press, 1987.

Foot P. "Morality, Action, and Outcome." In: P. A. Woodward (ed.) *The Doctrine of Double Effect: Philosophers Debate a Controversial Moral Principle*. Notre Dame: University of Notre Dame Press, 2000.

Foot P. "The Problem of Abortion and the Doctrine of the Double Effect." In: J. M. Fischer and M. Ravizza (eds) *Ethics. Problems and Principles*. Fort Worth: Harcourt Brace Jovanovich College Publishers, 1992.

Frankfurt H. "Alternate Possibilities and Moral Responsibility." *Journal of Philosophy* 66, no. 23 (1969): 829.

Frankfurt H. "An Alleged Asymmetry Between Actions and Omissions." *Ethics* 104, no. 3 (1994): 620–23.

Fukuyama F. *Our Posthuman Future: Consequences of the Biotechnology Revolution*. New York: Picador, 2002.

Fuller L. L. "The Case of the Speluncean Explorers." *Harvard Law Review* 62, no. 4 (1949): 616–45.

Galewicz W. "Wstęp tłumacza." In: św. Tomasz z Akwinu (ed.) *Traktat o ludzkim działaniu*, transl. W. Galewicz. Kęty, 2013.

Gardner J. "Introduction." In: H. L. A. Hart (ed.) *Punishment and Responsibility: Essays in the Philosophy of Law*, wyd. 2. Oxford: Oxford University Press, 2008.

Gardner J., and Jung H. "Making Sense of Mens Rea: Antony Duff's Account." *Oxford Journal of Legal Studies* 11, no. 4 (1991): 282–85.

Godność i prawa osoby ludzkiej. Watykan 1983, Międzynarodowa Komisja Teologiczna. http://www.vatican.va/roman_curia/congregations/cfaith/cti_documents/rc_cti_1983_dignita-diritti_pl.html (dostęp 11.10.2019).

Goldman A. "The Paradox of Punishment." *Philosophy and Public Affairs* 9, no. 1 (1979): 42–58.

Golser F. "The Concept of a Special Criminal Law as a Weapon Against 'Enemies' of the Society." *Studia Iuridica* 67 (2016): 65–77.

Grabowski A. *Prawnicze pojęcie obowiązywania prawa stanowionego. Krytyka niepozytywistycznej koncepcji prawa*. Kraków: Księgarnia Akademicka, 2009.

Greene J., and Cohen J. "For the Law, Neuroscience Changes Nothing and Everything." *Philosophical Transactions of the Royal Society of London* 359 (2004): 1775–85.

Habermas J. *Communication and the Evolution of Society*. Boston: Beacon Press, 1979.

Haidt J. *Prawy umysł. Dlaczego dobrych ludzi dzieli religia i polityka?*, transl. A. Nowak-Młynikowska. Sopot: Smak Słowa, 2014.

Hale M. *History of the Pleas of the Crown* 1 (1736).

Hall J. *General Principles of Criminal Law*. Indianapolis: Jerome Hall Law Library, 1960.

Harel A. "Economic Analysis of Criminal Law: A Survey." In: A. Harel and K. Hylton (eds) *Research Handbook of the Economic Analysis of Criminal Law*. Cheltenham and Northampton: Edward Elgar Publishing, 2012.

Harel A. Punishment and the State. http://dx.doi.org/10.2139/ssrn.2280755 (dostęp 10.10.2019).

Harel A. "Reply." In: P. H. Robinson, S. P. Garvey, and K. Kessler-Ferzan (eds) *Criminal Law Conversations*. Oxford: Oxford University Press, 2009.

Harel A. "The Duty to Criminalize." *Law and Philosophy* 34, no. 1 (2015): 1–22.

Harel A. "Why Only the State May Inflict Criminal Sanctions." *Comparative Research in Law & Political Economy* 3, no. 4 (2007).

Hart H. L. A. *Law, Liberty and Morality*. Stanford: Stanford University Press, 1963.

Hart H. L. A. "Prolegomenon to the Principles of Punishment." *Proceedings of the Aristotelian Society. New Series* 60 (1959–1960).

Hart H. L. A., and Honore A. M. *Causation in the Law*. Oxford: Oxford University Press, 1959.

Hart H. M. "The Aims of the Criminal Law." *Law and Contemporary Problems* 23, no. 3 (1958): 401–41.

Helios J. "Modele legitymizacji prawa europejskiego." *Zeszyty Naukowe Państwowej Wyższej Szkoły Zawodowej im. Witelona w Legnicy* 3 (2008): 27–55.

Helis J. "Hannah Arendt and Human Dignity: Theoretical Foundations and Constitutional Protection of Human Rights." *Journal of Politics and Law* 1, no. 3 (2008).

Henry L. M. "The Jurisprudence of Dignity." *University of Pennsylvania Law Review* 160, no. 1 (2011): 169–233.

Hertzberg L. "Blame and Causality." *Mind. New Series* 84, no. 336 (1975): 500–515.

Hervada J. *Prawo naturalne*, transl. A. Dorabialska. Kraków: Wyd. Petrus, 2011.

Hofmański P., and Wróbel A. "Komentarz do art. 6." In: L. Garlicki (ed.) *Konwencja o Ochronie Praw Człowieka i Podstawowych Wolności*, t. 1, *Komentarz do artykułów 1–18*. Warszawa: Dom Wydawniczy „Elipsa", 2010.

Hołówka J. "Relatywizm i obiektywizm etyczny." *Etyka* no. 17 (1979): 209–53.

Hughes G. "The Concept of Dignity in the Universal Declaration of Human Rights." *Journal of Religious Ethics* 39, no. 1 (2011): 1–24.

Hunt D. P. "Moral Responsibility and Unavoidable Action." *Philosophical Studies* 97, no. 2 (2000): 195–227.

Hunt L. *Inventing Human Rights: A History*. New York: WW Norton & Co., 2008.

Husak D. N. "Strict Liability, Justice, and Proportionality." In: A. Simester (ed.) *Appraising Strict Liability*. Oxford, 2005.

Ingarden R. *Książeczka o człowieku*. Kraków: Wyd. Literackie, 1987.

Ingarden R. *Wykłady z etyki*. Warszawa: Wyd. PWN, 1989.

Inwagen P. van. "The Incompatibility of Free Will and Determinism." *Philosophical Studies* 27, no. 3 (1975): 185–99.

Jabłoński M. "Klasyfikacja wolności i praw jednostki w Konstytucji RP." In: M. Jabłoński (ed.) *Wolności i prawa jednostki w Konstytucji RP, t. 1, Idee i zasady przewodnie konstytucyjnej regulacji wolności i praw jednostki w RP*. Warszawa: C.H. Beck, 2010.

Jackson J., and Tyler T. "Future Challenges in the Study of Legitimization and Criminal Justice." *SSRN Electronic Journal*, marzec (2013).

Jaeger W. *Paideia*, t. I, transl. M. Plezia. Warszawa: Wyd. PAX, 1962.

Jan Paweł II. "Orędzie na XXI Światowy Dzień Pokoju." In: Paweł VI and Jan Paweł II (eds) *Orędzia papieskie na Światowy Dzień Pokoju*. Rzym and Lublin, 1987.

Jedlecka W. *Legitymizacja prawa Unii Europejskiej. Legitymizacja demokratyczna czy cywilizacyjne?* Łódź: Wyd. Uniwersytetu Łódzkiego, 2014.

Jezusek A. "Domniemanie winy w prawie karnym materialnym a procesowe domniemanie niewinności." *Ruch Prawniczy, Ekonomiczny i Socjologiczny* 78, no. 2 (2016).

Jones M. "Overcoming the Myth of Free Will in Criminal Law: The True Impact of the Genetic Revolution." *Duke Law Journal* 52, no. 5 (2003): 1031–53.

Juzaszek M. *Paradoks trafu prawnego. Studium filozoficznoprawne*, Unpublished doctoral dissertation written under the supervision of prof. dr. hab. Tomasz Gizbert-Studnicki and the assistant supervisor, Dr. Adam Dyrda, Kraków, 2017.

Kaczmarek T. "Metodologiczne aspekty sporów wokół pojęcia czynu w polskim prawie karnym." In: T. Kaczmarek (ed.) *Rozważania o przestępstwie i karze. Wybór prac z okresu 40-lecia naukowej twórczości*. Warszawa: Uczelnia Łazarskiego, 2006.

Kallen H. M. "Responsibility." *Ethics* 52, no. 3 (1942): 350–76.

Kamiński S. *Jak filozofować?* Lublin: Wyd. KUL, 1989.

Kamir O. "Honor and Dignity in the Film Unforgiven: Implications for Sociolegal Theory." *Law and Society Review* 40, no. 1 (2006): 193–234.

Kant I. *Kant on Education*, transl. A. Churton. London, 1899.

Kant I. *Uzasadnienie metafizyki moralności*, transl. M. Wartenberg. Kęty: Wyd. Antyk Marek Derewiecki, 2013.

Kardas P. *Zbieg przepisów ustawy w prawie karnym. Analiza teoretyczna*. Warszawa: Wolters Kluwer Polska, 2011.

Kaufmann A. "Problemgeschichte der Rechtsphilosophie." In: A. Kaufmann and W. Hassemer (eds) *Einführung in Rechtsphilosophie und Rechtstheorie der Gegenwart*, 1985 (b.m.w.).

Kaufmann A. "Vorüberlegungen zu einer juristischen Logik und Ontologie der Relationen. Grundlegung einer personalen Rechtstheorie." *Rechtstheorie. Zeitschrift für Logik, Methodenlehre, Kybernetik und Soziologie des Rechts* 17, no. 3 (1986). Cuvillier Verlag Göttingen.

Kim J. "The Myth of Nonreductive Materialism." In: P. K. Moser and J. D. Trout (eds) *Contemporary Materialism*. New York: Routledge, 1995.

Kinzler K. D., Dupoux E., and Spelke E. S. "The Native Language of Social Cognition." *Proceedings of the National Academy of Sciences of the United States of America* 104, no. 30 (2007): 12577–12580.

Kleinfeld J. "Reconstructivism: The Place of Criminal Law in Ethical Life." *Harvard Law Review* 129, no. 6 (2016): 1485.

Kmiecik. "Perspektywy depenalizacji 'przestępstw bez ofiar' w USA." *Palestra* 1 (1980): 103–11.

Konieczniak P. *Czyn jako podstawa odpowiedzialności w prawie karnym*. Warszawa: Wolters Kluwer Polska, 2002.

Konstytucja Niemiec, transl. B. Banaszak, A. Malicka. Warszawa: Wyd. Sejmowe, 2009.

Kowalewska-Łukuć M. *Wina w prawie karnym*. Warszawa: Wolters Kluwer Polska, 2019.

Kozerska E. *Państwo i społeczeństwo w poglądach Piusa XI*. Wrocław: Wyd. Uniwersytetu Wrocławskiego, 2005.

Krąpiec M. A. *Ludzka wolność i jej granice*. Lublin: Wyd. Polskie Towarzystwo Tomasza z Akwinu, 2008.

Król-Bogomilska M. *"Formy winy" w prawie karnym w świetle psychologii*. Warszawa: Wyd. Uniwersytetu Warszawskiego, 1991.

Kuhse H. "Is There a Tension Between Autonomy and Dignity." In: P. Kemp, J. Rendtorff, and N. Mattsson (eds) *Bioethics and Biolaw, t. 2*. Copenhagen, 2000.

Kurek Ł. *Obraz człowieka w prawie karnym a nauki kognitywne*. https://www.academia.edu/32533446/Obraz_cz%C5%82owieka_w_prawie_karnym_a_nauki_kognitywne (dostęp 16.7.2019).

Lachowski J. "Strona podmiotowa czynu zabronionego." In: R. Dębski (ed.) *Nauka o przestępstwie. Zasady odpowiedzialności "System Prawa Karnego,"* t. 3. Warszawa: C.H. Beck, 2013.

Lachowski J. "Wina w prawie karnym." In: R. Dębski (ed.) *Nauka o przestępstwie. Zasady odpowiedzialności "System Prawa Karnego," t. 3.* Warszawa: C.H. Beck, 2013.

Law Commission. *Criminal Responsibility in Regulatory Contexts.* 2010. https://www.lawcom.gov.uk/project/criminal-liability-in-regulatory-contexts/ (dostęp 8.11.2019).

Leszczyński L. *Stosowanie generalnych klauzul odsyłających.* Kraków: Wolters Kluwer Polska, 2001.

Libet B. "Are the Mental Experiences of Will and Self-Control Significant for the Performance of a Voluntary Act?" *Behavioral and Brain Sciences* 10, no. 4 (1987): 318–19.

Lobel O. "New Governance as Regulatory Governance." In: D. Levi-Faur (ed.) *The Oxford Handbook of Governance.* Oxford: Oxford University Press, 2012.

Locke J. "Two Treatises of Government." In: *The Works of John Locke. A New Edition, Corrected. In Ten Volumes. Vol. V.* London, 1823.

Lowe E. J. "Substance Causation, Powers, and Human Agency." In: S. C. Gibb, E. J. Lowe, and R. D. Ingthorsson (eds) *Mental Causation and Ontology.* Oxford: Oxford University Press, 2013.

Luban D. "After the Honeymoon: Reflections on the Current State of International Criminal Justice." *Journal of International Criminal Justice* 11, no. 3 (2013): 505.

Łuków P. "Metafizyka wolności i odpowiedzialności." In: S. Kołodziejczyk (ed.) *Przewodnik po metafizyce.* Kraków: Wyd. WAM, 2011.

Macklin. "Dignity is a Useless Concept." *British Medical Journal* 327 (2003): 1419–20.

Majewski J. *Prawnokarne przypisywanie skutku przy zaniechaniu. Zagadnienia węzłowe.* Kraków: Wyd. Księgarnia Akademicka, 1997.

Makarewicz J. *Polskie prawo karne. Część ogólna.* Warszawa: Wolters Kluwer Polska, 2017.

Maritain J. "Introduction." In: *Human Rights: Comments and interpretations.* UNESCO, Paris, 1948.

Mayberg H. "Does Neuroscience Give Us New Insights into Criminal Responsibility?" In: M. S. Gazzaniga and J. S. Rakoff (eds) *A Judge's Guide to Neuroscience: A Concise Introduction.* Santa Barbara: University of California, Santa Barbara, 2010.

Mącior W. *Czyn ludzki i jego znaczenie w prawie karnym. Zagadnienia podstawowe.* Warszawa: Wydawnictwo Prawnicze, 1990.

McCrudden Ch. "Human Dignity and Judicial Interpretation of Human Rights." *The European Journal of International Law* 19, no. 4 (2008): 655.

McCrudden Ch. "On Portraying Human Dignity." In: D. Grimm, A. Kemmerer, and Ch. Möllers (eds) *Human Dignity in Context.* Baden-Baden: Hart Publishing, 2018.

McInerny. *Aquinas on Human Action: A Theory of Practice.* Washington: The Catholic University of America Press, 2012.

Meier R. F., and Geis G. *Victimless Crime? Prostitution, Drugs, Homosexuality, and Abortion*. Los Angeles: Wyd. Roxbury, 1997.

Metz T. "African Conceptions of Human Dignity: Vitality and Community as the Ground of Human Rights." *Human Rights Review* 13 (2012): 19–37.

Mill J. S. "O wolności." In: J. S. Mill (ed.) *Utylitaryzm. O wolności*, transl. M. Ossowska, A. Kurlandzka. Warszawa: Wyd. PWN, 1959.

Mirandola G. P. della. *Oratio de hominis dignitate. Mowa o godności człowieka*, transl. Z. Nerczuk, M. Olszewski. Warszawa: Wyd. IFiS PAN, 2010.

Molendowska M. "Ewolucja chrześcijańsko-demokratycznej wersji zasady pomocniczości." In: A. Pawłowska and S. Grabowska (eds) *Zasada pomocniczości. Wymiar europejski, narodowy, regionalny i lokalny*. Rzeszów: Wydawnictwo Uniwersytetu Rzeszowskiego, 2011.

Moore M. S. "A Taxonomy of Purposes of Punishment." In: L. Katz, M. S. Moore, and S. J. Morse (eds) *Foundations of Criminal Law*. Oxford: Oxford University Press, 1999.

Moore M. S. "'Nothing But a Pack of Neurons': The Moral Responsibility of the Human Machine." In: B. Donnelly-Lazarov (ed.) *Neurolaw and Responsibility for Action: Concepts, Crimes and Courts*. Cambridge: Cambridge University Press, 2018.

Moore M. S. *Placing Blame: A Theory of the Criminal Law*. Oxford: Oxford University Press, 2012.

Moore M. S. "The Moral Worth of Retribution." In: F. Schoeman (ed.) *Responsibility, Character, and the Emotions: New Essays in Moral Psychology*. Cambridge: Cambridge University Press, 1987.

Morell V. "Evidence Found for a Possible 'Aggression Gene.'" *Science* 260, no. 51155 (1993): 1722–23.

Morris H. "A Paternalistic Theory of Punishment." In: M. Tonry (ed.) *Why Punish? How Much? A Reader on Punishment*. Oxford: Oxford University Press, 2011.

Morris H. *On Guilt and Innocence: Essays in Legal Philosophy and Moral Psychology*. Berkeley, Los Angeles, and London: University of California Press, 1976.

Morris N. *Madness and the Criminal Law*. Chicago: University of Chicago Press, 1982.

Morse S. J. "Avoiding Irrational NeuroLaw Exuberance: A Plea for Neuromodesty." *Mercer Law Review* 62 (2011): 837–59.

Morse S. J. "Brain Overclaim Syndrome and Criminal Responsibility: A Diagnostic Note." *Ohio State Journal of Criminal Law* 3 (2006): 397–412.

Morse S. J. "Determinism and the Death of Folk Psychology: Two Challenges to Responsibility From Neuroscience." *Minnesota Journal of Law of Science and Technology* 9, no. 1 (2008): 1–36.

Morse S. J. "Failed Explanations and Criminal Responsibility: Experts and the Unconscious." *Virginia Law Review* 68, no. 5 (1982): 971–1084.

Morse S. J. "Genetics and Criminal Responsibility." *Public Law and Legal Theory. Research Paper Series*. Research Paper No. 11–34.

Mrozek J. J. "Godność osoby ludzkiej jako źródło praw człowieka i obywatela." *Civitas et Lex* no. 1 (2014): 41–47.

Mueller D. C. *Public Choice II: A Revised Edition of Public Choice*. Cambridge: Cambridge University Press, 1989.

Nagel T. "Moral Luck." *Proceedings of the Aristotelian Society, Supplementary Volumes* 50 (1976): 115–51.

Nozick. *Anarchy, State and Utopia*. Philadelphia: Perseus Books, 1974.

Ossowska M. "Normy moralne w obronie godności człowieka." *Etyka* no. 5 (1969): 7–25.

Packer H. *The Limits of the Criminal Sanction*. Stanford: Stanford University Press, 1968.

Papachristos A. V., Meares T. L., and Fagan J. "Why Do Criminals Obey the Law? The Influence of Legitimization and Social Networks on Active Gun Offenders." *Journal of Criminal Law and Criminology* 102, no. 2 (2012).

Pardo M. S., and Patterson D. *Minds, Brains, and Law*. Oxford: Oxford University Press, 2013.

Parent W. A. "Constitutional Values and Human Dignity." In: M. J. Meyer and W. A. Parent (eds) *The Constitution of Rights: Human Dignity and American Values*. Ithaca: Cornell University Press, 1992.

Paton H. J. *The Categorical Imperative: A Study in Kant's Moral Philosophy*. London: Cambridge University Press, 1947.

Patterson D. "Neuroscience and the Explanation of Human Action." In: B. Donnelly-Lazarov (ed.) *Neurolaw and Responsibility for Action: Concepts, Crimes and Courts*. Cambridge: Cambridge University Press, 2018.

Paust J. J. "Human Dignity as a Constitutional Right: A Jurisprudentially Based Inquiry into Criteria and Content." *Howard Law Journal* 27 (1984): 145–225.

Peristeridou Ch. *The Principle of Legality in European Criminal Law*, 2015

Pettit P. *Republicanism: A Theory of Freedom and Government*. Oxford: Oxford University Press, 1999.

Philips M. "Rationality, Responsibility and Blame." *Canadian Journal of Philosophy* 17, no. 1 (1987): 141–54.

Piechowiak M. *Filozofia praw człowieka. Prawa człowieka w świetle ich międzynarodowej ochrony*. Lublin, 1999.

Piechowiak M. *W poszukiwaniu ontologicznych podstaw prawa. Arthura Kaufmanna teoria sprawiedliwości*. Warszawa and Poznań: Wyd. Towarzystwo Naukowe Katolickiego Uniwersytetu Lubelskiego, 1992.

Pinker S. "The Stupidity of Dignity." *New Republic*, May 28, 2008.

Pius XI. *Encyklika Quadragesimo Anno*. https://opoka.org.pl/biblioteka/W/WP/pius_xi/encykliki/quadragesimo_anno_15051931.html (dostęp 8.11.2019).

Plato, *Laws*, The Project Gutenberg EBook of Laws, by Plato, https://www.gutenberg.org/files/1750/1750-h/1750-h.htm (accessed 28 March 2022).

Pohl Ł. "Czyn w prawie karnym." In: R. Dębski (ed.) *Nauka o przestępstwie. Zasady odpowiedzialności*, System Prawa Karnego, t. 3. Warszawa: C.H. Beck, 2013.

Poręba M. *Wolność i metafizyka. Eseje z filozofii pierwszej*. Warszawa: Wyd. PWN, 2017.

Potrzeszcz J. "Godność człowieka w orzecznictwie polskiego Trybunału Konstytucyjnego." *Roczniki Nauk Prawnych* 15, no. 1 (2005): 31–32.

Powszechna encyklopedia filozofii, wersja internetowa, hasło "akt i możność," opr. M. A. Krąpiec. ptta.pl/pef/pdf/a/aktim.pdf (dostęp 6.9.2019).

Powszechna encyklopedia filozofii, wersja internetowa, hasło "antropologia filozoficzna," opr. M. A. Krąpiec. www.ptta.pl/pef/pdf/a/antropologia.pdf (dostęp 4.12.2018).

Powszechna encyklopedia filozofii, wersja internetowa, hasło "etyka," opr. T. Styczeń. ptta.pl/pef/pdf/e/etyka.pdf (dostęp 8.10.2019).

Priel D. "The Place of Legitimization in Legal Theory." *McGill Law Journal* 57, no. 1 (2011).

Pulka Z. *Legitymizacja państwa w prawoznawstwie*. Wrocław: Wyd. Uniwersytetu Wrocławskiego, 1996.

Rejman G. *Teorie i formy winy w prawie karnym*. Warszawa: Wydawnictwo Prawnicze, 1980.

Renzo M. "State Legitimization and Self-Defence." *Law and Philosophy* 30, no. 5 (2011): 575–601.

Report of the Departmental Committee on Homosexual Offences and Prostitution, w całości dostępny na stronach internetowych Brytyjskich Archiwów Narodowych. http://discovery.nationalarchives.gov.uk/details/r/C1386377 (dostęp 21.8.2018).

Richards D. A. J. *Sex, Drugs, Death, and the Law: An Essay on Human Rights and Overcriminalization*. Totowa, 1982.

Ricoeur P. *Symbolika zła*, transl. S. Cichowicz, M. Ochab. Warszawa: Wyd. PAX, 1986.

Robinson P. H., and Darley J. M. *Justice, Responsibility and Blame*. Boulder, San Francisco, and Oxford: Oxford University Press, 1995.

Rodzynkiewicz M. "Fenomen odpowiedzialności w refleksji filozoficznej a prawnokarne zasady odpowiedzialności." *Przegląd Prawa Karnego* 16 (1997).

Rodzynkiewicz M. *Modelowanie pojęć w prawie karnym*. Kraków: Wyd. Uniwersytetu Jagiellońskiego, 1998.

Ross D. W. *Kant's Ethical Theory: A Commentary on the Grundlegung zur Metaphysik der Sitten*. Oxford: Oxford University Press, 1954.

Schabas W. A. *The European Convention on Human Rights: A Commentary*. Oxford: Oxford University Press, 2015.

Schur E. M., and Bedau H. A. *Victimless Crimes; Two Sides of a Controversy*. Englewood Cliffs, 1974.

Searle J. *Umysł. Krótkie wprowadzenie*, transl. J. Karłowski. Poznań: Wyd. Rebis, 2010.

Segev. "Moral Rightness and the Significance of Law: Why, How, and When Mistake of Law Matters." *The University of Toronto Law Journal* 64, no. 1 (2014): 26–63.

Seifert J. *What is Life? The Originality, Irreducibility, and Value of Life*. Amsterdam, 1997.

Sensen O. "Human Dignity in Historical Perspective: The Contemporary and Traditional Paradigms." *European Journal of Political Theory* 10 (2011): 71–91.

Shoemaker D. "Attributability, Answerability and Accountability: Toward a Wider Theory of Moral Responsibility." *Ethics* 121, no. 3 (2011): 602–32.

Shoemaker D. "Moral Address, Moral Responsibility, and the Boundaries of the Moral Community." *Ethics* 118, no. 1 (2007): 70–108.

Shulztiner D., and Carmi G. E. "Human Dignity in National Constitutions: Functions, Promises and Dangers." *The American Journal of Comparative Law* 62, no. 2 (2014): 461–90.

Sifferd K. "Non-Eliminative Reductionism: Not the Theory of Mind Some Responsibility Theorists Want, But the One They Need." In: B. Donnelly-Lazarov (ed.) *Neurolaw and Responsibility for Action: Concepts, Crimes and Courts*. Cambridge: Cambridge University Press, 2018.

Skąpska G., and Stelmach J. "Współczesne problemy i modele legitymizacji prawa." *Colloquia Communia*, t. 6, nos. 41–42 (1988–1989).

Skinner Q. *Liberty Before Liberalism*. Cambridge: Cambridge University Press, 2014.

Slaughter J. *Human Rights, Inc. The World Novel, Narrative Form, and International Law*. New York: Oxford University Press, 2007.

Ślipko T. *Zarys etyki ogólnej*. Kraków: Wyd. WAM, 2004.

Smilansky S. *Free Will and Illusion*. Oxford: Oxford University Press, 2000.

Smith A. *Teoria uczuć moralnych*. Warszawa: Wyd. PWN, 1989.

Smith D. J. "The Foundations of Legitimization." In: T. R. Tyler (ed.) *Legitimization and Criminal Justice*, 2007

Sokół W. "Legitymizacja polityczna." In: B. Szmulik and M. Żmigrodzki (eds) *Wprowadzenie do nauki o państwie i polityce*. Lublin: Wyd. UMCS, 2006.

Spyra T. *Granice wykładni prawa. Znaczenie językowe tekstu prawnego jako granica wykładni*. Kraków: Wyd. Zakamycze, 2006.

Sroka T. "uwagi do art. 42 ust. 1." In: R. P. Konstytucja (ed.) *t. I, Komentarz do art. 1–86*, red. L. Bosek, M. Safjan. Warszawa: C.H. Beck, 2016.

Stanford Encyclopedia of Philosophy. https://plato.stanford.edu/entries/paternalism/ (dostęp 20.8.2018).

Stępień M. "Legitymizacja prawa w różnych modelach demokracji." In: A. Preisner (ed.) *Prawowitość czy zgodność z prawem. Legitymizacja władzy w państwach demokratycznych*. Wrocław, 2010.

Strawson P. F. "Freedom and Resentment." *Proceedings of the British Academy* 48 (1962): 187–211.

Sulikowski A. *Posthumanizm a prawoznawstwo*. Opole: Wyd. Uniwersytetu Opolskiego, 2013.

Szczucki K. "Ethical Legitimization of Criminal Law." *International Journal of Law, Crime and Justice* 53 (2018): 67–76.

Szczucki K. "O miłosiernym lekarzu, czyli o moralnych podstawach prawnego obowiązku." In: B. Namysłowska-Gabrysiak, K. Syroka-Marczewska, and A. Walczak-Żochowska (eds) *Prawo wobec problemów społecznych. Księga Jubileuszowa profesor Eleonory Zielińskiej*. Warszawa: C.H. Beck, 2016.

Szczucki K. "Prawo karne jako instrument przeciwdziałania zachowaniom niemoralnym." In: M. Różański and R. Sztychmiler (eds) *Wychowanie religijne i moralne*. Olsztyn: Wyd. UWM, 2015.

Szczucki K. "Relacja między odpowiedzialnością etyczną i karną na przykładzie zasady podwójnego skutku." *Państwo i Prawo*, no. 3 (2019).

Szczucki K. *Wykładnia prokonstytucyjna prawa karnego*. Warszawa: Wyd. Sejmowe, 2015.

Święcicka P. *Proces Jezusa w świetle prawa rzymskiego. Studium prawno-historyczne*. Warszawa: Wyd. PWN, 2012.

Teichman D. "Why the State May Delegate the Infliction of Criminal Sanctions." In: P. H. Robinson, S. P. Garvey, and K. Kessler-Ferzan (eds) *Criminal Law Conversations*. Oxford: Oxford University Press, 2009.

Thomas Aquinas st. *Commentary on Aristotle's Nicomachean Ethics*. Notre Dame 1993, transl. C. J. Litzinger.

Thomas Aquinas, Summa Theologiae, Second and Revised Edition, 1920 Literally translated by Fathers of the English Dominican Province, Online Edition 2017.

Thorburn M. "Criminal Law as Public Law." In: R. A. Duff and S. Green (eds) *Philosophical Foundations of Criminal Law*. Oxford: Oxford University Press, 2011.

Thorburn M. "Why Only the State May Decide When Sanctions Are Appropriate." In: P. H. Robinson, S. P. Garvey, and K. Kessler-Ferzan (eds) *Criminal Law Conversations*. Oxford: Oxford University Press, 2009.

Tomasello M., Carpenter M., Call J., Behne T., and Moll H. "Understanding and Sharing Intentions: The Origins of Cultural Cognition." *Behavioral and Brain Sciences* 2 (2005): 5.

Twardowski K., *Etyka i prawo karne wobec zagadnienia wolności woli*, "Etyka" 1983, no. 20.

Tyler T., and Blader S. L. "Can Business Effectively Regulate Employee Conduct? The Antecedents of Rule Following in Work Settings." *The Academy of Management Journal* 48, no. 6 (2005): 1143–58.

Tyler T. R. "Legitimization and Criminal Justice: International Perspectives." In: T. R. Tyler (ed.) *Legitimization and Criminal Justice*, 2007.

Utrat-Milecki J. *Podstawy penologii. Teoria kary*. Warszawa: Wyd. Uniwersytetu Warszawskiego, 2006.

Vasiliev S. "Between International Criminal Justice and Injustice: Theorising Legitimization." In: C. Bailliet and N. Hayashi (eds) *The Legitimization of International Criminal Tribunals*. Cambridge: Cambridge University Press, 2016.

Waal F. B. M. de. *Good Natured: The Origins of Right and Wrong in Humans and Other Animals*. Cambridge: Cambridge University Press, 1996.

Waldron J. "A Right to Do Wrong." *Ethics* 92, no. 1 (1981): 21–39.

Walker M. U. "Moral Luck and the Virtues of Impure Agency." In: D. Statman (ed.) *Moral Luck*, 1993

Wallace R. J. *Responsibility and the Moral Sentiments*. Cambridge: Cambridge University Press, 1994.

Wąsek A. "Prawo karne – minimum moralności?" *Annales Universitatis Mariae Curie-Skłodowska. Sectio G. Ius*, 1984, t. 31.

Wąsek A. *Recenzja książki J. Majewskiego, "Prawnokarne przypisywanie skutku przy zaniechaniu. Zagadnienia węzłowe, Wydawnictwo Księgarnia Akademicka, Kraków 1997,"* *Państwo i Prawo* 1999, z. 3.

Weber M. "Trzy typy prawomocnego panowania." In: W. Derczyński, A. Jasińska-Kania, and J. Szacki (eds) *Elementy teorii socjologicznych. Materiały do dziejów współczesnej socjologii zachodniej*. Warszawa: Wyd. PWN, 1975.

Weldon T. D. *The Vocabulary of Politics*. London, 1953.

Wierzchowska A. "Konceptualizacja pojęcia "legitymizacja." In: K. A. Wojtaszczyk (ed.) *Legitymizacja procesów integracji europejskiej*. Warszawa: Wyd. Uniwersytetu Śląskiego, 2006.

Wiliński P. *Zasada prawa do obrony w polskim procesie karnym*. Kraków: Wolters Kluwer Polska, 2006.

Williams B. A. O. "Moral Luck." *Proceedings of the Aristotelian Society, Supplementary Volumes* 50 (1976): 115–51.

Williams G. "Sharing Responsibility and Holding Responsible." *Journal of Applied Philosophy* 30, no. 4 (2013): 351–64.

Witkin H. A. "Criminality in XYY and XXY Men." *Science* 193, no. 4253 (1976): 547–55.

Wojtyczek K. "Ochrona godności człowieka, wolności i równości przy pomocy skargi konstytucyjnej." In: K. Complak (ed.) *Godność człowieka jako kategoria prawa*. Wrocław: Centrum Handlu i Poligrafii, 2001.

Wojtyła K. *Osoba i czyn oraz inne studia antropologiczne*. Lublin: Wyd. Towarzystwo Naukowe KUL, 2011.

Woleński J. "Analiza i odpowiedzialność." *Znak* 1995, z. 10.

Woroniecki J. "Etyka." In: *Zarys filozofii: Praca zbiorowa*, t. 2. Lublin, 1929.

Zakrzewski P. *Stopniowanie winy w prawie karnym*. Warszawa: Wolters Kluwer Polska, 2016.

Zieliński A. "Pojmowanie godności ludzkiej w świetle praw ekonomicznych i socjalnych." In: *Godność człowieka a prawa ekonomiczne i socjalne. Księga jubileuszowa wydana w piętnastą rocznicę ustanowienia Rzecznika Praw Obywatelskich*. Warszawa, 2003.

Zieliński M., and Ziembiński Z. *Uzasadnianie twierdzeń, ocen i norm w prawoznawstwie*. Warszawa: Wyd. PWN, 1988.

Ziembiński Z. *Etyczne problemy prawoznawstwa*. Warszawa: Wyd. PWN, 1972.

Ziembiński Z. *O stanowieniu i obowiązywaniu prawa. Zagadnienia podstawowe*. Warszawa: Wyd. Sejmowe, 1995.

Ziembiński Z. *Wstęp do aksjologii dla prawników*. Warszawa: Wyd. Prawnicze, 1990.

Zimmerman D. "Reasons-Responsiveness and Ownership-of-Agency: Fischer and Ravizza's Historicist Theory of Responsibility." *The Journal of Ethics* 6, no. 3 (2002): 199–234.

Zoll A. "O wartościowaniu czynu w prawie karnym." *Państwo i Prawo*, no. 4 (1983).

Zygmunt A. "Zasada pomocniczości w nauczaniu Jana Pawła II." In: A. Pawłowska and S. Grabowska (eds) *Zasada pomocniczości. Wymiar europejski, narodowy, regionalny i lokalny*. Rzeszów: Wydawnictwo Uniwersytetu Rzeszowskiego, 2011.

JURISPRUDENCE OF THE CONSTITUTIONAL TRIBUNAL IN REPUBLIC OF POLAND

Judgment of 28 May 1997, K 26/96.
Judgment of 1 June 1999, SK 20/98.
Judgment of 8 December 1999, SK 19/99.
Judgment of 4 April 2001, K 11/00.
Judgment of 25 February 2002, SK 29/01.
Judgment of 15 October 2002, SK 6/02.
Judgment of 5 March 2003, K 7/01.
Judgment of 7 February 2005, SK 49/03.
Judgment of 7 February 2006, SK 45/04.
Judgment of 24 October 2006, SK 41/05.
Judgment of 7 March 2007, K 28/05.
Judgment of 10 July 2007, SK 50/06.
Judgment of 23 June 2009, K 54/07.
Judgment of 9 July 2009, SK 48/05.
Judgment of 22 January 2013, P 46/09.
Judgment of 23 November 2016, K 6/14.

JURISPRUDENCE OF THE SUPREME COURT AND COURTS OF APPEAL IN REPUBLIC OF POLAND

Bialystok AC Judgment of 6 December 2012, II AKa 210/12, LEX nr 1246605.
Judgment SN of 11 April 2006, I PK 169/05, OSNP 2007, nr 7–8, poz. 93.
Judgment SN of 28 May 2008, SNO 34/08, LEX nr 1288868.
Judgment SN of 2 October 2007, II CSK 269/07, OSNC-ZD 2008, nr 3, poz. 75.
Lodz AC Judgment of 16 October 2014, II AKa 230/14, LEX nr 1649014.
Lublin AC Judgment of 7 September 2017, II AKa 175/17, LEX nr 2369743.
Postanowienie SN of 7 February 2007, III KK 236/06, OSNKW 2007, nr 6, poz. 50.
SC Judgment of 25 April 1989, I CR 143/89, LEX nr 5282.Wroclaw AC Judgment of 6 March 2014, II AKa 34/14, LEX nr 1451862.

JURISPRUDENCE OF THE EUROPEAN COURT OF HUMAN RIGHTS

Judgment of 23 November 1976, *Engel and Others vs Netherlands*, 5100/71, 5101/71, 5102/71, 5354/72, 5370/72.
Judgment of 21 February 1984, *Özturk vs Germany*, 8544/79.
Judgment of 28 June 1984, *Campbell and Fell vs United Kingdom*, 7819/77 i 7878/77.

Judgment of 25 August 1987, *Lutz vs Germany*, 9912/82.
Judgment of 24 February 1994, *Bendenoun vs France*, 12547/86.
Judgment of 23 October 1995, *Schmautzer vs Austria*, 15523/89.
Judgment of 22 February 1996, *Putz vs Austria*, 18892/91.
Judgment of 29 August 1997, *A. P., M. P. i T. P. vs Switzerland*, 19958/92.
Judgment of 2 September 1998, *Lauko vs Slovakia*, 26138/95.
Judgment of 23 September 1998, *Malige vs France*, 27812/95.
Judgment of 29 September 1999, *Smith i Ford vs United Kingdom*, 37475/97 i 39036/97.
Judgment of 28 September 1999, *Escoubet vs Belgium*, 26780/95.
Judgment of 29 September 1999, *Moore i Gordon vs United Kingdom*, 36529/97 i 37393/97.
Judgment of 26 October 2000, *Kudła vs Poland*, 30210/96.
Judgment of 6 February 2001, *Wilkinson i Allen vs Zjednoczonemu Królestwu*, 31145/96 and 35580/97.
Judgment of 5 June 2001, *Mills vs United Kingdom*, 35685/97.
Judgment of 15 July 2002, *Ezeh i Connors vs United Kingdom*, 39665/98 and 40086/98.
Judgment of 9 October 2003, *Ezeh and Connors vs United Kingdom*, 39665/98 and 40086/98.
Judgment of 11 March 2004, *Yankov vs Bulgaria*, 39084/97.
Judgment of 8 July 2004, *VO vs France*, 53924/00.
Judgment of 20 October 2006, *Muršić vs Croatia*, 7334/13.
Judgment of 12 April 2007, *Dzwonkowski vs Poland*, 46702/99.
Judgment of 10 February 2009, *Sergey Zolotukhin vs Russia*, 14939/03.
Judgment of 22 October 2009, *Orchowski vs Poland*, 17885/04.
Judgment of 3 November 2011, *S. H. and other vs Austria*, 57813/00.
Judgment of 9 July 2013, *Vona vs Hungary*, 35943/10.
Judgment of 11 March 2014, *Abdu vs Bulgaria*, 26827/08.
Judgment of 17 July 2014, *Svinarenko and Slyadnev vs Russia*, 32541/08 and 43441/08.
Judgment of 24 July 2014, *Al Nashiri vs Poland*, 28761/11.
Judgment of 27 August 2015, *Parillo vs Italy*, 46470/11.
Judgment of 28 September 2015, *Bouyid vs Belgium*, 23380/09.
Judgment of 12 April 2016, *R. B. vs Hungary*, 64602/12.
Judgment of 6 September 2016, *W. D. vs Belgium*, 73548/13.

JURISPRUDENCE OF THE COURT OF JUSTICE OF THE EUROPEAN UNION

Judgment of 5 October 2000, *Komisja vs France*, C-337/98, ECLI:EU:C:2000:543.
Judgment of 18 October 2011, *Oliver Brüstle vs Greenpeace eV*, C-34/10, ECLI:EU:C:2011:669.
Judgment of 2 December 2014 r. *A, B, C vs Staatssecretaris van Veiligheid en Justitie*, Joined Cases, C-148/03 to C-150/03, ECLI:EU:C:2014:2406.

U.S. SUPREME COURT JUDGMENTS

Alden v. Maine, 527 U.S. 706, 802–803 (1999).
Alderman v. United States, 394 U.S. 165, 203 (1969).
Bates v. State Bar Arizona, 433 U.S. 350, 368 (1977).
Board of Educ. Island Trees Union Free School Dist. No. 26 v. Pico 457 U.S. 430, 462 (1974).
Brown, et al. v. Plata, et al., 563 U.S. 493 (2011).
Burstyn v. Wilson, 343 U.S. 250, 263 (1952).
Carroll v. United States, 267 U.S. 132, 154 (1925).
Chisholm v. Georgia, 2 U.S. (2 Dall.) 419 (1793).
Cohen v. California, 403 U.S. 15, 24 (1971).
De Veau v. Braisted, 363 U.S. 144, 148 (1960).
Estes v. Texas, 381 U.S. 532, 549 (1965).
Fed. Mar. Comm'n v. S.C. State Ports Auth., 535 U.S. 743, 760 (2002).
First National City Bank v. Banco Nacional de Cuba, 406 U.S. 759, 769 (1972).
Goldberg v. Kelly, 397 U.S. 254, 264–265 (1970).
Gonzales v. Carhart, 550 U.S. 124 (2007).
Gregg v. Georgia, 428 U.S. 153 (1976).
Griswold v. Connecticut, 381 U.S. 479, 482–483 (1965).
Haley v. Ohio, 332 U.S. 596, 617 (1948).
Heart of Atlanta Motel v. United States, 379 U.S. 241 (1964).
Heath v. Alabama, 474 U.S. 82, 88 (1985).
Homma v. Patterson, 327 U.S. 759, 761 (1946).
Hope v. Pelzer, 536 U.S. 730 (2002).
Hudson v. Michigan, 547 U.S. 586, 594 (2006).
In re Yamashita, 327 U.S. 1, 29 (1946).
Indiana v. Edwards, 554 U.S. 164, 176 (2008).
James v. United States, 366 U.S. 213, 225 (1961).
J. E. B. v. Alabama ex rel. T. B., 511 U.S. 127 (1994).
Kennedy v. Louisiana, 554 U.S. 407, 419–420 (2008).
Lawrence v. Texas, 539 U.S. 558, 567, 578–579 (2003).
Louisiana ex rel. Francis v. Resweber, 329 U.S. 459 (1947).
Mandoli v. Acheson, 344 U.S. 133, 139 (1952).
Marbury v. Madison, 5 U.S. (I Cranch) 137 (1803).
Milkovich v. Lorain Journal, 497 U.S. 1 (1990).
Miranda v. Arizona, 384 U.S. 436, 460 (1966).
Morisette v. *United States*, 342 U.S. 246, 250 (1952).
NAACP v. Claiborne Hardware Co. 73 L Ed 2d 1215 (1982).
Payton v. New York, 445, U.S. 573, 617–619 (1980).
Planned Parenthood v. Casey, 505 U.S. 833 (1992).
Powell v. State of Tex., 392 U.S. 514, 536 (1968).
Powers v. Ohio, 499 U.S. 400 (1991).
Rhodes v. Chapman, 452 U.S. 337, 359–360 (1981).
Rice v. Cayetano, 528 U.S. 495, 517 (2000).
Roper v. Simons, 543 U.S. 551, 560 (2005).

Skinner v. Ry. Labor Execs' Ass'n, 489 U.S. 602, 613–614 (1989).
The Exchange v. McFaddon, 11 U.S. (7 Cranch) 116 (1812).
Thornburgh v. American College of Obstetricians and Gynaecologists, 476 U.S. 747 (1986).
Trammel v. United States, 445 U.S. 50, 52, 913 (1980).
United States v. Ramsey, 431 U.S. 606, 618 (1977).
Wainwright v. City of New Orleans, 392 U.S. 598, 607 (1968).
Winston v. Lee, 470 U.S. 753, 760, 766–767 (1985).
Wolff v. McDonnell, 418 U.S. 539, 597 (1974).

UNITED KINGDOM COURTS JUDGMENTS

Reg. v. Clarence (1888) 22 Q.B.D. 23.
Reg. v. Miller (1954) 2 Q.B. 282.
Reg. v. O'Brien (1974) 3 All E.R. 663, 665.
Reg. v. Steele (1976) 65 Cr App R. 22.
R. v. Brown (1993) UKHL 19.
R v. Dudley and Stephens (1884) 14 QBD 273 DC. *R. v. R.* (1991) UKHL 12.*Southwark London Borough Council v. Williams* (1971) 2 WLR 467, 467.
Turk (Deceased) v. R. (2017) EWCA Crim 391 (6 April 2017).

OTHER JUDGMENTS

Canada SC Judgment, *Kindler v. Canada* (Minister of Justice), (1991) 2 SCR 779, 1991 CanLII 78 (SCC).
District Court of Columbia, *Flemming v. Nestor*, 80 S. Ct. 1367 (1960).
Judgment MTS of 18 July 1966, *Ethiopia v. South Africa* oraz *Libera v. South Africa* (Second Phase), (1966) ICJ Rep 6, at 308, 312.
United States Court of Appeals, District of Columbia Circuit, *United States* v. *Carter*, 436 F.2d 200, 210 (D.C. Cir. 1970).

Name Index

Subject Index

About the Author

Krzysztof Szczucki is assistant professor at the Faculty of Law and Administration of the University of Warsaw and president of the Government Legislation Center in Poland. He is the author of publications in the field of criminal law, constitutional law, and philosophy of law, including *Proconstitutional Interpretation of Criminal Law*.

www.ingramcontent.com/pod-product-compliance
Ingram Content Group UK Ltd.
Pitfield, Milton Keynes, MK11 3LW, UK
UKHW041833031026
15587UKWH00002B/735

9 781666 908053